JACOB A. RUBIN

PARTNERS IN STATE-BUILDING

AMERICAN JEWRY & ISRAEL

SBN 9210 - 0036 - 8

LIBRARY OF CONGRESS CATALOG CARD # C-68-19662

Published by

DIPLOMATIC PRESS, INC., NEW YORK, N. Y.

PANETH PRESS LTD.   LIVING BOOKS LTD. LONDON, E.C. 2

FOR ALL STATES' BOOKS PRESS, NEW YORK, N. Y.

Manufactured in the United States of America

by the M. P. Press, Inc., New York, N. Y.

Books by the same Author

PICTORIAL HISTORY OF ISRAEL
PICTORIAL HISTORY OF THE UNITED NATIONS
COUNTRY WITHOUT A CURTAIN
YOUR HUNDRED BILLION DOLLARS
MINORITY PROBLEMS IN POSTWAR EUROPE
AT THE GATES OF HADES
POLAND REVISITED, etc.

To Americans whose Supreme Sacrifice and many other forms of contribution to the cause of Zion Reborn made the Third Jewish Commonwealth possible.

CONTENTS

FOREWORD

THE TITLE of this book, PARTNERS IN STATE-BUILDING, was chosen after much painstaking consideration. Its purpose is to present a full narrative of the great story of American involvement in the rebirth of Jewish Statehood. But, as the title tries to convey, it is also very much related to the two decades old dispute as to whether the State of Israel is the historical creation and the peak of national aspirations of those only who settled in Israel, or a result of cooperation, of a historic partnership between the first-line pioneers in the ancient land of the Jews and those who, while staying abroad, in the Diaspora, gave their share in the efforts for the establishment of the third Jewish Commonwealth. As such—it is a book very much related to a long lingering dispute centered around the question whether the Diaspora Jews were only *helpers* in the building of the State, or *partners,* with all the implications a partnership of that kind represents.

The facts of history confirm, beyond any doubt, the assertion that it was the partnership between Diaspora Jewry and the pioneers in *Eretz Israel* that made the attainment of the dream of sixty generations of the Jewish people possible. And among those Jewish Communities of the Diaspora that gave their share in the upbuilding of a Jewish Palestine and the strengthening of Israel, the American Jewish Community played a most important, sometimes, even an almost decisive role.

This role remained, to a great extent, a rather well kept secret. The Jews of the country which gave birth to the concept of Public Relations and Advertising and turned it into a virtual art, failed completely in this special field of presenting their own share in one of the most important phenomena of our century, the rebirth of Israel. In this respect American Jews seem to be faithful partners in the general American failure to project the true image of America on the world scene.

The only well publicized American Jewish contribution—the financial help in rebuilding a Jewish Palestine—is only one of the aspects of this assistance. There was no field of human endeavor, of creative initiative, in the seven decades of building a Jewish Palestine, in which American Jews have no conspicuous share.

To make these many facts better known and have them registered in proper context is therefore a task of historic importance. The spreading of the awareness of this partnership and the details about its development, appears to the author, as well, a task of foremost, topical validity. The bonds of brotherhood between Israel and American Jewry that were so strikingly manifested in the days of crisis which preceded the *Six Day War,* during the war and thereafter, assume their full grandeur on the background of historical facts that prove that these bridges of common interest and common destiny were built over decades, hewed out of the solid rock of Jewish solidarity, and centuries old national aspirations. The excitement, concern and unprecedented measure of commitment apparent in the days of the May and June, 1967, crisis, appear a natural result and culmination in the awareness of this partnership, intensified due to the specter of total annihilation that threatened the two and a half million Jews in Israel.

But as every partnership, every commitment, this as well needs constant reviewing and deepening in order to remain a living force and foundation of cooperation. There is no doubt that such need exists on both poles of this partnership, both in Israel and in the United States.

To nourish such understanding, to deepen the mutual commitment is a most topical task of our days.

If this book will serve, to any extent, this purpose, the author will consider the labor invested in writing it, rewarding.

*　　*　　*

It is hard to close these remarks without proper recognition given to those who encouraged the author in his efforts, supplied vital information which was not available in written form, assisted in guiding him in the search for historical data and pictorial material. The thanks of the author go to Mr. Jacob Blaustein, honorary president of the American Jewish Committee, Rabbi Herbert A. Friedman, Executive Vice-President of the United Jewish Appeal, Dr. Nahum Goldman, president of the World Zionist Organization, Dr. Israel Gold-

stein, president of *Keren Hayessod* (Foundation Fund), Dr. Emanuel Neumann member of the Jewish Agency Executive, Mr. Meyer Steinglass, head of the Public Relations Department of the Israel Bonds, Mr. Israel Stolarski, Associate Director of the *Histadruth* Campaign, Mr. Morris Weinberg, the publisher of the Day-Morning Journal and many other leading officers of Jewish organizations who were most cooperative in opening archives and advising where source materials could be found. Among those the foremost thanks go to the staff of the Zionist Archives and Library in New York, the Central Zionist Archives in Jerusalem, the Library of Congress, and the archives as well as libraries of other institutions and organizations. Special thanks go to the author's wife, Aliza Rubin, for checking the material and preparing the index. It was the assistance of all those mentioned and of many others that enabled the author to persist in spite of the many hardships he had to encounter in the quest for historical materials that are scattered, often unorganized, and almost always well hidden.

It is the hope of the author that he will have the opportunity to extend each Part of this volume into a full book, as the material treated in them really deserves.

JACOB A. RUBIN

New York, N. Y.

PART ONE

PART ONE

THE DAWN OF NATIONAL ASPIRATIONS

THE BEGINNING

THE DREAM of Zion reborn followed the first Jewish immigrants to the New Continent. To preserve this tradition on the New Continent was not easy. The small Jewish community in America enjoyed a much greater measure of equality and freedom than Jews in any other part of the world. In 1795 Solomon Simpson and Alexander Ben Zvi, two leaders of the Jewish community in New York wrote to the Chinese Jews in Kaifung

> We wish to inform that we live here in the country of America, in New York and in other places, in complete security.

The Revolutionary War and the winning of independence further strengthened the Jews' sense of participation and equality in the new Republic. Literature, propaganda and correspondence in those days were replete with Biblical references. "War of the Lord", "Steps of the Messiah",—slogans used by the revolutionary forces—were only an external expression of the beliefs of many that the liberation from British rule was a kind of repetition of the victorious struggle of ancient Israel against its oppressors. Many of the communications of the Revolutionary leaders, including Washington, were written in this vein. The Jews had every reason to see in the new Republic the haven their race had been seeking for centuries. And though there have been, at that time, already some Jews who really viewed the positions achieved as the ultimate goal of Jewish redemption, the majority refused to forsake the ancient heritage and refused to give up the age-old dream of the return to Zion. Mendes Seixas, the first minister of America's oldest Congregation, *Shearit Israel* (the Spanish-Portuguese Synagogue) did not hesitate, at the end of the 18th century, to speak frankly on this problem.

> Though we are, through divine goodness, made equal partakers of the benefits of government by the Constitutions of these States, with the rest of the inhabitants, still we cannot but view ourselves as captives in comparison to what we were formerly, and what we expect to be hereafter, when the outcasts of Israel shall be gathered together, as it is said in Isaiah.

This was stated in one of his sermons, one of many in which the return to Zion was a constantly recurring theme.

In such an atmosphere, a call and a plan for the restoration of Israel's political independence was only natural. It came at almost the same time when Mendes Seixas was using his pulpit to preach the ancient dream of Jewish restoration.

Mordecai Manuel Noah

The personal history of the man who next expounded this idea served as an appropriate background for the daring plans. Journalist, lawyer, surveyor, playwright, army officer, American consul in Tunis, sheriff of New York, Mordecai Manuel Noah exploded his Jewish State bombshell in an atmosphere which had been preconditioned by years of Seixas' preaching. Speaking in the very same synagogue in which Seixas had preached his early "Zionism," Noah called for the re-establishment of the Jewish State in Palestine through the united effort of the Jews themselves. The idea of a Jewish political entity on Grand Island, about five by thirteen miles in size, in the Niagara River, near Buffalo, which Noah launched dramatically some seven years after his call for a Jewish State in Palestine, was, we may assume, conceived as a kind of dramatization of his real and deep conviction, that there is no other solution for the Jewish problem but a Jewish state. That this was his real belief, that he had full understanding of the political implications and of the importance of support for his ideas by people at the

The cornerstone of "Ararat", now in the Buffalo Historical Museum. The inscription reads: Ararat, A City of Refuge for the Jews, founded by Mordecai Manual Noah, in the Month of Tizri 5,514, September 1825, in the 50th Year of American Independence.

helm of the new Republic, was proven by the fact that he sent his *Discourse at Shearit Israel* to Thomas Jefferson, John Adams, and James Madison. This was in fact the first instance of political action among non-Jews, a precursor to Theodor Herzl's political activities, and the later political offensives of the Zionist movement.

Noah's activity for the realization of his idea was not ephemeral, nor was such his understanding of the political implications and imperatives of the ideas he expounded. In 1844, nearly twenty years after his somewhat quixotic Grand Island plan, and a quarter of a century after his Discourse, Noah again delivered in New York a *Discourse on the Restoration of the Jews.* Displaying a complete grasp of all the refinements of public relations and propaganda imperatives, he had this Discourse printed and widely distributed. Some of its paragraphs read even today as if they were excerpts from the writings of Theodor Herzl. Noah wrote:

> The first step is to solicit from the Sultan of Turkey permission for the Jews to purchase and hold land; to build houses and follow any occupation they may desire, without molestation and in perfect security. . . . The whole territory surrounding Jerusalem . . . will be occupied by enterprising Jews. The valleys of the Jordan will be filled by agriculturists from the North of Germany, Poland and Russia. Merchants will occupy the seaports. . . . Those who desire to reside in the Holy Land and have not the means will be aided by these societies to reach their desired haven of repose.

Noah's call did not effect any practical results. Though some non-Jews took initiatives for the restoration of the Jews to Palestine and of Palestine to the Jews, the Jewish community in America was, in this respect, no different from those in Europe. The love of Zion prevailed—but it lacked the strength not only to fire the imagination but it also failed to inspire action.

But the burning torch of dreams of redemption was not dropped. The Jewish sufferings at the hands of the Russian pogromists and bigots inspired thinking on a national political solution of the Jewish problem not only in Europe but also in America. It was again a person of Sephardic ancestry, such as were Seixas and Noah, who made the ancient dream of freeing the Jews from bondage a central theme of her spiritual creation. Emma Lazarus, a descendant of Gershon Mendes Seixas, whose poetry had won for her the acclaim of Emerson and Bryant and recognition of the general public, used her pen in *Epistles to the Hebrews,* in 1882, to plead for "a home for the homeless . . . a free Jewish state" inasmuch as "all suggested solutions of the Jewish problem other than this are but temporary palliatives."

Emma Lazarus,
first American poet of Zionism.

The author of the verses which have been acknowledged as symbolizing the American ideal and therefore chosen to be enshrined on the Statue of Liberty, continued to write what she considered the timely call to Jews, "Wake, Torah, wake, Recall today the glorious Maccabean rage . . ." This call for the awakening of Israel was supplemented by a much more specific expression of her thoughts underlying this call. In *Banner of the Jew* Emma Lazarus called proudly

> *O for Jerusalem's trumpet now*
> *To blow a blast of shattering power*
> *To wake the sleepers high and low*
> *And rouse them to the urgent hour!*
> *No hand for vengeance—but to save*
> *A million naked swords should wave.*
> *Oh, deem not dead that martial fire,*
> *Say not the mystic flame is spent!*
> *With Moses' law and David's lyre*
> *Your ancient strength remains unbent.*
> *Let but an Ezra rise anew*
> *To lift the banner of the Jew.*

Emma Lazarus died ten years before the "Banner of the Jew" was lifted high and proudly by Theodor Herzl with the publication of the *Judenstaat* and the opening of the first Zionist Congress. But she lived to see the first sprouts of the awakening, to observe in action the precursors of the political Zionism.

FIRST ZIONIST SOCIETIES

ALL OVER THE COUNTRY they made their appearance. Not organized through a central body, these Zion Societies were the purest expression of a real grass-root reawakening, which was ripe for some kind of formal manifestation of the longing for Zion.

No doubt, these societies paralleled what was happening on the "Old Continent" where the *Hovevei Zion* groups assumed a gradually growing influence in Jewish life. To a great extent, they were even physically a kind of an extension of the *Hovevei Zion* movement in Europe. The growing stream of Jewish immigrants from across the Atlantic brought to America people who had already been stung by the thrust of ideas about Jewish national regeneration and restoration.

The difficult conditions under which these immigrants had to live, served for many, no doubt, as a stimulus for the idealistic impulses of all sorts. The sweatshoppers and peddlers proved themselves again the unmovable rock of national fidelity. That which would have appeared much more natural, the exclusive immersion in the daily pursuits, the total concentration on finding a way and an economic niche in the new country, did not happen to these Jews. They knew how to preserve, in spite of hardships, the Sabbath of their lives; and the Sabbath was Zion, the dream about Zion, Jerusalem rebuilt, the Jewish nation restored to its ancient glory.

There was no single name for these organizations as there was no firmly stated program and defined activities. *Dorshei Hasifrut Haivrit,* the Hebrew Literary Society, was organized in Chicago in 1883. Some years later, a *Hovevei Zion* Society in the same city was formed. Dorshei Zion, Ohavey Zion, Shovei Zion, were

Chicago Zion Gate of Knights of Zion, August, 1900.

The first Zionist Flag displayed in this country.

some of the other names these societies began to adopt when a certain number of "Lovers of Zion" came together.

As could have been expected, the early Hovevei Zionists made some attempts towards formulation of their ideas in print. As early as 1886, Dr. Joseph J. Bluestone edited a supplement to the *New York Yiddische Zeitung,* titled "Hovevei Zion." Three years later Dr. Bluestone saw fit to begin the publication of *Shulamith,* a Yiddish language weekly devoted to the problem of Jewish colonization in Palestine, which kept its readers abreast of the progress of the first Bilu colonies in Palestine.

It was therefore no surprise that Herzl's *Judenstaat* found ready hands to grasp the meager booklet and minds only too eager to translate their spiritual readiness into political-ideological formulas, to be followed by practical organizational measures.

The way of contacting the author of the revolutionary idea who proposed to translate the dream of Zion into a plan of action, was not hard to find. Under the dateline of May 23, 1897, we find the following entry in Herzl's diary:

The movement is starting in America. Michael Singer, publisher of a new weekly, Tolerance, sends me reports of meetings in New York. A conference of Rabbis, headed by Dr. Gottheil, declared itself in favor of the movement. The New York Sun of May 10, published an article on Zionism. When I showed the clipping to Benedict (Moritz B., one of the publishers of the *Neue Freie Presse* for which Herzl wrote) he good-naturedly remarked, "You are driving the whole world crazy—a veritable Pied Piper of Hamelin."

Indeed, the "Pied Piper" drew growing numbers of people to his banner. He was

especially interested to draw them here, in the United States of America. His prophetic political acumen did not fail him in correctly appraising the role American Jewry would be able to play in his struggle for the implementation of Zionist ideals. Herzl wrote:

A crucial moment has arrived in the history of the Jews. . . . Will the Jews of America in particular forget in their own happiness how heavy is the bondage of their brothers?

As far as the conditions under which the majority of American Jews lived at that time, they were still far from achieving abundance and affluence. The crowded tenements of the lower East Side, of certain sections of Brooklyn, manifested misery rather than happiness. The boatloads of new immigrants from the East were bringing people whose first day in the "golden country" used to be a day of hunger, thirst, and lack of shelter. And though the rapidly expanding economy managed to absorb gradually these masses of new immigrants, they hardly found, at the beginning, the time, energy and interest in the activities of the Zionist Societies. The complaint, voiced by Zionist leaders in Europe, who used to ask the pertinent question, "what is happening to the thousands of Zionists whom we are sending?" was well justified. The Zionists from Lemberg, Uman, Minsk, who arrived at last in America, had more vital problems to solve before they looked for an address of a Zionist Society. They had to find out how to nourish their wretched bodies before they could think about their spiritual needs.

It was only natural that they looked, first of all, to the many organizations transplanted from the communities they left behind. In the organization of their *landsleit,* of the people who came from the same community, they felt at home. There they could speak their language, Yiddish; there they were "somebody"; there some assistance, some advice could be obtained. For a stranger in a new land, these were quite important considerations.

These objective facts of life were not the only deterrents from an immediate Zionist identification by the newcomers. America was not a wasteland as far as competing ideologies for the Jews' allegiance were concerned. The flow of immigrants brought not only former members of Zionist groups in Eastern Europe, but quite a considerable number of immigrants, who carried with them ideas of social revolution. Many of them were refugees from political oppression. Socialists of various de-

Rabbi Jacob Askowitz—reputed to be the originator of the Zionist flag, in 1891. The blue and white banner, later accepted throughout the world as the Zionist flag, and often as the Jewish flag, was introduced in this country six years before the First Zionist Congress.

nominations, anarchists of various degrees, set out to continue and expand their activities. The new, free country appeared to them a God-given opportunity for the success of their doctrines. And the process of proletarization of the Jewish masses seemed to fit completely into the pattern of their thinking. Here they had a vivid justification for their theories, a growing army of supporters driven into their ranks by the necessities of life. The sweat-shop was an excellent breeding ground for dreams about "another better tomorrow." This was a dream centered right there where they were, in the country they were living in. And the implementation of that dream seemed to be close, as it seemed that only their zeal, and ideological fervor could assure its realization.

Of course, these were not the only factors in the evolvement of ideological-political attitudes of the Jewish masses in America at the turn of the century. Though social theories made an important dent in the overall structure of traditional Judaism, the Judaism, the immigrants had grown and matured in, orthodoxy, was no negligible quantity among the Jewish masses. To many of these religious Jews, the talk about redemption of Palestine through human efforts was anathema. For them, the Zionists were now no better than the socialists, perhaps even worse, as they seemed to be attempting to defy the Messianic belief in redemption to come not by man's making. The workers for the Zionist cause had to overcome innumerable difficulties in their efforts to penetrate into the citadels of orthodox Jewry— the Synagogues.

Many a veteran Zionist could relate stories about the treatment he received at the hands of congregation presidents, board members, and the Rabbis. Led by a sound instinct, these young Zionist idealists clustered around the Synagogues, seeking their natural allies. Many were the forms of allegiance they sought. In the first place, the Synagogue seemed the most appropriate place for Zionist convocations. It had all the advantages organizers of mass movements might desire, the audience was ready-made, the worshippers, who in those days were quite numerous, were on the spot to listen to the exhortations of the Zionist speakers; there was no charge for renting the hall, a consideration of prime importance in days when the budget of all the Zionist Societies united, the Federation of American Zionists, reached the amount of $2,312 and some cents for an entire year of activities.

The Synagogue seemed also the natural place for the first fund collections for Zionist pur-

Rabbi Bernard Felsenthal, of the first Zionist leaders in Chicago.

poses. What could be more natural than adding a donation for the redemption of the land of *Eretz Yisrael* to the donation for the Synagogue made by the worshipper who was honored by getting an *aliyah?* And, on the eve of the High Holidays, wasn't it natural to place a Jewish National Fund stamp on the ticket admitting one to the services? And at the traditional *Elul* visits to the cemeteries, when multitudes used to come, repeating the ritual patterns they had brought from the Old Country, there, too, excellent opportunities seemed to offer themselves for ardent young Zionists to bid, for a Zionist cause, for a part in the magnaminity traditionally displayed at these occasions.

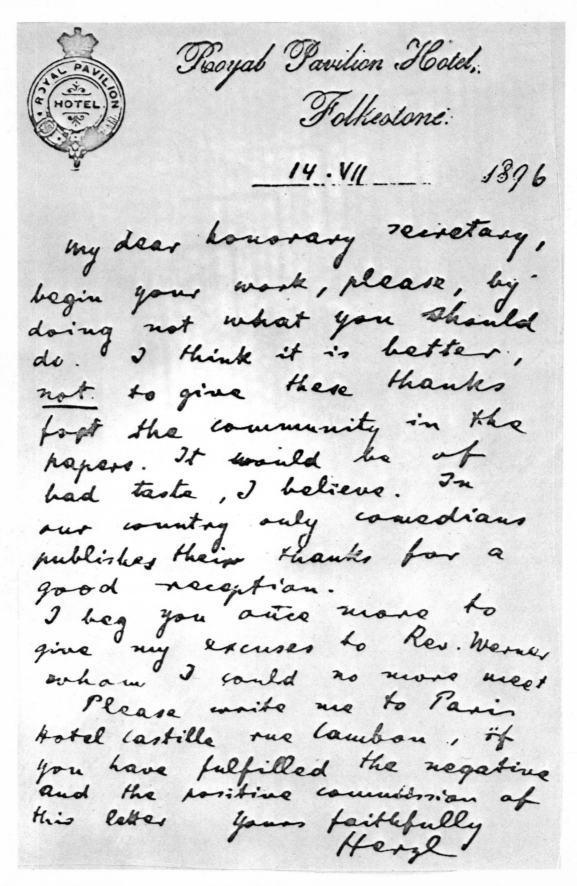

Royal Pavilion Hotel,
Folkestone.

14 . VII   1896

My dear honorary secretary,

begin your work, please, by
doing not what you should
do. I think it is better,
not to give these thanks
for the community in the
papers. It would be of
bad taste, I believe. In
our country only comedians
publishes their thanks for a
good reception.

I beg you once more to
give my excuses to Rev. Werner
whom I could no more meet.

Please write me to Paris
Hotel Castille rue Cambon, if
you have fulfilled the negative
and the positive commission of
this letter   Yours faithfully
         Herzl

Herzl's first letter to an American Zionist, a year before the first Zionist Congress. As
the letter indicates there was some discussion of acknowledging the attitude of the masses
toward the new leader. Herzl's distaste for such popular recognition is made clear in this letter.

But all these considerations seldom worked. The emissaries of Zionism were often chased away, and when sometimes admitted to bid for the generosity of the worshippers, they often came away with pennies, only seldom with a few dollars, an incomparable achievement in those days. How many times they were chased away, cursed, suspected and even accused of pocketing the few cents collected, treated as beggars for personal needs, many a veteran Zionist could tell.

In this two-pronged pressure, early American Zionism had to contend with an additional, most potent problem that appeared very soon. The Lower East Side (or "downtown" in other cities) represented only part of the Jewish Community of America. When the hundreds of thousands of immigrants from Eastern Europe began flooding the New York harbor, a second generation of their co-religionists, as they liked to call themselves, from Western Europe -- mainly Germany -- was already well established. They differed from the East European newcomers in all respects. They lived in different areas of the cities; they had their own congregations, the Reform Temples; they already occupied the higher strata of America's economic life, and through that moved closer to the upper classes of the country, to the new nobility of the New World.

To these circles Zionism was not only strange, it appeared dangerous, a threat to the hard-won positions. Though Zionism appeared to Orthodox Jews as a kind of apostasy, to Socialists a delusion, to the German Jews of influence and economic standing it appeared an imminent threat to the positions they had managed to achieve. When not engaged in direct struggle against the Zionists, they did their utmost to keep themselves sealed off from influences of the new movement. Wherever idological arguments were missing, they had a derisive epithet at their disposal, in which the word "immigrant" was supposed to substitute for logic, ideology, truth.

The small band of Zionist devotees understood well the character of the forces they had to cope with. The yearbook of the Philadelphia Zionist Organization, founded on June 25, 1897, thus preceding by two months the convocation of the First Zionist Congress, summarized editorially the difficulties Zionists had to encounter in those days:

We had much to contend with uptown and downtown, with Yehudim (the rich, assimilated Jews) and Yidden. The uptowners have dubbed us Russians, and in the eyes of the

Prof. Richard Gottheil, the first president of the Federation of American Zionists.

downtowners we are German. But we are neither Germans nor Russians. We are Jews, and Zionists.

In this division of the American Jewish Community of those days, an even more peculiar phenomenon made itself felt among Jews. The "uptowners," the *Yehudim*, the "Germans," became the main reservoir of leadership which in fact was more imposed than stemming from the will of the flock, a kind of benevolent patronage which considered the immigrants rather an object of charity, than a subject of a will for Americanization. In this general trend for human, social co-responsibility for the well-being of the newcomers, some of the well-established, second and third generation Americans, found their way to the Zionist movement. The first president of the Federation of American Zionists was an "uptowner," a professor at Columbia University, Professor Richard Gottheil; his successor was Dr. Harry Friedenwald. Cyrus L. Sulzberger, of the publishing family, was vice-president, Dr. Judah L. Magnes was secretary.

In the composition of forces supporting and opposing Zionism in America in its earliest stage, an important change occurred when Dr. Solomon Schechter assumed the leadership of the Jewish Theological Seminary. An ardent Zionist himself, Dr. Schechter soon made his influence felt in this institution of Jewish learning. The Zionist indoctrination became an integral part of the education rabbinal candidates received at the Seminary. Louis Lipsky, the decades-long leader of American Zionism, acknowledged this fact in one of his essays on American Zionism when he stated:

To them (the Rabbis of the Jewish Theological Seminary) we owe the later development of the Zionist movement.

The character, and one could say "ethnical" composition, of the followers of the Zionist idea in America was considered of interest not only by local American Zionists, but also by the Zionist leadership at the center of the Zionist movement, in Europe. In Herzl's regular and frequent communications with the American Zionists, the question of the identity of the Zionists by country of origin, came up constantly. The assurances of growth, of organizational advances, about which American Zionists reported to Herzl, did not satisfy him. In many of his letters an oft-recurring question was asked:

Are there Americanized young men and women in the ranks of the Zionist Societies? And whenever such society could be observed, with English as the language of discussion, as its most definitive mark, the leaders were quick to report it to Herzl. As in many other instances, on many other problems, Herzl's prophetic wisdom did not fail him. He knew over six decades ago, as we all know well today, that Zionism's future in America is a direct function of its acceptability, adaptability among the completely Americanized Jews, of which in a short time the entire Jewish Community of America would consist.

These inquiries about the composition of the Zionist groups in America, important as they were in Herzl's eyes, did not, even briefly, obscure the major problems of Zionist activities in the United States. The man who understood that his call for national redemption would be worthless if not accompanied by an organizing effort did his best to have the scattered Zionist Societies in America united. The prominence which he gave to the reports of Dr. Singer were not based on the appraisal of Dr. Singer's activity. It was simply that Singer was Herzl's first informant about the status of the Zionist movement in America, and whoever he was, whatever his influence, he was most welcome.

But Dr. Singer was by no means the only one to report to Herzl. Wolf Schnur of Chicago informed Herzl that his *Judenstaat* had reached America, was being translated and read with the greatest of attention all over the country. These first two reporters, though they kindled hope that the American continent would live

Ohavei Zion Society, 1899. The Society functions till this very day, as one of the constituents of Bnai Zion.

up to expectations and needs of the World Zionist movement, were by no means misunderstood for the Zionist movement in America Herzl was hoping for.

And really, these reports were only a far cry from the already existing intensity of Zionist life in America. The first Zionist organization in the United States, the Chicago Zionist Organization No. 1, was founded in 1896. The officers and organizers of this Zionist organization, Bernard D. Horwich, Wolf Sudowski, Elias Epstein, the noted journalist, and editor of Chicago's Yiddish language paper, Leon Zolotkoff, Dr. A. P. Kadison, Wolf Schnur and the Reform Rabbi Bernhard Felsenthal, were in earnest a group engaged in organizing Zionists, in winning supporters whose number reached in the first few years into the thousands. Similar societies were active in Baltimore (the Baltimore Zionist Association), Philadelphia, Los Angeles, Syracuse and of course New York where a dozen and more Zionist societies were formed. The prominence of American Zionism in Herzl's eyes could best be gauged by the large space devoted in the first issue of the Zionist weekly, *Die Welt*, to a report on Zionist activities in America: the weekly which officially launched the Zionist organization and was to serve as a visible symbol of organizational unity of purpose and a central tribune for expounding the Zionist ideas to the world, devoted two and a half pages to Zionism in the United States.

This formal expression of Herzl's interest in American Zionism was a part of a scheme to do the utmost in pushing American Zionism to the forefront of the world Zionist movement. Wherever and whenever possible, Americans were given the best possible treatment. Thus, though at the first Zionist Congress only one official, duly elected American delegate registered, Rev. Dr. Scheftel Schaffer of Baltimore, and all in all only four Americans were registered as delegates, Miss Rose Sonnenschein, editor of the *American Jewess,* of St. Louis; David Frisch, and Adam Rosenberg, Herzl asked Mr. Rosenberg to serve on the most important committee of the First Congress entrusted with the central task of the movement, namely the shaping of its program. It was an American Zionist who had the honor, together with such giants of Zionism as Dr. Max Nordau, Dr. Max Bodenheimer and Dr. Nathan Birnbaum, to shape what became the best known and most decisive program in the two thousand years' history of the Jewish Diaspora, the Basle Program. Whenever possible, Herzl

The call for the constituent Convention of the Federation of American Zionists, 1898.

did his utmost to assure the distinction of American Zionists. He maintained personal, permanent contact with American Zionist leaders, most often in long, hand-written letters. When he moved to limit the time allocated at the Congress for participants in the discussion, he always found a way to circumvent the rule to let an American deliver his report, at length, on the American Zionist movement. At Congresses, he cultivated personal relations with American delegates and took some of them, such as Dr. Gottheil, Dr. Stephen S. Wise, Cyrus Sulzberger, into his closest confidence.

All this was done with a view towards the then existing problems of the Zionist movement, and even more so, the farsighted appraisal of the future of the Zionist movement. As in many other instances, it seems that Herzl intuitively foresaw the eventual hegemony of America in world affairs, and the plight of European Jewry. Considering other political prophecies Herzl made, one must acknowledge that his statement, "our strength lies with the Jews of America, I hope that they will not fail us," was not just a phrase, put down on paper by an easy flowing pen and a mind sparkling with ideas, but an expression of a deep conviction that in the West, in the Jewish community planted in the Western hemisphere, will be vested the decisive influence on the realization of the Zionist dream.

At the 1899 Convention of the Federation of American Zionists: Henry Jackson, Rabbi A. Alexander, Dr. Judah L. Magnes, Prof. Max Schloessinger, Dr. Harry Friedenwald, Prof. Solomon Schechter.

But prophecies and appraisals were not deluding Herzl in his organizational drive. While hoping for a leading role for American Zionism on an international scale, daily organizational pursuits appeared to him in their full importance. Reports on the organizational progress of Zionism in America started to reach Herzl some months before the First Zionist Congress convened, and after. There was a report on a Zionist mass meeting held in May, 1897, in New York, on Zionist meetings in St. Paul, Des Moines, Kansas City, Boston, Louisville.

But a coordinated Zionist effort was still missing. The first news about such an effort reached Herzl some weeks after the First Zionist Congress. Written by Prof. Richard Gottheil, the letter informed him that plans were being made to organize Zionist Societies of Americanized Jews in New York. This letter was no mere report on a plan. Within a short time the Federation of Zionists of New York City became a fact. The list of the Federated Societies was not negligible: Young American Zionists, *Hovevei Zion* of New York (downtown), *B'nai Zion* of New York, *B'nai Zion* of Brownsville, Brooklyn Sons of Zion, *Hovevei Zion* of New York (uptown), *Shavei Zion,* Uptown East Side Zion Society, Uptown West Side Zion Society, *Dorshei Zion l'Sefath Ebber,* Patriots of Palestine, *Hovevei Zion* of Brownsville, *Ohalei Shem,* Zion Social Club, Ziona, *B'noth Zion I, B'noth Zion II, Ziona, Matteh Levi, Knesseth Zion, Dorshei Zion, Pirkhei Zion, Tifereth Zion,* Daughters of Zion. The new Federation chose its officers: President: Professor Richard Gottheil; Vice-Presidents: Herman Rosenthal, Rev. Dr. Bernard Drach-

man, Dr. Joseph T. Bluestone; Treasurer: Dr. William Cowen; Recording Secretary: B. C. Ehrenreich; Corresponding Secretaries: I. D. Morrison, Abner Tannenbaum; Financial Secretary: Max Bukansky.

The first step was taken: an office was set up to make further action for coordination and organization possible. The Central Bureau, as the executive body of the Federation called itself, at a meeting on February 28, 1898, decided to invite Zionist Societies all over the country "to unite with it for arranging for a Convention of American Zionists to be held on May 10 and 11, 1898." There was no attempt to dictate. The invitation made it clear that "the following cities have been suggested as the place of meeting: Washington, New York, Philadelphia, Boston and Baltimore," with the final choice to be determined "on the basis of a plurality of votes, counted according to Societies." And as it fitted a democratic organization, the basis for strength of representation was set down clearly:

> every Zionist Society composed of from twenty-five to one hundred members (25 being the minimum) shall be entitled to a representation of two delegates, with an added delegate for every hundred members, but no Society shall be represented by more than five delegates.

The birth of a nationally based Zionist movement was close. Though the convention was not held on time and convened two months later, on July 4, 1898, at 201 Henry Street in New York City, it had accomplished a basic function in the process of growth of American Zionism. Out of scattered Societies, each working independently, without a central direction, an organized body emerged. The World Zionist Organization gained a constituent member, American Jewry, a central Zionist address and a central Zionist authority. The National Federation of American Zionists adopted a constitution and elected its first officers: Prof. Richard Gottheil, president; five vice-presidents: Rabbi Bernhard Felsenthal of Chicago, Dr. Marcus Jastrow of Philadelphia, Rabbi Scheftel of Baltimore, Dr. Joseph I. Bluestone and the Rev. Dr. Hirsch Masliansky, both of New York; Stephen S. Wise, secretary, and C. D. Birkhahn of New York, treasurer.

Organizational details on this constituent convention indicate that the Zionist movement was already a force to be reckoned with. The thirty-six participating New York Societies alone represented a membership of about 5,000, and the two delegates representing the New

England Zionist Federation, Rev. Silver of Worcester, Mass., and Rev. Esakowitz of Boston, claimed a membership of 1,900. These figures are mentioned only as an example but are by no means exhaustive as far as the numerical strength of the Zionist Societies, participating in the Convention, was concerned. The eight Societies of the Knights of Zion of Chicago themselves claimed a membership of thousands, and considerable numbers of members were reported by delegates from Baltimore, Washington, Philadelphia, Syracuse, Troy, Paterson, N.J.; Trenton, N.J.; Hartford, Conn., and others. Delegates from 14 states attended the convention.

This organizational triumph encountered at the very beginning serious difficulties. The Societies which responded to the call and participated in the Convention were by no means representative of all Zionist groups active at that time in America, nor even of all the Zionist Societies in New York. The fact that the name of Dr. Singer, the first American Zionist to correspond with Herzl and to lay foundations for an organization, did not appear in the roster of participants in the founding Convention of American Zionists, was no accident. Dr. Singer had his own scheme of organization. As early as November, 1897, he reported to Dr. Herzl that a conference was called for organizing the "United Zionist Societies of the United States." And he was not alone. In his report he mentioned names of people with standing in the Jewish community. Rabbis Philip Klein, Bernard Drachman, Zionsler, Zadikoff, Yache, Friedman, and the publisher of the Yiddish daily *The Tageblatt* (Jewish Daily News), Ezekiel Sharasohn. Soon after this initial report in January, 1898, Dr. Singer cabled to Herzl, GREETINGS TO THE ENERGETIC FIGHTER FOR ZION DR. THEODOR HERZL. THE CENTRAL OFFICE OF THE NEWLY ORGANIZED UNITED ZIONIST SOCIETIES OF THE UNITED STATES WAS JUST OPENED. THE BASIS OF OUR ORGANIZATION IS THE BASLE PROGRAM AND ZION EVENTUALLY.

A group of organizers and canvassers for the first Shekel Day proclaimed for Sunday November 9, 1902.

We
Call Your Attention
to
Our Zionist Button

$15.00 per 100, post-paid
20c. each, post-paid
Address Maccabæan
320 Broadway

The first Zionist button, 1904.

The Zionist Societies comprising that organization were scattered all over the country. This organization enlisted the support of Zion Hamezuyeneth (Zion Armed), Ohavei Zion, Dorshei Zion, in New York, Brooklyn Hovevei Zion, Zionist Society of Newark, Hovevei Zion of Bayonne, N.J., B'nai Zion, Hovevei Zion and B'noth Zion of Cleveland, Ohio, Mevaseres Zion in Philadelphia, and the Zionist Society of Savannah, Georgia.

The fledgling Federation had to face the challenge of the United Zionist Societies. This challenge endangered the basic purpose of the efforts towards the creation of one central group and one united instrument of Zionist activity in the United States. Even before the establishment of the Federation of American Zionists, its forerunner, the Federation of Zionists of New York City and Vicinity, under the signature of its president, Prof. Richard Gottheil, tried to enlist Herzl's assistance for eliminating the schism which threatened the entire effort at unification. On January, 1898, Prof. Gottheil wrote to Herzl:

I suppose Dr. Leon Kellner (the man who dealt with organizational affairs of the World Zionist Movement) will show you the letter I wrote to him yesterday. I write to you directly now to ask you to put a stop to the disintegrating work which your representative here, Dr. Michael Singer, is doing. I enclose a letter which I have just received from Mr. W. Schnur. It represents the feeling which is common in Zionist circles here in America. I shall feel much obliged if you will give the matter your immediate attention.

Herzl did not dismiss the matter lightly. Within two weeks or so, he replied to Dr. Gottheil's letter, saying:

I received the official advice of your forthcoming conference to organize a central bureau of the Zionist Federation of Greater New York. . . . I very much dislike the Singer affair. I received reports from him for a long time and believed that he was very active on behalf of our Zionist movement. Although I noted a certain tendency, in his reports, which showed overeagerness, I see from your letter that Singer's activity aggravates you. I believe it would be best if you would send me official reports. I cannot take any side in this matter inasmuch as I do not know the conditions in America. Please send me unbiased reports to be published in the official organ, *Die Welt*. . . .

In addition to the United Zionists, another group as well refused to join the Federation. *Agudath Hakehiloth le-Zion*, which claimed to represent 80 congregations in the metropolitan area, continued to act as a separate unit. Another group, the Knights of Zion of Chicago, after initially joining the Federation, decided to keep up their separatism and even to expand their hegemony over all the midwestern states and assume the name of the Western Federation of Zionists. The seriousness of this problem was again demonstrated through the fact that the Third Annual Convention of the Federation, held June 11, 12, 1900, in New York, with 99 accredited delegates participating, adopted a resolution urging the Zionist Actions Committee to decline accepting Shekolim from individual American Societies, but from the Federation as a Landesverband. This resolution did not influence the Actions Committee. In spite of the protests of the Federation, a resolution was adopted acknowledging the independence of the Order of Knights of Zion. The only concession the Actions Committee made was a proviso limiting the right to separate action and representation at the Congress to groups which had a minimum of 3,000 shekel payers.

The organizational problems stemming initially from clashes of personalities, or geographical division, were soon to assume a completely new and different character.

AGONY OF ORGANIZING

3

IDEOLOGICAL PROBLEMS began to emerge. The first to appear was that of religious Jewry. Agudath Hakehilloth le-Zion was not merely a splinter group of a few dissidents who could hardly find justification for their separation. As the name indicated, this was a federation of congregations which professed to be followers of Herzl's political Zionism, without relinquishing any of the precepts of orthodox Judaism. Theirs was a Herzlian Zionism, plus adherence to the Torah, an additional principle the Federation of American Zionists could not accept formally. Such ideological principle would have endangered the broad basis of the Zionist appeal to the general American Jewish community, which hardly could be considered religious.

To overcome this schism, a religious substitute had to be offered within the framework of the Federation. This substitute came into being quickly. Initially it was the Sabbath Cooperative Society, soon to be replaced by the *Mizrahi Societies.* "The Mizrahi Societies, the conservative wing of the Zionist Organization," as the *Jewish Yearbook* called them, with their ascendance at the beginning of the century (1903), were a most welcome newcomer to the family of Zionist Societies associated with the Federation. Contrary to the Agudath Hakehilloth, Mizrahi affiliated without reservations with the Federation. Called by different names -- *Tifereth Hamizrahi, Agudath Hamizrahi, B'Noth Yerushalayim Mizrahi; Ahayoth Mizrahi*—these groups were eagerly supported by the administration of the Federation, and especially by its secretary, Jacob de Haas, who came to America from England on Herzl's recommendation. Their program, *Eretz Israel* for the people of Israel in the spirit of the Torah of Israel, was no obstacle to their full absorption within the ranks of the Federation. Though small in numbers, comparatively less than two thousand members, the Mizrahi, whose organ was *The Sabbath Journal,* manifested an extraordinary vitality, drawing admiration from all quarters in Zionist circles. Even non-religious Zionists acknowledged their potential in opening up, for active Zionism, the great reservoir of European immigrants who still preserved their religious devotion and zeal. Mizrahi Societies experienced no discrimination: they were part and parcel of the Federa-

A building housing a Zionist Club on 226 Lenox Ave. in Harlem which was, at that time, a place of Jewish concentration.

tion, which soon decided to utilize Mizrahi's ideological attributes for the benefit of the entire Federation.

This unusual trust was demonstrated as the Federation reached the point of its organizational development when sheer existence was no longer a problem and care had to be taken for cementing the organization through an ideological intrastructure and preparation of young cadres. It was only natural that in these efforts, foremost attention was given the problem of education.

Herzl's Last Message to America

The following letter, dated some two months before Herzl's death, was his last message addressed to the Zionists of America. At this time the agitation with regard to East Africa was at its height, and Herzl was anxious to clear up any misunderstanding that might have arisen in America with regard to his position. Herzl was deeply affected by the accusations which had been hurled at him that he had abandoned Palestine and the Zionist ideal. The great struggle that ensued left him in a shattered physical condition.

Vienna, April 28, 1904.

To the Convention of the Federation of American Zionists, Assembled in Cleveland, Ohio.

Worthy Colleagues:

You reassemble after the passing of many anxious days. Our friends throughout the world have been burdened by a fear that a national organization for the completion of a national work, created with so much difficulty, could be injured. The cause of this uneasiness was miscomprehension of the offer of the British Government.

We were compelled to lay before the Congress the fact that the British Government had offered us a tract of land for our suffering brethren, because we had no right to refuse the bread offered our poor. No one, however, has the right to conclude from this that we have departed from the Basle Program which we have formulated. I was deeply pained to note that it was believed that I had given up Palestine. I endeavored in my closing address at Basle to tranquilize all agitation by repeating our old oath.

East Africa offers us no solution of the Jewish problem. The Jewish question remains, but this plan would save for the house of Israel the poorest among the masses, who are now borne down by national and economic conditions and who would otherwise be lost to us. There is no political question as complicated as ours. But we have accepted no charity, and our policy is not the policy of philanthropy. A nation does not accept philanthropy—and our policy is a national one. As a nation, we have entered into negotiations with the British Government, as a nation, we shall continue treating of these affairs. The importance of the East African question lies in the fact that the Congress is publicly recognized by the greatest territorial power on earth as the representative of the Jews. Our history knows no analogy, and therefore it was right and proper that the Congress should reach the decision to send a Commission to gather the material for a practical decision on the issue, so that our people could be properly informed, and that our resolutions might be based upon fact, and not upon phrases. It was and is our duty adequately to carry out the decision of the Congress, as it was an obligation upon the Conference of the Greater Actions Committee to secure the unity of our organization by assuring the execution of the Congress resolutions. The Conference has carried out its mandate by the acceptance of resolutions already well known. The decision of the Sixth Congress to send an investigating Commission to East Africa therefore remains as decided by the Congress, and the unity of our organization is secured. We desire that Zionism shall go forward, that Zionism shall be the representative of the Jewish people. Why do we wish this? Because we believe that to attain a great end great power is needed. No private organization and no assembly can provide this force. Only the organization of the people can bring this power, and the medium of creating it is the Congress.

Dear colleagues, I greet you heartily. I expect from your labors not only that the organization in America will stride forward, but I hope also that the Federation of American Zionists will, like other Federations, immediately devote its attention to obliterating the injuries done our cause in the last few months by the refusal on the part of some to obey the mandate of the Congress, to safeguarding the decisions of the Congress and to increasing the propaganda in favor of our national ideas.

With Zion's greetings,

Th. Herzl

Herzl's last message to American Zionists as published in The Maccabean.

American Zionism deserves the greatest credit that so early in its existence, it accorded the education problem a position of highest importance. In the early American Zionist program, education meant not only the education of the adult members who flocked to the Zionist groups; much greater attention was paid to the problem of educating the younger generation, teenagers and even children, who had to assure the future of the Zionist movement in America. It is most amazing to learn that these early American Zionists, who themselves were not too far from their teens, were concerned with the preparation of another generation of Zionists in America.

It is most indicative of the harmony between the Mizrahi Societies and the rest of the Federation that this most vital task of educating the young was entrusted to Mizrahi. The seventh convention of the Federation, held in Cleveland, June 3-7, 1904, made this trust public and official, when it stated in its resolutions on education that

the Mizrahi, as a conservative body, in which the Jewish public places much confidence, be confided with this (educational) work, and authorized by the Federation of American Zionists to establish, organize and reorganize public Hebrew schools and *Talmud Torahs* for boys and girls in every city in the United States where there is a Jewish population not less than 50 families . . .

The masthead of the first Zionist publication of the Federation of American Zionists.

Mizrahi should supervise and dominate all the Hebrew schools and *Talmud Torahs* throughout the country.

In addition to this "conservative wing" of the Federation, there appeared almost simultaneously what the *Jewish Yearbook* of those days called "the radical wing of the nationalist party."

This "radical wing," the *Poale-Zion*, had, similarly to Mizrahi, a natural reservoir from which to draw. Among the European Jewish immigrants, quite a few professed socialist ideas together with devotion to Zion. Members of *Poale-Zion* in Eastern Europe laid the foundations for an American version of this group as early as 1903. The twenty-three delegates, representing twelve Societies, who assembled for their first Convention on April 29, 1903, in Philadelphia, followed the accepted pattern of those days and sought affiliation with the Federation. However, although they were officially associated, they created problems due to the very character of

Zionist Convention at Tannersville, N. Y., 1906.

their organizational and ideological individuality. Their quarterly journal, *Die Neue Stimme*, the separate conventions, the specific demands with which they faced the Federation's administration, put special strains on the Federation's leadership. But in spite of these differences it was apparent that with the pitfalls, these different organizations, co-existing under the umbrella of the Federation, were strengthening, not weakening the Federation.

This awareness led, at times, to more than sheer tolerance of organizational diversity. The leaders of the Federation acknowledged, at the very beginning of the nationally organized Zionist movement, that special groups could serve more efficiently when working through separate units. Another special group at which such effort was wittingly directed were the women.

The American Zionist leadership was able to take this initiative on the highest authority. At the second Zionist Congress, Mrs. Richard Gottheil, the wife of the first President of the Federation of American Zionists, was approached by Theodor Herzl with the behest that she organize the Jewish women of America for the Zionist cause. Following this advice, Dr. Gottheil stated in his presidential address at the Third Annual Convention of the Federation, in 1900, "It would not only be negligent on my part to make no reference to the various women's Zionist groups, which have grown up during the past years; it would be unjust in view of the splendid example they have given us all."

Groups of the Daughters of Zion, who chose names of women in Jewish history such as Rebecca, Deborah, Miriam, Esther, spread all over the country auguring correctly the tremendous Zionist potential, which the American women harbored. The future emergence and growth of the Zionist women's organization — *Hadassah* — became a natural development. So eager were the men to have the women organized that they assigned one of the leading Zionists, Bernard D. Rosenblatt, to the duty of organizing these groups, as they seem to have been dissatisfied with the pace of progress the women themselves had been able to assure.

In these organizational efforts, one aspect demonstrated a most amazing degree of foresight and social-political perception: this was the approach to the problem of organizing Jewish youngsters. The Federation was only five years old when it turned toward this problem. The definition, "youth organization," was not yet known. But the idea behind such an organization was more than clear for the Zionist leaders of those days. Intuitively they felt that the great promise of the American Zionist movement rested with these youngsters, nine to fifteen years old, in their incorporation in special organizational forms, into the Zionist Federation.

The First Company of the Boys' Brigade.

Typical promotional page in the Maccabean. Compared with today's dimensions of contributions for Israel causes, the donations for the Jewish National Fund, 1904, are most interesting.

National Fund Collection at Manchester, N. H.

Mr. S. Bloom, .50; Rose Mirsky, .25; A. Mirsky, .25; N. Sinberg, .25; D. Cohen, .50; M. Cohen, .25; S. Cohen, .25; Mr. Bauerman, .30; Jacob Lewis, .25; M. Allen, .05; I. Shurub, .50; S. Kaplan, .25; Miss Ainberg, .05; Mr. Katz, $1; Mr. Goldberg, .50; Mr. Allen, .50; L. Siegel, .25; Master Schlossberg, .05; Mr. Kaplowitz, .25; H. Siegel, .05; Master Feldsher, .05; I. Miller, .25; Mr. Sidel, .25; Mr. Fielding, .10; Mr. Spector, .05; William Rosenberg, .25; J. Kramm, .25; S. Teitelbaum, .05; Mr. Simms, .30; Mr. Mushlin, .25; Mr. B. Jaffe, .25; Mr. Hilsher, .25; Master Allen, .10; Mr. Keidansky, .25; M. Sessman, .50; A. Kneiser, .25; Mr. Hoffman, .25; Mr. Rosenberg, .25; B. Cohen, .25; L. Spector, .25; Miss Feldsher, .05; Mr. Blackburg, .50; Mr. Teitelbaum, .25; Mr. Siegel, .25; Mr. Levin, .25; Mr. Lowenstein, .50; Mr. Ressnick, .25; Mr. Ralkowsky, .50; Mr. H. Feldman, .25; Mr. Tallieur, .25; Mr. Strattle, .25; Mr. I. C. Lutz, .25; Mr. Resnick, .25; Mr. Rosenberg, .50; Mr. Jaffe, .50; H. Spector, .50; S. Fildman, .25; Mr. Teitelman, .25; Mr. Custin, .25; Mr. Santz, .25; Mr. Weissman, .25; Mr. Green, .25; Miss Feldman, .05; Mr. Simon, .25; Mr. B. Custin, .25; Mr. B. Jaffe, .10. Total.......... $18.35

NATIONAL TRIBUTE.

Mr. Cyrus L. Sulzberger, Treasurer of the National Tribute to the Children of Dr. Herzl, begs to acknowledge the following additional contributions:

Previously Acknowledged	650.00
Jos. Friedenwald	100.00
Patriots of Zion, Providence, R. I.	50.00
Louis Marshall	25.00
Rev. A. M. Ashinsky	$2.00
B. Miller	1.00
Rev. M. M. Eichler	2.00
Prof. S. Schechter	5.00
Max Finkelstein	2.50
Miss Henrietta Szold	3.00
Ab. Goodman	1.00
Defenders of Zion, Boston, Mass.	5.00
Louis S. Cohen	5.00
Ahawath Zion Gate, Bay City, Mich.	5.00
Dr. Julius Friedenwald	5.00
Eugenie Friedenwald	2.00
Tikwath Zion Assn., Baltimore, Md.	3.00
Sons & Daughters of Zion, Buffalo, N. Y.	25.00
Mr. and Mrs. Goody Rosenfeld	5.00
Miss Josephine Lazurus	25.00
Edgar J. Nathan	10.00
Elmira, N. Y., Sons of Zion	11.70
S. Braude	10.00
Rev. Dr. M. H. Harris	5.00
Per Rochester Council of Zionists:	
Ladies' Zion Endeavor Society	15.00
Young Men's Zion Club	10.00
Ohavei Zion "	8.00
Bnal Zion "	5.00
Ladies' Zion Friendship League	5.00
Nechomas Zion	3.00
Daughters of Zion, Norfolk, Va.	5.00
A Widow's Mite	1.00
Rev. H. Masliansky	2.00
H. Bayard	1.00

Mr. Cyrus L. Sulzberger, American Treasurer of the National Tribute, and Vice-President, F. A. Z.

Z. London	1.00
Philip White	1.00
Ohavel Zion Society, New Bedford, Mass.	10.00
Sons and Daughters of Zion, Chattanooga, Tenn.	5.00
Ohavie Zion, Chattanooga, Tenn.	5.00
Total Receipts to Sept 26, '04	$1,035.20

Further contributions may be sent to Mr. Cyrus L. Sulzberger, Treasurer, 58 W. 87th Street, New York City, and will be duly acknowledged.

In view of the later American Zionist history, this chapter of organizing youth for Zionism appears almost legendary, unbelievable. The basic principles adopted for this organization were patterned much more after military formations than the scout movement. The name it assumed left no room for misconceptions: the Jewish Boys Brigade, sometimes called the Jewish Lads Brigade. The Zionist publications of those days imply rather clearly that if these groups of youngsters "are divided in military units; squads, companies, regiments and brigades," the task they are called to fulfill will be greatly simplified.

These tasks were clearly defined. The Jewish Boys' Brigades had to become the instrument for implanting among Jewish youth the Zionist program of physical culture, military formation and Jewish education. Louis Lipsky, editor of the Federation's official organ, *The Maccabean,* presented a concise and clear formulation of what these groups symbolized:

> The Boys' Brigades mean the physical regeneration of the Jewish people. It means more than physical strength. It means the sanity of the Jewish race when it will collide with new experiences. It means the freshness of athletes infused into the Jewish people.

The founders and ideologists of this formation did not overlook making precautionary statements to prevent accusations that they were fostering the spirit of militarism in the Jewish youth. "Militarism will not be fostered. The showy features of cadets will not be countenanced," Lipsky continued, in an effort to counteract the impression these units had been making despite the anti-military assertions. The boys wore blue, brass-buttoned uniforms while in session or on parade, which contributed towards arousing self-respect and a pride of Jewishness which our boys lack today.

"For the purpose of physical training, they are to use wands of some weight." An enthusiastic Zionist publicist did not hesitate to add: "Such a brigade will assure the future American Jewry and the maintenance of the national idea."

The practical results justified fully the exalted hopes. Within weeks, hundreds, thousands, flocked to the Jewish Boys Brigades, organized under the supervision of the Federation. Professional men took over the implementation of the program of the Brigades. When they first made their public appearance, marching in formation at the Herzl memorial procession, astounded New York Jewry applauded the scions of the Maccabean spirit.

It was no wonder that the Seventh National Convention of the Federation in Cleveland, July, 1904, devoted a great deal of its deliberations on educational affairs to the idea of the Jewish Boys Brigade and estimated that

> it would be easily possible for the committee to increase the number of 10,000 in Greater New York alone.

All major cities were included in the plans for the establishment of the *Boys Brigades.* "To rise sufficent money for this desired unit should be a Zionist aim," stated one resolution.

The high hopes did not materialize. The noble and most promising concept of organizing Jewish youngsters for the Zionist idea disappeared suddenly from the agenda of Zionist activities. It fell into complete oblivion. There was left only a taste of what could have happened if those who gave birth to this idea would have persevered in it.

Early Histadruth Ivrit convention in Philadelphia

Members of the Austro-Hungarian Zionist Society on an outing in the Bronx Park, 1908.

Some years passed until a new attempt was made for reaching the youth. The new youth organization had no relation to the first attempt at such organization. Though not actually saying it, the new organization, *Young Judea,* was rather aimed at Jewish youngsters who were attending school. Whereas the Jewish Boys Brigades had the character of a mass movement of youngsters "taken from the streets," as the organization of the Boys Brigade professed, Young Judea drew its members from among the Jewish student body of those days. Organized in 1908, it defined its purposes clearly: to advance the cause of Zionism, to further mental, moral and physical development of the Jewish youth; to promote Jewish culture and ideals in accordance with Jewish tradition. Working in schools, with a leadership of excellent quality, Young Judea grew constantly in numbers, influence and standing.

Amidst this organizational outpouring, other groups emerged, groups which seemed to augur that American Zionism was destined to become the breeding ground and main reservoir of Zionist realization in the land of the fathers. In the same auspicious year of 1904 when the Seventh Cleveland Convention of the Federation outlined grandiose plans for a Zionist offensive on all fronts of Jewish life in America, a group of enthusiasts laid the foundation of Hehalutz, the Pioneer movement, which pronounced proudly that it intended to prepare its members for emigration to the Land of Israel. *Halutzei Ha-Am,* as the groups of these pioneers called themselves, also organized groups of *Tayarei Ha-aretz,* Scouts of the Land, an organization whose members expressed their intention to spend some time in the Land of Israel to assist the settlers, without any final commitment for permanent settlement in Palestine.

In this rush of organizational activities, the year 1908 brought also another interesting innovation into the ranks of organized Zionism in America: in 1908 the Order of the Sons of Zion, *B'nai Zion,* came into being. Among the many other Zionist groups the Order of the Sons of Zion introduced the fraternal factor into the area of Zionist activities. In view of the growing number of Masonic and other fraternal organizations which invaded American public life in those days, the Zionist order supplied a Zionist outlet for a then fashionable form of organization. The lodges, called "camps," of the Order of Sons of Zion were not inferior to the lodges of Masons or any other general fraternal organization. In defining its Zionist character, the Order Sons of Zion adopted as its aims "to help Zionist Congresses to provide our people with a publicly assured, legally secured home in Palestine."

Judging from this thriving organizational life, it is easy to draw conclusions which could be somewhat misleading. The young movement sprawling all over, towards all segments and sectors of Jewish life in America, represented only inconspicuous members of American Jews. The consecutive National Conventions listened to reports of the Zionist administration which did spell out the naked truth about the power or rather, the weakness, of organized Zionism in America. In 1900 the Federation of American Zionists counted in its ranks 8,000 members, organized in 135 Zionist Societies, this figure to be augmented by another 5,000 members organized in the ranks of the Knights of Zion, the independent and later autonomous Federated Zionist Societies of the Midwest. Though this number grew to 21,000 within four years, it later started to fluctuate, falling again to almost half of this number. When at later Conventions the count of members was made on the basis of shekel holders, the figures were much more modest than before. The Tenth Annual Convention of the Federation, for instance, of June, 1907, represented only 16,892 *shekel* payers, organized into 208 Societies. This figure fell later to around 14,000, grew again but never leaped towards an increase which would indicate that American Zionism accomplished an organizational breakthrough and encompassed real masses of Jewry.

Details of the budgetary problems of the Federation speak even more clearly the truth about the strength of the Zionist movement of those days. The financial report submitted at the Third National Convention, in which ninety-nine accredited delegates participated, showed receipts in the amount of $2,699 for the entire year 1899-1900. Two years later, at the Convention in Philadelphia, there were $3,465.24 in income and only $3,095.49 in expenses, a laudable balance. It is interesting to note that the budgets grew much more constantly than the numerical strength. Organizational activities were gradually extended, new programs envisaged, their implementation started, and the first professional staff members hired. The financial report submitted to the Seventh National Convention which shows $5,927.88 in income indicates already among the expenses $1,000 for a secretary, $266.50 for stenographers, $52.95 for telephone service. Of course, these figures should be viewed not from the perspective of the annual budgets of the Jewish national organizations of our days. But even compared with income and expense figures of organizations over half a century ago, these figures reveal one of the sources of the weakness of the Zionist organization in the first years of its existence in America. The item of

Banquet in honor of Dr. Shmaryahu Levin upon his initiation as member of a Zionist Society in New York, 1915.

American Jewish Committee delegation to Washington at the beginning of the AJC activities on behalf of Jewish interests overseas. In the picture left to right: Louis Marshall, Herbert Friedenwald, Judge Mayer Sulzberger, Harry Cutler, Oscar S. Straus, Judge Leon Sanders, Henry Goldfogle, Samuel Dorf, Leon Kamaiky.

$38.40, appearing among the expenditures under the heading "Propaganda Committee and Literature," indicates the ills of the Federation much more than the limited funds that were at the disposal of the Zionist movement. Here is a proof that Zionist propaganda was almost non-existent, that the new idea which had to conquer the masses, in Herzl's words, to "conquer the Kehilloth," had no financial means for its attack on the citadels of assimilation, indifference, and ideological enmity. In spite of that, the national conventions of the Federation of Zionist Societies were nationally followed and reported. And this bore proof that the ideas this Federation represented were much stronger than any figure could indicate, much more influential than any form of propaganda and promotion could impress on the public.

4

IDEOLOGICAL ENCOUNTERS AND DIFFERENTIATION

THE LEADERS of the Federation did not consider sufficient the allegiance the Federation professed for the Herzl Zionism, for the Zionist Congress, for the World Zionist Organization. The Federation tried, since the earliest days of its existence, to elaborate on the Zionist program, to unfold its entire meaning, adapt it to the specific needs and conditions of the American scene. The natural drive for ideological formulation and for deepening the ideological tenets of the new movement was very much accelerated due to the most stormy developments in the World Zionist movement itself. American Zionists were forced to commit themselves in the vital disputes which almost rocked the young Zionist world movement. They had to take sides in the discussion on the colonization of Cyprus, on the Uganda Plan, on political versus practical Zionism, on controversies about the role of Hebrew in new Palestine, and in the Zionist movement in general.

Delegates to the eleventh Zionist Convention, Atlantic City, July, 1908.

The Uganda Plan did not catch American Zionists off guard. In his cable to the annual Convention of June 1903, which took place after the Kishenev pogrom, Herzl alluded to the forthcoming Uganda Plan by saying, "I shall bring to the Basle Congress a program which, we believe, will help our people." When the great controversy broke into the open, when the Russian Zionists threatened to split the Zionist movement in case the Zionist Organization would adopt the British plan for Jewish colonization of Uganda, the Federation of American Zionists stood by Herzl with all the fervor and devotion they were able to mobilize. Though there were among the American Zionist leaders individuals who abhorred any idea of weakening, be it only illusory, of the exclusive allegiance to Palestine, officially the Federation supported Herzl without reservation and condemned the split tactics of those Russian Zionists who assembled in Kharkhov, Russia, to give their threat of splitting the Zionist movement, some tangible character. But one should by no means misunderstand this unlimited trust in Herzl's judgment and political wisdom as any sign of slackening attachment to Palestine. Herzl's dramatic vow, "If I forget thee, O Jerusalem . . ." was taken literally by the American Zionists and they saw no contradiction to this belief of theirs in their support for the appointment of a commission of inquiry of the conditions in Eastern Uganda. This basic tenet of Zionist credence they manifested at another occasion when in instructions given to American delegates to the London Zionist Congress, the annual Convention stated that

> The Convention does not consider Cyprus a place to colonize Jews and it firmly adheres to the idea of establishing colonies in Palestine and Syria only.

Such avowal in Herzl's conception of Zionism precluded any deviation from other principles of this conception. The fact that Herzl's Zionism was identical with the struggle for a political charter which had to condition any practical Zionist work in Palestine, made such approach to Zionism generally prevailing in American Zionism. When the first sprouts of practical Zionism appeared on the American scene, reaching even a point of most practical action in the form of personal Zionist attachment to the Land of Israel, through a purchase of a tract of land there, they were most vehemently opposed by the leaders of political Zionism. National Conventions became the forum for heated discussions on this problem. At one of such heated disputes, the intervention of Henrietta Szold was necessary to quiet down the excited proponents of the twin Zionist approaches to problems of implementation of the Zionist idea. How serious this controversy was is best illustrated by the fact that the official organ of the Federation, *The Maccabean,* had to devote an editorial to this problem in which it stated that

> political Zionism must be practical Zionism and practical Zionists must work to create an autonomous Jewish people in Palestine.

These formal classifications, though correct in whatever concerns the real approach to the ways of Zionist implementation, did not necessarily express any real understanding of what political Zionism stands for, what the conception of a "political charter" meant in the terms of Herzlian political Zionism. The lack of any sophistication in this respect was demonstrated to an amazing degree at the time of the Young Turks' revolution in 1908, which was supposed to open a new era in the history and policy of the Ottoman empire. Leading American Zionists considered the new program of the Turkish revolutionaries which spoke about liberalism, parliamentary democracy, autonomy, a sufficient guarantee for free Zionist activity in Palestine.

The most outspoken proponent of this opinion, Dr. Judah L. Magnes, even moved a resolution to this effect at the national Convention of the Federation. That this was in fact the general consensus of the delegates was proven in a vote taken on that resolution, which implied that the new Turkish constitution should be considered the realization of Herzl's conception of a political charter: only six votes were cast against the resolution, which was then adopted almost unanimously. The awakening had come very soon. The new rulers of Turkey turned out to be much more nationalistic, much less tolerant than the regime of the Sultan. They suppressed even those vague forms of autonomy which the old regime permitted in its many, multi-national provinces. Within months it became clear that Zionism had nothing to expect from the Young Turks, and that the political charter was as far from realization as it ever was. It is clear this overeagerness to see Zionism reaching a state of political conditions which would make its implementation possible was dictated by the strong desire to see Zionism work and emerge sound and strong from just theory and political discussion. This Zionist zeal was demonstrated on another occasion when the problem of the official language in the young Jewish school system in Palestine became the center of discussion. In the struggle for the preservation of Hebrew as the language of instruction at the Technion in Haifa, American members of the Technion's curatorium played

Henrietta Szold with first graduating class of Hadassa Nurses Training School

a decisive role. The Federation's Executive Committee intervened decisively at a moment when there was real danger that German might substitute for Hebrew at the Technion, that the will of the German *Hilfsverein,* which supported the Technion, would prevail. The American Zionist influence proved decisive in the first *kulturkampf* forced upon the young Yishuv.

The American Zionists went all out for Hebrew, even though they were not so sure that the language was modern enough to permit instruction in it. Their resolution supporting Hebrew stated clearly that it should be the language of instruction with "the exception of courses that demonstrably cannot be taught in Hebrew."

This special understanding for the role of Hebrew in the renaissance of the Jewish people was an ingredient, an integral part of American Zionism from its very beginning. Years before the Federation of American Zionists came into being, before Herzl's call reached America, Hebrew circles became the rallying point of dreams about Zion reborn. The first Hebrew literary society of Chicago, *Dorshei Ha-Sifruth Ha-Ivrith,* was founded in 1883, three years before the first branch of *Hovevei Zion* was established in that city. Chicago was no exception. The first official Hebrew organization in the entire world, *Schoharei Sefat Ever,* was founded in New York in 1881. It was preceded by a Hebrew periodical; *Hatzofe Ba-Eretz Hadasha,* first published in 1871.

The foundations laid, fostering of Hebrew in various forms became a permanent feature of Zionist activity in America. Periodicals in Hebrew, Hebrew courses, Hebrew circles appeared and . . . disappeared, to open the way for new efforts in this field. This was no easy task. Though many among the new immigrants had some knowledge of Hebrew from the Heder, the struggle for a living in the new country seemed not to be inducive for indulging in Hebrew reading, or speaking. Enthusiasts were not missing. When in 1910 the first issue of *Hadoar,* edited by Reuven Brainin, came off the press, a crowd of over 1,200 gathered despite heavy rain to greet the first issue. But the first Hebrew daily in America, *HaYom,* in 1910, did not last more than four months, and *Hameorer* of Daniel Persky had to close publication and announce in its eighth issue to "the tens of its subscribers that it would no longer take up their time . . ."

These touching examples of the struggle for Hebrew were not exceptions. Examples and proofs of these appeared periodically almost in every Jewish community with some semblance of a Zionist Society. Old and young tried their luck in this field. When a group of youngsters about Bar Mitzvah age organized itself as *Pirkhei Zion* (Flowers of Zion) they started publishing their own paper. There were publications for children, *Aviv,* by the Hebrew Teachers Union, and *Shaharith,* by the New York Bureau of Jewish Education. The financial demands for starting such publication must not have been too exorbitant if the founders of the monthly *Hatoren* were happy to report that after a year of soliciting, "a decent sum of between $400 and $500 was collected and the launching of the magazine made possible."

Though many of these attempts at the dissemination of Hebrew were rather spontaneous, independent of the organized Zionist movement, all were a corollary of the Zionist awakening and a function of the Zionist awareness throughout the country. But it would, of course, be unfair to conclude that organized Zionism did not consider Hebrew an integral part of Zionist education and Zionist conscience. The fourth annual Convention of the Federation, in 1901, adopted a resolution calling upon all Zionist societies to organize Hebrew study groups for their members and to support schools teaching Hebrew.

In this last respect of assuring Jewish education to Jewish youth, the Federation demonstrated a most remarkable grasp of the imperatives of Jewish survival in America. Educational problems figured prominently on the agenda of the consecutive Conventions. Care for education was not a superficial slogan. It stemmed from deep idological convictions about the role of Hebrew, of Jewish education in the rebirth of the nation. The resolutions adopted on this subject at the Seventh National Convention in Cleveland in 1904, were in fact a kind of a summing up of years that passed and years to come of Zionist concern for Jewish education. Among the many paragraphs on education, the formulation of an ideological base seemed to be important in the eyes of the Zionist leadership when they resolved:

"Whereas Zionism is not merely a political movement of the Jewish people, but also a natural striving to uplift its national spirit and revive its culture; and whereas Jewish culture was and is the highest aspiration of the Jewish nation, and the strength of its life, for the task of its fostering, it is resolved that the Federation of American Zionists undertakes the task of fostering the knowledge of the Hebrew language, Jewish history, ethics and awareness, giving the Jewish youth a thorough training in the Jewish national spirit as well as in physical culture."

Such approach to education was common to the spirit of the organized Zionists, whatever their formal organizational allegiance. The Federated Zionist Societies of the Midwest, in one of the annual reports of their administration, reported proudly,

One of the brightest developments of our movement is the building up of Sabbath schools for our children. The clamor for such institutions becomes the loudest in such Jewish communities where the Zionist movement has gained a foothold. The creation of Sabbath schools follows the organization of Zion societies with almost unfailing certainty.

From the perspective of over half a century of Zionist activities in America, and in view of the present-day state of Jewish education, it is somewhat hard to understand how it happened that the Zionist movement as such is so inconspicuously related to the highly developed net of the Jewish educational system of our days, how it lost so much of its influence in a vital field of Jewish life, in which it can proudly raise claim to being a pioneer and groundbreaker. Perhaps the fact that the Federation from the very onset abdicated its prerogatives in the field of education to one of its constituents, the Mizrahi, could, to some degree, explain the phenomenon of a pioneering organization which, instead of growing in stature in the field it pioneered, continued to lose influence in it to a degree of almost complete self-liquidation.

This preoccupation with Jewish education was well fitted into the pattern of the realities of Jewish life in America, and the serious encounters the fledgling Zionist movement had to meet in the early years of its existence.

The opponents of the Jewish national revival, of Zionism, on the American scene, were correctly influenced by their instincts when they mobilized their full strength at the moment Herzlian Zionism started finding root on the new continent. The Hovevei Zion societies which made their appearance in America years before the establishment of the World Zionist Organization were no threat to their ideology. They were limited in their appeal, and harmless in their actions. They constituted no political danger.

But Herzlian Zionism, political Zionism, was immediately acknowledged as the danger par excellence of the assimilationist theories.

Zion reborn, Jewish sovereignty reconstituted, were considered a direct threat not only to the ideological precepts of the assimilationists, but to their status in the general American community as well.

This basic enstrangement from the Zionist organization fed as well on another most potent factor: the distinction of geographical origin which characterized the protagonists of both inimical ideologies. The overwhelming majority of the early Zionist movement came from among the new immigrants from Eastern Europe. The anti-Zionists were almost exclusively recruited from among the "Westerners," Jewish immigrants of decades before, coming mainly from West Europe. The conflict between Zionists and anti-Zionists thus became to a large degree a conflict between "East and West." *The American Israelite* of January 13, 1898, stressed this point clearly:

The whole noise is made by some persons of recent immigration, with which we American Jews have absolutely nothing to do.

Brandishing Zionism as a movement alien to American Jews was therefore among the main tactical measures anti-Zionists adopted. They were not prone to be too sensitive in selecting arguments and even less in using proper language. Vituperation, abuse, upbraiding and insult were the common weapons of the anti-Zionists. The fact that the majority of those fighting anti-Zionists were Rabbis, casts a special light on the intensity of this fight, and the extremity of emotions it was to express.

The press, the sermons in the most important reform temples, the resolutions of the Central Conference of American Rabbis (Reform) are a most vivid illustration of the concentrated attack to which early American Zionism was exposed.

Leading this anti-Zionist crusade was the *American Israelite*. Quotations from this paper speak volumes:

These are fantastic dupes of a thoughtless Utopian fata morgana, momentary inebriation of morbid minds, and a prostitution of Israel's holy cause to a madman's dance of unsound politicians. . . . Zionism is a public lie and together with anti-Semitism comprises twin engines of Jewish destruction, with Zionism potentially the more dangerous.

To support these arguments, the anti-Zionists made use of quotations from statements of people who fought Herzl on his native ground, in Vienna. Dr. Moritz Guedeman, the Chief Rabbi of Vienna was quoted as having said -- that "Zionism is a suicide attempt on the part of Judaism. If anti-Semitism sets the brain of Herzl on fire, must we act as madmen too?"

Press attacks were not isolated excursions of the enemies of Zionism into the field of public discussion on what appeared, at that time, a burning problem of American Jewry's outlook on its future, on the future of the Jewish people in general. The representative organization of the Reform Rabbinate, the Central Conference of American Rabbis, considered Zionism a problem deserving its utmost attention. A resolution adopted at the Convention of 1897 stated:

> Resolved that we totally disapprove of any attempt for the establishment of a Jewish State. Such attempts show misunderstanding of Israel's mission, which, from the narrow political and national field has been expanded to the promotion among the whole human race of the broad and universalistic religion first proclaimed by the Jewish prophets. . . . We reaffirm that the object of Judaism is not political nor national, but spiritual.

The dissemination of the Zionist idea made further references to it a recurrent theme of the conventions of the Reform Rabbis. Their main concern was explicitly political Zionism. "We are unilaterally opposed to political Zionism," stated another resolution, adding, "The Jews are not a nation but a religion. Zion was a precious possession of the past, the early home of our fathers where our prophets uttered their world-subduing thoughts and our psalmists sang their world-enchanting hymns. As such it is a holy memory, but it is not our hope for the future. America is our Zion."

The argument which decades later used to be known as the "dual loyalty" issue became very soon a potent weapon in the hands of anti-Zionists.

". . . such (Zionist) attempts do not benefit but infinitely harm our Jewish brethren where they are still persecuted by confirming the assertion of their enemies that the Jews are foreigners in the countries in which they are at home, and of which they are the most loyal and patriotic citizens,"

stated another resolution of the Central Conference of American Rabbis. Individual leaders of the Reform Rabbinate were no less zealous. They tried to coin slogans. They attempted to frighten the newcomers from joining the Zionist movement unless they wished to cast doubt on their Americanism.

> America is our Palestine, the flag of this country is our banner, that Statue of Liberty in our harbor is the symbol of patriotism.

This onslaught had to be met. Though it was of concern to all Zionists, those who had been closest to the critics felt obliged to speak up in defense of Zionism's legitimacy and consistency with American patriotism. By some peculiar coincidence of American Jewish history, the leadership of early American organized Zionism came, to a considerable extent, from the ranks of the Western Jews, from the reform temples, from circles which had earned their name as "Yehudim." The division between "Westerners," and "Easterners" stopped at the leaders' table. The first president of the Federation of American Zionists, Prof. R. Gottheil, was a well-established personality in American intellectual life, a son of the rabbi of the important reform congregation, Temple Emanu-El. Dr. Judah L. Magnes, the secretary of the Federation, came from a similar environment, as did Cyrus L. Sulzberger, Vice President of the Federation and member of the well known family of publishers of the The New York Times. For them, accusations of lack of patriotism were a matter of serious concern. They engaged in ideological exchanges on this subject.

In the center of this argumentation was the example of American commitment in the struggle for national independence of Cuba, of Ireland. Why, they asked, is nobody casting doubts on the American patriotism of an Irishman who is supporting Ireland's struggle against England -- or, for that matter, why is it permitted that the best Americans risk their lives in the fight for the Cuban independence from the Spanish crown while only Jews who dare to support similar aspirations of their fellow Jews are castigated as doubtful Americans. In an article on "Patriotism and Zionism," published in The Maccabean, Sulzberger wrote:

> Patriotism is the crowning argument of the anti-Zionist.

After repeating the arguments concerning Ireland and Cuba, he expounded a full affirmation of Zionist goals. "There is a need in the world for a state which, by the nature, cannot aspire to be a great physical power, but which by its inherited tendencies and the principles to which it has tenaciously clung, is pre-eminently fitted to be among states what its people have been among peoples -- the exponent of justice, morals, of righteousness."

The idea of the mission which the Jews have to carry in the world, uttered by opponents of Zionism and accepted, with a different interpretation even by many American Zionists, as Sulzberger's article indicates, was not the only anti-Zionist argument. Exponents of anti-Zionism tried to engage in their struggle much more practical arguments, some of which showed deep perception in comprehending the intricate political, economic and social problems which the rebirth of a Jewish State might create. The leader of the Reform Conference of American Rabbis, Dr. Kaufmann Kohler enumerated the difficulties, the establishment of the State would encounter:

The Christian powers will not concede Palestine to the Jews; the hot climate of the land will hamper immigration; the State, even when established, will have poor prospects of becoming a leading state and will not be able to attract Jewish capital; the incongruous elements of which the Jewish State would be composed would initiate against harmonious blending into one commonwealth.

Nor was biting satire absent in the struggle against Zionism. The well known joke about the Zionist who manifests his Zionist devotion by sending to Eretz Israel a fellow Zionist on the account of somebody else's funds was originally coined in those days of the incipient Zionist movement. In its April 1903 issue, *The American Israelite* joked:

The safest kind of Zionist is the Zionist who urges the other man to go to the land flowing with milk and honey while the advocate is willing to remain just where he is.

In this chorus of anti-Zionist contempt, within the reform movement, voices of dissenters coming from this very group also made their mark. Reform Rabbis have been among the leading Zionist enthusiasts: to mention only a few of the most outstanding, Rabbi Gottheil, father of the first Federation President; Rabbi Stephen S. Wise, Rabbi Bernhard Felsenthal of Chicago, and many others.

In the great dispute on the virtues and foibles of Zionism, even declared opponents of the Zionist Organization had to admit its greatness. *The American Hebrew*, officially anti-Zionist but pretending nevertheless to be an objective press organ, reported on a Zionist meeting in New York:

It was the greatest meeting (the reporter) ever attended . . . Elements of greatness and majesty . . . The Jews of New York are thoroughly and wholly Zionistic.

There was no sign of the ghetto upon them. And in a report from the Zionist Congress of 1903, the same paper wrote: "Whatever we may think of Zionism . . . it attracts the most distinguished representative gathering. Compared with them, Alliance Israelite Universelle and Rabbinical conferences are pitiable."

Supporters of Zionism, whether members of the Zionist Federation or not, used arguments which reflected hitherto unadvertised approaches to the Zionist idea. Zionist endeavors were praised for the possibility they harbored to establish large colonies of Jews in Palestine, which in turn would help to relieve the congested Jewish quarters of Russia, Rumania, and even of London and New York. In other circles, Zionism was considered practical because "all that is involved is gold. And if gold is the substitute for arms, then Zionism can be realized even by a weak and dispersed people.

In spite of the numerical weakness of the organized Zionists, the general feeling was rather of strength, of power which could well contest any other force in the Jewish community. The Helsinki Program which established Zionism as a political force, able and called to contend for political influence in the countries of Jewish concentration in the Diaspora, found some resonance in America as well. The Zionists who came from Eastern and Central Europe carried not only the memory of deprivation, economic misery and the Zionist vision: they were imbued with the vision of the political awakening in the lands of their birth where Jews for the first time, were able to elect representatives to Parliament on Zionist tickets; they thought it therefore only natural to have a similar experience in the new land. Though officially American Zionists never reached more than the state of discussion whether a Zionist slate in congressional elections is at all feasible, active Zionists, interested in American politics, had tried to utilize Zionism -- and were quickly discouraged from any such ambitions. Tammany Hall strong-armed politicians had no scruples in using fists to tear down election posters put up in the windows of Zionist clubs on the Lower East Side.

The ephemeral escapade into *landespolitik,* became quickly an escapade nobody paid attention to, or remembered. The American way of making politics which excluded alliances on ethnic lines, the tradition of the American two-party system, the freedom and equality of opportunity afforded no fertile ground for a Zionist, or any other specific Jewish party. There were no specific Jewish problems to be solved, and no singular Jewish political interests, within America, to be expounded.

But developments in countries of Jewish concentrations made specific Jewish political action, even in America, imperative. The pogrom in Kishenev electrified and horrified the Jewish community in America. In this general awakening to the responsibility of American Jews towards the fate of their fellow Jews, suffering at the hands of the Russian anti-Semites, the Zionists felt that theirs was a primary obligation. The national awareness which Zionist ideas carried had predestined the young American Zionist movement to play the role of the herald in matters of concern with Jews in foreign countries.

It was therefore no wonder that in the actions on behalf of Russian Jewry, the Zionists assumed a leading role. With all its organizational weakness, the Federation of American Zionists was the only Jewish organization with chapters throughout the country, with a central leading body, with an ideology which represented not only the dream for national redemption and statehood, but also the awareness of national unity and the validity of unified political action.

Into such action they went. For the first time since the establishment of the Federation, American Zionists were called on to show their strength and manifest their will in mass meetings, parades, demonstrations. Kishenev, which seemed to have justified the Zionist theory on the necessity for a territorial concentration of Jews, of a Jewish State, gave American Zionists the first tangible issue for political muscle-flexing, for asserting its existence as an influential factor in Jewish life, reaching for a voice in affairs affecting the Jews as a nation, everywhere. And from this mass political action of demonstrating against the pogromist policies of the Russian government, and for the intervention of the American government, resulted the idea of self-defense, of armed resistance to physical attacks against Jews.

It would be an exaggeration to ascribe the cry for a Jewish self-defense force, which arose in the American Zionist movement of those days, to any clear, concise and planned conception of supplementing the political aims of Zionism with an element of enforcement, in the form of Jewish units equipped with arms, able and prone to use them. But there can be no doubt that the fact that such demand emanated from the Zionist ranks, that the Zionist Convention that took place in the year of the Kishenev pogrom devoted part of its deliberations to self-defense, was a direct and natural result of the general atmosphere Zionist ideas have generated.

That the call for a Jewish self-defense was something extraordinary was best proved in the fact that the only speech reported from the Federation's Cleveland Convention, in special detail, by the Associated Press, was the speech on Jewish self-defense, delivered by Dr. Judah L. Magnes.

In view of Dr. Magnes' later conversion to extreme pacifism, his championing of the self-defense idea reveals an interesting characteristic in the personality of the man who played such a leading role in America's early Zionism. This championing of the idea that force has to be met by force became an exalted call to American Jews. It was a call to tangible action. American Jews were called to provide funds for the self-defense units of the Russian Jewry. Though the call came from a Zionist leader and was voiced at a Zionist national convention, many non-Zionists and even some avowed opponents of Zionism responded eagerly to the call. The self-defense idea became a kind of symbol of an awakening Jewish national awareness that surpassed any, even the most audacious, expectations. Writing about it, about the kind of call which Dr. Magnes had voiced, Louis Lipsky remarked in an article in *The Maccabean*:

> The courageous word of Dr. Magnes held new content -- it was the Jew courageous, the Jew self-reliant, the Jew protestant that appeared on the American scene for the first time. . . . The ideas of self-defense led inevitably to self-emancipation and self-government. Democracy was an inevitable corollary.

Zionism, the ideas which emanated from Zionism, thus contributed unexpectedly to the democratization of the Jewish community in America. The delegates to the National Conventions of the Zionist Federation were the only Jewish leaders who were democratically elected. There was no other organization in Jewish life which could have pretended to have even a semblance of democratic principles observed in the selection of its leaders, in a more or less mass movement.

In contrast to the prevailing realities of Jewish public life, in which notables occupied the highest positions, and concentrated the overwhelming influence on the affairs of the Jewish masses, the Zionist movement introduced principles of democratic elections and democratic representation. Though the Kehilla in New York had formally no relation to organized Zionism, and the leaders of the American Jewish Committee were active in it, it was the brainchild of Zionists and Zionist influence that made its initial success possible. It was to some extent due to misunderstandings in the Zionist movement as such that the Kehilla, the general representation of New York Jewry, did not withstand the stormy onslaughts of those circles, who saw a death threat to their leadership aspirations, and sometimes even economic interests, in the estabishment of a representation of New York Jewry, which would have, by force of an inevitable process, become in time a truly democratic institution.

It is not hard to guess that with the success of the *Kehilla* experiment in New York, similar developments would have had to follow in other Jewish communities in American cities, and American Jewry would have followed the tradition of English Jewry where a central Jewish body represents the entire Jewish population. Many problems would have never arisen, first and foremost among them the problem of an American Jewish representation, to this day one of the most important questions of any action to be undertaken by or in the name of the entire American Jewish community. And there is no doubt that the entire history of American Jewry, in the last fifty years, would have followed a different path, that Jewish life in America today would have been much more coherent than it is, that the Hiobic lamentations on the future of the American Jew would have had no ground to stand on, and no source to stem from. Some hindsight observations published recently, such as the one contained in the memoirs of the Poale-Zionist leader, Baruch Zuckerman, who expresses regrets for his party's opposition to the New York Kehilla idea, only confirms the opinion that the Kehilla idea harbored revolutionary possibilities for the American Jewish community which were never fully exploited, though sporadic attempts have been made to recoup the loss and create in spite of it, some form of general, democratic representation of American Jewry.

In view of these realities, the Herzlian slogan of the "conquest of the *Kehiloth*" was evidently immaterial in the American Jewish community. As there were no *Kehiloth*, there was no object for a Zionist conquest. The proselytization efforts of American Zionism had to be concentrated around those circles which had already some organizational allegiance, and the great mass of Jews with no evident address.

The sweat-shop workers, the peddlers, the small artisans, the small merchants were the natural field of Zionist conquest. Here not only opposing ideologies contested the efforts of Zionism. In many of the youth circles Zionism was castigated as a "too idealistic movement" demanding too much from the individual. Veterans of the Zionist movement can tell many stories about the conflicts between the idealists, the Zionists, and the *"Ballniks,"* those who preferred a good time on the dance floor over those Zionist youngsters who called for sacrifices in the name of a Jewish State in Palestine.

In this contest with anti-Zionist assimilationists and convinced socialists grouped around the socialist Jewish press led by *Der Forward*, Zionism had to assert itself within its own ranks, torn by ideological divergencies. Though Poale-Zionism and Mizrahi posed no challenge, at that time, to the unity of the American Zionist movement, they nevertheless became catalysts of an ideological differentiation which resulted in the appearance of problems hitherto unknown in the Zionist movement. There was questioning of the priority of the Hebrew language in Zionism; the Poale-Zionists protested the use of German in the central organ of the Zionist movement and demanded that Yiddish get its proper share in the official publications of the Zionist movement. During the Uganda controversy, some of their most noted leaders, including Dr. Nahman Syrkin, took the stand that any territory could fulfill the Zionist aim of Jewish territorial concentration. Even the Golden Book of *Keren Kayemeth*, the Jewish National Fund, was a target of critical attacks and demands for complete disposal because it was rather a bourgeois institution which a decent Poale-Zionist should no recognize, much less support.

In this striving for ideological reforms in the Zionist movement even the Sabbath was not spared. There was a proposal that the Zionist movement abolish the institution of Sabbath and thus an additional argument was given for the self assertion of the other extreme within the Zionist Federation, the Mizrahi.

Fortunately these ideological disputes never transgressed the limits of organizational unity. The centrality of the Federation continued to be generally acknowledged. This spirit of unity was nourished not only by the awareness of its importance for the success of the young movement. The leadership of the Federation was tolerant enough to make any break-away superfluous. In this attitude, it was greatly assisted by the general atmosphere in the World Zionist movement and by the Zionist emissaries who started visiting the Zionists of the New

World, in whom Herzl himself vested so many and such important hopes.

The influence of these first Zionist *"shlihim"* (emissaries) was most important for the development of the American Zionist movement. The fact that these *shlihim* were of the highest caliber, enhanced the stature of the Zionist movement, branded either as a movement "of immigrants who do not understand America," or as a "movement of firebrands" whose minds were set aflame by anti-semitism, anti-semitic outrages of reactionary regimes in Europe. Nobody, not even the most rabid opponents of Zionism were able to dispute the authority and reputation of Dr. Shmaryahu Levin, when he set his foot on American soil. He came with the aura of a political leader who had achieved membership in the Russian Duma, the first Russian parliamentary institution, which resulted from a bloody revolution, and who dared to defy the Czarist regime, and was thus forced to become a political exile. "Former member of the Duma," a title invariably used by Dr. Levin, opened many doors hitherto closed to Zionist leaders. Even the circles, of what was considered a kind of Jewish aristocracy, at any rate, moneyed aristocracy, were willing to receive Dr. Levin and to listen to his "Zionist propaganda." His eloquence, intelligence, wit, personal charm, served extremely well the Zionist cause. And the fact that Dr. Levin asked for support for tangible projects in Israel, as the technical school in Haifa, made his pleas acceptable even to the ears of those rich American Jews who abhorred the very name of political Zionism.

Dr. Levin was only one of the first of Zionist emissaries, who represented in America the highest body of the Zionist movement. His mission was strengthened by Levin Epstein, the representative of the first practical efforts for the establishment of a Jewish economic entity in Palestine, and last but not least, Nahum Sokolov, whose fame as a Hebrew scholar, writer and Jewish leader could not have been overlooked or ignored by anyone. Even the citadels of assimilation, the most exclusive congregations of the reform movement, opened their doors to listen to Nahum Sokolov, and hear his message of a Jewish striving for national rebirth, and its first successes in Palestine.

This oral propaganda effort, in the form of meetings which drew increasing audiences, lectures in closed circles, banquets -- all this was supplemented by the Federation's Zionist literature. As early as November, 1901, the monthly publication of the Federation of American Zionists made its appearance. Under the editorial guidance of the "young, brilliant Zionist" as Louis Lipsky was characterized in a report to Herzl by Gottheil, *The Maccabean* accorded the Zionist movement in America a platform. The budget set aside for the new periodical did not indicate that excessive funds were available for this new venture for a permanent publicity and ideology organ of American Zionism. The amount of five-hundred dollars had to come from generous Zionists, and the existence of the periodical had to be assured through subscriptions by the Federated Societies, each paying five dollars annually and receiving in return, five copies.

The new magazine enhanced greatly the stature of the Federation. The editor observed strictly the programmatic resolution which proclaimed that *The Maccabean* will be a monthly of Jewish life and literature in Yiddish and in English. Ideological discourses, short stories, poems, essays were supplemented by extensive reports on the activities of Zionist Societies throughout the country. The gradual shrinking of the Yiddish section which led to its complete disappearance increased the pressure for a separate Yiddish publication. In 1909, *Das Yiddische Folk* was established, and the Zionist movement was given an organ of self-assertion in the world of the Yiddish press, in its best period of bloom and influence. Names like Senor Abel and Abraham Goldberg became associated, and in time identified, with *Das Yiddische Folk*, which opened a great chapter of Yiddish-Zionist journalism. Opponents of Zionism from the left, from the circles professing their allegiance to Yiddishism, were fought in the columns of *Das Yiddische Folk*, and Jewish immigrants who were still in the first stages of their linguistic absorption in America, found in the Zionist Yiddish press Zionist inspiration and information.

The leaders of the Federation of American Zionists were by no means satisfied with the Zionist missionary work done by the periodicals. They understood well that a successful political movement must provide its followers with more than a few articles and essays once a month. To solve this problem they opened the pages of the *Maccabean* to a permanent feature which listed existing books of consequence for the concept of Jewish national rebirth. *The Maccabean* would recommend "One Hundred Books For The Zionist Library," and facilities were provided for the purchase of such books. These cultural educational efforts were supplemented by a series of special publications sponsored by the Federation itself. The Federation sponsored publication of an English translation of Leo Pinsker's *Autoemancipation;* a special edition of Emma Lazarus' *An Epistle to the Hebrews; Aims of Zionism,* by Gottheil; *The Progress of Zionism,* by Norman Bentwich, a pamphlet of information on Palestine and the Jewish colonies. It promoted writings on Zionist subjects through establishing prizes of $50 for essays such as *"Disraeli and George Eliot," "Emma Lazarus and Michael Heilprin," "Pinsker and Mohiliver."*

Expounding Zionist principles in such publications supplied Zionist followers with the necessary arguments for their daily encounters with opponents. But it did not provide them with a detailed program of action, with clear directives as to how to react to the many problems of actual Zionist work facing the Zionist movement. The resolutions of the annual convention of the Federation had to provide these guide-posts. These resolutions supply a most detailed information of what really occupied the minds of American Zionists in those days. Great issues of the day such as the political charter and plans for Jewish colonization outside Palestine, of political versus practical Zionism were, in these resolutions, intermingled with practical tasks and programs the Federation considered important. It is surprising how deep was the understanding for the real needs of Zionist realization in Palestine in those first years of incipient American Zionism. American Zionists were instructed to urge the Zionist Congress to "set up an international exposition of Palestine products, agricultural and otherwise, to be transported from city to city and from country to country, so as to give ocular demonstration of the products of the Jewish colonies in the Holy Land"—an excellent exposition of the understanding for the idea of support for *"Totseret Ha-Aretz,"* way back, before this idea became of official concern to the Zionist movement as a whole. Calling for the provision of a Hebrew education for Jewish youngsters, the resolutions were imaginative enough not to use the misnomer of "Sunday Schools," using instead the name Sabbath Schools, while not refraining from taking up the problem of tuition, the basic problem of Jewish education till this very day.

Even care for agricultural education in Palestine was not omitted and a resolution of the Second Annual Conference of the Federation of American Zionists, held in Baltimore in 1899, allocated one hundred dollars as a nucleus of a fund to be secured through general appeal to the public and a special appeal to the Federated Societies to give at least ten dollars each, this fund to be devoted to the purchase of the sites in Modiin, for the purpose of creating a Maccabean memorial in the form of an agricultural college and settlement.

As important as all these resolutions and organizational measures might have been, and really were, for the progress of American Zionism towards the leading role it was destined to play in the decisive stages of the struggle for a Jewish state, they were supplemented by the first cautious steps towards political action whose importance was fully appraised by Herzl's political genius. In his struggle for opening Palestine for Jewish colonization, Herzl conceived a plan for making American influence instrumental in his pressures on the Turkish government. In a kind of prelude to future American interventions on behalf of Jewish immigration to Palestine, Herzl requested American Zionists to intercede with the American Congress, suggesting that it take up the Turkish restrictions against Jews entering Palestine. In a lengthy letter to Dr. Richard Gottheil of February 25, 1901, Herzl suggests that the question be raised "whether the Turkish government has the right to prevent American citizens, whether Jews or Christians from entering Palestine" Herzl went even further and requested him to intervene with President McKinley, such intervention to be undertaken after consultation with leading Jewish personalities, not necessarily of the Zionist leadership, such as Cyrus Adler, Straus, Sulzberger, Judge Rosenthal.

In his political perception, Herzl tried to make use of the discrimination against American citizens of the Jewish faith, as practiced by the Turkish government, for breaking the principle of anti-Jewish legislation concerning immigration to Palestine. Through this tactic he hoped to challenge non-Zionist Jews as well into action in view of their professed desire and readiness to fight anti-Jewish discrimination wherever it appeared. It was basically a repetition of this Herzlian tactic when some years later the Federation of American Zionists submitted to the American government a memorandum requesting intervention on behalf of the economic rights and interests of American citizens in Palestine.

Herzl was no exception among European Zionist leaders in his perception of the role American Zionists could and should play. In his message to the Cleveland Convention, Dr. Marmorek, one of Herzl's closest collaborators, stated:

Zionism in America gives the answer to those who want to make us believe that it is only those Jews groaning under the yoke, who are devoted to our national idea.

This idea was even more elaborated by Israel Zangwill when he wrote in The *Maccabean*, Zionism may have little to offer to the prosperous American Jew except moral dignity, as it would have had little to offer to the Jewish grandees of Spain before the days of the expulsion and Inquisition . . . I venture to think, the 313 American Zionist Societies are really stronger proof of our progress than the Russian, for not only is their ratio to the population somewhat higher, but they are founded by Jews free from the lower consideration of personal persecution. Thus America stands morally at the head of the Zionist movement, and because yours is the only Jewish population in the world which is both large and powerful, our suffering brethren are beginning to turn to America not merely as of old for a place of refuge, but as a center of political force for the solution of the Jewish question.

In its first one-and-a-half decades, American Zionism enjoyed exceptional stability. The Federation was led by only two Presidents, Prof. Richard Gottheil from its inception until 1904, and Dr. Harry Freidenwald of Baltimore for an entire decade, till 1914. With all its successes and the attention the Federation succeeded to attain on the American scene, it did not manage to break out of the relative isolation it was confined to. The Jewish community grew by leaps and bounds, and the membership of the Federation hardly registered any considerable increase. The enthusiasm of the Zionists was overwhelming, but did not fire the imagination of the many. Compared with Zionist organizations in other countries, the Federation of American Zionists was far from reflecting the relative strength of the Jewish community in America. It did even less live up to the expectations European Zionists had harbored concerning the role American Zionism had to play in the struggle for the implementation of the Zionist program. It was the war emergency, the outbreak of World War I, which brought a revolutionary change. When the Zionist organizations on the old continent were either destroyed or paralyzed as a result of the war, the American Zionists grasped the seriousness of the hour and the meaning of the Zionist mission which destiny had placed on their shoulders. American Zionism lived up to the greatness of the historic call. The words of the memorandum of the Zionist leadership in Galicia,

We don't know when the war will end, we don't know whether any of this committee will survive . . . the war will end some day and 2000 years of Jewish history will call upon American Jews to fulfill the Jewish aspiration for a Jewish Homeland

were destined to fall on receptive ears.

The Provisional Committee, representing all Zionist factions from left to right: Henrietta Szold, Dr. Stephen S. Wise, Jacob de Haas, Joseph Kesselman, Louis Lipsky, Charles A. Cowen, Shmaryahu Levin, Harav Meyer Berlin.   Standing: Blanche Shepard, Adolph Hubbard, A. H. Fromenson.

PART TWO

5

AMERICAN JEWRY MOVES TOWARD LEADERSHIP

EXECUTIVE COMMITTEE FOR GENERAL ZIONIST AFFAIRS

WITHIN WEEKS after the outbreak of World War I, the Zionist movement in Europe was struck at its very roots. The center of Zionist devotion, the Jewish communities in Central and Eastern Europe were paralyzed. War and its devastation hit millions of European Jews. The Zionist movement, based on the premise of the unity of the Jewish people, was faced with an unexpected development: Zionists confined within the borders of the warring parties no longer had ways to cooperate. And the Zionists leadership, the Zionist Executive, became suddenly the prisoner of political developments it could not influence. Located in Berlin, it lost its contacts, by force of events, with the Zionists in Eastern Europe, in fact, with the prime force and spiritual reservoir of the entire World Zionist movement. The historical creation of Herzl, the World Zionist Organization, the organizational framework of Jews aspiring to national redemption, lost its basic precept of existence -- its organizational unity, its ability for unified action. The World Zionist movement was thrown into the status of an army cut by enemy forces into small units, with no possibility of normal communication, and no central command.

Much sooner than anybody could have anticipated, American Zionists were called upon to be equal to the trust deposited with them by Herzl and other Zionist leaders, that in time of need and stress they would not fail their brethren.

The call came much too soon. The Federation of American Zionists had not yet attained capability for coping with the historic responsibility which political developments had thrust upon it. Although over a decade had passed since the establishment of the Federation, neither considerable growth in numbers nor new personalities of special standing were in sight. The last National, Annual Convention of the Federation before the outbreak of the war, held in June 1914, in Rochester, represented only 14,860 *shekel* holders. The budget this Convention adopted reached what was then considered the exorbitant amount of $12,150. And although spirits were high and the Convention decided to use its strength to fight the attempts of the *Hilfsverein* to foist the German culture on the *Yishuv*, signs of weariness were already visible. Speeches on new Zionist plans, on Zionist offensives were accompanied by expressions of doubt and impatience at the indifference of American Jews "who have forgotten the ancient hope of their people."

The failure of American Jewish masses to join the organized Zionist movement was not the only disappointment to befall the Federation. The self-confidence and outspoken enthusiasm which unity had lent the movement, after it finally overcame the first attempts of a schism, were put to the test in view of the new developments within the Zionist ranks. The *Poale-Zion* which started as a kind of subdivision of the Federation, and the *Mizrahi* which was considered a completely integrated part of the Federation, performing special functions in the name of the Federation, moved purposefully into the direction of complete organizational independence. Leading personalities of these two movements, who arrived from Europe, pressed for such separa-

Louis D. Brandeis with Dr. Shmaryahu Levin at a meeting of the Provisional Executive Committee for General Zionist Affairs.

tion with vigor. American Zionism stopped representing a monolithic political movement. The customary political nomenclature of right, left and center, which was alien to American Zionism in the first years of its existence, became common.

The renewed efforts of Louis Lipsky, the dynamic and imaginative chairman of the Federation's Executive Committee, to have the Poale-Zion reinvigorate its bonds with the central Zionist structures of the country, the Federation of American Zionists, went by unheeded. American Zionism headed towards political differentiation, which was bent on influencing the ability for action of the Zionist movement in America. The only consolation such developments harbored were the chances of expansion of Zionist influence into circles that had hitherto been shut off from such influence. Poale-Zion worked diligently at piercing the wall of enmity of the Jewish labor circles, and Mizrahi tried to extend its influence among the orthodox Jewry, which was at that time still the most powerful segment, numerically, of the Jewish Population. But all these organizational developments remained rather an internal problem of the Zionist movement. The Federation of American Zionists remained not only the power in the center of the Zionist movement, it was the only organizational Zionist framework which really counted in relations with Jewish non-Zionist groupings, as it was the only authoritative address for Zionist dealings with non-Jewish factors, first and foremost the non-Jewish public opinion, in and outside the government circles.

It is to the credit of these separate Zionist organizations that they actually never questioned the centrality of the Federation. The preponderance of the mother organization of American Zionism was not challenged by them, especially not by Mizrahi.

The outbreak of war in Europe was soon to put this special position of the Federation to test. The scattered and paralyzed leadership of the World Zionist Organization had to find

some substitute for two purposes: the continuation of care for the beginnings of Jewish colonization in Palestine, especially for the Zionist institutions there; and the provision of leadership for the World Zionist movement.

To move into the positions of leadership, American Zionism had to have some formal title of legality. To act without such title could have been branded as usurpation. An incident of history made such title available. Shmaryahu Levin, a member of the Zionist Executive, was on his way to South America, when on August 19, 1914, the ship suddenly changed direction and steamed into the New York harbor. The news that England and Germany were at war caused the ship's captain to change course, and thereby bring to America the man whose initiative was to open a new chapter in the history of American Zionism, and extend its influence far beyond the confines of the American continent.

With the concurrence of the executive of the Federation, under the chairmanship of Louis Lipsky, Dr. Levin sent out calls for an emergency meeting which said:

The Zionist Central Bureau in Berlin, established upon an international basis, is utterly destroyed. The organization in Europe is shattered. It is our first and most holy duty to hold and maintain in this critical moment the Zionist Organization and especially the positions we won in Palestine.

On August 30, 1914, an Extraordinary Conference of representatives of American Zionists met in New York, in the Hotel Marseilles. One hundred and fifty delegates participated in the conference. Poale-Zion sent three delegates as did Mizrahi. The representation of Poale-Zion had to fight its way to the general conference against internal opposition which fought the prospects of lending general Zionist authority to a conference which was called by and was supposed to strengthen the Federation of American Zionists.

The conference assembled in an atmosphere of crisis and emergency. American Zionists were well aware of the responsibilities they would have to bear. They knew that they were the only Zionist organization of consequence, which had the good fortune to act in a country not involved in war operations. Such position should have opened before them avenues of action on both sides of the war front, and certainly in Palestine. There was no need for lengthy deliberation before the assembly agreed upon the three basic tasks which American

Zionists were to take upon themselves: (a) the collection of a $100,000 fund for the Zionist institutions in Palestine; (b) the organization of relief work for Palestine in the Anglo-Saxon world and in Latin America, and (c) the representation of the World Zionist Organization before the American government, and every other government, when necessary.

The American Zionist movement had been catapulted into the forefront of Zionist endeavors. Financial assistance, relief, political action suddenly had been thrust upon an organization whose status in these areas appeared rather inconspicuous in relation to the triple task it aspired to undertake. The organization, which hardly covered its own annual budget of some $12,000, now set out to collect $100,000; a group that had no real avenues of contact with its own government, had now decided to become the political spokesman of the entire world Zionist movement, and to deal not only with the American government, but all the governments of the world whose positions and policies might have any bearing upon Zionist interests in the fate of Palestine, and the well being of its Jewish settlers.

It is against this background of American Zionist realities, and the overwhelming tasks American Zionists dared to undertake, that the appearance of a new Zionist leadership should be viewed. It seems that the old theory, that extraordinary times produce extraordinary personalities to deal with them, proved itself in American Zionism. A person of special standing, gifted and influential, practical and idealistic, appeared on the American Zionist scene. Louis Dembitz Brandeis captured the imagination of the delegates to the Extraordinary Conference. Without hesitation they grasped the opportunity to make use of his readiness to serve the Zionist cause. Brandeis was elected chairman, and Dr. Stephen S. Wise, co-chairman, of the Provisional Executive Committee for General Zionist Affairs, the body created by the conference for the implementation of the three point program suggested by Dr. Levin.

The choice of Brandeis to an official leading position in the Zionist movement electrified public opinion, Jewish and non-Jewish alike. The lawyer from Boston, already in his fifties, had built up a reputation of excellence, idealism, ability far beyond the confines of the Boston courtrooms, and the bar association of the Eastern States. The fame of the "people's advocate" had spread all over the country. His progressive utterances in

Jessy Sampter, the Jewish-American poetess, on the nature of Zionism, 1916.

defense of the common man, for a greater degree of economic democracy, against the rabid forms of American capitalism of those days, his influence on many of President Wilson's social ideas, were well known. And his successful mediation in one of the decisive strikes of the New York garment industry accorded the personality of Brandeis an aura of esteem and appreciation in circles for whom the Boston lawyer was as strange as any of the railway barons.

It is no wonder that a man of Brandeis' caliber, joining officially the Zionist movement, assuming in it a leading, highly responsible position, was associated with some kind of a revolution in the social and political standing of the Zionist movement. "The noise of immigrants" as the non-Zionist and anti-Zionist influential circles of the upcoming Jewish oligarchy called American Zionism, became suddenly the affair, the central preoccupation of a man to whom they themselves had to look up with respect and appreciation. Brandeis was not only prominent, successful in his profession, he had something they could not even dream of -- ancestry rooted in the United States, much more than they, many of whom had not yet managed to dispose of their German accent in the pronunciation of their own names. Brandeis' maternal uncle, Louis Dembitz of Louisville, Kentucky, was one of the three nominators of Lincoln at the Republican National Convention in 1860, while other members of the family were also well-rooted in American life for decades.

Overnight, Zionism became fashionable. Within a short period new personalities of standing joined the Zionist movement in various capacities of responsibility. Among them were Julian W. Mack, a judge of the U.S. Circuit Court; Felix Frankfurter, prominent professor of law at Harvard who was to follow Justice Brandeis on the U.S. Supreme Court bench; the philanthropists Nathan Straus of New York and Mary Fels of Philadelphia; Benjamin Victor Cohen, who became later one of the most important members of President Roosevelt's "brain trust"; Louis E. Kirstein, a prominent businessman and communal leader in New England; Colonel Harry Cutler of Providence, manufacturer, soldier and civic leader; Eugene Meyer, one of the most brilliant financial experts in America, later publisher of the *Washington Post*; Robert Szold, prominent lawyer and industrialist; and many others of lesser importance.

American Zionism gained a voice people wanted to listen to, the government had to pay attention to. It was a voice which detested compromise, and which was unconcerned with anything non-Zionists or non-Jews would say. To dispel the spectre of the "dual loyalty" accusation, Brandeis threw into the open his now historical statement that "to be good Americans, we must be better Jews, and to be better Jews we must become Zionists. Multiple loyalties are objectionable only if they are inconsistent." These basic ideological statements were accompanied by a call to action which American Zionists were long waiting for:

I know nothing about sacrifice -- I only know duty.

And this duty he instantaneously translated into terms of practical tasks:

Organize, organize, organize, until every Jew in America must stand up and be counted -- counted with us or prove himself, wittingly or unwittingly, of the few who are against their own people.

The call was heeded. Within less than a year the number of shekel purchasers more than doubled, reaching the number of 30,178; the number of affiliate Societies also practically doubled. But the greatest surprise was yet to come -- an organization which had struggled hard to meet an annual budget of some twelve thousand dollars succeeded within less than ten months to transfer to Palestine the sum of three hundred and fifty thousand dollars.

The assertive mood of American Zionism drew intensive fire from the anti-Zionists. For the first time in organized American Zionist history, an important segment of the American public joined the attack against Zionism. Representatives of vested interests in the American money aristocracy, antagonists of Brandeis on many other counts than his Zionist professions, thought that he laid himself open to a shattering attack by his Zionist activities. His Zionism made him — in their opinion -- open to an accusation of dual loyalty, of allegiance to a cause alien to American interests. Jewish anti-Zionists led by Reform Judaism's disciples of Isaac M. Wise, supplied ample arguments for such anti-Zionist, anti-Brandeis crusades. Brandeis seemed to have enjoyed this attack upon himself, as if intent upon drawing new fire, for he continued making ideological pronouncements pertaining to Zionism:

Noblesse oblige requires a Jew not only to live nobly as an individual but to reject assimilation as national suicide. It obligates him to strive for a land where the Jewish life may be naturally led, the Jewish language spoken and the Jewish spirit prevail. And that land is our fathers' land; it is Palestine.

Brandeis thus spoke up clearly not just in favor of Zionism, of Jewish settlement in Palestine; he cast his vote with political Zionism, the bogey of anti-Zionists of all sorts. An editorial in a leading daily newspaper suggested that Brandeis ought to "catch the first boat to the Mediterranean" and the organs of the Conference of American Rabbis thought this phrase an excellent one and deserving of repetition.

But these were the least serious worries of the Provisional Executive Committee for General

Zionist Affairs. Those who took pride in bringing Brandeis to Zionism were well justified in the hopes they laid in him. Jacob de Haas once said that Providence seemed to have chosen him to bring Herzl's word to the wide public, and later give American Jewry its Herzl, in the person of Brandeis. The growing demands for assistance to save the fledgling *Yishuv* from extinction under the persecuting whip of the Turkish authorities, prompted financial efforts far above and beyond the capacities of the Zionist movement, even compared with its unprecedented achievement in those first ten months of the existence of the Provisional Executive Committee. And together with the care for the preservation of the practical base for the future development of a Jewish Palestine, problems of political action started moving into the forefront of the Committee's concern. The task of representing the World Zionist movement before the American government and the governments of other nations entrusted to the Committee by the Extraordinary Conference, assumed special significance and urgency.

Performing the duties of a representative of the political aspirations of world Zionism became a most complicated task. Though the United States preserved officially its neutrality, the real sympathies of President Wilson were not obscured. German atrocities in Belgium and Northern France alarmed American public opinion. The relief effort undertaken under the leadership of Herbert Hoover met general support. Although formally based on humanitarian responses, the success of the relief action resulted from the vast reservoir of popular sympathy most Americans felt towards the Allied nations. This attitude was alien to the Jewish community.

The fact that Russia was part of the Allied front became the decisive factor in determining the Jewish position on war, and the relationship toward the fighting forces. For the Jewish masses in America, Russia was the symbol of reaction, rabid anti-Semitism, and pogroms. And as such, it deserved, in their opinion, only defeat. At the Boston Convention of the Federation in June 1915, the executive committee of the Federation issued a declaration of neutrality that read:

On the particular issues of war, the Zionist Organization of course passes no judgments and takes no sides. Its members are citizens of every embattled side.

. . . The Zionist Organization is neutral and cannot be otherwise.

At the same convention, Henrietta Szold, by then a leading Zionist personality, stated from the rostrum:

I do not believe that the allies are fighting in favor of the principle of independence for small nations.

And one of the Yiddish dailies exclaimed:

America has no business allying herself with an Asiatic barbarian.

This general anti-Allies mood had to be taken into consideration by the leadership of the Provisional Executive Committee. The Yiddish press, the four dailies, the periodicals, all represented the anti-Russian point of view. Russia's defeat -- they argued -- will mean the end of the pogrom regime, and therefore salvation for over five million Jews, living under the Czarist yoke. By circumstances of political conditions and interests, the Jewish masses found themselves in one group with the German-Americans, and became allies of the forces which were engaged in an effort to keep America out of the war.

Formally such position of neutrality was most convenient for the Provisional Executive Committee. The rump World Zionist executive which was established in neutral Copenhagen, called upon all Zionist groups to preserve their neutrality in war. Neutrality appeared to be the most appropriate political line to be taken by a movement whose adherents were scattered on both sides of the fighting fronts. And the situation prevailing on the fronts scarcely gave any definite indication as to which side would be the winning one. If fortunes of war had to influence political orientation, the probability of a victory of the Central Powers seemed to be much closer than any other outcome of the war. In these political considerations one more factor weighed heavily in Zionist minds: Palestine was a part of the Ottoman empire, and Turkey was a member of the German war coalition. To gain favors with the Central Powers could have meant a real hope for the realization of Zionist aims in Palestine. To make such hopes stronger, the German government did not spare pro-Zionist propaganda efforts, whenever such efforts were able to reach Jewish communities.

Neutrality was therefore the easiest solution for this perplexing political dilemma faced by Zionists the world over and in America. Hardly anyone in the Zionist leadership in America deceived himself into believing that neutrality would win any friends for Zionism. They understood the obvious -- that a neutral Zionist movement would be non-existent in the struggle of political powers, and certainly could count on no political gains to be derived from such attitude.

It was therefore neutrality with uneasiness, with apprehension, caused by the awareness that the dreamed-of Zionist charter for Palestine could be achieved only if and when the Zionist movement decided upon some clear position in the world conflict. Suddenly, the few thousand American Zionists realized that, in fact, they represented much more than the fifteen thousand individuals who had spent some dimes to purchase the Zionist shekelim. The mighty of the world let them know that they counted, that their opinion was of interest, even in this world-wide conflagration.

The internal dispute on political orientation became therefore even more heated. An incident which occurred in 1915, some two years before the American declaration of war against Germany, and before the Balfour Declaration, illustrates vividly the problems the American Zionist movement had to cope with. In that year, a well known active member of the Zionist movement in Germany arrived in America with the professed aim of going into business in the publication field. Mr. A. Strauss, well known to Dr. Shmaryahu Levin, looked for his first contacts in the ranks of the Zionist movement. Together with Dr. Levin he founded a new periodical for Jewish national Zionist thought. In a subtle manner, the new periodical attempted to infuse the idea that a German victory held promise for the Zionist cause. Such ideas expounded under the authority of Dr. Levin, the initiator of the Provisional Executive Committee for General Zionist Affairs stirred up the Zionist circles. At one of the meetings of the Executive Committee of Poale-Zion, which Dr. Levin was invited to attend, Dr. Nahman Syrkin, a staunch supporter of the Allied cause, vehemently attacked all those who collaborated with Mr. Strauss. Turning to Dr. Levin, he shouted angrily, "Dr. Levin, you are eating a spy's bread!" The uproar caused by such an accusation, the fist-fight which ensued, the throwing of ink bottles, is of no consequence in this instance. It only indicates, as does Dr. Syrkin's accusation, how emotionally loaded was this discussion on the course Zionism was to choose in determining its political orientation. The fact that Mr. Strauss was a week later interned by the American authorities as a German spy only underlines the interest Germany had in the political attitudes of American Zionists.

In the midst of this fateful discussion, differences of opinion emerged resulting from the hardening organizational and ideological divisions in American Zionism. The Provisional Executive Committee was the creation of the Federation of American Zionists, still by far the most decisive organizational framework of American Zionism. The fact that among the one hundred fifty delegates to the Extraordinary Conference which established this Provisional Executive Committee, only six represented Poale-Zion and Mizrahi combined, was indicative of the strength of these two Zionist groups, as compared with the main body of American Zionism, the Federation. But although acknowledging such relationship of strength, Poale-Zion and Mizrahi were not ready to be relegated to the role of passive observers of actions undertaken by the Provisional Executive Committee. They demanded real influence. To assure for themselves this influence, they demanded what they called "proportional representation" in the organs of the Provisional Executive Committee, and after this was granted, in the executive bodies of the Committee.

Here the first clash occurred with the chairman of the Provisional Executive Committee. Brandeis could not grasp how anybody could visualize an executive body to be composed of various party representatives, and thus lacking the unity of approach and decision necessary for real action. Steeped in principles of American democracy, Brandeis considered such demand outrageous and was not ready to accept the request of Poale-Zion and Mizrahi. Even their threat to leave the Committee did not influence his position. Brandeis was not ready to sacrifice principles and ability of action for political expediency, even if it meant Zionist unity. Efficiency in action meant to Brandeis more than formal unity, hampering decision-making. Soon this demand for proportional representation in the Executive branch was complicated by the discussion on the prerogatives of the Provisional Executive Committee. The leaders of the Committee aspired to supervisory powers over the Zionist activities of all Zionist formations in the United States. Poale-Zion wanted these prerogatives limited to problems related to the World Zionist movement, and its wider interests.

The first split in the united Zionist front was unavoidable. At the conference called by the Provisional Executive Committee, on June 28, 1917, the Poale-Zion and Mizrahi decided to leave the Committee. Efforts to heal the rift, made due to the intervention of the World Zionist Actions Committee which instructed to give Poale-Zion and Mizrahi a representation on all the working committees, with the exception of the political committee worked only in part. Mizrahi was satisfied with the concessions, while Poale-Zionist leaders refused to accept the compromise. Among the Poale-Zionist leaders who strongly opposed any compromise and called for final secession from the United Zionist forum, was David Ben Gurion, who joined the Poale-Zion leadership in America after going into exile from Turkish-ruled Palestine. It was at that time that the ideological differences in American Zionism came to light. When the Poale-Zionists stated their case and threatened secession, their representatives heard a remark by one of the intellectual authorities of American Zionism, Professor Horace Kallen:

"You are hyphenated Zionists," Zionist Socialists. In American realities such definition bore the mark of some kind of lesser allegiance to the central cause, as this term was originally used by former President Theodore Roosevelt, who called "hyphenated Americans" all those Americans who were not ready to drop from their Americanism their allegiance to the countries of their origin.

These developments, as aggravating as they were, remained somewhat outside the main stream of the American Zionist movement and its response to the needs and opportunities which World War I created. In broad terms and in basic endeavors, American Zionism remained united, ready for the historic mission it was called upon to fulfill.

The first contingent of nurses of the Hadassah Medical Unit sent to Palestine after World War I. Miss Henrietta Szold (first right, sitting, front row). At her left leading members of Hadassah.

6

TOWARD THE BALFOUR DECLARATION AND THE PALESTINE MANDATE

THE INTENSIFICATION of the Zionist activities heralded by the doubling of the Federation's membership within a year of the assumption of leadership by Brandeis, spilled over to all other fields of concern for the future of Palestine, and the Zionist movement. The National Convention in Baltimore, in 1916, which launched a fund-raising drive for $1,000,000 for a stock company to finance the upbuilding of Palestine, formulated a challenging slogan for American Zionism: "More money through more societies, having more members." Such slogan was in conformity with Brandeis' general evaluation of the components of Zionist strength and the resulting measure of influence. "Organize, organize, organize" — these three words of Brandeis' basic advice to fellow Zionists were to become the order of the day for the Zionists, to have them readied for the political role American Zionism will have to play. The chairman of the Provisional Committee, Brandeis; the Committee's co-chairman, Dr. Stephen Wise; the executive secretary, Jacob de Haas, had no difficulty in preparing for the political action they knew they will have to undertake in the name of American Zionism, as an exponent of American Jewry in general. They knew that they could justify their claim for representing the sentiments of the majority of Jews in America only through multiplying the number of organized Zionists.

But in readying themselves for the role they were called to play in the implementation of the Zionist charter idea, they seemed to have been too much concerned with the general attitude of the American government toward the nations involved in the world struggle. Though the basic sympathy of the Wilson Administration toward the cause of the Allied Powers was no secret, in spite of the official policy of neutrality, Wilson and his Administration were reluctant to encroach upon the interests of one of the partners of the Central Powers' bloc, of Turkey. And any plan of support for Jewish Zionist interests in Palestine was in direct contradiction with the Turkish sovereignty over that part of the Turkish empire. At a time when Britain and France had already concluded a pact for the division of spheres of influence in the territories of the Turkish empire, the American government was still dreaming of weaning away Turkey from the Central Powers, and of a separate peace with that country. America hoped to make, through such an accomplishment, a major contribution to its professed intentions of serving the interests of peace, and cutting the war short—at least on the Eastern front, across the entire Middle East.

From this point of view, Zionist interests were rather in formal clash with American "war aims." Though the official policy of the Zionist leadership was still observing neutrality the most vital centers of the Zionist movement had long declared the identity of the Zionist cause with that of the Allies. Zionist military units had already fought at the side of the Allied forces in Gallipoli, the British Zionist movement was already engaged in intensive efforts for gaining the sympathy of the British War Cabinet for a pro-Zionist declaration of policy, and the idea of Jewish military formations, fighting with the Allies against Turkey, the Jewish Legion, was officially supported by many Zionist leaders. The July 22, 1916, statement of the British Secretary for Foreign Affairs, Sir Edward Gray, that

> The British Government has made it known officially that the Powers will strive after the war towards the restoration of Palestine by the Jews

had removed any doubt concerning the side in the World War with which Jewish-Zionist interests were deposited.

These interests were already far advanced in the direct negotiations of the Zionist leaders in Great Britain, headed by Dr. Haim Weitzman, with the British War Cabinet. In Britain's quest for assuring the Imperial Road to India and the Suez Canal, hegemony over Palestine was a vital pre-condition. But Palestine was a part of the Turkish empire. To extend British influence to this area two obstacles had to be overcome: Britain had to do away with its own war propaganda which kept on assuring that Britain had no plans for annexation of foreign territories; the Sykes-Picot agreement, which divided spheres of influence, in the Middle East, between France and Britain, had to be somehow annulled to make void the provision according to which Northern Palestine had to become part of the French-ruled area, and the rest of Palestine internationalized. Of course, all this had to be done in addition to achieving the basic condition—that of a victory over the Central Powers, over Turkey, which was by no means yet assured, and of gaining American support, which was slow in coming.

In such general political situation Jewish support for Britain's war aims in the Middle East was of serious importance. Under the veil of supporting the Zionist demand that Palestine become open for an internationally guaranteed Jewish National Home, an opening could have been found for bringing British national aims into the Middle East. A Jewish demand that Great Britain become the trustee over Palestine to assist and supervise the process of the building of the Jewish National Home appeared as the best instrument for overcoming most of the existing obstacles. In addition, Jewish support for Britain's war aims meant also active support of Jews all over the world for the Allies' cause in the war.

In this overall scheme of Zionist-British cooperation, the support of American Zionists was most important, and in certain respects, almost decisive. The fact that American Zionism was headed by Brandeis, a Justice of the Supreme Court, and close friend of the President, made the approach to American government circles easier, self-evident. The three and

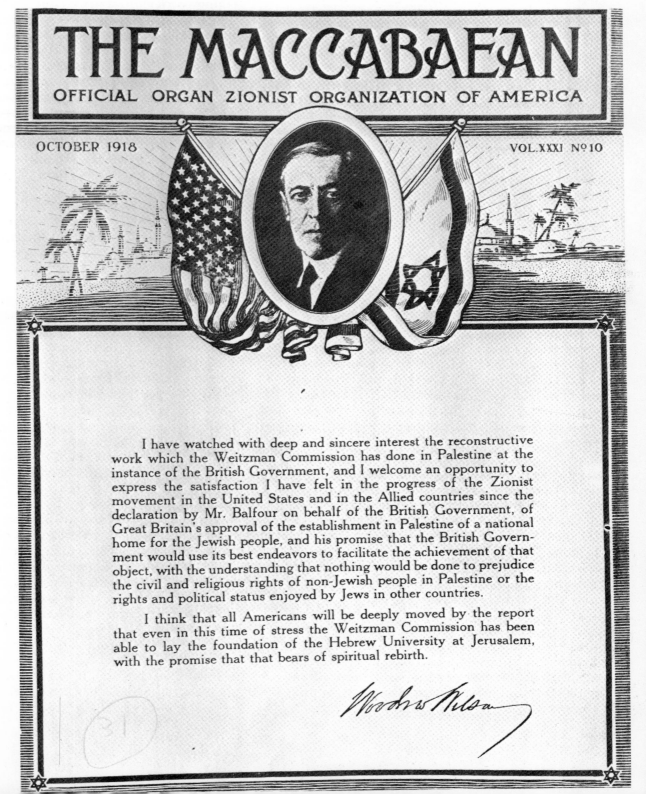

President Wilson's pro-Zionist declaration as displayed on cover-page of The Maccabean.

THE MACCABAEAN

OFFICIAL ORGAN ZIONIST ORGANIZATION OF AMERICA

OCTOBER 1918   VOL. XXXI No 10

I have watched with deep and sincere interest the reconstructive work which the Weitzman Commission has done in Palestine at the instance of the British Government, and I welcome an opportunity to express the satisfaction I have felt in the progress of the Zionist movement in the United States and in the Allied countries since the declaration by Mr. Balfour on behalf of the British Government, of Great Britain's approval of the establishment in Palestine of a national home for the Jewish people, and his promise that the British Government would use its best endeavors to facilitate the achievement of that object, with the understanding that nothing would be done to prejudice the civil and religious rights of non-Jewish people in Palestine or the rights and political status enjoyed by Jews in other countries.

I think that all Americans will be deeply moved by the report that even in this time of stress the Weitzman Commission has been able to lay the foundation of the Hebrew University at Jerusalem, with the promise that that bears of spiritual rebirth.

Woodrow Wilson

Members of the Zionist Commission arrive in Jerusalem, in 1918. Left to right: Van Vriesland, Rudolf Sonnenborn, Robert Szold, Dr. Harry Friedenwald, Jack Mosseri, Dr. David de Sola Pool. As photograph shows American Zionists were eminently represented on that Commission.

a half million of American Jews appeared to be an important factor in influencing American public opinion, and the American government, in the formation of their attitudes towards the warring sides. It was therefore natural that British Zionists, and first of all the man primarily responsible for the negotiations with Britain, Dr. Haim Weitzman, turned time and again to Brandeis, Wise and de Haas urging them to achieve some kind of American commitment for supporting the British-Zionist cooperation and agreement concerning the future of Palestine.

The political conditions prevailing in America were not too conducive for such public American intervention. There was a need for a political enlightening effort to make American Jews understand that in spite of their attitude towards one of the partners of the Allied camp, Russia, they were nevertheless bound to support the Allies' cause if they really hoped, as a result of the war, for some political gains for Zionism. And dealing with the American government, American Zionists had to overcome not only America's formal policy of neutrality before America declared war on Germany, April 2, 1917, but as well America's efforts to reach some understanding with Turkey. American apprehensions that outright support for Great Britain's devices in the Middle East could alienate other partners in the Alliance, France and Italy, were also bound to be considered.

It is in these special political circumstances that the American Zionist leadership had to carry the burden of mobilizing support for the British declaration of cooperation with Zionist efforts in Palestine.

The American government understood well the real intentions of Great Britain in her dealings with the Zionists. In one of the discussions of the Zionist demand that President Wilson state publicly his sympathy for the Zionist hopes in Palestine, President Wilson's adviser, Colonel House, remarked:

The English naturally want the road to Egypt and India and Lloyd George is not above using us to further their plans.

This reluctance of "being used by the British" was not the only reservation the American government had concerning the Zionist demands for public support of Zionist aims in Palestine. America considered such support open interference in the affairs of a state it was trying to wean away from the Central Powers. These desires were no pious intentions. Henry Morgenthau, a former American ambassador in Turkey, was sent on a clandestinely official mission to Turkey to start negotiations for having the Turkish government quit the Central Powers' camp. Such efforts ran contrary to the political plans of the Zionist movement. Turkey's compliance with the American inducement would have meant exempting Turkey from the consequences of defeat at the hands of the Allied Powers. The chain of events in such case was clear: The integrity of the Turkish empire would have been saved and the entire plan of British-Zionist cooperation in Palestine would have lost its base; its pre-condition, the chance for British rule over Palestine would have become null and void.

The American Zionist leadership had therefore a most immediate task: to spurn the Morgenthau mission. Morgenthau's assertions that he had already support for his mission in government circles in Turkey were in fact completely baseless. In conversations with President Wilson, Colonel House, and the State Department, Morgenthau was unable to produce any semblance of proof that his mission was not a product of imagination, which had happened to meet the desires of the Administration. There was therefore no difficulty to impress on the Administration that Morgenthau needed to be watched and controlled, to assure that his mission would not discredit the Wilson Administration. Thus, Justice Brandeis had no difficulty in inducing Secretary of State Lansing to include Felix Frankfurter in the Morgenthau mission. Frankfurter's Zionist devotion was sufficient guarantee that Zionists would not be stymied by Morgenthau's statements. The inclusion of Frankfurter, at that time assistant to Secretary of War Newton D. Baker, was also befitting the Administration's tactic in its efforts to keep secret the real purpose of the Morgenthau mission. Press reports presented the mission, which ultimately included also the treasurer of the Federation of American Zionists, E. W. Levin-Epstein, as an investigation of the conditions in which Jews in Palestine, and in other territories of the Turkish empire were living. Surprisingly, these news reports stressed the fact that though this mission had the sympathy of the U.S. government, it had nothing to do with the prospect of the establishment of a Jewish State.

These precautionary steps against Morgenthau's diplomatic fancies indeed prevented the damage his mission was bound to cause the Zionist interests. The two Zionists in Morgenthau's mission, Frankfurter and Levin-Epstein, kept Dr. Weitzman informed of Morgenthau's actions and movements. They were also instrumental in having Weitzman come to Gibraltar for a meeting with Morgenthau, a meeting that proved to become an important factor in scuttling entirely the Morgenthau mission.

This service which the American Zionist leadership had done for the strengthening of the plan for Zionist-British cooperation in the solution of Palestine's political future, was no more than a preliminary step in the political efforts that had to come. Though the British Zionists had reached, basically, agreement with leading members of the British War Cabinet, to turn this understanding into a binding formal government statement, it was still a most serious and difficult task. Assistance of the American Zionist leadership was of primary importance for achieving this goal.

The reasons for American siding with a British statement of support for Zionist aims in Palestine were manifold. The United States had already moved into the position of the leading, almost decisive power in the Allied camp. American support for such statement appeared tantamount with overcoming the opposition of the other Allied powers, primarily France and Italy, which were not at all eager to cede Palestine completely to British influence. And the over three and a half million Jews in America of those days were not an unimportant target in Britain's devices for the political gains Britain hoped to derive from a pro-Zionist statement.

The British Zionists were therefore insistent in urging an American declaration of support for the Zionist-British cooperation in achieving Zionist aims in Palestine. James Rothschild, acting on behalf of the British Zionists, urged Brandeis to meet the British Secretary for Foreign Affairs, James Balfour, on his visit to the U.S., in the spring of 1917, and speak with him on Jewish aspirations in Palestine. Similarly, Weitzman urged Brandeis to gain President

Henrietta Szold to her relatives in the U. S. on her travels in Palestine and meetings with new immigrants, September, 1920.

Wilson's support for these aspirations. Of course, there was not too much need for prodding Justice Brandeis into such efforts. Brandeis saw Balfour twice, and on May 6, 1917, on a Sunday, he had a lengthy meeting with President Wilson, which he registered in the form of notes dictated to Jacob de Haas, the secretary of the Provisional Executive Committee:

The interview lasted three-quarters of an hour, in the course of which Brandeis explained to the President the general Zionist policy . . . and the difficulties involved in the settlement of the Zionist question in Palestine as between French and English policy. . . .

The President answered him that he was entirely sympathetic to the aims of the Zionist movement, and that he believed the Zionist formula to establish a publicly assured, legally secured homeland for the Jewish people, would meet the situation . . . that the President would at the proper time make a statement, but that he would first bear in mind the situation arising in France and would exercise his influence in that direction, and that only thereafter would he consider making public his views, and that his utterances under that head would be drafted by Mr. Brandeis. . . . Further, the President expressed himself in agreement with the policy, under England's protectorate, for a Jewish homeland.

This report on the decisive intervention on behalf of the Zionist plan, with the American President, revealed as well the basic shortcoming of the American attitude. At a time when the success of the Zionist plan necessitated to a certain degree open, public support on the American side of the ocean, the American Zionists were unable to deliver. It seems that in the appraisal of the importance of that public support, Brandeis himself lacked the full measure of conviction that such public statement was really of most vital importance for Zionism.

Throughout the entire period of late spring and fall of 1917, which preceded the publication of the British document on the support for the Zionist aspirations in Palestine, consecutively called the Balfour Declaration, a lively exchange of correspondence and cables was going on between the leadership of the Provisional Executive Committee and Dr. Weitzman. Brandeis played the role of the somewhat reluctant partner in getting American support and in exerting his influence to make public the historic action which had to give Zionism its charter, and create the publicly secured base for the implementation of Zionism.

Brandeis' associates, Dr. Wise, his co-chairman in the Provisional Executive Committee, and the executive secretary of the Committee, de Haas, who were much more eager to fulfill Weitzman's demands for making public the American support, had to acquiesce with Brandeis' definite position not to do a thing which could have been interpreted as an attempt to force the hand of the American Administration on this question. Brandeis seemed to have been satisfied with the support, given in principle, by the American Administration, for the Zionist plan. He considered relating this support to the British government, in a confiden-

tial form, completely sufficient for the Zionist aims. He must have thought that his actions on behalf of this plan, his interview with President Wilson, meetings with Wilson's adviser Colonel House, his lengthy conversations with Lord Balfour, gave results which didn't need any elaboration. And he must have certainly considered clear and decisive enough the summary of the Zionist aims as phrased by the British Zionists that:

Palestine be recognized as the Jewish National Home; Jews of all countries to be accorded full liberty of immigration; Jews to enjoy full national, political, and civil rights; a charter be granted to a Jewish company for the development of Palestine; local government to be granted to the Jewish population; the Hebrew language to be officially recognized,

formulations which he had submitted to the State Department with a personal note, on the stationery of the Provisional Executive Committee for General Zionist Affairs, reading:

I think you will be interested in enclosed formulation of the Zionist program by Weitzman and his associates and which we approve.

But in spite of Brandeis' reluctance to exert too much pressure on the Wilson Administration for an open, public statement of support for the Zionist aims, this pressure was building up all over the country at a growing pace. By October, 1917, this pressure reached such a degree that Colonel House decided, on October 13th, to complain privately to President Wilson that:

The Jews from every tribe descended in force, and they seemed determined to break in with a jimmy if they were not let in.

Great Britain had thus achieved one of the main purposes of the support given the Zionist cause, which Lloyd George, the British Prime Minister, at the issuance of the Balfour Declaration, thus appraised 20 years later, in his testimony before the Palestine Royal Commission:

The launching of the Balfour Declaration was done for propagandist reasons . . . It was believed that Jewish sympathies or the reverse would make a substantial difference one way or the other to the Allied cause. In particular Jewish sympathy would confirm the support of American Jewry, and would make it more difficult for Germany to reduce her military commitments and improve her economic position on the Eastern front. The Zionist leaders gave us definite promise that, if the Allies committed themselves to give facilities for the establishment of a National Home for the Jews in Palestine they would do their best to rally Jewish sentiment and support throughout the world to the Allied cause. They kept their word.

This preoccupation with political action on behalf of Zionism has not limited American Zionist and general Jewish support for action on behalf of general Jewish interests in the post-war era. The plight of European Jewry, the destruction Jewish communities suffered in war, the problem of their legal standing had put before the largest Jewish community which remained intact, a historical mission of world-wide significance. American Jews did not intend to shirk the responsibility. As early as in 1914 voices had been raised for the organization of a representative body of the entire American Jewish community. The American Jewish Congress idea was conceived.

Originating in circles close to the Jewish masses, the Congress idea exercised a growing appeal. Zionist leaders, the Yiddish papers, led the crusade. Though Brandeis himself showed, initially, some reluctance, he and the entire Provisional Committee acknowledged the role, a body representing the entire American Jewish Community, could perform in the coming political struggle for Zionist implementation. Zionism was not the only concern of theirs. Relief work for Jewish communities in wartorn Europe and in Palestine, assurance of political rights for those Jewish communities was of concern as well. Compared with the Provisional Executive Committee, a Congress held promise of broadening the base for Zionist demands, which no Zionist leader could have neglected.

Of course, they were politically mature enough to see also the political dangers such Congress could bear for Zionism, as nobody could guarantee that in a general Jewish representative assembly Zionists would carry enough weight to assure the inclusion of the Zionist program in the Congress resolutions. Amazingly enough, some leading Zionists did not hide their worry that a Congress, which would adopt the Zionist program would make the Zionist Organization superfluous . . .

But all these hesitations and apprehensions were not strong enough to withstand the pressure of the public clamor for a Jewish Congress. The feeling that post-war Europe would not be more the same as before the summer of 1914, that American Jews bore a responsibility for the political emancipation of European Jews, was common. In fact, the Jewish Congress movement was part of the preparations all suppressed nationalities had started for the presentation of their demands after the war, at the Peace Conference. America was abounding then with congressional movements of Poles, Armenians, Ukrainians. But the Jewish Congress idea was an innovation, as it had, for the first time, striven to claim for Jews equal rights with any other nationality.

No wonder that such approach met with strong opposition from the circles of the Reform Rabbinate and the American Jewish Committee. The idea of Jewish nationhood ran contrary to all beliefs they had held. It was basically a Zionist concept. In their fight against the Jewish Congress idea they used each and every available argument. The bogey of "double loyalty" didn't seem convincing and sufficient enough. The spectre of sheer national treason was raised. To use the definition "Congress," they argued, will infringe on the prerogatives of the United States Congress, and is bound to shed a most negative light on the allegiance of Jews to American institutions. As an interesting illustration of this state of mind, could serve an episode in a meeting, at which the Jewish Congress was discussed, when Judah L. Magnes sent a note, in Hebrew, to one of the supporters of the Congress idea reading:

Al tikra Congress, ela Conference. (Don't call it Congress—but Conference.)

The word Congress was not the only concern of opponents of the entire idea of a democratically elected representation of American Jewry. They were not ready to acquiesce to the formulation of Congress aims as striving to assure the national rights of Jewish communities in the Diaspora, and Jewish national aspirations in Palestine.

American Zionists were called upon to play, in this dispute, a decisive role, by far exceeding their formal numerical strength. The Executive Committee was already a power the entire Jewish community had to reckon with. It played a decisive role in the negotiations for assuring the participation of the entire Jewish community in the Congress. When at last, in March, 1916, a preliminary conference for the American Jewish Congress was held in Philadelphia, Justice Brandeis, the chairman of the Executive Committee for General Zionist Affairs, appeared as the most natural choice to serve as chairman of the "Jewish Congress Organization Committee." A resolution concerning Palestine stated that the Congress would labor "for the furtherance of Jewish rights in Palestine and for Zionist development in all its phases." Adopted at this Conference, at which 367 delegates represented some six thousand Jewish organizations throughout the country, it gave the Zionist program a backing the Zionist movement could have hardly dreamed of a year or two ago.

But in spite of this obvious political success, the desire for full Jewish unity weakened the Zionist determination to exploit fully the achieved result. Under the pressure of the American Jewish Committee, the Zionist representatives on the Jewish Congress Organization Committee agreed to have the Palestine resolution watered down and replaced by a formula which spoke only of "securing and protecting Jewish rights in Palestine." The struggle against this curtailment of the Zionist section of the Congress platform, spearheaded by the Poale-Zionists resulted in a referendum among the delegates who rejected the compromise and accorded both a victory for the interests of political Zionism, and a rebuke to the leadership of the Jewish Congress Organization Committee which succumbed to the pressure of American Jewish Committee. Thus the restoration of the original formulation of the Palestine platform proved above doubt how strong are the Zionist feelings in the American Jewish community. But this success did not suppress many of the political squabbles around the Congress idea, and organization. Even the successful election act of the Congress delegates, on June 10, 1917, in which 325,000 Jewish voters participated, after paying a nominal tax poll, did not put an end to the attempts to minimize the impact of the Congress and its influence. After all efforts to stymie the Congress idea had failed, new obstacles were raised to postpone the date of the Congress, in order to have its impact wear out and weaken. "Not before cessation of hostilities" became the slogan of opponents of having the Congress convened. Again arguments of loyalty to the American government were raised. Formulation of demands of the Jewish community, to be submitted to the Peace Conference, was proclaimed as hampering the Administration's freedom. Even an alleged communication from the White House to that effect was used as an argument.

But the delaying tactics did not undercut the basic importance of the Congress as a democratically elected representation of American Jewry. All shades of Jewish opinion, all organizations, including the American Jewish Committee, became partners in the American Jewish Congress. When it finally assembled in Philadelphia, on December 15, 1918, it was proclaimed as the constituent body of the American Jewish Democratic representation and its resolutions were considered the Magna Charta of American Jews in their worldwide Jewish responsibilities.

From the Zionist point of view, the Congress was a major success. At the moment of political decisions on the future of Zionism, the Zionist program gained the support of a united American Jewry. Judge Julian W. Mack, a leading Zionist, was elected president of the Congress, and two other leading Zionists, B. Harry Friedenwald and Henrietta Szold, vice-presidents. The basic decisions of the Congress were most important for Zionism's quest for American Jewry's support in the final stages of its struggle for winning an internationally guaranteed title for a Jewish Palestine.

The resolutions about sending a delegation to cooperate with representatives of other Jewish communities at the Peace Conference in Paris, instructed the delegation to cooperate with

> representatives of other Jewish organizations, and specifically with the World Zionist Organization to the end that the Peace Conference may recognize the aspirations, and historic claims of the Jewish people with regard to Palestine, and declare that in accordance with the British government's declaration of November 2, 1917, endorsed by the Allied governments and the President of the United States, there shall be established such political, administrative and economic conditions in Palestine as will assure, under the trusteeship of Great Britain, acting on behalf of such League of Nations as may be formed, the development of Palestine into a Jewish Commonwealth.

As could have been expected, the last paragraph of the resolution repeated the provisions of the Balfour Declaration, concerning the rights of the non-Jewish communities in Palestine, and the civil rights of the Jewish communities all over the world. American Zionists appeared to be adhering faithfully to the position taken during the negotiations on the wording of the British declaration. They had supported those two provisions in the Balfour Declaration, that were to become major obstacles in the implementation of the purposes for which the Balfour Declaration was issued.

But basically, the resolution adopted by representatives of the entire American Jewry, including the American Jewish Committee, was a Zionist achievement of paramount importance. Moreover, irrespective of the Balfour Declaration it spoke of the "development of Palestine into a Jewish Commonwealth," thus stating clearly that all of Palestine has to become a Jewish Commonwealth.

It is clear that the Balfour Declaration facilitated greatly the Zionist efforts for winning general Jewish support. American Jewry was jubilant. The Balfour Declaration relieved sentiments which the number of shekalim sold have never reflected even faintly. The complete disproportion between the number of Zionists organized, and the enthusiasts of the Zionist idea, was never so clear and obvious as it was at that time. Jewish masses were carried away with the historic events they witnessed. They used every occasion to demonstrate their joy. Meetings and parades were attended by tens of thousands. Representatives of other nationalities showered the Zionists with expressions of encouragement and recognition. Some of these congratulations had political connotations bearing on the future of Zionist work in Palestine. Under the title "Neighborly Greetings" wrote the *Maccabean*:

> One of the most gratifying accompaniments of the Balfour Declaration has been the whole-hearted and sympathetic congratulations conveyed to the Zionist Organization by Armenian and Arabian organizations. The Zionist Organization will know how to express its appreciation of the good wishes of the representatives of these two nationalities, who are destined to be neighbors of the New Zion. . . . Our interests run parallel and at certain points meet.

The spirit of Zionist elation affected many other Jewish organizations. When the Jews of New York, together with other national groups, demonstrated their American loyalty on the Fourth of July, the Zionist colors came first, and the Zionists were leading the Jewish contingent, followed by all elements of the Jewish people, including the Jewish labor unions and landsmanschaften. But the Zionist flag was not confined only to the Zionists. In the Allied demonstration on July 14th, Bastille Day, it

> was the Zionist contingent that represented the Jewish people, and represented them worthily.

Thus the American Jewish delegates to the Peace Conference in Paris had behind them not only the democratically elected Jewish Congress, they had popular support no Jewish cause ever had. The composition of the delegation was reflecting fully all shades of opinions. Though the Zionists were in overwhelming majority with Julian W. Mack, chairman, Bernard S. Richards, secretary, Joseph Barondess, Col. Harry Cutler, Jacob de Haas, Rabbi B. L. Levinthal, Dr. Nahum Syrkin, Dr. Stephen Wise, the American Jewish Committee had its representative in Louis Marshall, and the non-Zionist left in the writer, Morris Winchewsky.

The American Jewish delegation to the Peace Conference in Paris asserted itself very soon. Within the Committee of Jewish Delegations to the peace Conference the Americans had won easily a leading place. They were after all close to the chief power at the Conference, the United States, and they represented the most powerful Jewish Community, unaffected by war, uninhibited in its political actions. And as such they were the delegation that carried the greatest influence with the French and British Jewish delegations, whom the Americans succeeded to induce not to make an open issue of their anti-Zionism, and not harm the efforts for assuring national rights to Jewish minorities in European countries. Such influence on the Jewish delegations, from France and England, was certainly the result of another, somewhat peculiar situation: within the American delegation a leading role was played by Louis Marshall, a non-Zionist, the central personality of the American Jewish Committee, an organization with an ideology basically identical with that of the British and French Jewries' delegations.

In such circumstances, the entrusting of the preparation of the Palestine memorandum to Louis Marshall was an almost unprecedented act of trust in his loyalty which must have prevailed in the American delegation. Similarly such trust was demonstrated when Marshall was elected chairman of the Committee that had to formulate the Palestine subject, as well when he was elected one of the consecutive, in rotation, chairmen of the entire Committee of Jewish delegations. The faithful implementation of the Palestine resolution of the Congress was for Louis Marshall a natural imperative. At the moment he accepted the mission and subscribed to the resolutions, he considered his duty to serve the cause he represented to the best of his ability.

The American Jewish Congress delegation utilized every and each contact its members had had. Its members appeared before the American delegation to the Peace Conference, Secretary of State Lansing, Colonel House, General Bliss and Mr. White. The presentation of the resolutions adopted by the American Jewish Congress was accomplished by emphatic efforts for enlisting the support of the official American delegation. This formal meeting was followed by a series of conferences held by Judge Mack and Mr. Marshall with Colonel House, and with the legal advisers of the Council of Five, the de facto ruling body of the Peace Conference. Utilizing its own contacts was only part of the role played by the delegation of the American Jewish Congress. Following the instruction of the first Congress session, the delegation gave its full backing to the representatives of the World Zionist Organization, Dr. Haim Weitzman, Nahum Sokolov and Menahem Ussishkin. At a hearing before one of the committees of the peace conference, the representative of the Zionist Organization, Sokolov, presented the Palestine resolution of the Jewish Congress as well as that of the Zionist Organization. Such identity of purpose, purportedly promoted by the Congress delegation, gave special weight to the demands as formulated by the Zionists.

Americans also played a most influential role in the Zionist delegation itself. Felix Frankfurter, a former member of President Wilson's Administration and outstanding law authority, served as legal adviser to the Zionist delegation. He was soon thrust into the very midst of one of the most sensitive encounters with the opposition to the inclusion of the Balfour Declaration into the official decisions of the Peace Conference. It certainly was not a mistake, or a result of misinformation, that the head of the Arab delegation, Emir Feisal, the oldest prince of the Hashemite family, son of the Sherif of Mecca, had chosen Felix Frankfurter as the addressee for his letter of Arab support for the cause of Zionism, in fact, the most important document disproving Arab contentions that there was never, and never could be, any chance for harmony between Jewish and Arab national aspirations. Feisal's statements, that Arabs "look with deepest sympathy on the Zionist movement" and "will wish the Jews a most hearty welcome home," carried their weight in the discussions among the powers, set on determining the fate of the provinces of the Ottoman empire.

The American Zionists had thus lived up to the expectations of the world Zionist leaders. Dr. Weitzman, who headed the political struggle of the Zionist movement attested to the historic role played in those days, by American Zionists. In a cable to the National Convention of the Federation of American Zionists which assembled in December, 1917, almost two months after the issuance of the Balfour Declaration, Dr. Weitzman stated:

You American Zionists have shown yourselves worthy of all hopes founded on your ideal. In the sphere of organization and sacrifice you displayed all the force of Jewish realism sustained by the indestructible faith that Palestine must become a Jewish Homeland.

But the role of American Zionists in assuring Jewish national rights to Palestine was far from finished. The political charter achieved was by no means yet Zionism implemented. Conditions had to be created in Palestine that would make the building of a Jewish Commonwealth possible. Zionist authority in Palestine had to make itself present. And here again the active participation of American Zionists was of utmost importance. The world Zionist leadership knew well that American involvement would help to overcome obstacles and enmity, which certain circles of the British colonial administration hadn't even attempted to hide. Such American involvement was established when leading American Zionists had been appointed to become members of the Zionist Commission which followed in the footsteps of the advancing British army in Palestine. The presence of the Americans on the Commission, Dr. Harry Friedenwald, Robert Szold, Rabbi De Sola Pool, Rudolph Sonnenborn, made it clear, to whoever was still in doubt, that Americans considered to be their business the proper implementation of the Balfour Declaration.

The Americans on the Commission left no doubt that they knew what they wanted and that they saw in their tasks a mission for preparing Palestine to become a Jewish State. Dr. Harry Friedenwald, who became the head of the political department of the Commission, made it clear in each and every contact with the British occupation authorities. He impressed these ideas as well on the representatives of the small Jewish *Yishuv*. How elaborated the state-building plans of the American members of the Commission were was best illustrated in their decision to transfer the central office of the Commission from Jaffa to Jerusalem. They had done it not withstanding the loud opposition of the representatives of Jewish labor, Yoseph Sprinzak, the latter speaker of the Knesseth and Meyersohn of the Jewish Settlers' Union. These leaders of the *Yishuv* had valid, practical arguments against the move to Jerusalem: the vast majority of the *Yishuv* was concentrated in the coastal area and Jerusalem was isolated, at a distance of at least a full day's journey by horse and wagon. But the

Dr. Stephen S. Wise pledges support ot American Jewry to Dr. Weitzman

Americans stuck tenaciously to their decision. They moved the offices of the Zionist Commission to Jerusalem and thus laid the foundations for the future Zionist office, Zionist Executive, and eventually the Government of the State of Israel.

Because the opposition of the British administration to the policy of the Jewish National Home was growing stronger, the need for continued political support of American Zionists was not lessened. It was again the American influence that was instrumental in the historic decisions of the San Remo conference, April, 1920, at which the mandate for Palestine was assigned to Great Britain. American Zionists had formal justification for their intervention in the decisions of the San Remo conference. The United States took an active part in the deliberations on the future of Palestine. The insistence of the American delegation on the provision for adequate guarantees for American interests in Palestine, gave the American Zionists an opening for promoting the Zionist interests. They used this opportunity to the maximum extent. As the Balfour Declaration, the San Remo decisions could have been credited, to a great extent, to the intervention of the American Zionist leaders. They were aware of these achievements, and felt entitled to have an important say in the next decisive step that had to follow, the exploitation of the political framework for the practical effort of building the Jewish land.

It was most unfortunate that at the threshhold of this second stage in the implementation of the Herzlian Zionism, the inner Zionist harmony that characterized the period of political struggle was destined to be turned into a most serious cleavage.

7

THE GREAT RIFT

THE "DRAMATIS PERSONAE" of this cleavage, have prejudiced its character and intensity. Weitzman and Brandeis represented not only two sections of the world Zionist movement, whom geography and historical destiny had set oceans apart, but they were different in personality and cultural background as well. Brandeis, whom many likened to Lincoln, resembled the great President. The clean chiseled face, the deep-set eyes, the serious look, the austere appearance, were only an external expression of the innermost character of this great Jewish leader. Principles were to live by, and not for propaganda purposes, honesty was the highest distinction of men, who should not debase himself even for the price of popularity. Aloofness in relations with people, with masses, was closer to Brandeis' way of life than mingling and becoming part of the many. If such behavior and philosophy of life are marks of inborn aristocracy, then Brandeis was the symbol of the Jewish aristocrat, an exception among the many claiming such title, an exception that did not turn his aristocracy into a shield for precluding any identification with the real interests of his people. It was a kind of theoretical Jewishness, of philosophical attachment to Zionism as the essence of Jewish nationalism, as the vehicle which had to give Jews dignity and a place where this dignity and the Jewish genius will come to play without external restrictions and foreign obstacles.

Weitzman was the complete opposite. Born in Pinsk among the Jewish masses of Eastern Europe, he remained part and parcel of their outlook on life, their philosophy, even in the days when destiny and Zionist zeal had pushed him into the forefront of Zionist leadership. His was a quick temper, quiet and contemplative reaction were rather strange to him, his readiness for some circumstantial compromises was always present. Weitzman was Jewish, Eastern Jewish in every expression of his being. Weitzman acknowledged this distinction when he wrote about himself during the gruelling hours of decision at San Remo:

> In a quiet corner of the lounge there sat, while we talked, Sir Herbert Samuel and Dr. Sokolov, both exquisitely groomed, very calm and collected, absolutely undisturbed. I was very conscious of the contrast we presented, in appearance, background, manner, and above all, frame of mind. So,

apparently, was Kerr, my personal friend of many years, for he said, glancing toward them: 'When you look a little more like those two, I shall be pleased to fix an appointment for you' (with Lloyd George, Britain's Prime Minister). There was much wisdom in that suggestion, though at the time I dismissed it as unwarrantably frivolous.

Contemporaries had a brief definition for this contrast: "Pinsk *versus* Washington," "East *versus* West."

From a distance of almost half a century, these imponderables of personal characteristics, and background, appear to be much more decisive in the rift between Weitzman and Brandeis than differences of opinion on problems of Zionist tasks, purposes, and methods. Only such background of the rift explains the many misunderstandings and misinterpretations of statements, and programs, made at that time by both sides. Reading these statements today, without the passion of those days, one can hardly understand how it happened that no compromise was found, that the divisive elements have prevailed over those which were common to both camps.

These personal animosities were fed on other important elements. The Zionist masses in America remained in fact much closer to Weitzman's folkways, Weitzman's philosophy of life than to that of Brandeis. The "immigrants" thus branded by the anti-Zionists, remained "immigrants" in their mentality which remained identical with that of their brethren in Eastern Europe. Brandeis and the entire group of leaders which supported him, and which constituted the administration of the Zionist Organization of America, were basically alien to those Zionist masses. Their initial joy at having won the approval and support of "uptown" was tempered by a certain resentment that they were wards of their leaders rather than a democratically constituted group. Brandeis' type of leadership strengthened considerably such feelings. After a period of direct immersion in Zionist affairs, Brandeis disappeared from Zionist councils. He led through intermediaries. Jacob de Haas became his "chief apostle," and with him others accepted the role of "representatives." Brandeis' leadership became only a voice, the lips from which it came were invisible. "The Voice," this was how his leadership came to be called. His was a kind of leadership by proxy. The reasons for such behavior whether acknowledged or ignored, or even detected by the Zionist masses, were of no consequence. Decisive was the fact that Brandeis created the impression of even greater aloofness and detachment than his leadership actually was. The result of such relationship between the leader and the led could have been only one: estrangement.

Against such background each and every, even the most inconspicous, difference of opinion was bound to assume the proportions of an insurmountable cleavage. The fact that the differences concentrated on rather weighty problems of Zionist activity added to the intensity of the feelings of alienation.

Like in a classical Greek drama, the elements of the coming rift were building up gradually. When on his way for his first trip to Palestine, in June 1919, Brandeis stopped for a few days in London. Attending the Actions Committee of the World Zionist Organization he had a first taste of Zionist realities. There was nothing to even vaguely resemble the American way of "doing business." The parliamentary procedures were strange, European, the discussion, the "general-debatte" was un-American in its forms and length of speeches, the forms of adopting decisions was different. And on top of all that, which made Brandeis feel a kind of a stranger in Zionist councils no special attention was paid to him, to his opinions. Though Brandeis was anything but vain, he nevertheless felt somewhat left out by the matter-of-fact treatment he received in London at the hands of the European, mostly East-European Zionists. The language barrier, Brandeis spoke only English, strengthened the feeling of isolation.

All this ran contrary to all expectations, and let's say, justified hopes for proper recognition. For five years, since the outbreak of World War I, the American Zionists carried the main burden of Zionist work. American Zionists assured Zionist continuity, at a time when the World Executive was paralyzed, and the territorial Zionist organizations were completely incapacitated. And though the political achievements were credited, to a great extent, to European Zionists, to Dr. Weitzman, nobody could have denied that the role American Zionists, and especially Brandeis, played in assuring those political victories, was decisive. This awareness of historical achievements was enhanced by the generally accepted axiom that American Zionists will have to

The Zionist delegation to the U. S. in 1921. From left to right: Menachem M. Usishkin, Dr. Chaim Weitzmann, Mrs. Weitzmann, Prof. Albert Einstein, Mrs. Einstein, Dr. Benzion Mossensohn.

assume the leading, really decisive role in the second phase of Zionist implementation, the practical building of a State, a free Jewish nation in Palestine. Each and every speaker made it clear that there will and can be only one source of funds for exploiting the political victories, for practical work in Palestine: American Zionists, American Jewry.

The facts, Brandeis observed in Palestine, were also somewhat disappointing. The country enchanted him. He wrote:

It is a wonderful country. . . . The age-long longing -- the love is all explicable now. . . . The way is long, the path difficult, but the struggle is worthwhile. It is indeed a Holy Land.

At Rachel's Tomb, on the Bethlehem Road, he said:

I know now why all the world wanted this land, and why all peoples loved it.

But the practical aspects of the Jewish settlement all but satisfied him. He was appalled by many of the economic features of the Jewish colonies. They seemed to appear remote from anything which could resemble American efficiency and self-reliance. They were too much dependent on budgets based on outside subsidies, and too little on simple economic premises of efficiency, income, balance between expense and profit.

This situation shocked him. He became convinced that a change in this respect is imperative. He saw in the continuation of such prevailing methods a major obstacle in the development of a Jewish Palestine. In his usual manner he decided to speak up with candor. He wrote:

As for the work in Palestine and the large number of people engaged in administrative work there: I am not of course criticizing their motives in any respect. . . . Unless our people recognize that the greatest public service they can perform in Palestine is to earn there an honest living and not be dependent upon the Organization, we shall not accomplish our work. The highest work that can be done for Palestine is to earn a living in Palestine. That is real patriotism.

Such general indictment of the methods of Zionist colonization were sufficient to provoke anger of all those who were responsible for instituting, and guarding such approcah to practical work in Palestine. This sweeping criticism of the colonization methods was soon supplemented by remarks which have been clearly directed against the Zionist leadership, the Zionist offices. Brandeis demanded sweeping reforms. He spoke of balanced budgets. He suggested that efficiency decides in the selection of people to the highest offices. He spoke about it bluntly:

The only consideration which we are at liberty to regard is efficiency in (that) public service, and not to pick men because of what they may have done in the past. The only proper test that can be applied in respect to the filling of offices is fitness and efficiency.

Thus the first shots were fired. Though names were not mentioned -- there was no mistake as to the addressees of these remarks. Their number was not negligent. In the over two decades of existence of the Zionist Organization, a Zionist bureaucracy became well entrenched. The Brandeis conception of Zionist administration was not of their choosing.

The first rumbling of criticism against Brandeis' administration were felt at the Chicago Convention of the Zionist Organization of America. Though the absentee leadership of Brandeis was not the direct aim of the attack -- the criticism of the administration which in fact represented everything Brandeis stood for, was the first sign of popular disappointment.

But this was no more than a sign, ignored by the administration and unrecorded by the general membership of the Zionist Organization. The great drama was still many months away. Many months were still necessary until it unfolded in its full grave consequences for American Zionism, and the World Zionist movement in general. It had still to be preceded by the serious confrontation between Brandeis and the Weitzman forces, at the London Conference of July, 1920.

The American delegation of forty included the most illustrious figures of American Zionism. They had acquiesced in the reversal of previous plans for holding the Zionist Congress in America, envisaged with Weitzman's initial concurrence, and later revised in view of the opposition of European Zionists, who had demurred to being majorized by 750 American delegates who, according to shekel records, could have attended a World Zionist Congress held in America. Though some members of the delegation complained for not being taken into Brandeis' confidence as to the plans he was bringing to the London Conference, and suspected that Brandeis had no clear vision of action, Brandeis plunged into activity at the moment of his arrival in London on the board of "Lapland". Disagreements were not lacking at the outset. Brandeis considered inadequate the opposition of the European Zionists to the British plans for territorial curtailment of the future Jewish National Home. There was some measure of rapport between him and Max Nordau who considered all the political achievements a far cry from the real goals of real Herzlian, political Zionism.

But these reservations had no bearing on Brandeis' actual plans for an accelerated effort of Zionist implementation in Palestine. Concern with the conditions of practical work in Palestine led to a concept of involvement of non-Zionists in the upbuilding of Palestine. In consultation with Dr. Weitzman, an agreement was reached to entrust with these responsibilities a group of leading British Jews with Lord Reading and Sir Melchet (later Lord Mond) at their head. For three years all problems of economic Zionist work in Palestine were to remain the domain of this group. The overall supervision of this work by the Zionist movement was to be preserved. In fact, this was the first attempt for a kind of an extended Jewish Agency which became fact nine years later. Behind the scene maneuvering shattered the plan. Dr. Weitzman, pressed by his European colleagues, withdrew his support from the plan. In turn, the non-Zionists changed their mind too. Members of the Brandeis group still among us have most harsh words for this development. They consider it a betrayal, especially in view of the latter charges of their opponents that Brandeis was the one who torpedoed any plan for non-Zionist involvement in Palestine work.

Other programmatic clashes followed. The need for amelioration of the Palesttine swamps, for the eradication of malaria was uppermost in Brandeis' mind. The unsanitary conditions which he observed in Palestine left on him a most serious impression. At one time Brandeis even concluded that no practical work should be done until this killing disease, malaria becomes a matter of the past. Though this could have been considered a kind of an extravagant overstatement, in the tense atmosphere of distrust and incrimination, Brandeis' opponents raised the spectre of some "idea fix" which should shed doubts on the entire Brandeis approach to the problems of Zionist work in Palestine.

In truth, some principles of the Brandeis program that became known as the Zealand Program (name derived from name of boat on which it was, basically, phrased) lent themselves to much more serious misinterpretations. His formulation of the immediate Zionist tasks had put political action into a somewhat undefinable position. It did not exclude the possibility of relegating it to a most inconspicuous role in the framework of Zionist action. Speaking to members of the American delegation at the London Conference, on July 14, 1920, Brandeis stated:

There has been a tremendous amount of talk in the past, and properly, of the political question, of political Zionism. The political question will be important hereafter, but to my mind, practically, the whole of politics lies in proceeding efficiently in the building up of Palestine. That is the only political act which can effectively produce the results and make of our opportunity -- success, instead of failure. Politics as such may now be banished; certainly politics may go into suspense. . . . We have come to the time when there are no politics that are valuable, except the politics of action. We must be in a position to act in Palestine and we have to be strong outside of Palestine.

Whoever looked for a pretense to oppose Brandeis found in such statements sufficient substance. The cry went out: "Brandeis is against political action." And this was the year 1920, when the British military occupation authorities had already manifested their hostility towards the Balfour Declaration, and the policy it embodied, when Arab opposition was openly promoted by the British command, and the British authorities in Cairo, whose influence in Palestine was still decisive.

The formulation of Brandeis' policies on other Zionist problems was not less ambiguous, and not less prone to attack. The problems of

New York Mayor John F. Hylan greets Dr. Weitzmann at City Hall, in 1921, at the beginning of Weitzmann's mission for launching the first American Keren Hayessod campaign.

organization of the world Zionist movement were acute. The role of the world Zionist Organization, the relationship between the world movement and the Zionist National Federations, the role of the world Zionist Executive, the question of the Executive's seat, of Palestine's role in the organizational set-up, all these appeared as well of vital importance. The implementation of the Zionist program depended upon their solution. Brandeis had a clear conception for such solution: the needs of building of a Jewish Palestine must precede any other consideration. Maximum concentration on this goal was his credo. Such concentration had to be achieved by concentrating each and every bit of energy on this goal. And there was, in Brandeis' opinion, no better way of achieving this goal than by utilizing to the maximum Zionist energies harbored within the Territorial Zionist organizations.

"I believe," he said, "that any organization that we are to create now must recognize that the World Organization is, in one way at least, no more important than the Great Hinderland." That no misunderstanding prevail as to the real motives of such formulation, Brandeis added:

"Without that which will be done in the Federations of the several countries, our task is impossible of accomplishment." And accomplishment had for him one meaning, "to bring into Palestine as rapidly as we can as many persons as we can. That really comprises the whole work before us."

Out of this central goal of building a strong Jewish community in Palestine, in the shortest possible time, resulted the demand that the seat of the Zionist Executive be only and alone in Jerusalem, with no allowance for any major, second political Zionist center, in London. Colonizatory efforts had to have absolute priority over any other aspects of Zionist work like education, propaganda; national Zionist Federations had to preserve maximum authority and the role of the World organization reduced to the necessary minimum. This last opinion was a clear transposition of the American principle of "State rights" as confronted with the authority of the Federal Government, the principle of decentralization. Brandeis, considered these principles not only constitutionally right, but also best fitted to serve Zionist democracy, and the interests of maximum Zionist effort by Zionist Territorial Federations.

Such approach to the organizational problems resulted in strong opposition of the European Zionists. In their view the measure of authority of the World Organization, and for that purpose of the World Executive, vis-a-vis the Territorial Federations, was not only a matter of an organizational scheme. The World Zionist Organization was, in their opinion, not only an organization for building a Jewish Palestine, in it was the expression of Jewish national unity, of the concept of Jewish peoplehood in spite of the dispersion, and territorial division into separate Jewish communities, according to the countries of Jewish abode. The spectre of turning the Zionist movement into a colonization organization alarmed many Zionists for whom Zionism was the embodiment of a Jewish national movement, for national regeneration, in which the Jewish State was only one, though the most important goal.

Judging these Brandeis formulations from the point of view of generally accepted Zionist principles, as formulated by the European Zionist movement, the opposition to the Brandeis concepts appears understandable. But there was another set of Zionist problems, that belonged to the realm of economic measures for the upbuilding of Palestine, which according to Zionist tradition were in conflict with the Brandeis concepts, though in fact such opinions have hardly found justification in Brandeis' pronouncements. The question allegedly in conflict was the role of private investment versus national capital. According to such a simplified concept of the Brandeis-Weitzman conflict, Brandeis pleaded for the preponderance of private capital, of private investment in the upbuilding of Palestine, while Weitzman concentrated his hopes on national funds, on *Keren Hayessod* (Foun-

dation Fund) then still in the planning stage. Such conception, or rather misconception of the economic aspects of the Brandeis-Weitzman rift is accompanied by, what seems to be only a logical derivation, an alleged reactionary character of Brandeis' social philosophy.

To the extent that documents are prevailing such assumptions were completely baseless. Brandeis, the social reformer who influenced many progressive policies of President Wilson, preserved the same awareness of the imperatives of social justice in matters of Zionist implementation, of building the new Jewish society in Palestine. The Pittsburgh Zionist Program, adopted at the National Convention of the Federation of American Zionists in 1918, bore Brandeis' spirit, and was in fact written under his influence and direction. Its principles can well be identified with any most progressive, one could say an almost socialist ideology. As early as January 1918 Brandeis thus defined the principles on which the Jewish Palestine should be built:

> The utmost vigilance should be exercised to prevent the acquisition, by private persons, of land, water rights and other natural resources, or any concessions for public utilities. These must all be secured for the whole Jewish people.

Interestingly, -- even in appraisal of the branches of economy that should prevail in Palestine, Brandeis' view was identical with that of the Zionist Executive. "Our pursuit," stated Brandeis, "must be primarily of agriculture in all its branches."

As to the financing of Jewish settlement in Palestine, Brandeis' conception was close to that of the majority of the Zionist leadership. In his programmatic speech to the members of the American delegation, at the London Conference, Brandeis stated clearly,

> It is absolutely necessary that a large part of the money which is going to develop Palestine is to come in the form of gifts from Jews throughout the world. There is no such thing as investment, in a proper sense of that term, unless there is either security or the prospect of a large return, which is the alternative, in the investors' minds, for security.

There were therefore all the premises for overbridging the differences, for harmonizing the views and for the selection of a unified leadership for the World Zionist Organization in its trying hour of confrontration with destiny for a speedy progress in building a Jewish Palestine. Existing documents, and depositions of participants in the historical London Conference, all indicate that would have Brandeis been ready to assume the leadership of the World Zionist Movement, he would have been acclaimed to lead the Jewish people towards the restitution of its independence. At the decisive hour, Brandeis shunned away. There was a dramatic meeting in the council chamber of 77 Great Russel Street, the seat of the Zionist Executive, at which Louis Lipsky, Israel Brodie, Abraham Tulin, Morris Rothenberg, appealed to Brandeis that he accept the election to become one of the Triumvirate, which in practical terms meant his personal leadership of the World Zionist movement. Brandeis refused. Though he did not spell out clearly the reasons, his arguments implied above any doubt that he was not ready to give up his post of Supreme Court Judge, leave the United States and become the leader of the Jewish freedom movement. The considerations were not only personal in nature. There was the additional apprehension that Brandeis' abandonment of his high position in the United States could be exploited by anti-Semites of all vocations who would catch on the argument that when a choice appeared, the Jew chose to cast his lot with his people, with political Zionism, and abandon the country of origin, which gave him one of the highest positions it could give to its sons.

With this decision of Brandeis, the role of the American delegation was, practically, at its end. Weitzman was elected President of the World Zionist Organization. The Conference, which opened July 7, 1920, drew to an end. The Americans lost their sense of direction as their leader made it clear that he was not ready to assume responsibility.

What followed was a natural result of what happened in London. Brandeis' leadership by proxy lost its mystery, lost its meaning. Voices critical of this leadership and of the administration which consented to the role of Brandeis' "voice," grew in numbers and intensity. The psychological elements of estrangement between the Zionist masses and the Brandeis followers became more and more evident. The Zionist Organization of America was ripening for an open rift. The existing administration of the Federation of American Zionists, which was renamed the Zionist Organization of America at the Pittsburgh Convention, precipitated the process of alienation between itself and the majority in the movement. Though pledging token support for *Keren Hayessod* (The Foundation Fund), it adopted resolutions for concentrating

on mobilizing investment funds for individual economic enterprises in Israel. The two central organs of the American Zionist movement, *Dos Yidische Folk* and *The Maccabean*, ceased publication. The auxiliary Zionist organizations, like Young Judea and the Intercollegiate Zionist Association, were abandoned. And the service American Zionism was expected to render the world movement through making available funds for the upbuilding of Palestine was not forthcoming. It appeared obvious that the administration of the Zionist Organization of America was bracing itself for some form of autonomous dealing with Zionist affairs, without too much attention to the directives and policy advice of the World Zionist Executive.

An open conflict seemed unavoidable. It was in the air. Avoidance of an open clash appeared impossible as the importance of American cooperation became more and more evident. Without American support not even a slightest chance existed that any appreciable percentage of the $25,000,000 envisaged as the goal of *Keren Hayessod,* within five years, would be collected. Jewish Palestine was in growing need. Old settlements which suffered during the war had to be restored. New immigrants had to be taken care of. In view of the political adversities, speed in practical efforts in Palestine, appeared imperative.

It was in this general atmosphere that the World Executive decided to force its way onto the American continent. A delegation on behalf of *Keren Hayessod* set out for the United States. The composition of the delegation was most impressive. Dr. Weitzman, the president of the World Zionist Organization, stood at its head. With him were Menahem Ussishkin, the iron man of Zionism, whom many in America still remembered from the days of the Uganda controversy, Dr. Mossinsohn, the principal of the first Hebrew high school in Palestine, *Herzliyah,* and first and foremost among them all, Professor Albert Einstein, then in the heyday of his glory as the author of the theory of relativity. The delegation came without being formally invited by the American Zionist administration. The official purpose was the establishment of the *Keren Hayessod* in America and the collection of funds for the Hebrew University. The authority to do so stemmed from the statutes of Keren Hayessod as adopted at the London Conference.

The approaching arrival of the Zionist delegation gave new opportunity for demonstrating the rift. While the American Zionist administration did not show eagerness to arrange a demonstrative reception for the delegation, a Jewish Reception Committee was organized. With the support of the Yiddish press, landsmanschaften and fraternal organizations, an atmosphere of popular excitement was easily created. American Jewry, American Zionists, were still in the stage of national excitement with the Balfour Declaration and San Remo, and they were eager to demonstrate their appreciation for the man who was one of the prime movers of the historic struggle for Jewish redemption.

Indeed, when Weitzman arrived at the New York harbor on Saturday, thousands streamed to the harbor. Due to the Sabbath, disembarkation was delayed till the stars appeared. At that time, tens of thousands were already assembled. Rabbis, pious Jews with beards, women, youth, a great mass of New York Jewry, blocked all entrances to the pier and all adjoining streets. When the great caravan of cars moved to the Commodore hotel, it was close to midnight when the delegation arrived at the hotel. The enthusiastic reception could, by no means, deceive the members of the delegation. Dr. Weitzman had already in his hands a memorandum delivered to him in person by the president of the Zionist Organization of America, Judge Julian Mack.

The memorandum had set out the conditions under which the Zionist Organization of America would be ready to cooperate in raising of funds for *Keren Hayessod*. The basic premise of this memorandum was concerned with the need of distinction between various purposes for which the fund had to be raised. The memorandum tried to build Zionist finances on principles of public budgeting, where money assigned for one purpose could not easily and without ceremony be transferred to another purpose. It demanded economy, thrift. It disapproved methods of financing of the Palestine work which could in practice be turned into sheer subsidizing, a kind of a a new modern *"Halukah."* It used time and again the term of "conmingling of funds," which meant that funds collected by *Keren Hayessod* should be separated according to the purposes they were to be assigned to: for investment, for development, for subsidies. For a while it seemed that a compromise could be reached. According to certain sources, at one phase of the negotiations, Weitzman agreed with small reservations, acceptable by the Brandeis group, to the basic tenor of the memorandum. According to the same sources

he changed his mind before a final settlement was reached. He had allegedly done so under the influence of other members of the Zionist delegation and some members of the American Zionist administration who opposed the entire approach of the administration to Zionist problems.

After sixteen days of negotiations, on April 18, 1921, Weitzman published his appeal to American Jews and launched the campaign for the Keren Hayessod. The administration, over the signature of its president, Judge Julian Mack, made immediately public its position. It notified the public that the administration would not participate in the fund-raising efforts and would not bear any responsibility for any form and phase of this effort. The long simmering cleavage came into open. The reception which the administration of the Zionist Organization of America arranged for Weitzman and his delegation in the Metropolitan Opera House became only a deceiving episode. The announcement of the Zionist administration that it would start raising funds independently, for practical work in Palestine, made clear that the administration intended not only to withhold support from Keren Hayessod, but would embark on a competitive fund-raising venture. Loyalties were put to the test. A group of leading members of the administration resigned and started to organize the opposition. Led by Louis Lipsky, the group developed an intensive enlightening campaign throughout the country. *The New Maccabean,* under the managing editorship of Meyer Weisgal, gave the dissident group a powerful mouthpiece. The work for *Keren Hayessod* started with full swing. The fund started growing into an efficient instrument for support of Zionist work. Funds started flowing in amounts Zionists never dared to dream of. The sums collected reached millions. The old controversy on the measure of financial support American Jewry would be willing to give to Zionist goals was resolved. Contrary to the appraisals of the Brandeis group that hundreds of thousands would be the maximum attainable, millions had started to flow to *Keren Hayessod.*

When the 24th National Convention of the Zionist Organization of America opened in early June 1921, in Cleveland, the outcome of the contest between the Weitzman and the Brandeis groups was no more in doubt. Brandeis was absent, as he was from every Zionist gathering for the past few years. Weitzman kept away from the American convention not to injure the sensitivities of American Zionist pride; and not to be accused of "foreign intervention." The election of the chairman of the Convention gave the occasion for the first test of parliamentary strength; a little known candidate of the opposition, Henry J. Dannenbaum of Texas won over the acknowledged leader of American Zionism, Judge Julian Mack. Louis Lipsky, Emanuel Neumann, Morris Rothenberg, Peter Schweitzer, Bernard Rosenblatt and Abraham Goldberg led successfully the struggle against such luminaries of the American Zionist leadership like Julian Mack, Stephen Wise, Felix Frankfurter, Robert Szold, Samuel Rosensohn, Dr. Abba H. Silver. By a vote of 158 to 71, the opposition asserted victory for everything it stood for. In an atmosphere electrified with emotions, the defeated President of the Zionist Organization of America, Judge Mack, read a letter from the honorary President of the organization, Judge Brandeis. Its contents spoke for itself:

With the principles and policies adopted by the national Executive Committee under your leadership I am in complete agreement. Strict adherence to these principles is demanded by the high Zionist ideals. Steadfast pursuit of those policies is essential to early and worthy development of Palestine as the Jewish Homeland. We, who believe in these principles and policies cannot properly take part in any administration of Zionist affairs which repudiates them. Upon the delegates in convention assembled rests the responsibility of deciding whether those principles and policies shall prevail in the immediate future. If their decision is adverse you will, I assume, resign, and in that event, present also my resignation as honorary President. Our place will then be as humble soldiers in the ranks where we may hope to hasten, by our struggle, the coming of the day when the policies in which we believe will be recognized as the only ones through which our great ends may be achieved.

An era in American Zionism was closed. Though many of the leaders of the Brandeis group returned successively to Zionist work, the first among them, Dr. Silver, and later, Dr. Wise, Judge Mack, Robert Szold, Brandeis never again assumed any official Zionist position. For some years after the Cleveland Convention, attempts had been made to implement sections of the Brandeis program in the realm of practical work in Palestine.

The Brandeis group had organized Palestine Development Leagues, a Palestine Cooperative Company for investing in cooperative efforts in Palestine, a Palestine Development Council and a Palestine Endowment Fund. Though these institutions (except the Palestine Endowment Fund) which were later merged into the Palestine Economic Corporation (P.E.C.) have drawn millions of dollars into practical work in Palestine, they were very far from justifying the hopes deposited in them. With all the good these funds have done for the economic development of Palestine, they could not pretend to being, an important addition to the official Zionist effort in building a Jewish economic sector in Palestine.

But with all limitations, these economic institutions created a resourceful Zionist instrumentality into which Brandeis' and his friends' Zionist zeal could have been channeled. Brandeis cared to address personally meetings of these institutions. He revealed in those speeches his real Zionist devotion. He did not refrain from stating that real Zionist zeal meant "taking a direct part in the upbuilding of Palestine through settling there", calling those Zionists who are not doing it "not so fortunate" and therefore bound to "effectively aid in carrying forward Zionist goals by their contributions made here, of money and time." But giving money and time, in Brandeis' opinion, should not be considered sufficient.

It (participation in the building of Palestine) cannot be done merely by giving, or investing money. To have a vital part we must add to investment a willingness to take the trouble to learn what the needs of Palestine are, and how they are being and should be met. To achieve for Palestine what the American Jew can do for it, and for the American Jew what Palestine can do for him, we must make the development of the Homeland a part of the daily thought of the Jew.

Such periodical Zionist utterances kept alive the belief that some day a way would be found for the restoration of Zionist unity. The return of Brandeis to Zionist leadership remained a cherished hope. Mediators and men of good will never gave up. When Zionism encountered obstacles, the clamor for Brandeis' return grew in intensity. Such period of extreme stress came in 1930 when the British government embarked on a policy of almost complete annulment of the Balfour Declaration and the Palestine Mandate. Brandeis' personal relations in Washington appeared of prime importance if put in service of the Zionist cause. Brandeis' official leadership of American Zionism held the promise of vigorous American support for the Zionist cause in its encounter with Great Britain. Many saw in it a kind of a providential coincident that this clamor for Brandeis' return arose on the eve of the National Convention which had to be held in Cleveland. Zionists hoped that the Cleveland Convention of 1930 would do away with the split which occurred at the Cleveland Convention of 1921. "From Cleveland to Cleveland" became a slogan carrying hope for the restoration of Zionist unity. The administration delegated a committee consisting of David Freiberger, Rabbi Israel Goldstein, Rabbi James G. Heller and Dr. Nathan Rattnoff to meet with Brandeis and invite him to return to the fold of organized Zionism. They were not turned down. Brandeis and the three of his associates who were with him, Judge Julian Mack, Robert Szold and Jacob de Haas, asked for details of the status of the organization. This demand was complied with.

A second meeting followed. At this meeting Brandeis handed over a lengthy memorandum on the conditions under which unity could be restored. It was harsh in wording and uncompromising in tone. It amounted to a demand for complete and unconditional surrender of the existing Zionist administration. It restated basic postulates of the Brandeis group. In its opening paragraph it stated unequivocally:

> The experience of the last ten years has confirmed the views, expressed on July 14, 1920, in the Zealand Memorandum, that the efforts of the Zionists should be directed primarily to the economic development of Palestine. In our judgment the best guarantee which we can create is our widespread cooperation in a carefully devised plan of economic development, which will make practical immediate increased settlement by Jews in Palestine.

Organizational terms that followed boiled down to one clear condition: the existing administration of the Zionist Organization of America has to go; its activities have to be subject to thorough scrutiny; the new administration has to be composed of nine neutral persons who were identified neither with the Brandeis group nor with the administration. All these harsh terms in ultimative form would have perhaps been accepted had these conditions been followed by a clear statement that after their acceptance Brandeis would be willing to assume, personally, the leadership of the Zionist Organization of America. Such statement was missing. The contrary was clear: Brandeis had no intention of becoming again the formal and official leader. The existing leadership had no difficulty in gaining support for the rejection of the Brandeis group terms. Thus the renewed effort for the restoration of Zionist unity resulted in renewed rancor.

And for rancor the time was the least opportune. The policy of the Mandatory power became a challenge to everything Zionism achieved after World War I. American Jewry's stand became again essential in the struggle for the implementation of Zionism. Though Brandeis did not assume officially any responsibility, his doors remained always open for Zionist leaders who desired his advice, or intervention with the U.S government. He gave of his financial means in measures unprecedented among Zionist leaders.

Among the first to recognize the importance of Akaba-Eilath, he donated a considerable sum of money for pursuing this plan; he provided means for Zionist propaganda purposes among Arabs; he was most helpful in promoting the efforts of the *Histadruth* campaign; his bequest endowed the Palestine Endowment Fund with half a million dollars; his influence in Washington was always for service to the Zionist cause; he continued to pay his dues as a member of the Zionist Organization of America, but never again appeared as a contender for leadership in the Zionist movement. The "voice" was never again used for advising disciples and followers. Most of them gradually found their way into direct Zionist activity. Several of them assumed again leading roles in the Zionist movement. The first to rejoin was Dr. Abba Hillel Silver, followed by Rabbi Stephen Wise and Judge Julian Mack, who took over the leadership of the United Palestine Appeal, Robert Szold, who became chairman of the Executive, and others. But even after they rejoined the mainstream of American Zionism, they often did not see eye to eye with the World Zionist Executive. They were not too enthusiastic about the extended Jewish Agency, which was supposed to accord non-Zionists an influence equal to that of the Zionists in the affairs related to the upbuilding of Palestine. Dr. Wise was a leading opponent of such policy as were others of the *Brandeis group*, as Brandeis followers came to be called long after the Justice retired into the quiet halls of the Supreme Court, and the serene atmosphere of legal findings which made history in American constitutional law.

The fact that many of the non-Zionist personalities, who were supposed to become partners of the Zionist movement in upbuilding a Jewish Palestine, turned their sympathies to a completely different direction, by abandoning help for Jewish colonization in Palestine, and, concentrating on collecting funds for the communist program of colonizing Jews in the Russian Crimea, vindicated the suspicions of the "Brandeis group." From this group came the strongest opponents of Weitzman's policies toward the mandatory power, Great Britain. They were not ready to acquiesce with the first partition of Palestine in 1922, when the "Churchill" White Paper severed the territory East of Jordan from the realm of the Jewish National Home. From among them came the strongest opposition to the plan of the second partition of Palestine, in 1937, and Brandeis, according to Mr. Robert Szold, supported financially the action against the British partition scheme. But in these, his

actions, and despite them, Brandeis continued to adhere to the opinion which, on some occasions, appeared divorced from any real insight concerning the policy of the British Government in Palestine. After the Arab anti-Jewish riots in the summer of 1929, when the rumblings of the British anti-Zionist policy could not be more mistaken, at an Emergency Palestine Economic Conference of November, 1929, Brandeis repeated a statement he had made many times before in various forms, but basically identical in content:

> The road to a Jewish Palestine is economic -- the opportunity is open... The happenings during each of those ten years, including the present, have served to deepen this conviction.

The facts of political life did not seem to confirm Brandeis' political analysis. The British Government left no doubt any more that it has embarked on a policy of betrayal of the obligations it undertook in the Balfour Declaration, and the Palestine Mandate. American Zionists, American Jews, were again called to action.

Mass demonstration, in New York against the British, 1929, White Paper on Palestine.

8

THE STRUGGLE AGAINST BRITISH TREACHERY

THE GUNS on the Palestine front had hardly been silenced and the ink on the signature of the Balfour Declaration had hardly dried when a conspiracy against the policy of a Jewish National Home in Palestine made the first serious attempt to scuttle this policy, to turn the Balfour Declaration into a scrap of paper. The fact that between the pro-Zionist declaration of the British Government and its international endorsement by the League of Nations almost half a decade had passed, opened the field widely for anti-Zionist maneuvers. And the complete disavowal of President Wilson's foreign policy followed by America's return to isolationism, encouraged Britain to renege on its policy obligations concerning the Jewish National Home.

The Jewish National Home policy encountered growing opposition. The military administration in British occupied Palestine was at the outset opposed to the "fancy" plans of establishing a Jewish National Home. Those who were not anti-Semites, and the majority of those in positions of power were, felt simply uncomfortable with the Jews. They preferred the Arabs. They preferred the "native" whom they could treat as such, with whom they could keep up a relationship of master and obedient servant. Those with some administrative experience acquired it in the vast realm of the British colonial empire. They were reluctant to acknowledge that Palestine was not a new possession of the British crown, but rather an international trust to be administered with the clear aim of bringing about the establishment of a Jewish State. The Jew was too equal, too self-confident, and too aware of his historical relationship with the country, and its recognition in the Balfour Declaration.

Such practical reluctance to promote the policy envisaged in the Balfour Declaration had found excellent encouragement in London. The press was overwhelmingly anti-Zionist. Anti-Semitic overtones were not missing in the campaign against the policy of the Balfour Declaration. The House of Lords had a majority of anti-Zionists; and in the House of Commons, those opposed to the establishment of a Jewish National Home in Palestine were gaining influence with each day that passed from the termination of war actions.

In confrontation with those unfavorable political developments American Zionists were bound to be called upon to intervene. President Wilson's standing among the leaders of the Alliance, America's overwhelming power, made any American intervention of enormous importance. American Zionists were fully aware of their obligations and their political potential. They willingly assumed duties on exposed positions of political responsibility. They had done so in full understanding of the special weight their intervention, as Americans, had to carry. They were therefore given a leading role in the Zionist Commission in Palestine. And they had tried their best to have this anti-Zionist course of the British administration reversed. Dr. Harry Friedenwald, who, for a time, served as head of the political department of the Zionist Commission in Palestine, saw no other remedy for the anti-Zionist atmosphere prevailing in Palestine but a general replacement of the high officials. Brandeis' intervention with the London authorities after his visit in Palestine was similarly aimed at the removal of some of the extreme anti-Zionist members of the Palestine administration.

These irritations proved soon to be of rather sparing character compared with the problems that the Zionist Organization had to face in years subsequent to the Balfour Declaration. The Palestine British administration was not more satisfied with its own mischief. Arab opposition was encouraged, if not instigated. The resulting anti-Jewish riots of May, 1920, were a frightening awakening. The killing of Jews in the Jewish National Home, with the passive sufferance of the authorities, was more than even most hard-headed optimists could take.

The days were auspicious for the future of a Jewish Palestine from another point of view as well. French and British diplomats discussed the boundaries of Palestine. They were interested only in spheres of influence, in British and French interests. The viability of what had to be carved out as Palestine did not concern them at all. They drew a line across Palestine from the Ladder of Tyre to the north of Lake Kinnereth. The headwaters of the Jordan, the watershed, the Hermon and the Litani were completely excluded from the Palestine territory. One must not have been an expert in national economy to grasp that a Palestine within such boundaries had no chance of becoming a viable Jewish State or, for that matter, any state at all.

The United States of America still had a political lever in matters concerning the final disposition of the former territories of the Turkish empire. The "Big Four" had still not said their last word on the post-war territorial divisions. The British mandate over Palestine was not yet a fact. Though President Wilson was incapacitated and his foreign policy under concentrated attack by the isolationists, his voice was still decisive in the councils of the Allies. His intervention appeared the only remedy in the precarious situation. American Zionists decided to enlist, again, President Wilson's response. The letter which the American Zionist leadership had addressed to President Wilson on the subject was simply adopted by Wilson as his own version of a communication to be related to the British Cabinet. It left no doubts where the United States stood. The contents speaks for itself. It read:

Negotiations in Paris on the Turkish settlement have reached so critical a stage in their efforts upon the realization of the Balfour Declaration in Palestine as to compel me to appeal to you. My associates of the Zionist Organization wire me from Paris that in the conferences on the Turkish Treaty, France now insists upon the terms of the Sykes-Picot agreement—one of the secret treaties made in 1916 before our entrance into the war. If the French contention should prevail it would be disastrous to the realization of the establishment of the Jewish Homeland in Palestine, inasmuch as the Sykes-Picot agreement divides the country in complete disregard of historical boundaries, and national necessities. The Zionist cause depends upon rational northern and eastern boundaries for a self-sustaining, economic development of the country. This means on the north, Palestine must include the Litani River, and the Watersheds of the Hermon, and on the east, it must include the plains of the Jordan and the Houron. Narrower than this is a mutilation. If the Balfour Declaration, subscribed to by France as well as the other Allied and Associated Powers, is to have more than paper value, there can be no compromise as to the guarantees by which the Balfour Declaration is to be secured.

I need not remind you that neither in this country nor in Paris has there been any opposition to the Zionist Program, and to its realization the boundaries I have named are indispensable. The Balfour Declaration which we know you made possible was a public promise. I venture to suggest that it may be given to you at this time to move the statesmen of Christian nations to keep this solemn promise to the hope of Israel . . .

Facsimile of the draft of the letter presented February, 1920, to President Wilson, who from his sickbed authorized its cabling to Lloyd George as expressing his own views on the Palestine boundary question.

In this memorandum, adopted by Wilson, the Zionists concluded their appeal to Wilson in these words:

It is your word at this hour to Millerand (France) and Lloyd George (Great Britain) which may be decisive.

The American Zionists were very much aware of the problems of the boundaries of the future Jewish National Home. During the deliberations in Paris, at the Peace Conference, the American Zionist delegation played a most important role in elaboration of this part of the Zionist proposals to the Supreme Council of the Peace Conference. According to these proposals,

to the north, these boundaries had to reach a point south of Sidon, at the sea, stretching to the east along the line reaching the slopes of Hermon, close to and west of the Hedjaz Railway. In the east a line close to and west of the Hedjaz Railway terminaing in the Gulf of Akaba . . .

In the closing paragraphs of these proposals it was stated that,

the details of the delineations, or any necessary adjustments of detail, shall be settled by a Special Commission on which there shall be Jewish representation.

Though the final delineations of the Palestine boundaries were far from identical with those envisaged by the Zionist committees, at least they took into consideration one important prerequisite of economic viability of the country, the assurance of an adequate water supply by inclusion of most of the headwaters of the Jordan within the Palestine territory. But this partial success of Zionist efforts was soon to be shattered by the first major British assault on its war-time promises and obligations. In the very midst of the deliberations on the final approval of the draft of the Mandate for Palestine came a British Government decision that annuled, by one major stroke, the application of the provisions of the Balfour Declaration to the east bank of the Jordan which constituted half of the territory, originally considered the Jewish National Home territory, an integral part of what was to become the Jewish Commonwealth.

This decision bore the name of the Colonial Secretary, Winston S. Churchill: The first British White Paper on Palestine removed unilaterally almost two-thirds of the Palestine Mandate territory from the area to which provisions of the Balfour Declaration were to be applied. A new territorial entity was established under the name of Transjordan. An Arab ruler had to be appointed as its head. And even within the boundaries of what remained as the territory of Palestine, major departures from the Jewish National Home policy and obligations were envisaged. The consolatory statement of the White Paper that "The Jewish people will be in Palestine as of right and not of sufferance" was immediately followed by the statement that "Immigration will not exceed economic capacity of the country at the time to absorb new arrivals," a provision which had in time to become the source and alleged legal basis for Britain's final attempt to stop completely Jewish immigration into Palestine.

The fact that the Churchill White Paper of July 1st, 1922, was promulgated at the time of the feverish discussions on the final formulations of the Palestine Mandate, and its approval by Great Britain, was utilized by the British Government as an instrument of pressure on the world Zionist leadership. The British Government threatened openly that in case the Zionist Executive should refuse to approve the Churchill White Paper, the final British approval of the Palestine Mandate would not be forthcoming. The question whether such a threat should have forced the Zionist leadership into a stampede of submission is today of rather theoretical importance. The Zionist leadership, under Weitzman, approved Churchill's White Paper. It did so over the protests of influential American Zionists of the Brandeis group who were, at that time, already out of office, and thus had no way of using their political weight for influencing the course Zionist policy was taking.

But even with the formal support that American Zionists had given the World Zionist Executive in its dealings with Great Britain, they were soon to be forced into raising their voices in defense of promises given, and against detractions that were becoming too obvious. The procrastination of the discussion on the approval of the Mandate by the British Government caused growing anxiety in American Zionism. It seems that the adoption of the Joint Palestine Resolution by both Houses of Congress, which occurred at that very time, was not considered a sufficient guarantee for Britain's faithfulness to its obligations regarding the Jewish National Home. The news coming from London were not encouraging at all. The discussion, in the House of Lords, on the Palestine Mandate, revealed that influential sectors of British public opinion were inimical to the policies outlined in the Balfour Declaration and implemented in the international, League of Nations document, the Palestine Mandate. It appeared that there was imminent danger to all political achievements Zionism had scored in the closing months of World War I, and at the Peace Conference. The American Zionists were alarmed.

The 25th National Convention of the Zionist Organization of America assembled June 25, 1922, in Philadelphia, treated the British anti-Zionist devices as a most urgent and central problem. After lengthy discussion a resolution was adopted which left no doubt that American Zionists were very much aware of Great Britain's anti-Zionist maneuvering. In its operative paragraph the resolution states:

The ratification by the League of Nations of the Mandate of Great Britain over Palestine has been repeatedly delayed, which has led to an unfair and sinister propaganda, resulting in bloodshed and loss of innocent lives in Palestine, and has encouraged hostile forces in British life culminating in the vote taken in the House of Lords on June 22nd, which though not expressive of the majority sentiment of even that body, has given rise to fear lest the British Government falter in discharge of its solemn engagement, and to satisfaction among the enemies of Great Britain who are eager to discredit the good name and honor of the British nation.

This restrained language of the Zionists in conference assembled was not completely indicative of the vehement criticism British policy in Palestine had caused in America. The growing anger of those leading Zionists who were not part of the administration was well supported by that part of the liberal American press which had no special anti-Zionist ax to grind. The influential magazine, *The Nation*, of July 19, 1922, wrote in an editorial:

> The problem of Palestine has made strange bedfellows; it has tossed the Tory *Morning Post* under the same coverlet with the Mohammedan Arab chieftain; and the Holy See has crawled alongside. All of them are afraid, it appears, that the Jews will build up a powerful tyrannical state by the shores of the Jordan and that no one else will be allowed life or liberty or a free look at the Holy Places.

The Nation was not the only publication that dealt with British policy in Palestine. *The New York Times* had joined, it could be said, officially, the ranks of anti-Zionists after its publisher, Adolph S. Ochs, returned from a visit in Palestine. The September, 1922, issue of *New Palestine* noted sadly that:

> American Zionism, contrary to our expectation since Mr. Ochs' return from Palestine is slowly learning to look on *The New York Times* as the mouthpiece of regular anti-Zionist sentiment.

This anti-Zionist sentiment was not new for the leading New York newspaper.

The New York Times was a willing instrument for anti-Zionist statements for years. The successes of Zionism at the close of war, President Wilson's outspoken support for the renewal of Jewish independence, endangered the entire philosophy the Jewish publishers of *The New York Times* had stood for. The paper gave wide publicity to an appeal to President Wilson to terminate his support for Zionism, signed by some 200 Jewish personalities. A cable by Congressman Julius Kahn of California to President Wilson, suggesting that he consider the "protest by representative Jewish citizens of the United States against the organization of a Jewish state in Palestine," received undue prominence.

The vehemence of opposition to Zionism was in direct proportion to its success. Even those non-Zionists who supported Jews in Palestine during the war and who contributed to relief

Emir Feisal to Felix Frankfurter: Expresses his sympathy with the Zionist Movement and his support of Zionist proposals to the Peace Conference. 1 March 1919. This letter, of which the Arabs later denied any knowledge, was recently found in the Jewish Agency Office in London.

agencies assisting Jewish settlers in Palestine were shocked by the dimensions of the Zionist success. They were ready to accommodate themselves with a movement that helped Jewish refugees, eventually wanted to build some spiritual center, but they could not acquiesce in a state, a political symbol of Jewish national identity, which could, as their imaginary fears dictated, reflect negatively on their cherished status as American citizens. Personal spite was not missing. Henry Morgenthau, the former U.S. ambassador in Turkey who spared no effort to help Jews in Palestine persecuted by the Turks, could not forget that the Zionists exposed his self-aggrandizing efforts when his uncalled for political intervention threatened to undo years of delicate, thoughtful political efforts. Morgenthau's standing in America made his attack on Zionism a most irritating, if not damaging, experience. Hate of Zionism competed with blind vehemence of uncontrolled language.

Zionism is the most stupendous fallacy in Jewish history, wrote Morgenthau in his book, *All in a Lifetime.* I assert, he continued, that it is wrong in principle and impossible of realization; that it is unsound in its economics, fantastical in its politics, and sterile in its spiritual ideals. Where it is not pathetically visionary, it is a cruel hoax playing with the hopes of a people blindly seeking their way out of age-old miseries. . . . Zionism is a surrender, not a solution. It is retrogression into the blackest error and not progress toward the light. I will go further, and say that it is a betrayal; it is an eastern European proposal, fathered in this country by American Jews, which if it were to succeed, would cost the Jews of America most that they have gained in liberty, equality and fraternity. . . . I prophesy that it will not support more than one million additional inhabitants. We Jews of America have found America to be our Zion.

Such attacks were not isolated. Though they were not new to the American Zionist movement, seasoned in permanent ideological struggle, they nevertheless threatened to jeopardize the greatest political service American Zionism was able to give at that time to Zionist interests in Palestine. The Joint Resolution of both Houses of Congress, the so-called Lodge-Fish resolution which had incorporated the basic premises of the Balfour Declaration, was a refreshing development in view of the British official intransigence and the general anti-Zionist campaign in America. Weitzman's cable of congratulations addressed to Louis Lipsky, the Chairman of the executive committee of the Zionist Organization of America, was an additional boost to the weary American Zionists, who had not yet recovered from the serious split that cost American Zionism the active cooperation of some of the most influential personalities in American Jewry. Weitzman's cable assured American Zionists that their political work has again helped Zionism greatly in its new hour of trial. Wrote Weitzman:

Heartily congratulate you and all your friends on your historic achievement which helps our cause in this difficult hour. Am confident that with your support we shall soon enter upon a period of peaceful reconstruction in Palestine.

This "peaceful reconstruction" became the order of the day of American Zionism, which supported without reservation the official line of the World Zionist Organization. To hasten the pace of such reconstruction new forces were sought. The non-Zionists, leading members of the American Jewish Committee, were the natural target for the efforts to gain partners in the practical work in Palestine. Such practical work fitted in completely with the ideological approach of those circles. Their reservations towards Zionism were aimed only at the political concept of Jewish nationhood and statehood. But helping Jews already in Palestine to reach some kind of economic stability, and Jews suffering in Europe to emigrate to Palestine, was well within the realm and ideological comprehension of the non-Zionists. The Palestine Mandate provided for the establishment of "an appropriate Jewish Agency" to cooperate with the mandatory power on matters concerning "the establishment of the Jewish National Home and the interests of the Jewish population in Palestine and . . . to assist and take part in the development of the country." And though the Zionist Organization was recognized as this agency, the Mandate contained a provision, that it should seek the cooperation of "all Jews who are willing to assist in the establishment of the Jewish National Home."

The ensuing period of negotiations with those Jewish personalities, among whom leading ones were Louis Marshall, the acknowledged leader of the American Jewish Committee, Herbert H. Lehman, Dr. Cyrus Adler, Judge Horace Stern and Felix M. Warburg, lasted for over half a decade. These negotiations for finding some basic, constitutional form of utilizing the non-Zionist support for the reconstruction of Palestine were conducted independently of practical steps that were taken for making this support work. An all-day conference held in New York, on February 17, 1924, was called by a committee headed by Louis Marshall, Cyrus Adler, Herbert H. Lehman and Horace Stern. The conference adopted a resolution calling for the organization of an investment company to develop the economic resources of Palestine. Another resolution called for a study of the concept of the Jewish Agency for Palestine with the aim of preparing a blueprint for its extension, and inclusion of non-Zionists in its works. A second conference in March 1925 decided to create an economic instrument for the development of Palestine, and thus the Palestine Economic Corporation was brought into being with a capital of $3 million.

American Zionists have followed faithfully the official Zionist policy. The American delegations to the Zionist Congresses were always at the side of the World Executive whenever rumbling of discontent punctured the edifice of alleged Zionist unity. This discontent was well fed by the British policy in Palestine. The Churchill White Paper proved to be the official opening salvo against the real meaning of the Balfour Declaration. Anti-Zionist measures were multiplying. Among them the two most painful and damaging were: the restrictions on Jewish immigration, and an economic policy which has precluded the development of an industrial sector in Palestine.

The discontent had fed, in America, on the special internal situation of the Zionist movement. The Brandeis group had often voiced demands for a more daring and forceful policy toward the mandatory power. The fact that Brandeis remained in the background weakened immensely the influence of that group, though it did not make it disappear completely. Its opinions on Zionist affairs remained a permanent undercurrent in American Zionism.

The excesses of the British anti-Zionist policies had lent time and again sense and justification for the assertions of those who argued that it was time for a general political offensive against the British betrayal.

The breaking point was supplied by Britain itself. The August, 1929, riots and the ensuing series of surveys, investigations and finally the Passfield 1930 White Paper, left no doubt that unless Zionism gathers courage to make a stand against the British policy in Palestine, there will soon be nothing left to fight for. The Passfield White Paper tried to give a new meaning to Britain's international commitment toward Zionism by according the British obligations to the Jews and Arabs the status of "equal weight." Thus the basic premise of the Balfour Declaration and the Palestine Mandate was wiped out. The main purpose of these documents, to assure the establishment of the Jewish National Home, was put in question. On such a basic premise a whole superstructure of anti-Zionist policies was built. The so-called "economic absorption capacity" of Palestine was to be instituted as a decisive factor in the determination of the extent of Jewish immi-

Zionist delegation with President Warren G. Harding, 1922. Beginning second from left: Louis Lipsky, Abraham Goldberg, unidentified, Morris Rothenberg, Herman Conheim, President Harding, Prof. Mordecai M. Kaplan, Louis Robison, Judge Bernard A. Rosenblatt, Peter Schweitzer.

gration into Palestine; the findings of the report by a British land expert, Sir John Hope Simpson, about the unavailability of land for Jewish settlement had to make impossible further growth of Jewish colonization; a proposed legislative council established at a time when the Arabs were still an overwhelming majority had, under a screen of a democratic principle, to place the entire Zionist work in Palestine at the mercy of the Arab nationalists.

In these circumstances even the most compromising Zionist leaders could not remain silent any more. The uproar embraced all sections of the Zionist movement. The non-Zionists of the extended Jewish Agency had resigned in protest against the British breach of faith.

Felix M. Warburg, chairman of the Administrative Committee of the Jewish Agency, made public his message in which he explained his resignation. Warburg outrightly accused the author of the White Paper, Lord Passfield, of bad faith. Warburg wrote:

The assurances which Lord Passfield gave as to the forthcoming recommendations are at variance with what he has now publicly announced. At Lord Passfield's personal invitation, I went to London on August 22nd. During a two-hour talk, he authorized us to make certain statements to the Administrative Committee of the Jewish Agency at its forthcoming executive meeting in Berlin a few days later. In the light of documents just issued by Lord Passfield, I am compelled, however regretfully, to say that I was misled. Lord Passfield's representations to me made me the innocent vehicle of misstatements to my colleagues of the Jewish Agency.

Mr. Warburg's indictment of British policy in Palestine was not isolated in the camp of non-Zionists in America. Abraham Cahan, vet-

Delegation of the Zionist Organization of America in Washington, September 1929. The delegation met with President Herbert Hoover, Secretary of State Henry L. Stimson and Senator William Edgar Borah. From left to right: Charles Cowan, Bernard Deutsch, Bernard A. Rosenblatt, Emanuel Neumann, Nelson Ruttenberg, Max Rhoade, Judge Gustave Hartman, Dr. Israel Goldstein, Nathan D. Perlman, Mrs. Zip Szold, Dr. A. Goralnik, Dr. David Kaliski, A. Tannenbaum, Jonah Goldstein.

eran Jewish socialist leader, the seventy-year-old editor of the Yiddish, socialist daily *Forward,* joined the protesting forces. Cahan, who relinquished his opposition to the upbuilding of a Jewish National Home in Palestine after a visit to that country in 1925, wrote about the British betrayal not only as a Jew, but also as a socialist, whose socialist beliefs had been shattered by the perfidy of the socialist government of Britain. Wrote Cahan in his paper:

With a bleeding heart I must ask: How can a Labor Party issue such a policy? In the present tragedy of England, our comrades there have, it seems, lost their ordinary coolness, common sense and deep socialist sense of justice. They believe that the decision which they have made is in the interests of their country, of their people. We, the Jewish Socialists, can only have one standpoint in this sad moment. We must stand by our people, the Jewish people. . . . We demand our rights in Palestine. We demand that England should keep its word and not break its solemn vow. . . . Let us hope that the League of Nations will reject the decision of the Colonial Office and demand of England that it fulfill its contract.

The resignations came in the wake of the resignation of the president of the Zionist Organization, and of the Jewish Agency, Haim Weitzman. The authorative "interpretation" of the Passfield White Paper by the Prime Minister of the Labour Party government, Ramsay MacDonald, which reversed the official Zionist protest, did not appear to be too convincing for many Zionists. Prime Minister MacDonald's assurance, in his letter to Dr. Weitzman, that the Mandatory government does not intend to prevent the "acquisition of additional land by Jews," or to bar "Jewish immigration in any of its categories" appeared as a token for the mollification of the Jewish anger, with no guarantee of a real change in British policies. To many American Zionist leaders,

the 1930 White Paper appeared as an attempt at institutionalizing the anti-Zionist policy, rather than a passing formulation of such a policy, resulting from Arab anti-Jewish riots.

The Jewish press in the United States joined the clamour for a more aggressive Zionist policy. Wrote the *Jewish Morning Journal*:

A sacred promise has been sacrificed on the altar of political expediency. . . . Zionism is a mass movement and a blow, such as that administered by MacDonald's government, has wide ramifications. There are limits to national patience. And the British, by the last decision, have overstepped the boundaries of that patience.

The Day was even more vehement in its criticism:

The indignation of the Jews of the World, wrote the paper, cannot be controlled. This is a dastardly violation of promises made, of covenants agreed to, of policies repeatedly declared in international tribunals.

In conclusion, *The Day* hinted that the withdrawal of the Mandate from Great Britain should be considered.

Jewish masses were called to the streets to demonstrate. June 5th, 1930, saw tens of thousands of Jews demonstrating against the Passfield White Paper. According to a report in New Palestine:

Old men and women, young boys and girls, university students and day laborers, professional men and happy-go-lucky cobblers, all joined in a spontaneous, deeply felt protest against the attitude of the British government toward Jewish rights in Palestine.

The mass meeting set a new pattern of mass action on behalf of Zionist interests, to be repeated many times in the crucial years of the final struggle for a Jewish State after World War II. The meeting saw on the platform Felix Frankfurter, the coming man of American law, and Senator Borah, the most influential spokesman on foreign affairs in the United States Senate in his office as the chairman of the Senate Committee on Foreign Relations, whose statement, at that meeting, became a slogan: "Instead of a National Home we are given an international shamble."

Opponents of the administration of the Zionist Organization of America seized the opportunity to attack its policies of support for the policy line of the World Zionist Executive, which had, according to their opinion, resulted in the 1930 White Paper. Dr. Stephen S. Wise, who left, together with the entire Brandeis group, the position of leadership in the Zionist movement, used fully his wit and biting satirical phraseology to attack those who were, according to him, responsible for the political setback Zionism had suffered. On a visit in Palestine he gave an interview in *Hazman*, a Hebrew daily, in which he attacked the z.o.a. by saying that:

> The z.o.a. is no more than a sounding board for the voice of London. It has no independent existence, no voice of its own. Its motto rightly or wrongly has been, 'Amen.' It must now more or less gracefully accept the penalties of self-obliteration. . . . If the Agency becomes, in Palestine, the counterpart of the Joint Distribution Committee in Eastern Europe, the Zionist movement will speedily become a thing of memory.

Even those who disagreed with Dr. Wise's sharp criticism could hardly find words to defend the acquiescence with the British policy aimed at the liquidation of the last vestiges of obligations undertaken in the Balfour Declaration and the Palestine Mandate. Though the long-lasting negotiations between the administration of the Zionist Organization of America and the Brandeis group had not led to a formal agreement, the years of intensified political crisis in Zionism saw a closing of ranks when more than half of the Executive of the Z.O.A. came from the ranks of the Brandeis group, and the chairmanship of the Executive Committee was given to one of Brandeis' staunchest supporters, Robert Szold.

The struggle against the violations of the spirit and the letter of the Balfour Declaration and the Mandate entered a new phase. The mass demonstration in Madison Square Garden was only a beginning. The Committee on Public Information, headed by Dr. Emanuel Neuman, initiated a planned and widely spread mobilization of popular support for the Zionist cause. The American Palestine Committee, organized under the auspices of the Committee on Public Information, opened a new avenue of involvement in Palestine affairs of non-Jewish personalities, prominent in American political and religious life. Irrespective of this activity, a permanent Washington bureau nurtured contacts with Government and Congress. A new pattern of political action was set. The formation process of the Committee was by itself a political act of great political importance. On a Thursday, December 17, 1931, a group of influential political leaders met at the home of Justice Brandeis. Among those present were Senators King and La Follette, Assistant Secretary of State Rogers and Congressman Ham-

First Dinner Committee of American Palestine Committee, January, 1932. Left to right: Dr. Emanuel Neumann, Supreme Court Justice Harlan F. Stone, Vice President Curtis, Senator William H. King, Professor Felix Frankfurter, Congressman John Q. Tilson, and Majority leader Henry T. Rainey.

ilton Fish. The dinner of January 18, 1932, at which the creation of the American Palestine Committee was proclaimed, became a major demonstration of pro-Zionist sentiments. A message from President Hoover reaffirmed American support for the restoration of the National Home of the Jewish people. And the galaxy of Cabinet members, leaders of both Houses of Congress, Vice-President Charles Curtis, members of the Supreme Court, as well as leading personalities of all walks of life present at the dinner, demonstrated America's commitment to oppose the anti-Zionist policy of the British Government and the determination to make such British policy untenable.

Information on British policies in Palestine, mobilization of political support against British violations of the Mandate, became permanent activities of the Zionist leadership. Meetings with leaders of the Administration and Congress were held a number of times. At a meeting of a Zionist delegation with President Hoover and Secretary of State Stimson, a memorandum was submitted with the request for American intervention on behalf of the stipulations of the Mandate to which the United States became partner through the treaty of 1924. According to Dr. Neuman's recollection, the Department of State sent, at that time, a note to the British Government in which it called attention to the loss of lives and property of American nationals and the danger to other American nationals. Though this limitation of American intervention was far from satisfactory from the point of view of Zionist interests, it included a suggestion concerning the availability of American forces to restore order, a unique statement of American readiness for military involvement in the Palestine

Senator Borah.

issue, that became a kind of a bogey in American Middle Eastern policy for decades to come.

This new form of American Zionist activity had, no doubt, opened a new era in American Zionist, and not only Zionist, involvement in the political struggle for the implementation of the Balfour Declaration. It was, to a great extent, a major rehearsal for the coming great political battle for Jewish rights in Palestine in the forties.

American Zionism had thus set its place among those Zionist forces which were not ready to accept the British policy in Palestine. It joined the forces that called for political action, for struggle, for mobilization of Jewish and non-Jewish sympathies for such Palestine policy that would lead to the establishment of a Jewish National Home, in the original meaning of the word, which considered this term identical with a Jewish Commonwealth.

It was therefore no surprise that the overwhelming majority of the American delegation to the 17th Zionist Congress, in 1931, cast its votes with all those who opposed the policies of the President of the World Zionist Organization, Dr. Haim Weitzman. It was this American vote, together with the votes of Mizrahi, the Radical Zionists, and the Zionists-Revisionists that removed Weitzman from the Presidency of the World Zionist Organization.

But this fighting spirit of American Zionism was soon to be put to its test from within. Though the attack did not come from the Zionist ranks themselves, the source it came from carried considerable weight. The American non-Zionist partners of the Jewish Agency were not ready to sit quietly by at a moment when the formation of the political aims of Zionism was at stake. They never were ready to admit openly that they were supporting a political movement aimed at the restoration of Jewish Statehood. In view of the *Endziel*—"ultimate goal"—discussion which became the center of

the storm before and at the 17th Zionist Congress, they were forced to state their opinion. Acquiescence in the negative reaction to Dr. Weitzman's statements which disregarded the Zionist aim of establishing a Jewish state, could have been interpreted as meaning opposition to Weitzman's basic position and support for those who spoke openly that the Zionist aim is Jewish Statehood. To make their position clear in the raging dispute, they used the platform of the Jewish Agency Council. Presiding over the second meeting of the Jewish Agency's Council, on July 14, 1931, Dr. Cyrus Adler presented his and his colleagues' definition of the term *National Home,* adding that his interpretation was accepted by the Zionists as binding upon both Zionists and non-Zionists. Dr. Adler left no doubt that the interpretation he presented was the only formulation of the Agency's policy that non-Zionist members of the Jewish Agency were ready to support and work for.

Dr. Adler did not try to be original in this interpretation of what he considered the real meaning of the Balfour Declaration and the Palestine Mandate. Adler quoted a paragraph from Churchill's White Paper of 1922:

When it is asked what is meant by the development of the Jewish National Home in Palestine, it may be answered that it is not the imposition of a Jewish nationality upon the inhabitants of Palestine as a whole, but the further development of the existing Jewish community with the assistance of Jews in other parts of the world, in order that it may become a center in which the Jewish people as a whole may take, on grounds of religion and race, an interest and pride. But in order that this community should have the best prospect of free development and provide full opportunity for the Jewish people to display its capacities, it is essential that it should know that it is in Palestine as of right and not sufferance. That is the reason why it is necessary that the existence of a Jewish National Home in Palestine should be internationally guaranteed, and that it should be formally recognized to rest upon ancient historic connection.

It seems that this formulation of the first exercise in the British official statements of reneging on previous obligations did not appear to Dr. Adler clear enough for repudiating the idea of a Jewish State. Dr. Adler elaborated therefore by quoting a statement of the Attorney General of Palestine, a Jew, Norman Bentwich, that left no doubt that the term "National Home" could not mean at all the establishment of a Jewish State in Palestine.

A *National Home,* according to Bentwich, connotes a territory in which a people without receiving the rights of political sovereignty has, nevertheless, a recognized legal position and receives the opportunity to develop its moral, social and spiritual ideals.

In this atmosphere of scaling down the Zionist goals another factor arose among those who hoped for accommodation with the Arabs and the British at the price of discarding hopes for Jewish Statehood. Dr. Judah Magnes, then the Chancellor of the Hebrew University, whose public activities in America were still well remembered, assumed a leading position with Brith Shalom, a group that set as its goal an understanding with the Arabs on the basis of a bi-national state in Palestine. Dr. Magnes did not hesitate to use his connections in America for the propagation of his political concepts. Dr. Magnes' opinions seemed to have been well adjusted to the opinions then prevailing in a considerable part of the American press. With the first wave of indignation at the killing of Jews in Palestine over, a growing number of voices joined the chorus of understanding for the so-called motives of the Arab pogromists.

The misleading allegations of the British White Paper, and of the Report of a British land expert, Sir John Hope Simpson, which asserted that Jewish immigration displaces Arab land workers and that the arable land in Palestine is so scarce that it can't even suffice for the existing population, helped the enemies of Zionism. Enemies of Jewish statehood were joined by so-called liberals to present the Palestinian Arab as an underdog who had to be saved from the pressure of the Zionists, supported by the entire might of world Jewry. Voices like that of Magnes were therefore most welcome for these circles. They gave the semblance of objectivity and freed the anti-Zionists from the blame of Jew-hatred, or even Zion-hatred. Magnes' Zionist past appeared as the best argument that those who were taking the Arab side were objective in their appraisal of the Palestine situation.

In such circumstances the American Palestine Committee assumed a most important role. The Senators, Congressmen, Governors, Cabinet members, Vice-President Curtis, leading personalities in the academic world, and writers who became members of the American Palestine Committee, were an adequate counterbalance against the anti-Zionist voices. One of the basic and most convincing anti-Zionist argu-

THE WHITE HOUSE
WASHINGTON

June 27. 1929.

Mr. Philip Slomovitz,
President of the Zionist District of Detroit,
Detroit, Michigan.

My dear Mr. Slomovitz:

Please say for me to the members of the Zionist Organization of America, gathered in annual convention at Detroit on June 30th, that I pray their deliberations may be, as always, richly fruitful in that spiritual wisdom for which the Jewish race has been noteworthy in all ages.

Yours faithfully,

Herbert Hoover

President Hoover's greeting to the 32 Zionist Convention in Detroit, June, 1929.

ments concerning Palestine's limited economic absorptive capacity was given special attention in the enlightenment effort of the Committee. Conversations with leaders of the American Government left no doubt that what concerned them most was the question whether Palestine could serve as a solution for needs of Jewish immigration, whether it possessed the room to accommodate a mass immigration of Jews.

It was most unfortunate that the work of the American Palestine Committee did not last too long. With the first uproar over the Passfield White Paper over, with the growing preoccupation with the ascendance of Hitler to power, and the subsequent relaxation of immigration policies in Palestine, the feeling of urgency for such a committee seemed to be waning.

The renewal of Arab disturbances in 1936, the British Royal Commission, the Peel Commission, which suggested to limit again the area of implementation of the Balfour Declaration policies, again jolted the American Zionists from the state of relative complacency. The proposals of the Peel Commission for the establishment of a Jewish State in part of Palestine introduced a new element of controversy into American Zionist ranks.

Similarly to the division of opinions in Palestine, in the Yishuv itself, the attitude to the partition plan cut through all Zionist parties. In America the circles close to Brandeis, or to the Brandeis group, were overwhelmingly against partition. During the months of inquiry conducted by the Peel Commission, prior to the issuance of its final report, American organizations concerned with work in Palestine submitted a memorandum dealing with "American interest in the administration of the Palestine Mandate." The document signed by the Zionist Organization of America, Hadassah, the Palestine Foundation Fund, Jewish National Fund, the Palestine Economic Corporation, the American Economic Committee for Palestine and the Palestine Endowment Funds elaborated on the reasons for American concern with the situation in Palestine. The document dealt also, in detail, with the contributions American citizens had made to the development of Palestine. This memorandum was supplemented by a second document submitted to the U. S. Department of State, whose title indicates sufficiently the scope and purpose of the document. Entitled, "A brief statement of the basis and scope of the Right of the United States to participate in any disposition of Palestine," the memorandum appealed to the Department of State for a broad interpretation of American interestts in Palestine. It was an obvious attempt to extend American official interpretation of United States rights, resulting from the United States-British treaty of 1924, in which America assumed direct rights of intervention in the conduct of Palestine affairs by the Mandatory Power.

The final report of the Peel Commission introduced a new element of division not only in American Zionist ranks, but between the non-Zionist members of the Jewish Agency and the Zionists as well. The American non-Zionist members of the Jewish Agency Council opposed vehemently partition of Palestine and the establishment of a Jewish State in part of the country. At a meeting of the Council, in August, 1937, they fought against the acceptance of the Peel report. The argumentation behind this opposition was supplied in policy statements of the American Jewish Committee, the organization whose leaders were virtually the guiding force of the American non-Zionist partner in the Jewish Agency. The Committee proposed the restoration of the state of affairs before the Peel report, and the establishment of an international trusteeship embodying the substance of the Mandate. But in pro-

posing this, the Committee did not delude itself that such trusteeship could become a matter of practical politics. In the absence of a practical solution the Committee proposed vaguely that "within a reasonable period of years" Palestine should become a self-governing commonwealth, by implication, neither Jewish nor non-Jewish, under a constitution which "should protect, among other rights, the right of the Jewish National Home to grow by immigration and settlement to the full extent of the economic absorptive capacity of the country." The crux of the non-Zionists' concern with the Peel report was hardly concealed in this formulation of a new political program: this was the concern with the Peel suggestion for the establishment of a Jewish State. Faithful to its decades-long policy, the Committee considered Jewish Statehood anathema to its entire conception of Judaism and the political philosophy it had not promised to forfeit when giving its consent to join the Jewish Agency.

The dispute within the Jewish ranks did not last too long. The British Government took care to make the entire controversy immaterial. Before long it made clear that there was no intention whatsover of implementing the report of the Peel Commission. After the Arab rejection of the Peel partition plan, the acceptance of the plan by the Jewish Agency remained worthless. The return to the old British tactic of conferences between the interested parties at which Great Britain allegedly had only a role of an observer and arbiter brought no change in the situation in Palestine. The Arab nationalists had ground to believe that increased pressure, and more terror, would bring the results they desired. They were not mistaken. In May, 1939, a new White Paper was published on the future of Palestine. The ill-famed diplomat of the Munich agreement, British Prime Minister Chamberlain, delivered what he and the Arabs assumed could be the final blow to the Zionist hopes. Limitation of the Jewish immigration to 75,000 and making its future dependent on the consent of a Council with an Arab majority, closing of almost the entire country for Jewish settlement, were meant to spell the death-knell for all Zionist aspirations, even in its limited Churchillian interpretation.

The entire Zionist, Jewish world was thrown into an uproar. Palestine was swept by demonstrations, and American Zionists stood up in arms. Protest meetings, demonstrations and printed material carried the message of Jewish anger. Rabbi Stephen Wise appeared before the Secretary of State, Cordell Hull, at the head of a delegation of 250 Jewish leaders to protest the British action and request American intervention. The petition submitted to Secretary Hull read in part:

We, therefore, respectfully request that the United States Government . . . make representation to the British Government a) that no action be taken for the implementation of the new White Paper on Palestine until this Government shall have had an opportunity to examine its terms and to pass judgment on its bearing on American rights; and b) that the United States Government, on the basis of its convention with Great Britain . . . cannot recognize action taken under the new White Paper in view of the jeopardy for American interests.

This was not the only action taken. The Zionist Organization of America through its president, Dr. Solomon Goldman, appealed to the United States Government to take action; the National Council of Jewish Women appealed directly to President Roosevelt, "to prevent further tragedy." Prominent writers, 27 of them, signed a petition to the Government asking for intervention. But all that these appeals, protests and petitions were able to produce were expressions of general sympathy and promises to "study the problem."

The anti-Zionist character of the British policy in Palestine was demonstrated in the most tragic circumstances that developed in Europe. The triumphal march of Nazi Germany sent masses of Jews running for their life. Storming of the gates of Palestine by so-called "illegal" immigrants, and the draconic, repressive measures taken by the British Government, added a new dimension to the immigration clause of the White Paper. From a document of political assault against Zionism, and an outspoken breach of faith, it became a death verdict for thousands of Jews, for whom Palestine could have served as the only haven of safety. American Jews, led by the Zionist organizations, tried to use this humanitarian aspect of the Palestine problem, but to no avail. The Zion-

ist Organization of America, Hadassah, Poale-Zion, and Mizrahi were joined by the American Jewish Committee and the American Jewish Congress in appealing to the British Prime Minister, Neville Chamberlain, to stop the hunt for illegal immigrants. In a cable dispatched to Chamberlain they asked "the English people and their government to avert this punitive action against the innocent victims of an unparalleled persecution."

The problem of illegal immigration, which began to assume proportions of a major instrument of Zionist struggle, was to become a central political issue of the 21st Zionist Congress assembled on the very eve of the World War II. It was at this Congress that the coming leader of American Zionism in its struggle for a Jewish State, Dr. Abba Hillel Silver, revealed some of his inner thoughts this struggle had, according to his opinions, to assume. Disputing the Eretz Israel labor leader's (Berl Katzenelson) contention that illegal immigration should become the immediate battle cry of the Zionist movement against the May, 1939, White Paper, Dr. Silver warned: "I call upon you to refrain from desperate acts of resistance, as civil revolt, non-cooperation, and the like." This call, which many tried to present as an argument against Silver's reputation of an uninhibited, daring and fighting leader, Dr. Silver supplemented with the following qualification:

I can imagine that some day we might be faced by a situation that will demand revolutionary methods, but for that we have to prepare in advance, and to be equipped with appropriate means and forces, to await a propitious juncture. We must guard against a strategic blunder.

The outbreak of World War II catapulted, suddenly, a new all-out struggle against the British attempt at liquidating its political obligations toward Zionism. The *propitious juncture* seemed to be appearing on the horizon. American Zionism was facing again its moment of decision, greatness and struggle. The decisive phase in the struggle for a Jewish Commonwealth was opened.

PART THREE

9

NON-JEWISH AMERICA EXTENDS ASSISTANCE

JEWISH STATEHOOD: AN IMPERATIVE OF INTERNATIONAL JUSTICE AND MORALS

PRESIDENT JOHN ADAMS' utterance, "a Jewish nation in the land of its ancestors," did not come out of nowhere. Proclaimed in the first years of the Republic, it symbolized concern for the people of the Bible, which was deeply rooted in the hearts of the Puritan settlers. It could not have been otherwise. A people amongst whom Bible-reading was a popular pastime, and family Bibles a precious treasure, was bound to believe in the final realization of the Biblical prophecies. And belief did not appear sufficient. To right the wrongs done to the Jewish people seemed to be a most appropriate way towards redemption and deliverance. A people in search of God had to nurse an affinity for the land in which Jesus was born, and for the people of whom he was a son. This affinity assumed many forms. When the choice of the official language for the new nation was considered, the language of the Bible was one of those taken into consideration. When institutions of higher learning were laying the foundations for their advancement towards excellence, the language which the people of the Bible had spoken in their land was considered the language of nobility, and inscriptions in it a manifestation of allegiance worthwhile to be proud of.

The maximum religious freedom had to produce, at some point, religious denominations which tried to translate this affinity with the people of the Bible into some measures of tangible canons of belief. The names of the Churches were many. Scores of them appeared and disappeared after making some mark on the spiritual physiognomy of the American nation. The beliefs in Messiah used to be with the main article of their faith. "The second coming of God" was considered an unavoidable development. And the deliverance of the Jews from their bondage, a natural consequence of the coming of the Messiah. The most outspoken in this respect among them and the most sizable was the Church of Latter Day Saints, the Mormon Church. Joseph P. Smith, the Founder of the Mormon Church, made the return of the Jews to their ancestral land an article of faith for his followers. He spoke about it, he wrote about it, he propagated this idea wherever and whenever possible. He did it at the most solemn occasions for his Church. At the general conference of his Church, in April, 1893, his son the new leader included in his law-giving message the proclamation that *"Judah must return, Jerusalem must be rebuilt."* This was no mere talk. This statement was well thought over, practical action was taken upon it. As such program should be properly promoted, scouts were sent to the Holy Land to search and to inquire. Orson Hyde, one of Smith's associates, was chosen for the mission to go to Palestine to "dedicate there the land for gathering the Jews." And as was fitting a pathbreaker of a new religious revelation, Smith felt dutybound to announce that in due time, he would go to Jerusalem and "do great work which shall prepare the way and greatly facilitate the gathering together of that people."

Smith and his Mormon Church were no exception. In the annals of American religious history appear many more movements in whose center was prominently placed the return of the Jews to their land. Sometime after Smith's first proclamation on his Church's mission to promote the return of the Jews to Palestine, another religious group, Christ's Church of the Messiah, set out on its way to implement the prophecy of the Jewish return. A certain Reverend Thomas Adams, of the Adams' family, the family of American Presidents, left the shores of America in order to help, practically, the Jews to set foot on their land. Some two hundred Americans -- Adams' religious followers -- went with him. It was, I believe, the first such colonizing expedition in human history. Adams organized a com-

Rabbi Isaac Leeser.

munity which could well be considered self-sufficient. Every profession, necessary for a normal functioning community, was represented in this group of American Christian emigrants to the Holy Land. There was a doctor, a nurse, there were teachers, craftsmen, artisans and, of course, farmers with their farming implements. What was most unusual about them -- they carried with them prefabricated houses, the first prefabricated dwellings ever mentioned in modern history. In Adams' writings, in his correspondence with Jewish groups which preceded even Hovevei Zionists in their attempts to settle Jews on the land, he left no room for any misrepresentation of his real goal to help Jews to become toilers and tillers in their own land. It is a most amazing and fascinating chapter in the history of practical attempts to redeem the Holy Land from its desolation, and make it a haven for its persecuted children.

Adams' was a kind of a public, collective group effort. But there were also examples of individual decisions to help the Jews regain their land. These decisions were no less characteristic of the spirit which prevailed in this respect in America than the previously mentioned efforts of religious denominations. Outstanding among these individuals was a certain Mrs. Carolina Minor, who left behind her, in Philadelphia, a patrician home, comfort and social standing, in order to go to Palestine and try to build a Jewish settlement, an endeavor in which she tried to cooperate with Sir Moses Montefiore. As Adams after her, so did Mrs. Minor's attempt end in failure and personal tragedy. That the Adams experiment was not just an attempt of no significance, proves the fact that Mark Twain dedicated serious attention to these American colonists in Palestine in one of his books, *Americans Abroad,* and President Lincoln's

Secretary of State William H. Seward, on his trip to the Middle East, paid special attention to this American colony on what is today the outskirts of Tel Aviv. And perhaps no less interesting is the fact that in his notes on that journey, Secretary Seward saw fit to mention his meeting with American Jews in Jerusalem and wrote:

Mrs. Minor's and Reverend Adams' initiatives were to be followed by a man who had political vision and public courage to appeal for support of his ideas to wider circles of Jews and non-Jews alike. It is interesting that the man who carried this idea of helping Jews return to their land, Warder Cresson, also came from Philadelphia, as did the aforementioned Rev. Adams. Cresson made use of his writing ability to make people know what his ideas were. Before going to Palestine in 1844, he published a tract in which he tried to convince his readers that God must choose some medium and manifest through it in order to bring about his designs and promises in this visible world. . . . This medium or recipient is the present poor, outcast Jew. . . . God is about gathering them again.

Cresson's plan envisaged American government help in the implementation of his idea. The first such step in that direction, thought Cresson, would be the establishment of an official American representation in Jerusalem. And he knew how to go about winning support for his idea. He used his citizen's rights of lobbying with his Congressman. Congressman Edward Jay Morris of Philadelphia took upon himself to intervene with the Secretary of State. The Congressman wrote, in May, 1844, "Jerusalem is now much frequented by Americans. . . . a consulate there will be of service to our citizens." As was expected, Congressman Morris had a candidate -- Warder Cresson. The appointment was not to hard to receive: the consular position didn't have to become a burden in budgetary terms.

The official status did not make Cresson abandon his mystical idea. As soon as he arrived in Jerusalem, he demanded an interview with the Pasha at which he explained that according to his interpretation of the Apocalypse --

the five powers and America are about to intervene in Syrian affairs and assure the infallible return of the Jews to Palestine.

Cresson was not content with this political initiative. He tried to create funds for assisting the needy Jews already in Palestine, the *halukah* Jews in Jerusalem. As could have been expected, he turned to America for such financial help. Philadelphia was again the choice. The addressee was the editor of *The Occident*, Rabbi Isaac Leeser, a *Hovev Zion*, years before this name was coined in the annals of Jewish national rebirth. Rabbi Leeser had already experience. He tried to provide funds for the experiment of Carolina Minor, and failed.

The system, he wrote, for the collection of money suggested by Cresson, has been often tried, and has always signally failed.

But Cresson did not give up. When he embarked on an effort to establish an extensive farm in the vicinity of Jerusalem, in the Valley of Rephaim, Rabbi Leeser greeted the plan with joy.

A proper system of agriculture . . . (will) be introduced into our ancient heritage by which means these (Jews in Palestine) who now lack bread might be enabled to obtain for themselves from the bosom of the earth.

Cresson agreed with Rabbi Leeser that there is not too much of a chance to raise the necessary means through methods he had initially suggested. He tried to mobilize public opinion. In London he issued a "Circular Letter for the Promotion of Agricultural Pursuits and also for the Establishment of a Soup House for the Destitute Jews in Jerusalem." The main emphasis was on the productivization of the Jews on their return to the land. It is only want of land, he wrote, that

has prevented their energies becoming effectual for so many hundreds of years; for no people can become powerful while scattered over the whole earth because Unity and Consolidation is strength, but diffusion is weakness. . . . It is evident that agriculture is to be Israel's vocation, when restored to their own land.

These precursors of Christian American championship of the cause of Jewish return to the homeland were followed by even more definite and more eloquent spokesmen. General events on the world scene greatly promoted interest in the Jewish cause. The world was moving towards more liberalism and greater equality. National liberation movements were gaining recognition and support. Europe was in turmoil. New states were emerging. And amidst this change, only one people seemed to be deprived of any hope of liberation from oppression. Instead of progress, the Jews in great parts of Europe,

Anglo-American Commission on Inquiry on Palestine, upon arrival in Jerusalem.

in Russia, were faced with the danger of physical assault. The pogroms in Russia awoke the conscience of many Americans who considered themselves the guardians of equality and rights to a secure living everywhere. The idea of furthering emigration from countries of persecution was a natural result of this American concern with the fate of the Jews. One of the most outspoken proponents of the return of the Jews to Palestine, Reverend William E. Blackstone, a Protestant clergyman, added a religious undertone for what was already taking shape as a political idea: the establishment of a State for Israel, preached Rev. Blackstone, should be considered part of the Divine Plan. His idea of a Jewish State was only a prelude as in his opinion the issue became much too serious that it be confined only to a repetition of religious utterances of the middle of the 19th century. The world was different: different were the ideas about the solution of national problems, and different was the approach to the problem of the Jews in Europe which no humanitarian could evade.

The first political action on behalf of the oppressed Jews made its debut. It assumed the form of a memorandum (at that time called "memorial") to the President of the United States, Benjamin Harrison. The number of signers, their standing in the American community, were a most revealing development. Four hundred and thirteen leading personalities of the country signed the memorandum: J. Medill of the Chicago Tribune; Victor Lawson of the Chicago Daily

AMERICAN LABOR DEMANDS A JEWISH PALESTINE

250 delegates representing 114 International, State, City and local unions of the American Federation of Labor and the Congress of Industrial Organizations met at a three-day Trade Union Conference for Labor Palestine in Atlantic City, May 16th through 18th. These delegates, Jews and non-Jews, represented millions of organized workers in various parts of the United States and Canada. Out of their deliberations came this call to the American people and to the entire democratic world:

THE CASE OF THE JEWISH PEOPLE IS BEFORE THE CONSCIENCE OF THE WORLD. JUSTICE DEMANDS THAT THE DECISION BE: **A JEWISH HOMELAND IN PALESTINE**

WILLIAM GREEN, President of the American Federation of Labor, told the delegates:

"The 7,500,000 members of the American Federation of Labor are wholeheartedly in favor of a Jewish Homeland in Palestine. The AFL will fight by the side of the Histadrut, the General

JAMES B. CAREY, secretary-treasurer of the Congress of Industrial Organizations, told the delegates:

"The C.I.O. stands behind the Jew-

American Labor support for a Jewish Palestine—A New York Times report of May 23, 1947

News, Melville W. Fuller, Chief Justice of the United States Supreme Court, were among them. The memorandum left no room for misunderstandings. It did not indulge in hollow statements. It started with a question,

What shall be done for the Russian Jews? . . . But where shall two million of such poor people go? Europe is crowded. Shall they come to America? This will be a tremendous expense and take years. Why not give Palestine back to them again? According to God's distribution of nations, it is their home, an inalienable possession from which they were expelled by force. Under their cultivation it was a remarkably fruitful land, sustaining millions of Israelites. . . . They were agriculturists and producers as well as a nation of great commercial importance. A million of exiles, by their terrible sufferings, are piteously appealing to our sympathy, justice, humanity. Let us now restore them to the land of which they were so cruelly deported by our Roman ancestors!

For the Christian signers of this memorandum, this was a clear exposition of their opinions. But a number of Jewish signers considered it important to have the following addendum:

Several petitioners wish it stated that the Jews have not become agriculturists because for centuries they were almost universally prohibited from owning or tilling land in the countries of their dispersion.

As years passed by, compassionate expressions of support for a Jewish return to Palestine were continuously voiced by leaders of the Church, molders of public opinion, and statesmen. Elihu Root, John Hay, Theodore Roosevelt, made their support for the renovation of the Jewish commonwealth, in Palestine, part of their public pronouncements. The Russian pogroms, at the beginning of the present century, deepened understanding for the need of a solution for the Jewish problem. Humanitarian urges were strengthened by political considerations. When a committee for the support of the Jewish self-defense in Russia was organized in America, the largest contribution, $10,000, came from a non-Jew, the railroad magnate, Edward Henry Harriman, father of Ambassador Averell W. Harriman, a friend of the idea of a Jewish Palestine of long standing.

World War I and the actions, taken against the fledgling Jewish community of Palestine, by the Turkish authorities, spurred an outflow of American help over and above the usual call of humanitarian duty. American warships, among them the U.S. Cruiser *Tennessee,* transported Palestinian Jews expelled by the Turks, to their exile in Egypt. Many hundreds thus escaped squalor and suffering in Turkish concentration areas. From among those Jews, many of the first Jewish fighting unit with the British, the *Zion Mule Corps,* were recruited. When articles were collected for help to the persecuted and destitute Jews in Palestine and needed to be shipped, the Nickel Plate Railroad offered to place, without charge, at the disposal of a special committee as many freight cars as would be needed. Secretary of the Navy, Josephus Daniels, placed at the disposal of the rescue committee the U.S. Navy vessel, the *Vulcan.* He permitted that the shipment be accompanied by a Jewish representative, a leading Zionist figure, Dr. Harry Friedenwald, to whom even an officer's commission was offered so that his mission be facilitated. And what would appear today as almost a political apostasy, the Standard Oil Company undertook to remit all moneys to Palestine Jews without expense to the American senders.

The progress of war and political developments in England, and in the Middle East, started to shift the interest in a Jewish Palestine from the realm of pure humanitarianism and religious motivation into that of political considerations, dictated by the opportunities of the hour. Old reservations seemed to give way to more audacious political thinking. Only a few years before, February 1912, the State Department had refused a request that the President send a message to be read at a meeting of the Zion Literary Society on the grounds that ". . . problems of Zionism involve certain matters primarily related to the interests of countries other than our own." Four years later, in the second year of World War I, this position changed completely. While the first representations concerning the primary preparations for the issuance of the Balfour Declaration were still confined to Great Britain, influential Americans saw fit to renew the pressure on their government that it do something for the restoration of the Jews to their land. In May 1916 a memorial somewhat similar to that presented to President Harrison was submitted to President Woodrow Wilson. The memorandum called his attention to the powerful support which was given the first memorandum and reminded him that since 1891 the records of the U.S. Department of State had shown "the development of a remarkably benign activity on the part of our Government in behalf of the Jews." As in 1891, the signers included again such personalities as Andrew D. White, president of Cornell University, former Ambassador to Russia John Wanamaker, and many other persons prominent in all walks of American life.

This time their intervention had much better prospects of influencing American policy. These were chances of objective and subjective character: the times of war had created a situation in which the future of Palestine became again a matter of international bargaining, and the President to whom this memorandum was addressed, had a very clear conception as to what the future of

GI's at the Wailing Wall look with curiosity at chassid praying at the Wall.

Palestine should be, and how its fate should be related to Jewish hopes for their national redemption. It was only in line with the genuine American tradition that this conception was related rather to religious notions than to political accounting. President Wilson revealed the deep sources of his sympathy for Zionism in these words, uttered in a conversation with one of the chief leaders of early American Zionism, Rabbi Stephen S. Wise:

> I am a son of a manse, son of a Presbyterian clergyman, and therefore I am with you completely and I am proud to think that I may in some degree help you to rebuild Palestine.

This help was forthcoming. As time passed and deliberations on the future of the territories under Turkish rule became more detailed, this help turned into a most potent element in determining the Jewish rights to Palestine. Though President Wilson was reluctant to make his support public because he hoped to win over Turkey from the camp of the Central Powers, he left, nevertheless, no doubt in the political circles of the Allied Powers, that he stood fully behind the plans

Group of GI's visits, during World War II the campus of the Hebrew University in Jerusalem, on Mount Scopus.

Dr. Chaim Weitzmann discusses the Palestine problem with Herschel Johnson, United States representative to the United Nations, 1947.

for issuing a declaration in support of Zionist aims. In the first months of 1917, this problem moved to the forefront of the Allies' concern, especially of Great Britain.

In September 4, 1917, President Wilson's closest advisor, Colonel Edward House, informed the President that Lord Robert Cecil, the British Under-Secretary of State for Foreign Affairs, had sent the following cable:

We are being pressed here for a declaration of sympathy with the Zionist movement, and I should be very grateful if you felt able to ascertain unofficially if the President favors such a declaration.

The letter carried as well an additional note by House which said:

Have you made up your mind regarding what answer you will make to Cecil concerning the Zionist movement? It seems to me that there are many dangers lurking in it, and if I were British, I would be chary about going too definitely into that question.

After a month, in October, Wilson replied

I found in my pocket the memo you gave me about the Zionist Movement. I am afraid I did not say to you that I concurred in the formula suggested by the other side. I do, and would be obliged if you would let them know it.

These sentiments received later a clear exposition when it was stated, in an official Government document, that

It is right that Palestine should become a Jewish State, if the Jews, being given the full opportunity, make it such. It was the cradle and home of their vital race, which has made large spiritual contributions to mankind, and it is the only land in which they can hope to find a home of their own; they being in this last respect unique among significant peoples.

The pro-Zionist statements, and even more, the deep moral commitment of President Wilson, met for the first time in the history of American-Zionist relations, resistance from circles interested in the preservation of the Arab character of Palestine. Missionaries, the leaders of American educational institutions in the Middle-East, launched their offensive: It was their pressure that resulted in the dispatch of a Commission which had to investigate the sentiments of the local population, which meant the Arabs, concerning the Zionist policies. The results of such investigations by the King-Crane Commission, thus named after its principal members, could have been predicted well in advance: the people to whom they talked were only Arabs and such Arabs who had definite negative opinions on the prospect of Palestine becoming open to Jewish repatriation. In its findings the Commission stated that

Jewish immigrants should be definitely limited, and the project for making Palestine distinctly a Jewish Commonwealth should be given up.

But this was not a clear-cut report: out of the three experts attached to the Commission, two submitted dissenting opinions.

This first attempt of scuttling the definite policies of the President, which opened a new era in the formulation of American policies towards Zionist aims in Palestine, was soon turned into an episode of no consequence in President Wilson's policies towards the Jewish National Home. Even the subtle attempts of sabotaging this policy which made their appearance in practical acts of the State Department were of no consequence. The "Arab bloc" in the Department of State was only at the start of probing its way and its possibilities. Thus the practical preparations for the implementation of the promises, contained in the Balfour Declaration, were not influenced at all by these tempering influences of Zionism's opponents. When recommendations for the Peace Conference entered the stage of practical formulations, the Section of Territorial and Political Intelligence of the American Delegation to the Peace Conference prepared an outline of a tentative report for President Wilson which urged that there be established

a separate state of Palestine and that the Jews be invited to return to Palestine and settle there . . . being assured that it will be the policy of the League of Nations to recognize Palestine as a Jewish State as soon as it is a Jewish State in fact.

This report, submitted to the American Delegation to the Peace Conference on January 21, 1919, contained a series of other statements which left no doubt that this document resulted from a thorough investigation of the possibilities of its implementation. The Section composed of Dr. Isaiah Bowman, Dr. James T. Shotwell, Dr. Sidney Mizes, Dr. William Westerman, and for a time, Walter Lippman as secretary, gave full guarantees of sincerity and seriousness. The members of the Section did not absolve their function with perfunctory statements. They were careful to formulate their recommendations in detail. A historical review preceded the practical part of the document. It stated that

the separation of the Palestinian area from Syria finds justification in the religious experience of mankind. The Jewish and Christian Churches were born in Palestine; and Jerusalem was for long years, at different periods, the capital of each. And while the relation of Mohammedans to Palestine is not so intimate, from the beginning they have regarded Jerusalem as as a separate state can justice be done to a holy place. Only by establishing Palestine these great facts. . . .

Having thus reviewed the historical implications of the Palestine problem, the Section moved to more practical details: Boundaries, government, Jewish immigration, Holy Places were treated in definite terms. Speaking about boundaries, the document states,

as drawn upon the map, the new state would control its own source of water and of irrigation on Mount Hermon in the east of the Jordan; a feature of great importance since the success of the new state would depend upon the possibilities of agricultural development,

a recommendation which, if accepted at that time, would have spared the whole "water dispute" on the utilization of the Jordan River waters, one of the major sources of contention in the present Arab anti-Israel crusade. In

Dr. Chaim Weitzmann, Israel, first President presents a Scroll of the Law to President Harry S. Truman at the White House, 1949.

The Israel flag raised for the first time at Rockefeller Center, May 13, 1949. Participating left to right: Abba Eban, Israel's first representative to the U. N., Edward Warburg, Greater New York chairman of the United Jewish Appeal, and Nelson Rockefeller, president and chairman of the board of Rockefeller Center.

fulfillment of previous basic agreements and Zionist presentations a clear recommendation was included as to the choice of power to supervise the implementation of the Sections report:

It is recommended that this state be placed under Great Britain as a mandatory of the League of Nations. . . . Palestine would obviously need wise and firm guidance. Its population is without political experience, is radically composite, and could easily become distracted by fanaticism and bitter religious differences.

Later comes a section which assumes ironical proportions in view of the later record of British mandatory rule in Palestine:

The success of Great Britain in dealing with similar situations, her relations to Egypt and her administrative achievements since General Allenby freed Palestine from the Turk, all indicate her as the logical mandatory.

After such wholesale subscription to Great Britain's political integrity and administrative ability, written at the insistence of Zionist representatives, the document faces squarely the problem of the number of Jews within the Palestine population as a decisive factor in the implementation of its pro-Jewish recommendations.

At present, however, states the document, the Jews form barely a sixth of the total population of 700,000 in Palestine, and whether they are to form a majority or even a plurality of the population in the future remains uncertain. Palestine, in short, is far from being a Jewish country now. England, as mandatory, can be relied on to give the Jews the privileged position they should have without sacrificing the right of non-Jews.

With such a formulation of the recommendations for the American Delegation to the Peace Conference, President Wilson lived up to his part of pro-Zionist declarations. If any proof was necessary of the weight and character of American intervention on behalf of Great Britain's policy in the Middle East, which the Zionist movement undertook to support in

Zionist delegation meeting with President Eisenhower. From left to right: S. L. Kennen, James G. Heller, Mrs. Rose Halprin, Louis Lipsky, the President, Rabbi Irving Miller, Rabbi Jerome Ungar, Rabbi Mordecai Kirschblum, March, 1953.

Mrs. Eleanor Roosevelt with Mrs. Weitzmann visiting Offakim and meeting new immigrants.

exchange for the support of Zionist aspirations, this document of the American committee supplies it with the utmost clarity.

The evolution of British policies towards Palestine, after American support was achieved, proved very early that Great Britain did not intend to divest itself from its traditions, which earned it the dubious fame of being the "Perfidious Albion." At this juncture, President Wilson intervened again. When in 1920, the British Colonial Office started scheming the whittling down of the boundaries of Palestine, President Wilson, already stricken and embattled by the growing clamor of the opponents to his policies of involvement with the League of Nations, cabled the British Government a tersely worded letter as to the honor of Christendom being involved in providing the Jewish homeland with adequate boundaries.

This was not a isolated demonstration of President Wilson's continuous support of the Zionist cause. On August 31, 1920, in a letter to Dr. Stephen S. Wise, the President confirmed not only his interest in "the reconstructive work, which the Weitzman Commission had done in Palestine" but used as well the opportunity to "express the satisfaction in the progress of the Zionist movement in the U.S. and in the allied countries since the declaration by Mr. Balfour." The repetition in this letter of the basic provisions of the Balfour Declaration that followed had, no doubt, the very specific political aim of making it clear to Great Britain that America intends to insist on the implementation of that declaration. Such support was at that time of vital importance, as was the closing statement of the letter, that all Americans will be deeply moved by the report that even in this time of stress, the Weitzman Commission has been able to lay the foundation of the Hebrew University at Jerusalem with the promise that that bears of spiritual rebirth.

The Zionist leadership was not content with these expressions of Presidential sympathy alone. The understanding of the need for bi-partisan support became an undisputed principle of Zionist policies. The defeat of President Wilson's international policies, of his decision to make the United States part and parcel of the League of Nations, raised the spectre of defeat for other aspects of his international policy. America's commitment in the question of Palestine faced a most serious test. The fact that this policy was an integral part of the League of Nations system could have made the opposition to the Balfour Declaration, and the Palestine Mandate almost unavoidable. Wilson's letter of affirmation was no longer sufficient. To a certain extent, from the point of view of practical policies, it was almost meaningless. It was a defeated policy of a defeated President, physically incapacitated and politically rebuked.

To enlist the support of those who had defeated President Wilson's League of Nations policy became of utmost importance. Fortunately such support was forthcoming. Senator Henry Cabot Lodge, the Senate majority leader, who led the successful revolt against the policy of the Democratic President, understood the importance of his intervention on behalf of Zionist aims in Palestine. On November 23, 1919, Senator Lodge, in an authorized interview on peace terms published in the New York *World*, stated that

> by general accord with the announced British policy Palestine must be turned over to the Jewish people.

Thus was the pro-Zionist policy of the American Government extricated from the internal controversy which harbored a threat to the very roots of this policy. Senator Lodge's statement of sympathy and support for a Jewish Palestine had not remained isolated. Cardinal Gibbons of Baltimore issued to the Zionist Organization of America a statement of support of the Jewish National home; in January, 1920, Representative Elihu D. Stone, himself a leading Zionist, introduced in the Massachusetts State House of Representatives a resolution of endorsement of the establishment of a Jewish homeland in Palestine; the State Legislature of Wisconsin adopted unanimously

John Foster Dulles and Harold Stassen accompanied by Moshe Sharett review Israel guard of honor at Lydda airport, May, 1953.

a resolution favoring the establishment of a Jewish State as

> essential to the millions of people who have been faithful and loyal subjects of the several nations of which they are citizens and have been for centuries oppressed through racial prejudice and left without a parent country.

The State Legislature of Ohio voted a resolution which expressed the view

> that the national aspirations and historic claims of the Jewish people with regard to Palestine should be recognized by the Peace Conference in accordance with the Balfour Declaration

and that

> the American delegates at the Peace Conference should use their best endeavours to facilitate the achievement of this object.

A country-wide movement was set in motion to have the entire nation committed to what its President had made its official policy. No authority was neglected to gain the support for the Zionist goals in Palestine. Political leaders, clergy, and the intellectual elite were mobilized for the support of Zionism. Outstanding among such voices of the intellectual community was that of Upton Sinclair who made public a statement that, concerning his

> attitude towards Zionism, I would say that I believe in letting every people govern themselves, provided only that they are capable of so doing. I think the Jews are entitled to be classified among the capable ones. The Turks may be capable of governing themselves, but they are certainly not capable of governing other nations and so I should be glad to see Palestine turned

over to the Jews and placed under international guarantee. . . . I wish very much that the Jews of the world would take it up and agitate it.

The first major battle of Zionism for the support of the American people was won almost without recourse. The opponents of a Jewish Palestine, so-called representative Jewish citizens who were against the establishment of a Jewish state in Palestine published letters in the *New York Times,* found some Congressman to cable their opinions to President Wilson, but they did not succeed to

James McDonald, first U. S. Ambassador to Israel at reception in Tel-Aviv.

make even a dent in the proclaimed and genuine pro-Zionist sympathies of the American people.

This was no negligible achievement. The United States had entered a period of extreme isolationism and support of Zionism's aims in Palestine was in direct contradiction to that policy. The sympathies for a Jewish Palestine prevailed even over these isolationist sentiments. The Congress which only a brief time ago had repudiated the policy of the President of the United States, and had not hesitated to do such enormous injury to American standing in international politics, saw fit to adopt a joint resolution, which favored the establishment of a Jewish National Home in Palestine. This joint resolution of the 67th Congress, dated June 30, 1922, and signed into law by President Harding on September 21, of the same year, registered in a most formal way America's support for Zionism's aims as formulated in the Balfour Declaration. But the isolationist sentiments made themselves felt even in this document. In the debate it was argued that the resolution

> merely voices America's favorable opinion and will not involve the U.S. in any possible manner.

A HANDBOOK OF DIPLOMATIC HEBREW

Hebrew-English and English-Hebrew Vocabularies

Abbreviations

Bilingual List of International Organizations

by

LAWRENCE MARWICK
HEAD OF THE HEBRAIC SECTION
LIBRARY OF CONGRESS

Cover of a Handbook of Diplomatic Hebrew.

And the report to the House Committee on Foreign Affairs insisted

> it (the resolution) commits us to no foreign obligation or entanglement. . . . We may be assured no unfortunate diplomatic complications can or will occur.

In spite of these reservations; further American involvement in the Palestine affairs was forthcoming. With the British rule over Palestine formally acknowledged and incorporated into an international document, in the League of Nations' Mandate, the United States moved quickly towards a new association with this document. This association assumed the form of a bi-national convention signed into a binding international document in December, 1924. From the point of view of Zionist interests this was a most welcome development. The preamble cited in full the provision of the Palestine Mandate and the Balfour Declaration, thus making the United States a signatory to these political instruments. Article 4 made it mandatory that the Mandatory Power, Great Britain, submit to the United States a duplicate of its annual report to the League of Nations, thus making the U.S. a permanent guardian and controller of the measures and forms of implementation of the Mandate's provisions. And what proved later of decisive importance in American attitudes towards British attempts at liquidation of the basic provisions of the Palestine Mandate and the Balfour Declaration, the Convention

included an article (7) which stated clearly that

Nothing contained in the present convention shall be affected by any modification which may be made in the terms of the mandate as recited above, unless such modification shall have been assented by the United States.

This was the article that was later to be invoked when America's intervention was called upon to prevent the implementation of British White Papers which aimed at the complete termination of policies resulting from the obligations undertaken in the Palestine Mandate and Balfour Declaration. These provisions, subscribing to the policy that had to lead to the establishment of the Jewish National Home, were even further elaborated in the negotiation which preceded the final formulation of that Convention. Unlike its position on the other mandates, the United States demanded certain guarantees of commercial equality in consideration of the "special situation in Palestine," which according to the British made it impractical to give equal facilities for developing the natural resources of the country to persons or bodies motivated by considerations other than the establishment of the Jewish National Home.

John Foster Dulles, U. S. Secretary of State delivering his speech as last of seven Foreign Ministers to address the Security Council on the Suez problem when he said: "the essence" of the Suez Canal problem was "that the operation of the Canal should be insulated from the influence of the politics of any nation".

President Eisenhower with Mr. Moshe Sharett, the Foreign Minister of Israel, and Ambassador Abba Eban at the White House, 1955.

Fourteen years later, during trade negotiations with Britain, in 1938, the United States put on record a formal expression of willingness to facilitate the establishment of the Jewish National Home by waiving certain rights of commercial equality with Palestine in British markets.

In fact this set of documents, with all their legal validity as binding international treaties would not have meant too much, had it not been for the continuous sympathy of official and unofficial America for the Zionist cause. None of the Presidents, who followed President Wilson, failed to endorse the policy of support for the Jewish National Home. Occasions for such statements of sympathy were many: New Years messages to the American Jewish Community, cables to National Conventions of the Zionist Organization of America, and in time to other Zionist groups, the Labor Zionists, Mizrahi, Hadassah, Mizrahi Women, statements to Zionist delegations received at the White House. All of them carried the message of American sympathy to the cause of Zionism.

Israel's first President, Dr. Weitzmann, receives specially designed, luxurious car, gift of Ford.

Addressing himself to a conference of the Palestine Foundation Fund, President Warren G. Harding wrote in May 1922,

I am very glad to express my approval and hearty sympathy for the effort of the Palestine Foundation Fund in behalf of the restoration of Palestine as a homeland for the Jewish people. I have always viewed with interest, which I think is quite as much practical as sentimental, the proposal for the rehabilitation of Palestine, and I hope the effort now being carried on in this and other countries in this behalf may meet with the fullest measure of success.

President Calvin Coolidge followed in the footsteps of President Warren G. Harding. Two years after the latter's declaration of sympathy and support for Zionism, President

David Ben Gurion, Israel's Prime Minister meets President Eisenhower at the White House.

Coolidge, in June, 1926, reiterated such support and elaborated even more on the subject when he stated:

I have many times reiterated my interest in this great movement that anything which I might add would be a repetition of former statements, but I am nevertheless glad to have this opportunity to express again my sympathy with the deep and intense longing which finds such fine expression in the Jewish National Homeland in Palestine.

President Coolidge was not satisfied with such generalities. He further expressed his conviction that the Jewish National Homeland in Palestine will in effect give to the Jewish people the great opportunity they were waiting for, for the

John F. Kennedy on his visit to Jerusalem, at a reception given by the British High Commissioner, 1939.

national redemption, and full realization of their historical aspirations and qualities. To make it clear that his sympathies were not pious wishes, President Coolidge did not hesitate to commit the United States of America to a policy of

earnest and substantial aid to assure the Zionist enterprise a full measure of success.

It is interesting to note that the number of pro-Zionist statements by American Presidents was proportionate to the degree of their interest and involvement in international affairs, and their general influence and standing in American public opinion. Thus the Presidents who followed Herbert C. Hoover,

Franklin D. Roosevelt and later, Harry S. Truman -- were issuing numerous statements in support of Zionism, even though not all of these statements should be taken at their face value, as the case with President Roosevelt has proved so many times. These frequent Presidential statements on the Jewish National Home were also a result of the growing controversy between the Zionist movement and the mandatory power.

The 1929 Palestine disturbances which resulted in the major British breach of confidence placed in her by the Zionist movement, accorded special importance to such statements. President Hoover's statement, issued in September, 1929, was a reassuring attestation to America's continued support of the Jewish National Home policy. In a broader sense it was one of the first demonstrations of American disagreement with the British policy in Palestine. At the time when Great Britain's government was busy in preparing its anti-Zionist White Paper, President Hoover confirmed his confidence in the success of Zionism,

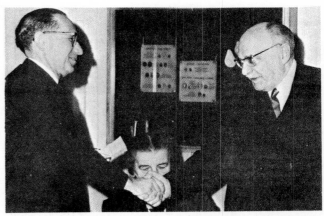

President Shazar presents Israel's contribution to the Eleanor Roosevelt Foundation to Philip M. Klutznick. In center Golda Meir, Israel's Foreign Minister.

Chief Justice Warren with members of the Israel Supreme Court during visit in Jerusalem. Left to right: Justices Etzioni, Halevi, Landau, Silberg, Agranat, and Warren.

I am confident, he wrote, out of these tragic events will come greater security and greater safeguards for the future, under which the steady rehabilitation of Palestine as a true Homeland will be even more assured.

President Hoover was even more outspoken in his pro-Zionist sympathies in 1930 when in a message to the National Convention of the Zionist Organization of America he assured the delegate of "his deep appreciation of their service to the spiritual life of the Jewish race," and referring again to the 1929 disturbances stated:

I have followed with deep interest the occurrences of the last year in Palestine, and wish to assure the Convention not only of my sympathy with them in their problems, but of my hope that the discouragements of the moment will presently be removed, and the work of advancing Jewish aspirations will go forward to even greater success.

No amount of pressure of Jewish anti-Zionist groups succeeded in preventing such statements. Even the fact, which nobody could have denied, that the Zionist movement had organized in its ranks only a minority of the Jews in America, did not affect this policy. The Presidents had an excellent perception of the real sentiments of the overwhelming majority of American Jews, whether organized in the Zionist movement or not, and of the vast majority of non-Jews, who wished to see Jerusalem rebuilt and Jews masters in their own land.

President Eisenhower visiting the Israel Pavilion at the International Fair in the New York Coliseum. With the President at right is New York Mayor Robert F. Wagner.

10

THE SPIRAL OF POLITICAL INVOLVEMENT

THE RAPID DEVELOPMENT of world events was soon to put to test the new American isolationism. The rising conflict in Europe, the challenges of fascist expansionism were too pressing problems that a nation like the United States could afford to ignore them. The Middle-East moved as well to the forefront of international affairs. These were not only the pressures of American Zionists caused by the British anti-Zionist policies that forced the American government to take positions on the Palestine question. The Congressional resolution of 1922, the Convention of 1924, notwithstanding the Wilson involvement in shaping the political future of Palestine made the United States a natural address for those who thought that its intervention could influence the course taken by Great Britain concerning its policy in Palestine. The conditions which induced President Wilson to intervene with the British Government, and the circumstances which precipitated these interventions, were not changed. On the contrary, the special conditions grew in intensity as far as the official British enmity towards the Jewish National Home was concerned.

The British White Paper of 1930 which followed the Arab anti-Jewish riots of 1929, was the culmination of a series of devices to curb the progress of the Jewish National Home, and arrest its development. American Zionists were incited by this trend of developments. The American Government had, in their opinion, not only a moral right to intervene, and try to bring about a change in that policy of Great Britain -- they considered the Convention of 1924 a document through which the United States became a guarantor of implementation of that document and all its stipulations. Did not Article 7 of the American-British Convention, they argued, state clearly that no modification in the terms of the Palestine Mandate will be admissible without the consent of the United States? Representations of this character were made many times, but hardly elicited real American intervention. But even in this state of reluctance to embarrass a friendly nation, the Department of State sent an inter-governmental communication to the British Government, calling its attention to the loss of lives and property of American nationals, and the danger to other American national interests. Curiously enough, in view of later developments in American Middle Eastern policies, that note included also a suggestion that if need be

American forces would be made available to restore order.

The limited character of this non-public American intervention could hardly have influenced British policy in Palestine. The Arab opposition to the policy of a Jewish National Home started to assume serious proportions. The Italian invasion of Ethiopia, the German expansionist policy aimed at undermining British influence in Africa and the Middle East, turned Palestine into a focal point of this Fascist-Nazi political drive. The policy of appeasement selected the Jewish National Home as one of the easiest means for the mollification of Arab appetites. The British scheme of partition of Palestine -- the recommendations of the Peel Commission, which were accompanied by a Government White Paper, were an open assault on the integrity of the Balfour Declaration and the Palestine Mandate. The British Government abandoned all moral scruples and inhibitions. Its White Paper of 1937 included a clear statement that the

irreconcilable conflict between the aspirations of Arabs and Jews in Palestine . . . cannot be satisfied under the terms of the present Mandate and that a scheme of partition on the . . . (suggested) . . . lines . . . represents the best, and most hopeful solution of the deadlock.

It did not take long before even this policy of partition was abandoned. With partition scuttled, only the basic assumption remained that because the aspirations of the Jews and the Arabs cannot be reconciled, the provisions of the Balfour Declaration and the Palestine Mandate were no more binding.

American intervention could not be avoided. On October 8, 1937, Secretary of State Cordell Hull issued a statement that

New York Mayor Robert F. Wagner issuing Israel Independence Anniversary Proclamation. From left to right: Rabbi Mordecai Kirschblum, Mrs. Rose Halprin, Charles Bick, the Mayor, Mrs. Yael Sharett Medini, Leon Kohn, Rabbi Jerome Unger. Not shown Paul Goldman, Louis Segal.

the American Government and people have watched with the keenest sympathy the development in Palestine of the (Jewish) National Home.

Whether such cautious statements could have had any influence on the British policy in Palestine is rather doubtful. But even this overly cautious wording was weakened by a new interpretation of America's prerogatives in handling the implementation of the Balfour Declaration and Palestine Mandate. The Department of State saw it advisable to add that the United States is not empowered to prevent

any modification of the Palestine Mandate, though it promised to

take all necessary measures for the protection of American rights and interests in Palestine.

It was at this occasion that the first major cleavage between the State Department and the American public opinion appeared on matters of attitudes towards Palestine. Fifty-one Senators, one hundred and ninety-four representatives and thirty state governors submitted a memorandum to the White House, protesting the British policy. Results were not forth-

Boy Scouts raising the Israel flag at ceremony of flag raising, in San Francisco, on the occasion of the tenth anniversary of signing the United Nations Charter, June 20, 1955.

coming. The State Department statement was fully endorsed by President Roosevelt. But far worse was the interpretation of Article seven of the American-British Convention of 1924. In what appeared to be the strongest argument supporting the American right to intervene on behalf of the implementation of the Palestine Mandate, Article seven, was completely ignored. To make things worse, Mr. Hull's statement asserted that none of the treaties concerning the Mandates

> empower the Government of the United States to prevent the modification of the terms of any of the mandates.

The intention was clear: this statement of policy included the Palestine Mandate as well.

Thus ended in defeat the first major battle for causing the United States Government to take a direct interest in the conduct of the Palestine affairs, not out of general humanitarian impulses, but based on clear, treaty obligations.

But even this statement, void of any practical political meaning, was interpreted differently by the Arabs and what became already known, their new allies, Hitler's Germany, and Mussolini's Italy. The Arab broadcasts from the Bari station, in Italy, branded the United

States as the ally of Zionism, and President Roosevelt the enemy of the Arab world. The German propaganda was eager to catch upon this Arab appraisal of the American attitude. When President Roosevelt invited on April 14, 1939, Hitler and Mussolini to settle all outstanding international disputes through peaceful negotiations, Hitler saw it convenient to include in his harangue, before the Reichstag, the following statement:

. . . the fact has obviously escaped Mr. Roosevelt's notice that Palestine is at present occupied not by German troops but by the English; and that the country is having its liberty restricted by the most brutal resort to force, is being robbed of its independence, and is suffering the cruelest maltreatment for the benefit of Jewish interlopers. The Arabs living in that country will therefore certainly not have complaints to Mr. Roosevelt of German aggression, but they do voice a continuous appeal to the world, deploring the barbarous methods with which England is attempting to suppress a people which loves freedom and is but defending it.

Thus, whether the democratic world wanted it or not, Palestine, the problem of implementation of the Palestine Mandate, was catapulted into the very center of international politics. The hand of anti-Zionists in the British government was strengthened. They knew,

President Truman and Mrs. Truman with Dr. Abba Hillel Silver.

President John F. Kennedy addressing a Convention of the Zionist Organization of America on the eve of his election to the Presidency, 1960.

At the celebration of Israel's Tenth Anniversary at New York's Polo Grounds. Left to right: Ira Guilden, Abba Eban, Mrs. Eleanor Roosevelt, Gen. Moshe Dayan, Herbert H. Lehman, Meyer Weisgal, Averell Harriman.

America would not try to influence their policy of appeasement in the Middle East. With the clouds of World War II gathering in growing intensity, such appeasement assumed proportions of a most vital interest of alleged worldwide proportions. The way was open for a complete betrayal of the Mandate obligations.

A White Paper of May, 1939, spelled out formally the long brewing intentions of a final blow at Zionist aspirations. A final limit to Jewish immigration to Palestine was set, 75,000 over five years, while the later continuation of such immigration was to be made dependent on Arab consent, land purchases were to be forbidden in most of Palestine which was divided for this purpose into three zones, a Council was to be elected and an independent Palestine State to be established after a period of ten years.

That this meant the final end of the Jewish National Home policies was clear. That it had to liquidate the obligations of the Palestine Mandate and institute in Palestine a Jewish ghetto instead, nobody doubted. The fact that the British Government had this breach of its international obligations approved by a slimmer majority of the House of Commons than expected (a majority of 89 votes, while the Government commanded a normal majority of 220), that two former Colonial Secretaries branded the document "a plain breach of a solemn obligation," "another Munich," gave little consolation to the World Zionist movement. No more consoling was the decision of the Mandates Commission of the League of Nations, which rejected the White Paper unanimously and declared that the policy set out in the White Paper was not in accordance with the interpretation which, in agreement with the Mandatory Power and the Council, the Commission had always placed upon the Palestine Mandate.

The British Government was not moved by all these statements. The outbreak of World War II within four months of the publication of the White Paper, made all these protests worthless. The Zionist movement was alone in its struggle against the White Paper. The *Yishuv* made the first serious attempt at sabotaging British anti-Zionist policy. Demonstrations, clashes with police forces marked the beginning of a policy of non-cooperation with the Mandatory Power. But the hoped-for assistance from America was not forthcoming. The State Department kept silent. So did President Roosevelt. Voices of protest were heard only in Congress and the press. Some Congressmen threatened an investigation of the State Department's silence. Some spoke about

Jew-haters who are also Roosevelt baiters, who grin like Cheshire cats at the abetting of this betrayal by some of our own officials in the State Department.

Editorials in the leading organs of the American press protested the policy of the May, 1939, British White Paper. The *St. Louis Post Dispatch,* the *New York Times,* the *New York Herald Tribune,* the *Los Angeles Times,* the *Chicago Daily News,* the *Cleveland Plain Dealer,* the *Boston Globe,* the *Baltimore*

Israel's President Zalman Shazar arriving for the funeral of President Kennedy. With him are U. S. Secretary of State, Dean Rusk, Mrs. Golda Meir and Israel Ambassador Abraham Harman.

Sun, led the attack. But the editorials were limited to pious exclamations. The *New York Times* wrote:

> Great Britain must protect these people to the end.

The *Chicago Daily News* asked:

> Was our assent secured? Was an effort made to secure it? If not, why not? These are the questions in which both Congress and State Department should take an immediate interest.

Only the *News of Birmingham,* Alabama, spoke about United States obligations

> The United States is not without duty under the circumstances.

None of the editorials suggested any specific policy.

Israel mourns the death of President Kennedy: Premier Levi Eshkol is escorted by U. S. Ambassador W. Barbour after signing the Kennedy condolence book.

The cause of American official silence was no longer a function of isolationist considerations which were still prevailing. A new factor assumed importance in forming American policies in the Middle East. The oil lobby made its appearance. The American-owned oil companies which, in 1928, owned 23.75 per cent of the Iraq Petroleum Company continued to expand their holdings in that area. American interests acquired in 1934 half ownership of the Kuwait oil fields, exclusive concessions in Bahrein in 1929, and 1940, and in Saudi Arabia in 1933, and 1939. Among the American companies, the California Arabian Standard Oil Company, which later became the Arabian-American Oil Company, *Aramco,* engaged very soon in serious political lobbying.

American entrance into the war, and the joining with the British Middle East Supply Center, involved the United States in the practical political problems of the Middle East. It became clear that the Middle East was assuming permanent importance for America's world-wide political interests and responsibilities. A tendency to buy the favors of Arab rulers was the result. *Aramco* promoted a policy of financial reward to Arabs by the United States Government in exchange for concessions this company was gaining. After some hesitation, dictated by consideration of the fact that

Arabia is in the British sphere of influence, a decision was adopted to construct a pipe line system for transporting petroleum from the Arabian Peninsula to the Mediterranean, at a cost estimated between $130,000,000 and $165,000,000. The alleged reason for such expense, was, of course, national necessity. In authorizing such expenditure Secretary of Interior, Harold L. Ickes, declared that its aim was to offset the dwindling American oil reserves "estimated to be adequate for this nation's needs for only a relatively few years." In exchange for such government support, the oil companies were supposed to set aside a reserve of oil to help

> assure an adequate supply of petroleum for the military and naval needs of the United States in view of the obligations which this country must assume for the maintenance of collective security in the post-war world.

Though the project was not implemented, its very initiation should be considered the turning point in American policies in the Middle East.

The fact that private interests were so vitally involved in having America set political foot in the Middle East, and having this policy based on the premises of need to win Arab sympathies, had only hastened American involvement in Middle Eastern affairs. These considerations have thrived on an unavoidable development related to America's broader strategic, economic, and political interests resulting from the emerging American global policies. Palestine, the political forces in Palestine, were no longer a matter of sheer sympathies. Practical considerations entered the scene. It was in this light that President Roosevelt's first exchange of correspondence with King Ibn Saud of Saudi Arabia has to be viewed. President Roosevelt's pledge, in his letter to Ibn Saud, that the situation in Palestine will not be changed "without full consultation with both Arabs and Jews," made the United States a direct partner in determining the future of Palestine. By implication this was an explicit anti-Zionist statement, because the existing situation, which President Roosevelt promised not to change, without consultation with the Arabs, was an anti-Zionist situation, based on the 1939 British White Paper. President Roosevelt's later detraction from this statement, when under pressure of American Zionists he permitted that it be stated in his name, in March 1944, that the United States had not given its consent to the 1939 White Paper and that "when fu-

President Johnson at the Weitzmann Institute annual dinner in New York. Left to right: Meyer Weisgal, the President and Walter Annenberg.

ture decisions are reached, full justice will be done to those who seek a Jewish National Home," was not the final word in this matter.

The statement which President Roosevelt made on March 1, 1945, after a meeting with King Ibn Saud, in 1945, on his way from Yalta, that he learned about "the Moslem problem and the Jewish problem" more by "talking with Ibn Saud for five minutes than I could have learned in exchange of two or three dozens of letters," did not indicate that President Roosevelt had not changed his mind since his statement of March 1944.

Whatever one can think, that seesaw of statements which followed again is an almost grotesque illustration of this duplicity in

President Lyndon B. Johnson accompanied by Mrs. Johnson welcomes Prime Minister Levi Eshkol and Mrs. Eshkol on their arrival at the White House, 1964.

Roosevelt's policy. After making his statement on the famous "five minutes," President Roosevelt again reassured Dr. Stephen Wise that he had not changed his pre-election promises regarding Zionist aspirations in Palestine, and assured the Zionist leader that he would "continue to seek to bring about their realization." When Ibn Saud hastened to send to the President a strongly worded letter, President Roosevelt, a week before his death, reassured Ibn Saud that his promises stand, and reminded him of their conversation some weeks earlier when Roosevelt promised that he

> would take no action, in the capacity as Chief of the Executive Branch of his Government, which might prove hostile to the Arab people.

Whatever one can think of the moral attributes of such conflicting statements it made abundantly clear that the United States made interfering in Middle Eastern affairs its official policy. The United States became a partner in deciding the fortunes of Palestine. American statements on Zionism, on the future of Palestine, departed from the realm of moral, humanitarian, and sentimental considerations. They became part and parcel of American foreign policy. They were a complete departure from the policy of some three decades before, when a American President declined to send

greetings to a Zionist literary society on the grounds of refraining from "intervening in affairs related to the interests of other states."

Thus the dilemma of duplicity in American policies in the Middle East, made its appearance. According to anti-Zionists only internal political considerations promoted giving a sympathetic ear to Zionist demands, while what was defined as alleged American interest in the Middle East, was supposed to dictate disregard of international obligations to which the United States was partner. What such policy has meant in practice was revealed by Bartley Crum, one of the American members of the Anglo-American Committee of Inquiry:

> When the Committee was on its way to Europe, after the initial hearings in Washington, the American members received contents of a file of confidential communications on Palestine, supplied by the Division of Near Eastern Affairs. It dealt with 17 items, despatches, cables, correspondence, memoranda and conversations. This was, revealed Crum, a resume of the State Department's secret file on Palestine, the extent of which apparently not even President Truman had known. According to this file, since September 15, 1938, each time a promise was made to American Jewry regarding Palestine, the State Department

Eighteen junior "Goodwill Ambassadors" from the United States received by the Israel President Zalman Shazar at his residence in Jerusalem. Paul Kevin Williams, aged 12 of Boston, read "letter of credence" from President Lyndon B. Johnson.

Israel President Shazar on brief stop-over in New York, on his way from a South American tour. From left to right: U. S. Senator Robert Kennedy, President Shazar, Max Fisher, National Chairman of the United Jewish Appeal, U. S. Senator Jacob Javits.

promptly sent messages to the Arab rulers discounting it and reassuring them.

Discussing these facts, Judge John Hutcheson, the chairman of the Committee remarked: "It seems that Great Britain is not the only power which promises the same thing to two different groups."

A new promise to the American Jews was soon to be forthcoming. The year 1944 was an election year and President Roosevelt decided to run for an unprecedented fourth term. To assure Jewish support, the Democratic platform, adopted at the Democratic Convention in Chicago, included a statement of policy which said:

We favor the opening of Palestine to unrestricted Jewish immigration and colonization, and such a policy as to result in the establishment there of a free and democratic Jewish Commonwealth.

President Roosevelt's personal commitment was not missing. In a letter to Senator Robert Wagner of New York, to be read at the National Convention of the Zionist Organization of America, President Roosevelt stated:

Efforts will be made to find appropriate ways and means of affectuating this policy as soon as practicable. I know how long and ardently the Jewish people have worked and prayed for the establishment of Palestine as a free and democratic Jewish Commonwealth. I am convinced that the American people give support to this aim and if re-elected, I shall help to bring about its realization.

Because this statement preceded the meeting with Ibn Saud, President Roosevelt did not hesitate to authorize Dr. Stephen Wise, after that meeting, to quote him:

I made my position on Zionism clear and shall continue to seek to bring about its earliest realization.

These democratic statements were immediately countered by the Republican candidate for the Presidency. Governor Thomas E. Dewey issued a statement that he "heartily endorses the Palestine plank in the Republican Party platform." Recalling his previous statements made to the "great leader of the American Zionist movement and distinguished American, Dr. Abba Hillel Silver," Governor Dewey as-

President Johnson and Premier Eshkol in intimate conversation.

sured that he is "for the reconstruction of Palestine as a free and democratic Jewish Commonwealth in accordance with the Balfour Declaration, and the resolution of the Republican Congress in 1922."

The statement continued:

I have also stated to Dr. Silver that in order to give refuge to millions of distressed Jews driven from their homes by tyranny, I favor the opening of Palestine to their unlimited immigration and land ownership. The American people have time and again declared themselves in favor of these principles. The Republican Party has, at all times, been the traditional friend of the movement. As President, I would use my best offices to have our Government working together with Great Britain to achieve this great objective for a people that have suffered so much and deserve so much at the hands of mankind.

It would be a simplification, as some anti-Zionists like to see it, to present such pro-

Philadelphia Mayor James H. J. Tate explaining history of Liberty Bell to Premier Eshkol.

Zionist statements as related only to election mathematics. Though one can see nothing wrong in the fact that in a democracy various groups try to impress their opinions on the general policies of the country, it should not be forgotten that such pro-Zionist statements were dictated not only by pressures of the American Jewish Community galvanized into action, and expressed by the American Zionist movement. In fact, a pro-Zionist policy was demanded by the overwhelming majority of the American people from all walks of life, of all religious denominations. Clergymen, university professors, labor, Governors, Senators, Congressmen, a real cross-section of the American people voiced in clearest terms their support for a Jewish Commonwealth. During the first three years since America's entry into the war, thirty-nine State Legislatures in states representing approximately 85 per cent of

U. S. Ambassador to Israel Walworth Barbour with American Young Judea contingent and guests at reception in the ZOA House, in Tel Aviv, preceding Thanksgiving Dinner.

the entire American population had gone on record, through resolutions, as favoring the establishment of Palestine as a Jewish Commonwealth.

On October 4, 1943, the American Federation of Labor unanimously adopted a resolution which stated that the A. F. of L.

urges that the restrictions on Jewish immigration and settlement contained in the British White Paper be withdrawn, and that the Balfour Declaration be so implemented that the hopes and aspirations of the Jewish people to build their own Commonwealth in Palestine be realized. Thus will this ancient people be enabled to take its rightful place among the democratic nations of the world, and make its full contribution to that progressive world which, we all pray, will emerge from the horrible sufferings of this global war.

Only a month later, the other major labor organization, the Congress of Industrial Organizations, expressed similar sentiments. The CIO addressed itself to the demands of Palestine Jews that they be given

all opportunity for unrestricted participation in the battlefield and for unrestricted opportunity to make a agricultural and industrial contribution to the war effort.

Forty State Governors signed a petition to President Roosevelt in which they expressed their support for the demand of making Palestine a Jewish Commonwealth. Initiated by Governor Herbert Maw of Utah, who acted as Chairman of the Conference of State

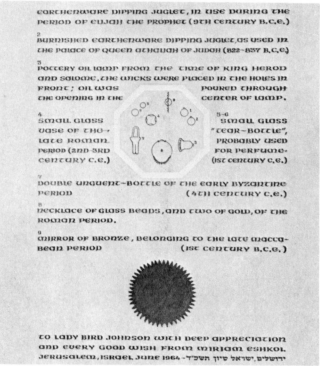

List of items presented by Mrs. Eshkol to Mrs. Johnson.

Governors, it received immediate support of the Governors of New York, Massachusetts, Rhode Island and Connecticut. At the same time, wide publicity was given to a "Letter to the President" signed by fifty-five Senators and 261 Congressmen who repeated, in varying phrases, the all-American demands for American Government support for a Jewish Palestine.

A most effective campaign for a Jewish Palestine was conducted by the American Palestine Committee, founded in 1941, under the joint chairmanship of Senator Robert Wagner of New York, and Senator Charles McNary of Oregon, and by the Christian Council on Palestine, composed of Chrisian clergymen and educators, organized in 1942 by

Premier Eshkol with children of Israeli trainees at Fort Bliss.

Dr. Henry A. Atkinson and Professor Reinhold Niebuhr. Explaining the basic aims of their organizations, both these public bodies expressed their conviction that

the destiny of the Jews is a matter of immediate concern to the Christian conscience, the amelioration of their lot, a duty that rests upon all that profess Christian principles.

The American Palestine Committee considered itself

the vehicle for the expression of the sympathy and good will of Christian America for the movement to re-establish the Jewish National Home in Palestine.

Israeli soldiers study the Hawk missile.

And the Executive Committee of the Christian Council on Palestine recommended that

> plans be made how to place Palestine under an international mandate of the United Nations and that the door of Palestine be opened at once to admit tens of thousands more of the persecuted Jewish people in war-torn Europe.

There was also an American Christian Palestine Committee, with thousands of members in local chapters in one hundred cities, throughout the country. They embarked on a wide campaign of information, collected signatures for petitions to the President, to Senators and Congressmen.

The slowly penetrating news about the mass liquidation of European Jewry made the demands for opening the doors of Palestine for Jewish immigration a matter of human conscience which no politician dared to question publicly. *"Days of Compassion for murder-*

ed Jews" organized by the American Christian Palestine Committee, brought the awareness of the murder of millions to millions.

On March 9, 1943, and on March 18, respectively, a resolution was introduced in the Senate and the House of Representatives which dealt with the German mass murders. After stating that "the American people view with indignation the inflicted atrocities upon the civilian population in the Nazi-occupied countries and especially the murder of Jewish men, women and children" it called that "those guilty directly or indirectly of these criminal acts shall be held accountable and punished in a manner commensurate with the offenses for which they are responsible." On July 26, 1943, Senator Edwin C. Johnson of Colorado called an emergency Conference to Save the Jews in Europe.

But all the demonstrations of public concern with the fate of European Jews failed to move

Mayor James H. J. Tate of Philadelphia and members of clergy at Independence Square rally, in support of Israel, June 11, 1967.

U. S. Ambassador to the U. N. Arthur J. Goldberg addressing Security Council during Six Day War, June 7, 1967.

the Administration. The British argument that admittance of any number of Jewish refugees into Palestine would cause an explosion in the Arab Middle East, and make the Arabs turn towards the German-Italian axis, seemed to carry weight with the American government, irrespective of the fact that wherever and whenever an occasion occurred, the Arabs had always supported the Axis cause. The tragic story of the boatload of Jewish refugees from mass murder who managed to escape on the ship *St. Louis* and reach American waters, and were then forced to return to their ultimate place of destruction, is only one illustration that this pressure of Christian public opinion hardly influenced government action. Henry Morgenthau, Jr., then Secretary of the Treasury, published a shattering accusation against officials (who) dodged their given responsibility, procrastinated when concrete rescue schemes were placed before them, and even suppressed information about the atrocities in order to prevent an outraged public opinion from forcing their hand.

Writing on this problem in the November, 1947, issue of *Colliers*, Morgenthau revealed that from August, 1942, the American government knew, from many sources, that the Germans "are killing Jews wholesale." Only as late as January 22, 1944, President Roosevelt issued an Executive Order establishing an official agency for saving Jews in Europe -- the War Refugee Board. The first meeting of the new agency, January 26, 1944, attended by Secretaries Hull (Dept. of State), Stimson (Dept. of War) and Morgenthau (Dept. of Treasury), instructed all United States diplomats and consular offices throughout the world to do everything possible to effectuate the Government's new war refugee policy as announced by the President, bearing in mind the urgency of the problem.

The 984 refugees brought to Fort Ontario, Oswego, New York, in July 1944, were only an example of what could have been done if concern for people killed en masse would have overcome other considerations.

Israeli trainees dance the Hora after completion of training at Fort Bliss.

These considerations, to a degree, were a result of inter-Allies policy. America's closest ally, Great Britain, was not ready to change, in any degree, its anti-Zionist policy. The statements of the American President, inasmuch as they included pronouncements of sympathy to Zionism, were very much resented by Great Britain. And the general tenor of American public opinion, which supported overwhelmingly the claim for a Jewish Commonwealth, was considered by the British a irresponsible intervention. Leading organs of the British press voiced these feelings openly. The pro-Zionist planks of both the Democrats and Republicans were in the opinion of the London *Times* "inspired no doubt by genuine sympathy with the Jews, but also by the evident necessity of carrying New York. *The Economist* was even more critical, stating that

Congress has afforded itself the luxury of criticizing where it has no intention of

Sign attesting to American-Israel cooperation in building the new Sdom-Elath road.

constructive action and proposing positive solutions which it has neither the power nor the intention to enforce.

As developments proved, Congress was not proceeding as quickly as expected with its resolution of support for the Zionist cause. The Palestine Resolution, which was introduced early in 1944, in both Houses of Congress, did not move swiftly towards approval, as expected. Though it was supported by an overwhelming majority of Congress, it was stalled before being put to final vote. Even the fact of bi-partisan sponsorship of the resolution, by Senators Taft (Rep.) and Wagner (Dem.) and Representatives Wright (Rep.) and Compton (Dem.), did not assure passage of the resolution that

U. S. Assistant Secretary of State (sitting right) George V. Allen and Israel Ambassador Abba Eban signing agreement for sale of American surplus food to Israel. Looking on, left to right: Senator Thomas E. Martin of Iowa, Senator Frank A. Barret of Wyoming, Senator Roman L. Hruska of Nebraska, Secretary of Agriculture Ezra Taft Benson, Senator Bourke Hickenlooper of Iowa, Senator George Bender of Ohio.

resolved, that the United States shall use its good offices and take appropriate measures to the end that the doors of Palestine shall be opened for free entry of Jews into that country, and that there shall be full opportunity for colonization so that the Jewish people may ultimately reconstitute Palestine as a free and democratic Jewish Commonwealth.

The resolution was not brought to a vote. The administration intervened in strongest terms. The resolution was opposed by the War Department because, in their terms, "further action on the resolution at this time would be prejudicial to the successful prosecution of the war."

After this pretense of military considerations was removed, in a letter from the Secretary of War Stimson to Senator Taft, the Roosevelt Administration did not hesitate to admit that

Signing of U. S.-Israel agreement of Technical Aid. From left to right: Ralph Goldman, Teddy Kollek, Bruce McDaniel, head of the U. S. Operations Mission.

its opposition to the Palestine Resolution had no relation to the military needs of the war conduct. Secretary of State Edward R. Stettinius Jr. appeared on December 11, 1944, before the Senate Foreign Relations Committee to argue in the name of the Administration against the resolution, because

> passage of the resolution at present time would be unwise from the standpoint of the general international situation.

Secretary Stettinius' arguments were in line with a statement by Secretary of War Stimson, who admitted that "political considerations now outweigh the military, and the issue should be determined upon the political rather than military basis."

These reverses did not discourage the friends of a Jewish Palestine. Though there were signs of dissension in the Jewish ranks that followed the activities of a group called American Friends of a Jewish Palestine (and later, American League for a Free Palestine), sponsored by representatives of the Irgun Tzvai Leumi in America, such dissension, whatever was the real strength of these separate groups, did not impede the general atmosphere of support for a Jewish Palestine. Senators, Congressmen, mayors of major cities, continued to exert

pressure on the President that he take the necessary steps leading to the establishment of Palestine as a Jewish National Home.

The change in the White House, after President Roosevelt's sudden death, was bound to bring a change, if not in policies then at least in the forms and tone of American pronouncements on the future of Palestine. Within weeks after President Roosevelt's death, the war was over. The horrors of the slaughter of six million Jews could no longer be absolved by assertions that this is mere "propaganda." The facts were there, the victorious American armies, the liberators of the death camps' inmates, witnessed the horrible truth. The upsurge of public American support for finding a home for the wretched remnants of European Jewry was strong and spontaneous. Former President Hoover spoke up again on behalf of a Jewish Palestine. In a statement published on November 19, 1948, in the *New York World Telegram*, President Hoover suggested a transfer of Arabs from Palestine to Iraq to make even more room for Jews in Palestine. He stated:

> There is room for many more Arabs in such a development in Iraq than the total of Arabs in Palestine. The soil is more

American Point Four representatives and Israeli officials visit phosphate mines in Makhtesh Hagadol, in the Negev.

fertile, they would be among their own race; which is Arab-speaking and Mohammedan. . . . The Arab population of Palestine would be the gainer from better lands in exchange for their present holdings. Iraq would be the gainer for it badly needs agriculture population. Today millions are being moved from one land to another. If the lands were organized and homes provided, this particular movement could be made the model immigration of history. It would be a solution by engineering instead of by conflict. . . I realize that the plan offers a challenge both to the statesmanship of the Great Powers as well as to the goodwill of the parties concerned. However, I submit, it does offer a method of settlement with both honor and wisdom.

The many committees which were supporting the cause of a Jewish Palestine had suddenly realized that the justification for their cause was much more human and imperative than they themselves had anticipated. The War Refugee Board was no longer the answer, now even less than it had ever been

from the day of its inception. The Christian conscience was bound to sweep away all the political arguments of the new President Harry S. Truman's Cabinet. In June, 1945, President Truman instructed Earl G. Harrison, the American representative in the Intergovernmental Committee on Refugees, to investigate the problem of the displaced persons in Europe. In the articles of reference of this instruction, President Truman requested that particular attention be paid to Jews who could not or do not want to return to their countries of origin, and to revealing their emigration preferences. Harrison's report of August 31, 1945, sounded an alarm. "We appear," charged Harrison, "to be treating the Jews as the Nazis treated them." In his estimation, there were about 100,000 European Jews outside the Russian zone. The Hitler persecution, he argued, had formed a group that must be treated as a unit, based on particular racial and religious considerations as repugnant as such categorizing must appear to an American. He had no doubt that none of the Jews would be ready to remain in Germany and Austria.

They have one preference in the choice of the country of emigration: Palestine is definitely and pre-eminently the first choice. Many have relatives there, while others having experienced intolerance and persecution in their homelands for years, feel that only in Palestine will they be welcomed and . . . given an opportunity to live and work.

The Harrison report set the pace and marked the direction, American policy was destined to follow, in regard to Palestine. On September 20, 1945, William O'Dwyer, retiring director of the War Refugee Board, urged immediate action to effect the opening of Palestine to immigration of stateless Jews. On September 29, 1945, President Truman ordered General Eisenhower to improve conditions of displaced persons in Germany. At the same time, he communicated directly with the British Government suggesting that the doors of Palestine be opened to such of these displaced persons as wished to go there. The British Labor Government headed by Prime Minister Attlee agreed to follow the American request on condition that the United States assume joint

The 150-mile road from Beersheba to Elath, built with the help of Israel Bonds as have many other communications arteries, development enterprises and basic industries.

responsibility, including the use of troops, if necessary. Such condition had no chance of being accepted. With the war over, America wanted its boys home. Even if he could have so desired, President Truman could hardly have afforded to accede to such condition.

The outburst of British anger had no bounds. Ernest Bevin, the British Minister of Foreign Affairs, in an address on June 12, 1946, to the Annual Conference of the British Labor Party, attacked vehemently the American agitation for Jewish immigration to Palestine. In the peak of his anger he stated ". . . they did not want too many of them in New York." The British press followed suit. President Truman was accused of being motivated by the "5,000,000 Jews who form so influential a body of voters in the United States," and another paper wrote that "America's request would be more impressive had she herself opened her doors wider to Hitler's victims."

Before America adopted finally a policy of support of Jewish immigration to Palestine, traditional expressions of vacillation in its Palestine policy could not have been avoided. The State Department did not relinquish its opposition to what had become already clear: the necessity of American commitment to practical steps related to the basic problems confronting Palestine. In October, 1945, Secretary of State James F. Byrnes stated that

> should proposals emerge from discussions with the British Government which in the opinion of the United States would change the basic situation in Palestine, the United States Government will not reach final conclusions without full consultation with Jewish and Arab leaders.

Secretary Byrnes was not isolated in his opinions. Other members of the Cabinet were equally disturbed by President Truman's open advocacy of Jewish immigration to Palestine. Secretary James V. Forrestal complained of the "tremendous task that is involved in the implementation of American policy," and cited the American Palestine policy as an example of the complex problems of racial, religious and social diversity which America tries to solve by application of moral, liberal yardsticks which have no bearing in this particular case. American attitudes in the Palestine question, he argued, caused a loss of American prestige in the Arab world.

But the direction of American Palestine policy could no longer be changed. The British, who, according to Forrestal, said that "they cannot do all they would like for the Arabs because of the pressure we (the U.S.) are able to exert," have decided to suggest a joint Anglo-American investigation of the problem related to Palestine. After President Truman accepted the suggestion, the stage was set for the first official and formal direct involvement of America in the Palestine question. In November, 1945, the Anglo-American Committee of Inquiry came into being. Its terms of reference, much discussed until formally accepted by both partners, were very much attuned to the real desires of the British government to accommodate the Arabs. The provisions speaking about immigration to Palestine were guarded by a series of reservations. These reservations were concerned with the responsibilities, the possibilities of re-integration of the Jews in the countries of Europe, while the estimation of the number of Jews to be admitted to Palestine had to be formulated after the Committee would reach the conclusion how many were "impelled by their conditions to migrate to Palestine or other countries outside Europe." Setting such numbers had to be accomplished in "consultation with representative Arabs and Jews, with concern for the prevailing political, economic and social conditions."

The ambiguity of this formulation, which opened in fact the way for a complete acceptance of the Arab point of view, did not augur well for the outcome of this inquiry. The composition of the American part of this Committee became therefore of primary importance. Only Americans who had some knowledge of the Palestine problem, and who would therefore be able to be a match for their British counterparts, held some promise of an objective inquiry, and objective conclusions. The Department of State was therefore very much concerned with not having on the Committee individuals whose past could, in any way, make them open to independent political thinking, to reasons of historical justice, fidelity to international obligations, and responsiveness to humanitarian considerations. How much these elements weighed in the selection of the American members of the Committee was best illustrated by the fact that one of these members of the Committee, Bartley Crum, was rejected three times by the State Department and approved only after President Truman cabled to the Secretary of State then in Moscow, and demanded compliance with his choice. The other American members represented a cross-section of American public opinion. There were Judge Hutcheson from Texas, Frank W. Buxton, editor of the *Boston Herald;* Dr. Frank Aydelotte, director of the Institute for Advanced Study at Princeton; James McDonald, League of Nations Commissioner for German Refugees; and William Philips, former Ambassador to Italy. Everyone understood that with the establishment of that Committee, something had occurred that would continue to occupy for months American public attention. At the luncheon given for the joint Committee by Secretary of State Dean Acheson, the chairman of the British group, Sir John Singleton, a Judge, saw fit to equal the importance of that Committee's work with the wartime collaboration of Britain and the United States, by saying:

> We must endeavor to capture, in peace, the wartime partnership of Mr. Roosevelt and Mr. Churchill.

The send-off given the Committee by the British Minister for Foreign Affairs was not too inducive to believing that the British Government saw in that Committee anything else than a delaying tactic, and an attempt to associate the United States Government with the British policy in Palestine. In his anti-Semitic rage, Bevin could not withstand the temptation of a direct anti-Semitic remark when he said:

> If the Jews with all their sufferings want to get too much at the head of the queue, you have the danger of another anti-Semitic reaction through it all.

In this atmosphere, the American members of the Committee had no difficulty in finding out that unless they were firm, they were going to become mere tools of British devices. If there were among them any who were apt to succumb, the months of investigation immunized them against such possibility. After opening the hearings in Washington and listening to the exposition of the case by the interested parties, they traveled to Europe and and to Palestine, to see on the spot the core of the problem. The Displaced Persons camps, harboring the remnants of European Jewry, were sufficient to move a rock. The intense and uncompromising clamor of these Jews to go to Palestine was more convincing than all the British arguments. And the results of the inquiry into the absorptive capacity of Palestine, the ability of the Jewish Community of Palestine to defend itself, and the right to keep Palestine's doors open, appeared to be more convincing than all the threats of Bevan about the danger of evoking the ire of the Arab world and that of 90,000,000 Muslims in India. They appeared to be just what they were -- the phantoms of a man who tried frantically to prevent the inevitable, and considered the defeat of Zionist aims in Palestine his personal ambition.

The considerations of the *Yishuv's* defense capability weighed heavily on the deliberations of the Committee, especially on its American members. This was illustrated in Bartley Crum's report of a conversation he had with the Chairman of the American group, Judge Joseph C. Hutcheson from Texas:

> 'You remember,' relates Crum, 'Judge,' I told him one afternoon, as we were having tea in our offices, 'that about a hundred years ago the people of Texas were in almost the same situation as the Jews in Palestine.' The Judge cocked his head and raised his eyebrows. 'Absolutely,' I said. 'The Americans were under Mexican rule. The Mexican Government got tough with them. It halted all immigration into Texas. It attempted to take away the arms and ammunition from the Texans. You know what happened. The Texans kicked out all the Mexicans and set up a state of their own.' Hutcheson: 'O, yes, but we were prepared to fight for our liberty.'

After the visit in Palestine, Bartley Crum had no difficulty in convincing Judge Hutcheson that the Jews were no less prepared to fight for their liberty.

This was not the only conversation with Crum that influenced Judge Hutcheson's thinking. It is well known that Judge Hutcheson was rather receptive to the British point of view. In one of his last confessions, before his untimely death, Bartley Crum revealed to me a story which he kept secret until that time. When the Committee came to Geneva to write the report, there was little unanimity not only between the two groups of Committee members, but even among the Americans themselves. The first draft of the report was very unfavorable to Jewish interests. Some American members, primarily Bartley Crum, threatened that they would not hesitate to prepare a minority report. After long deliberations, the Committee broke off its meeting for the weekend recess. Suddenly, Crum said, on Sunday morning he heard the telephone ringing. Judge Hutcheson was on the other end of the line. He urged Crum to see him without delay. Crum obliged. When they met, Judge Hutcheson read a letter he had received the previous

Saturday from Mrs. Hutcheson in Houston, Texas. Mrs. Hutcheson wrote about the blessing the DPs were showering on Mr. Crum for his humane behavior and understanding of their tragedy. There were enclosed clippings from the press of the DPs. Mrs. Hutcheson, a deeply religious person, closed her letter with an appeal to her husband to follow in Crum's footsteps and earn the gratitude and prayers and good wishes of the people of the Bible. When Judge Hutcheson finished reading the letter, he added: "Bartley, I am with you."

The report of the Committee was unanimous. To meet the conditions set by the British and American governments, formulated at the establishment of the Committee, was not easy. President Truman demanded that 100,000 Jews be admitted immediately into Palestine, and Bevin wanted Palestine turned into a trusteeship to become in time an independent "Palestinian, not Jewish, state." The President had his hand strengthened by the adoption of the Palestine Resolution, which became finally a fact in December, 1945, after a long off-and-on struggle between both Houses of Congress and the Administration. The Anglo-American Committee's report, released simultaneously in Washington and in London, May 1, 1946, called for admission of 100,000 Jews to Palestine. This recommendation followed by the statement that the, 1939, White Paper's immigration and land restrictions be rescinded, was approved by President Truman on the same day, though he reserved judgment on long-range political questions.

These long-range political questions became much more complicated than they were before. In January, 1946, *Aramco* received from the Palestine Government a concession to construct a pipe line from its oil fields in Saudi Arabia to the Palestine coast. The United States acquired air landing rights in Arab lands, a big airfield for the U.S.A.F. was being built in Saudi Arabia.

The interest shown by Soviet Russia in the Palestine question added to the growing awareness that the area was bound to become involved in international rivalries of ever-growing magnitude. The fact that the British Government reneged on the obligation of complying with the recommendation of the Committee of Inquiry complicated the question even more. President Truman's endorsement of the recommendation for the admittance of 100,000 Jews to Palestine didn't meet with British approval. Instead of taking action, or re-stating the American position, the State Department announced that no immediate action will be taken on behalf of these 100,000 without first acting on the other recommendations of the report.

After accepting in principle the position of the British Government, the State Department went even a step further in emulating the British methods of dealing with the Palestine problem: on May 20th, the State Department invited Arab and Jewish representatives to present their views on the recommendations of the Committee of Inquiry. This was an obvious departure from President Truman's stated policy.

While such maneuvering was continued, American delegations were shuttling back and forth between London and Washington. There was a delegation of technical experts to work out the logistics of the mass movement of the 100,000; there was later an American Cabinet Committee to work with British counterparts on the implementation of the Committee of Inquiry recommendations, other than the admittance of 100,000 Jews to Palestine.

The deliberations of the Committee resulted in a completely new device for liquidating Jewish rights and aspirations in Palestine, and perpetuation of British rule there. This was the so-called Grady-Morrison plan. It recommended a scheme of provincial autonomy with Jewish areas, Arab areas, and areas reserved for exclusive authority of the British Mandatory power. The Jews were to be restricted to an area of some 1,400 square miles. Even in that zone, Jewish immigration was to be permitted up to its absorptive capacity, which in turn would be determined by the mandatory power, or trustee government. Britain reserved for itself the sole option to become the mandatory power. This was the plan to which American representatives, headed by Henry F. Grady, a high official of the State Department, were to give their apprroval. And for this privilege, the American Government was to buy Arab cooperation with this plan, by a grant of $300,000,000. Secretary of State Byrnes advised President Truman to approve the plan.

How this was prevented is a story which is not yet to be revealed though President Truman's own statement in later memoirs gives some indication of the tug-of-war which was going on behind the scenes to prevent the approval of a plan that could have meant the death-knell for Jewish aspirations in Palestine for years, and perhaps even for decades. The behind-the-scenes pressure was supplemented by the American members of the Anglo-American Committe of Inquiry. Appearing in Washington at the request of President Truman, they testified that the Grady-Morrison plan was submitted to them and rejected, and that it was, in fact, a repudiation of findings of their report.

It was time for a renewed American endorsement of the basic findings of the Anglo-American Committee of Inquiry, concerning the immigration of the 100,000 Jews. On October 4, 1946, President Truman issued a 1500-word statement in which he reviewed the Administration's efforts regarding Palestine. In conclusion, he stated that:

> substantial immigration into Palestine cannot await a solution to the Palestine problem and it should begin at once. Preparations for this movement have already been made by this Government and it is ready to lend its immediate assistance.

This forceful statement made clear that President Truman really meant business. The majority of the American public backed the President fully. The Roper poll of November 16, 1945, showed that 80.1 pct of American Jews favor a Jewish State; 10.5 pct oppose it and 9.4 pct are undecided.

A later poll by Gallup of January 8, 1946, indicated that three-fourths of the American voters who were conversant with the Palestine question favored settlement of Jews there.

But the real test for the sincerity of President Truman, in his pro-Zionist statements, was still to come. Ominously enough, it was a letter to the Saudi Arabian king, Ibn Saud, the same from whom President Roosevelt learned, within five minutes, the entire truth of the complex Palestine problem, which really set the relationship between the Jewish and Arab rights to Palestine in clear perspective. On October 29, 1946, President Truman made public his answer to Ibn Saud who complained in a letter to the President that he reneged on the commitments of his predecessor. The letter read:

> The Government and people of the United States have given support to the concept of a Jewish National Home in Palestine ever since the termination of the First World War, which resulted in the freeing of a large area of the Near East, including Palestine and the establishment of a large number of independent states, which are now members of the United Nations. The United States, which contributed its blood and resources to the winning of that war, could not divest itself of a certain responsibility for the manner in which the freed territories were disposed of, or for the fate of the peoples liberated at that time. It took the position, to which it still adheres, that these peoples should be prepared for self-government and also that a national home for the Jewish people shall be established in Palestine. I am happy to note that most of the liberated peoples are now citizens of independent countries. The Jewish National Home, however, has not as yet been fully developed.

These were words no American President had as yet spoken. It was a clear acknowledgement that the policy of support for the establishment of a Jewish National Home still had a long way to go. Moreover, it rescinded one of the basic arguments of all enemies of a Jewish Palestine that there is a conflict between the promises given the Arabs and the Jews. President Truman made it clear that in his opinion the Arabs had received more than their share in the form of the many independent states in an area liberated by the Allies. It implied clearly that only the Jews had to strive for the implementation of promises concerning their National Home. From this point of view, this was a document of highest importance. It created the moral and political basis for opposing any policy that implied the termination of efforts for the establishment of the Jewish National Home. And thus it was a document diametrically opposed to the basic premises of the British policy in Palestine. Great Britain had to face not only the Jewish determination in obstructing British anti-Zionist policies but also the explicit policy of the United States Government. On April 7, 1947, the British Government requested the United Nations Secretary General

> to summon, as soon as possible, a special session of the General Assembly for the purpose of constituting and instructing a special committee to prepare for the consideration of the problem of Palestine and its future government at the next regular session.

The role President Truman played in the crucial days at the United Nations, and later at the inquiry conducted by the United Nations Special Committee on Palestine, was in full agreement with the position he had taken. On instructions of President Truman, the United States delegation to the United Nations played a leading role in defeating an Arab attempt to have the Palestine item on the U.N. agenda phrased in a way that would include

Congressman Emanuel Celler addresses a Brooklyn protest delegation on the steps of Capitol Hill.

in it not only "the termination of the Mandate over Palestine" but also "the declaration of its independence." Some months later, when the American delegation to the U.N. proposed to exclude the Negev from the Jewish State area, it was again President Truman's intervention, that assured viable boundaries for the future Jewish State. President Truman phoned personally to Hershel V. Johnson, the U.S. delegate to the United Nations, and instructed him to take care that the Negev be Jewish. It happened only minutes before the meeting of the U.N. subcommittee on boundaries was called to order.

And when the crucial vote on the majority recommendations of the U.N. Special Committee on Palestine (UNSCOP) for the partition of Palestine and the establishment of a Jewish state had to be taken at the end of November, President Truman again used the full influence of his office to assure the necessary two-thirds majority of the U.N. General Assembly for the passage of the UNSCOP majority report. There were dramatic days and hours of last minute calls at the White House, and there was the unflinching response of understanding and support.

The fact that Soviet Russia as well supported the resolution on partition of Palestine and the establishment of a Jewish State in part of it made President Truman's task easier.

But even after the vote was taken, after 33 states voted, on November 29, 1947, for the establishment of a Jewish state, the opponents of this policy in the Department of State were not yet ready to admit their defeat. They were supported by other powerful members of the Cabinet, first of all by James Forrestal, Secretary of Defense. Forrestal continued to employ his "Arab oil" argument.

Saudi Arabia, he said, is one of the three great oil puddles left in the world.

He easily won over to his side the Secretary of State George Marshall. The anti-Zionist front was powerful.

President Truman admitted later that, almost without exception, the State Department's Middle East specialists were "unfriendly to the idea of a Jewish State." Arab oil was for them as well the main motive."There were some among them," states Truman, "who were also inclined to be anti-Semitic."

At a meeting of the Cabinet on January 16, 1948, Forrestal repeated his oil argument. This time he decided to update it. Without the Arab oil, he argued, the Marshall Plan would fail, all of Europe would be lost to Communism, and the American economy could not be maintained. A new interpretation concerning the November 29, 1947, U.N. vote evolved. The State Department experts found that in fact this formal resolution of the General Assembly of the United Nations was only a form of a recommendation, and not a final decision.

With such findings from the State Department, the United States ambassador to the United Nations, Warren Austin, readily accepted the advice from Washington to call a general retreat from America's declared position on the partition resolution. When a meeting of the U.N. Security Council considered the situation in Palestine, already submerged in blood by Arab aggression, Austin made a surprising statement that the Security Council is not bound by the resolutions of the Assembly, although it should give it great weight. It took only another three weeks that Austin's intention become clear when on March 19, he declared flatly at the Security Council meeting:

> My Government believes that a temporary trusteeship for Palestine should be established until Jews and Arabs . . . reach an agreement regarding the future of the country.

American Jewry, the American Zionists, the entire country were shocked. Mrs. Eleanor Roosevelt, who served as a member of the United States delegation to the U.N., resigned. According to President Truman's press secretary, David Niles, the about-face of American policy in Palestine was done without

Banner headline in London Daily Express.

Truman's knowledge. Niles says:

> Truman was not even informed of his (Austin's) talk until he read about it in the papers. He was as angry as I ever saw him.

President Truman knew little of the plot concocted against his Palestine policy. The State Department worked hand in hand with the oil companies, first of all with *Aramco*. Within a fortnight of the partition resolution, a representative of *Aramco* assured the leaders of the Arab League that American Government experts are opposed to partition, and that the decision to support the U.N. resolution was made by the President, who did not grasp the consequences.

The oil company's representative even struck a deal with the Arab League leaders by promising to have the State Department accept the Arab compromise solution "that a 'Vatican State' be established for the Jews" and the Arabs in return promised to maintain American oil concessions. So eager was the man to please his negotiators and his bosses that he assured them that all good Jews were leaving Palestine, that the Red Flag was flying side by side with the Star of David and that Israel was being organized as a Communist state.

It is a matter of guesswork as to what would have happened if the Jewish Community in Palestine would not have acted according to the November 29th U.N. resolution without paying any attention to the anti-Zionist plot in Washington and Lake Success. It is equally a matter of guesswork as to what would have happened if American Jewry, American Zionists, would not have fully backed the *Yishuv* and even more, encouraged it to proceed with the preparations for the declaration of the establishment of the Jewish State.

The anti-Zionist forces in Washington were using all their influence and power to prevent what they knew was inevitable: The proclamation of the establishment of the Jewish State in Palestine on the day of the expiration of the British Palestine Mandate, May 14, 1948.

The threats of blockade, of cutting off of funds and other forms of American assistance came from the Secretary of State himself, from General George C. Marshall. Though there were some who wavered, firmness prevailed. On the day before the already stated date of the proclamation of the Jewish State, an emergency session was held in the President's office. Information on this meeting is some-what confusing. According to Truman's press secretary, David Niles, "Marshall and Lovett opposed recognition, while Clark Clifford and I urged it." But a communication from President Truman to Mrs. Roosevelt tells a different story. Truman writes:

> Since there was a vacuum in Palestine and since the Russians were anxious to be the first to recognizing, General Marshall, Secretary Lovett, Dean Rusk and myself worked the matter out and decided the proper thing to do was to recognize the Jewish Government.

Ten minutes after Israel came into being and the U.S. recognition was announced, David Niles called in Eliahu Elath, the Israel representative in Washington, and informed him about the President's decision. Says Niles, "He was so excited that he cried."

Excitement was not much different in Lake Success, where the news agencies flashed the information about the President's decision. The meeting of the Security Council was about to be called to order for discussion of the "Palestine Problem." The "problem" ceased to be a problem. There was a State, a viable government that commanded control over its territory, and a State recognized first by the mightiest power, the United States, and within minutes by another mighty power, the Soviet Union.

President Truman had completed his work. He had made good his many statements and deeds in support of the cause of the re-establishment of a Jewish Commonwealth, of the rebirth of the Jewish nation in its ancient homeland. He remained faithful to what he said many times, again and before the final act of recognition of the Jewish State, in a communication to Mrs. Roosevelt, "My sympathy has always been on the side of the Zionists." This statement was perhaps the most appropriate explanation of Truman's decision.

It was a decision of a grand vision, of a historic perception which lifts itself over and above so-called practical considerations of the hour. It was a decision of greatness which, in the final analysis, and count, proved itself more practical, from the point of view of America's vital interests than those considered with the help of facts and figures, maps and alleged strategic accounts in sight.

The Jewish State was born. Israel was a fact. Relations with the United States moved onto a completely different plane. The chapter of inter-state relations was opened.

11

INTER-STATE RELATIONS

THE TRIUMPH of the Zionist cause and the American Government's commitment to protect the existence of the young Jewish State, expressed in the act of recognition, soon were put to a most serious test. Israel was under attack by six Arab armies; it was still vulnerable and its existence not yet an assured certainty. America's ally, Great Britain, was still hoping for a dramatic turn of events. On the horizon of the Arab-Israel war loomed the specter of British intervention on the side of those Arab countries with whom Britain had formal, mutual defense agreements. And the British Government had not yet given up hopes that at some dramatic juncture the longed-for cooperation with the United States on matters pertaining to Palestine would materialize.

Peculiarly enough, the success of Israel's army appeared to have afforded this opportunity. When the victorious Israeli armies repulsed the Egyptian attack in the Negev, and, exercising the right of hot pursuit, penetrated into Egypt, Great Britain invoked her 1936 alliance with Egypt, and requested that Israeli armed forces evacuate the Egyptian areas behind the international border.

Britain did not dare to take any initiative without the backing of the United States. Information originating from the British Embassy in Washington tried to create the impression that the United States was exerting most serious pressure on Israel by threatening to withhold a pending loan, and even to withdraw its recognition of the young state. American official spokesmen tried to allay the growing concern of American public opinion and of the American Zionist movement. The Zionist Emergency Council was still a very active body. Interventions in Washington were followed by a broad public relations campaign in which the general public was informed of the impending danger for the young Jewish State.

The developments in this most dramatic moment of Israel's early history seem to be somehow baffling in the light of documentary evidence, published some years later. While the chairman of the Zionist Emergency Council, Dr. Silver, seemed to have been satisfied with the position taken publicly by the American Administration, and saw himself fit to state: ". . . the attitude of our Government has been good," the historic truth of those days appears different when checked against the revelations of America's first Ambassador to Israel, James McDonald. Recounting years later the story of American involvement in the British pressure on Israel in those days of January, 1949, McDonald says:

In Knox's hands was a top secret cable just from Washington. It was as sharp as it was unexpected, and especialy serious as it was sent in the name of the President. Such phrases were used as 'grave consequences,' 'review our attitude,' 'no desire to act drastically if . . . ,' and so forth. Knox and Klaus were despondent, their interpretation especially pessimistic; mine was a little less pessimistic. Whatever the case, immediate action was necessary. We had to get a reply from the Israelis as fast as possible. . . . Steadily the Israeli troops pressed the enemy farther and farther towards the Egyptian border. They captured the border town, Al-Auja, giving Israel control of the main road leading through the Sinai Peninsula to Suez and Cairo. . . . At this crucial juncture Washington instructed me to deliver immediately to the Israeli authorities the substance of a cable which radically changed the whole situation.

This direct intervention of the United States Government in the Arab-Israel relations was to prove a beginning of a long series of developments in which American official policy toward the State of Israel was to become a direct reflection of American policies before the establishment of the State. This policy of vaccilation, of periods of clear sympathy, and intervals of unfriendly actions, had once forced the Israeli Prime Minister, David Ben Gurion, to state before an American official:

You can crush us, but you can't force us to commit suicide.

This, 1949, unhappy episode in American-Israeli relations should by no means be considered as indicative of the relations between the two countries. Soon the Americans had the opportunity to learn that their intervention, on behalf of defeated Egypt, was completely misunderstood in the Arab world. The Arabs saw in it a guarantee of freedom to harass Israel, without facing the ultimate consequences of a military confrontation.

The Armistice Agreements between Israel and the Arab countries, considered as the first step toward peace talks, soon turned into a shield for Arab aggression and belligerency. The Arab governments made no secret of their intention to renew their war on Israel on the first given occasion. Though Egypt was yet years distant from opening the gates of the Middle East to Russian penetration, the threat of Russian intervention, in case of an open Arab-Israel conflict, was prevalent. To preserve the stability of the Middle East became therefore a prequisite of the best interests of the three Western powers, Great Britain, France, and of the United States foremost among them all. Thus came about the so-called Tripartite Declaration of the three Western powers, of May, 1950, which pledged the support of the three governments for the maintenance of the Arab-Israel armistice agreements and warned that if

any of these states was preparing to violate frontiers or armistice lines
they would
immediately take action, both within and outside the United Nations to prevent such violation.

The wording of the Tripartite Declaration did not, unfortunately, provide for the prevention of the special type of Arab warfare that was short of an open invasion, but nevertheless exposed Israel to a permanent war of attrition: infiltration and guerilla raids. The proviso of the Tripartite Declaration that "the Arab States and Israel . . . need maintain a certain level of armed forces" enabled Great Britain to continue its supply of arms to Arab States, while Israel had to shop for arms almost clandestinely. The ensuing developments on the borders of Israel, which forced Israel to assume self-defense measures in the form of retaliatory raids condemned by the three powers, convinced the Arabs even more that Israel was in fact isolated and open to attack.

The United States started missing every and each occasion, as they arose at the United Nations, to demonstrate its adherence to the Tripartite Declaration, and its backing of the Armistice Agreements. At almost every occasion of the U.N. dealing with what became known as "the Palestine problem," when Arab aggression and Israel retaliations were brought before the U.N. Security Council, the U.S. delegation would cast its votes against the country

that defended itself. The United States thus strengthened even more Arab intransigeance and conviction that after all, in spite of many American gestures of friendship toward Israel, when the real test occurs, they don't have to be apprehensive of the American position.

In this evolving pattern of Arab-Israel relations even the U.N. Security Council ruling of September 1, 1951, that Egypt has to open the Suez Canal to Israeli shipping, was not backed with the full force of American influence. The most extraordinary opportunity for receiving Egyptian assurances to preserve international obligations for free navigation through the canal was missed, and all urgent pleas with the United States Government by the Zionist movement, by the American Jewish Committee, to use its influence with Egypt, remained unheeded.

It was therefore somehow preposterous when on the assumption of office by the Republican Administration, after the Eisenhower landslide victory in the elections of 1952, the new Secretary of State, John Foster Dulles, enunciated the doctrine of "impartiality" towards the Middle East nations to

allay the deep resentment against the United States that has resulted from the creation of Israel.

The Arabs did not wait for elaboration in order to grasp what this statement meant, in practical terms. Secretary Dulles provided himself clear indications that the new policy of "impartiality" would find its expression in cuddling Arab friendship, in supplying arms to Iraq and Saudi Arabia, in supporting the Arab position in the treatment of the Jerusalem controversy, through the refusal to recognize Israel's decision to make Jerusalem the capital of the country.

The "new policy" was not limted to unfriendly acts towards Israel. High officials of the State Department ventured into the field of Zionist ideology. Assistant Secretary of State Henry A. Byroade chose no other platform than that of the American Council of Judaism to attack the very essence of the Jewish peoplehood that embraces Jews all over the world, with Israel as their spiritual center and beacon of brotherly love. The attempt to intimidate American Jews and force them to desist from supporting Israel was clear. There was rejoicing in the Arab lands at this attack on the "roots of the Zionist conspiracy." The intensified Arab raids into Israel and Israel's retaliatory actions earned condemnation only for Israel. The Arab policy of "belligerency," openly proclaimed by the Arabs at the United Nations, was never rebuked by the United States Government in unmistakable terms. The recurring declarations of American representatives at the United Nations that Israel should not retaliate but depend on the United Nations machinery, sounded rather awkward in view of the assured Russian veto in the U.N. Security Council that was bound to prevent any resolution unfavorable for the Arabs. Israeli spokesmen intensified the anger and harshness of their language in accusing the United States Government in "one-sidedness," "hypocrisy," inasmuch as there was no similarly strong condemnation of the Arab attacks. The fact that since the Tripartite Declaration of 1950 until 1959, four hundred twenty-one Israelis had been killed or wounded in Arab attacks must have weighed much more heavily than the moralizing statements of the United States that demanded Israeli restraint and statesmanship. In the very midst of this mounting crisis American and British arms shipments to Arab countries were accelerated in a growing pace. The many Israeli requests for arms were dismissed by laconic statements that the requests were "under active consideration."

Again, as on so many occasions in the history of American-Zionist relations, the policies of the President and the State Department were far from coordinated. While President Eisenhower reiterated United States' "firm friendship" towards Israel, the State Department left no doubt that Israel remained isolated in confronting incessant Arab aggression.

At a time when Arab leaders grew in boldness in their statements that they were set for the destruction of Israel and demonstrated their aggressive intentions by armed raids into Israel, a high American official, Deputy Assistant Secretary of State Jernegan saw fit to state that he does "not see evidence of any intent on the part of her neighbors to attack Israel."

The Middle East was thus set on a sure course toward a military explosion. Slogans of "impartiality" in Middle Eastern affairs, or statements intended for calming the growing tensions, appeared completely irrelevant to the existing situation. The need for something more than pious wishes appeared imperative. A major policy statement on August 26, 1955, by Secretary Dulles was to suggest a way out of the deteriorating situation in the Middle East. Although the statement was replete with promising suggestions concerning the Arab refugee problem, regional development, boundaries and security guarantees, it was in fact meaningless because it made each and every proposal dependent on Arab agreement.

It is amazing how, in view of Arab anti-Israel hostility, any practically thinking political leader could have launched a program for the solution of the conflict while knowing that whatever proposal he makes, it will be a priori unacceptable to the Arabs. All the positive details of the Dulles plan about America's willingness to

contribute to the realization of water development and irrigation projects which would, directly or indirectly, facilitate resettlement of the refugees; to join in formal treaty engagements to prevent or thwart any effort by either side to alter by force the boundaries between Israel and its Arab neighbors; to grant to Israel a large loan to help it compensate the Arab refugees and enable them through settlement and—to such extent as may be feasible—repatriation, to resume a life of dignity and self-respect

—and many other points of John Foster Dulles statement could have been no more than another declaration as long as the United States Government was not ready to state unequivocally that it guaranteed the territorial integrity of the Middle East countries.

Proof of the Dulles plan's uselesness was not late in coming. The Arab raids into Israel intensified. After the Nasser-Soviet Russia arms deal of the fall of 1955, the specter of Arab large-scale aggression was no longer the bogey of scared pessimists, but a reality of an imminent threat. The establishment of the unified command of the Arab military forces was the evident sign that the statements about "crushing Israel," "throwing its population into the sea," and "liberating Palestine," were meant to be translated into action. The Arab commando raids were growing in their audacity and reaching almost the outskirts of Tel Aviv; the Suez Canal anti-Israel blockade was a fact sanctioned by the world; the blockade of the passage to Israel's southern port of Eilath made this vital communication artery to the East worthless; the United States Government strengthened its policy of entrenchment behind the doctrine of impartiality. There was no doubt anymore that the encirclement was about to break into open warfare.

The Suez Canal crisis, which forced Great Britain and France to a showdown, seemed to have offered Israel a unique opportunity to strike at the bases of the Fedayin-commando units, and to shatter, at the onset, the Arab war preparations. Israel forces struck at Egypt. The spectacular Sinai campaign brought Israel forces, within seventy-two hours, to the banks of the Suez Canal.

In this crucial hour for Israel and for the future of political and military realities in the Middle East, the United States policy towards that area, and towards the principal factors in it, faced a historic test. As far as the Administration was concerned, this was not a test that proved the Arab argument of alleged American bias in favor of Israel. These were not the Israeli forces, it was not Israel whom the United States Administration under President Eisenhower had saved from utter defeat.

As in 1949, when Israeli forces were on Egyptian soil, on their way to inflict upon the Arab aggressors a decisive defeat, and were forced by President Truman to give up the chance for a lasting peace and to retreat, so nine years later the American Government had again saved the strongest Arab country from the Israeli forces, whose tanks had already reached the Suez Canal and were able to assure at long last a peaceful solution of the Arab-Israel conflict.

To what extent the United States Government was ready to exert pressure on Israel to have it comply with the American policy of saving Nasser, is best documented by the man who, as President of the United States, is certainly the most reliable source for such information. In his book *The White House Years: Waging Peace* 1956-1961, President Eisenhower admits that in order to pressure Israel into withdrawal from the Sinai in 1957, he preferred

> a resolution which would call on all United Nations members to suspend not just governmental but private assistance to Israel.

Such a move, continues Eisenhower, "would be no hollow gesture."

> As we discussed it, George Humphrey, the Secretary of the Treasury, put in a call to W. Randolph Burgess, Under Secretary of the Treasury for monetary affairs, who gave a rough estimate that American private gifts to Israel were about $40,000,000 a year, and sales of Israel bonds in our country between $50,000,000 and $60,000,000 a year. This information was in part based on Treasury figures on income tax deductions.

Eisenhower is also answering the question why his Administration had adopted this anti-Israel policy

> John Foster Dulles strongly expressed the view that we had gone as far as possible to try to make it easy for the Israelis to withdraw. To go further, he said, would surely jeopardize the entire Western influence in the Middle East, and the nations of that re-

gion would conclude that United States policy toward the area was, in the last analysis, controlled by Jewish influences in the United States. In such event, the only hope of the Arab countries would be found in firm association with the Soviet Union.

Compared with American statements by the then Secretary of State Dulles, and the United States representative at the United Nations, Henry Cabot Lodge, Jr., that America's intervention against Israel and in favor of the Arabs was dictated only by considerations of pure defense of the principle that no international conflict should be solved by arms, the Eisenhower book is really a revelation, shedding a much more serious light on that chapter in American-Israeli relations than any other statement and explanation. The moral attributes of such policy which was ready to sacrifice the most vital interests of Israel, perhaps its very existence as a viable State, should be viewed in the background of the realities of practical politics. But what is most amazing in the matter is the success of Arab propaganda to create such political concepts in most important circles of the American Government. The innumerable examples around the globe when the West lost influence completely in spite of the fact that there were not involved the "Palestine problem" and "Jewish influence in the United States," seemed to escape the comprehension of certain American officials.

Even the most ardent anti-Zionist and defender of that Eisenhower-Dulles theory of which other leaders of the United States were not free, would not assert that the loss of China to communism was due to "Jewish influence in the United States"; that this influence, or for that matter, the existence of Israel had anything to do with Indonesia almost going communist. Nobody can certainly contend that Israel is responsible for Nasser supporting the communist rebels in the Congo, intervening in Yemen, plotting against one of America's staunchest supporters in the Middle East, the present regime in Iran, or instigating the civil strife in Cyprus.

That this Eisenhower-Dulles doctrine in the Suez crisis days was not pursued to its extreme consequences was only due to a combination of international and internal American forces which saw somehow differently the dilemma of American policy in the Middle-East. Even the Eisenhower Administration had soon the opportunity to see the problems of the Middle East in a different context and light than as they appeared to them during the heat of the debate over the Suez campaign. America's hope to gain Egypt's Arab gratitude for its salvage operation of Nasser's regime and Arab prestige, did not materialize. The opposite occurred. The credit for saving Nasser went entirely to Soviet Russia.

The situation in the Middle East kept on deteriorating in disfavor of the United States, in spite of the fact that even the Eisenhower assurance that the Suez Canal will be opened to the shipping of every nation, remained hollow and nothing was done to make Eisenhower's word good.

The Eisenhower Doctrine of 1958 that America will assist every country defending itself against communist or communist-instigated aggression, brought about by the imminent fall of the Lebanese and Jordanian governments, was in fact an admission that sacrificing Israel's interests had no bearing on the anti-American forces which were at work in the Middle East, and which the United States, in fact, promoted, by deluding itself that if it wouldn't be for Israel, no problems would have arisen in the Middle East.

The sobering process in American appraisal of the Middle East situation entered a new phase with the beginning of the Kennedy Administration. Kennedy's assurance that when elected, he would bring about peace negotiations between Israel and the Arab countries augured new initiatives in the Middle East, though few in Israel really believed that even a serious effort of any American President could bring about a change in Arab intransigence. But the firmness of American resolve to prevent a new flare-up in the Middle East and Arab aggression against Israel was demonstrated in the beginning of the Kennedy Administration, when Israel was about to complete the central water carrier for the use of Jordan River waters for irrigation. Arab threats of military intervention became insistent, and a united Arab front was again forged against what the Arab States called "Israel aggression."

No doubt, labeling as "aggression" a peaceful project of putting water to work for the welfare of people was not the most convincing slogan the Arabs had, as was not sympathy-evoking the threat to divert the Jordan waters for only one purpose: to deprive Israel of its use. It was in this tense situation that President Kennedy indicated America's determination to support the attacked country. There is no doubt that such statement played a most pacifying role and perhaps even prevented an

outbreak of anti-Israel hostilities which seemed imminent.

The tragic death of President Kennedy introduced a factor of uncertainty in American-Israeli relations for only a brief time. President Johnson's policies towards the Middle East soon proved that Israel had in the new American President a man free of many of the inhibitions of his predecessors. The old school of thought ascribing all American difficulties in the Middle East to America's friendship towards Israel seemed to have faded, if not disappeared completely. Nasser's policies in expanding his aggressive devices to areas in which no relationship to Israel could be indicated, helped in this process immensely. So did Nasser's growing cooperation with Russia and his bolder and bolder assistance in opening the Middle East, Africa and West Asia to Russian influence.

The official visit of the Israel Prime Minister Levi Eshkol to Washington, in June, 1964, the first official visit of an Israel Premier, was a formal, external sign of the change of attitude of the United States to Israel. Prime Minister David Ben Gurion visited with American Presidents three times: Truman, Eisenhower, and most informally in New York, with John F. Kennedy. But these were visits without the fanfare and political meaning an official visit carries in political realities. And the rebuke given to Arab Ambassadors, who protested the official invitation to Israel's Prime Minister, when Under Secretary George Ball invited them, and taught them a lesson in diplomatic courtesy which excludes Ambassadors of foreign countries from lecturing the host government how it should behave and treat its guests, was perhaps more indicative of the new atmosphere which President Johnson created than many formal statements.

In plain diplomatic language, this rebuke meant a beginning of the end of an era when Arab blackmail made American Administrations most apprehensive and often submissive. It was also for the first time in American-Israel relations that an American President departed from the traditional line of blaming equally Israel and the Arabs for the tensions in the Middle East, and for the permanent threat to peace in that area. President Johnson spoke about Israel's desire for peace indicating clearly who should be blamed for the Middle East tensions. The agreement on a cooperative American-Israeli effort for the use of atomic energy for desalination of sea water was an additional proof that the United States government is not reluctant to state its cooperation with Israel openly, irrespective of Arab reaction.

But the real test of the U.S. policies towards Israel and the Middle East conflict had yet to come. The May, 1967, crisis left no room for evasiveness. Preparations for the Arab aggression were no more veiled. Threats of destroying the State of Israel entered a phase of practical military preparedness. Plans for the murder of a state were followed by plans for a mass genocide of the entire Jewish population in Israel.

In the gravest hour of its nineteen-year existence Israel seemed to stand alone. The efforts of the Johnson Administration to break the United Arab Republic's blockade of Israel's southern sea routes through the Strait of Tiran, proved fruitless. And when Arab aggression forced Israel to act in self defense, a spokesman of the Department of State stated the United States position as that of complete neutrality in thought, spirit and deed.

The quick resolve of the military conflict on the battlefield, Israel's stunning victory created a new situation in the Middle East. It gave the U.S. Administration the opportunity to prove whether it stands for the liquidation of belligerency in that area, or for a new makeshift arrangement that will prepare a new war. President Johnson chose to support peace. In a clear policy statement President Johnson formulated basic principles for peace in the Middle East which included: an end to belligerency; respect for political independence and territorial integrity of all states in the area as well as respect for the fundamental right of every nation to live; free and innocent passage through international waterways; justice for the refugees; curbing of the arms race.

In view of the Russian political onslaught, the Arab enmity and the outcry of Israel haters all over, the United States Government withstood all pressures inside and outside the United Nations. It remained faithful to its professed policy of assuring peace in the Middle East and putting an end once and forever to the permanent crisis in the Middle East. The United States leadership in the United Nations and on the international arena became the mainstay of support for the cause of peace and against belligerency, against the return to the status that prevailed prior to the Six Day War —the two main pillars of Israel's policy after the Six Day War.

Reviewing the history of American official policy toward Israel, one cannot limit himself to political pronouncements and acts of the Administration alone. From the very first days of Israel's existence, the American Administrations have continuously extended the bounty of their country to the benefit of the State of Israel. The fact that this was in concert with a broader American policy concept which started with UNRA, and, through the Marshall Plan, led to today's foreign aid programs, through which the United States helped foreign countries to the amount of one hundred and twenty billion dollars, does not affect by an iota the historic importance of American generosity for the strengthening of Israel's economy, for its advance towards economic viability. Here again Arab propaganda has succeeded to propagate certain inaccuracies which became rather part of common conviction among Jews and non-Jews alike, that no measure of factual information could affect.

Though it is true that the United States has helped Israel's economy, immensely, it is still a far cry from the contention of foe and even friend of Israel, that this American assistance is the only factor that kept Israel economically going. In fact, this aid which reached $882,-000,000 by June, 1962, is composed of a few forms of assistance, some of them on a rather commercial basis in the form of loans for which Israel has paid many millions of dollars in interest.

One of the first American acts of assistance to Israel was a loan of $135,000,000 by the Export Import Bank in 1949. When, in 1950, the foreign aid program, renamed from the Economic Cooperation Act to Mutual Security Act, reached an unprecedented amount of $ 885,000 000 0 , ten percent of $415,000,000, assigned for Greece, Turkey and Iran, were to be given by the President to the

> Arab States and Israel if he determines such action is essential to the security of the United States.

In the words of Assistant Secretary of State McGee, this percentage would be given

> to increase the indigenous defensive capabilities of the Jewish and Arab States, strengthen their internal security and reduce area rivalries.

These amounts were augmented by assistance "for the care of Jewish refugees in Israel" as a counterbalance to the sums earmarked for Arab refugees. Though direct grants in aid were gradually on the decline, other forms of economic assistance to Israel continued year by year.

The overall of American aid to Israel was given one-third in the form of agricultural commodities made available on a loan basis; another third in the form of long-term loans at commercial interest rates; technical assistance and other forms of grant aids accounted for the balance. One of these assistance forms, the technical aid, was discontinued completely in 1962 when it was considered that Israel needed such assistance no longer. The statement by the U.S. Operations Mission in Israel, *Mission Accomplished,* issued at the termination of its activities, was both a badge of honor for the efficiency of American aid, and a landmark in the process of Israel's economic development.

The second practical problem of American-Israeli relations, the problem of supplying arms for Israel's defense, passed many stages until it reached the decision of the Johnson Administration to supply Israel with A-4 Skyhawk bombers, that have a combat range of one thousand miles and can carry 5,000 pounds of bombs or missiles. During the twenty years of Israel's independence, this was at times the most crucial problem for Israel's survival. The arms embargo with which the United States "greeted" Israel's emergence as an independent nation, evolved into an adamant attitude when Israel was left to its own ingenuity and resources in finding sources for the purchase of arms.

In view of permanent Arab threats, arms acquisitions became a condition *sine qua non* of Israel's existence and of relative tranquility in the Middle East. The strength of Israel arms was the main, at times the only, deterrent against Arab aggression. But all Israel pleas for arms remained unheeded. The phrase coined by the State Department that the "U.S. is not a major supplier of arms to the Middle East" did not interfere with supplying American arms to Iraq and Saudi-Arabia. Only after Soviet Russia started to turn Egypt and other Arab countries into an ever-growing arsenal, did Secretary of State Dulles advise other NATO nations that they should supply arms to Israel. The fact that America used such device was defined by Jewish leaders as "not representing leadership or morality."

The decision of President Kennedy to supply Israel with Hawk ground-to-air missiles for Israel's defense against air attacks was an important departure from American policy in this field. It was for the first time that the United States had speedily and directly assumed the role of supplier for Israel's defense forces. The meaning of such decision was even more vital: the United States acknowledged that Israel can not depend only on American assurances that aggression in the Middle East will be prevented, and that the United States Sixth Fleet in the Mediterranean is a sufficient guarantee against it. The proximity of the aggressor nations which proclaim daily their intention to attack Israel, and the smallness of the country made Israel vulnerable to a first attack. It is the decision to supply Israel with the A-4 Skyhawk bombers that gave Israel a new offensive weapon and thus increased immensely the deterrent weight of Israel's army.

In these multiphased and multifaced fortunes of American-Israeli relations one factor stands out both as decisive and consistent in its declared, open, often almost passionate avowal of friendship to the State of Israel. The floors of the Senate and the House of Representatives were often the platforms for declarations of friendship to Israel that were warming the heart of every friend of Israel not only with their sentiments, but also with their political persuasiveness, clarity and conviction. And these were not only voices of individual members of Congress who expressed such sentiments. The long list of Congressional Resolutions pertaining to Israel is proof that this was a political line consequently pursued by the elected representatives of the American nation, thought over and meant to oblige the executive arm of the United States government in its practical dealings with Zionist and later, Israeli affairs.

In the interplay of the two branches of American Government, the legislative and the executive, the Congress served as a mighty rock on which Israel could lean and depend. Drawing their mandate from the American public, from the electorate, and depending on it directly for their mandate to speak in its name, the opinions of these legislators were the closest possible reflection of American sentiments, much more so than the statements and policies of heads of the State Department or even of Presidents, who had to in the last count, bow to the will of the people.

The Joint Resolution by both Houses of Congress in 1922 that the United States favors the establishment in Palestine of a national home for the Jewish people,

the concurrent Resolution of December 20, 1945, that urged the United States to

use its good offices with the mandatory power to the end that Palestine shall be opened for free entry of Jews into that country . . . so that they may freely proceed with the upbuilding of Palestine as the Jewish national home . . . and . . . establish Palestine as a democratic commonwealth,

were only the basis and the beginning of the many acts of Congress in support of Zionism, and consequently, of Israel.

It is true that such persevering support of the cause of Jewish statehood was deeply rooted in the strong ties of ideals, morality and emotion that bound America to Jewish concepts for 350 years, since this continent was settled by people for whom the Bible was inspiration, hope and moral law. There is no other country where the Bible is so much alive, and where so much romantic affiliation with the Holy Land was a permanent feature of life. And when the new pioneering spirit of the reborn Jewish nation started to redeem its ancient land, it was this spirit, the moral zest, the conquest of the desert, the respect for human dignity, and for freedom of the individual which characterized the young republic of the United States and were recreated in the new young republic of Israel, that have cemented this understanding and support for Israel.

It is fortunate that leading American legislators have seen in the support of Israel not only a moral imperative but as well a factor in purely American interests. The bipartisan bills for extension of American aid to Israel in 1949 sponsored by Senators Paul A. Douglas (D.) and Robert A. Taft (R.) described Israel as "a bulwark of world democracy" and urged that "the economic assistance to strengthen free nations . . . should now be extended to Israel." The House of Representatives majority leader, John W. McCormick, voiced even more outspoken remarks on Israel's potential as an ally of the United States, whose system of government and basic ideals were assuring for America a foothold in an area destined to play a leading role in international relations.

Opinions as those quoted were often heard on the platforms of both Houses of Congress. And though they did not always influence decisively the conduct of American policy in the Middle East, they served as an indicator of public sentiment towards Israel, which no Administration could afford to ignore completely.

One episode in the long history of Congressional support for Israel stands out as characteristic of this entire field of American-Israeli relations. At the time when President Eisenhower was fully set to employ, against Israel, a whole series of punitive measures, during the Israel, 1956, Sinai campaign, the Senate Majority leader, Lyndon B. Johnson, and the Senate Minority leader, William F. Knowland, bluntly warned President Eisenhower that the Senate would not approve economic sanctions against Israel. Reporting on these days of crisis in his book, *The White House Years: Waging Peace* 1956-1961, President Eisenhower quotes Senator Johnson and Senator Knowland as having argued that

cracking down on Israel is using a double standard—following one policy for the strong and one for the weak.

Senator Johnson went even further, stating that threats to impose sanctions on Israel were unwise and unfair, and that he was against "pressure on one side in a two-sided dispute." Deploring the attempted "coercion" of Israel as a "method of settlement," Senator Johnson told the Eisenhower Administration it had lost sight of basic facts in the Israel-Arab dispute.

This was not the only aspect of American-Israeli relations and of the policy divergences between the legislative and executive branches of the American government.

The Sinai campaign demonstrated another feature of American attitudes towards Israel which related to the very fact of popular pro-Israel sympathies that are not always to the liking of the Administration. It happened quite often that Administrations tried to denigrate this popular support, as expressed by legislators, by tainting it with the alleged stigma of political expediency which has nothing in common with real convictions. President Eisenhower quotes in the above mentioned book an opinion of a White House staff member (whose name is not identified) who "reflected on the pettiness" of those reluctant to sanction Israel. This Eisenhower associate found it

somewhat disheartening that partisan considerations could enter.

That this was the opinion of President Eisenhower himself was well demonstrated years later when he appeared in a TV series on his presidential years. Questioned by CBS-TV's chief commentator, Walter Cronkite, whether in view of later political developments in the Middle East, he would revise the position he took at the time of the Suez Canal crisis, President Eisenhower, instead of making a political comment related to the Middle-East, had only one reflection: that those who warned him that his attitude toward Israel would harm his chances as Presidential candidate in New York were wrong. The results of the elections, he said, proved that the Jews preferred the interests of their country over their sentiments toward Israel . . . It didn't occur to President Eisenhower that it was time to admit that his policy during the Suez crisis was far from serving justice, peace and American interests.

Although President Eisenhower's statement can not be considered typical of American attitudes toward Israel, it should as well be borne in mind as one of the components of American-Israeli relations. There are people, even in highest positions, who try to castigate Jewish sympathy for Israel as non-compatible with the real interests of the United States. For itself this Eisenhower opinion has indicated clearly an aspect of American-Israeli relations in which American Jews were ascribed a most important role. Though, in the Eisenhower formulation, this weight of the "Jewish vote" was presented in a light allegedly contrasting the interests of the United States, many controversies concerning American foreign policies, in which great segments of the population differ from the opinions of the Administration, have and are proving evidently that the Eisenhower approach to this question, as far as Israel is concerned, is far from objective.

No amount of fixed concepts can convince anybody that when Americans differ from their government's policy in Europe or in Southeast Asia, this should be considered their constitutional right resulting from American freedom of discussion and dissent, while when Americans differ from their government's policies in the Middle East this should make their patriotism questionable.

By the same token, this situation imposes on American Jewry a most important role in the framing and forming of American policies towards Israel and the Middle East in general. Judging from the past, it could be assumed that American Jews will not acquiesce with attempts at intimidation and will always speak up for the cause of justice and peace in the Middle East, as they understand it, even if and when it is not to the liking of a given Administration.

On the occasion of the issue of Israel's 1966 proof-like coins in current circulation, former President, Harry S. Truman was presented with a set by Robert Weber, (*left*), of the Israel Government's coins and medals division. Also shown is Charles Hipsh, (*right*), President, Empire State Bank, Kansas City, Missouri.

PART FOUR

PART FOUR

12

MASTERING THE POLITICAL STRENGTH

FIGHTING THE 1939 WHITE PAPER AMIDST WAR

THERE WAS NO NEED for special political acumen for the Zionist leadership to grasp the new opportunities that the outbreak of World War II afforded. There was no more room for illusions. It was clear that the 1939 White Paper was a decisive landmark in British policy in Palestine, in British attitudes toward Zionism, towards the international obligations it had assumed in the Balfour Declaration and the Mandate. The closing date for Jewish immigration set for March 31, 1944, after which further immigration was subject to Arab consent, the barring of Jews from land purchase in almost the entire country, and the provision to establish a Palestine State with an Arab majority, meant a death-knell to everything Zionism stood for. It meant to a great extent that Zionism had to resume the entire political struggle all over again, almost as in the days preceding the Balfour Declaration. But 1939 was not 1917.

This time Zionism had the advantage of international treaties; it had a Jewish community in Palestine that had already achieved the ability to form a nucleus of Jewish independence; it had a base for physical resistance against any scheme for liquidating the very aims and ideals for which these over five hundred thousand Jews had gathered in Palestine.

This clarity of the new political status of Zionism was accompanied by a full awareness that there was a central political front on which the sinister anti-Zionist devices of the British Government could be fought -- the United States of America. The basic premises of this awareness were anchored not only on the existence of the powerful Jewish community in America, but also on the evidence of British dependence on American support in its fight against the Axis powers.

While in World War I the British interest in winning American support appeared one of the central motives behind the issuance of the Balfour Declaration, in World War II, this support appeared much more vital; moreover, it appeared decisive for the success of British arms. These were therefore objective political circumstances which have thrust the United States of America into the very center of the Anglo-Jewish-Zionist controversy on the ultimate political fate of Palestine.

To a decisive degree Great Britain's own policies have opened it to a growing extent to American influence, and therefore to American pressure in matters concerned with the future of Palestine.

The contest between these two opposing forces -- Zionism and British policy -- for the sympathies and active support of America, could not have been postponed to the last days of the war as it happened in World War I. This time the contest was already on, in full force, on the day the opening shots of World War II were heard. The Zionist movement was at that time already besieged under what appeared, to the British, the final attack for its total submission. The decision of the Zionist movement to fight back left no doubt for Britain that to prevail with her anti-Zionist policy she must continue her pressure on one of the most vulnerable, for Britain, theatres of this war against Zionism, in the United States of America.

Britain appeared to have found in this struggle many eager supporters among influential officials of the State Department. Though America was not yet formally a belligerent, her sympathies in the war contest were evident. The fact that the Jews, that Zionism, had basically the same political priority in defeating the Axis, Nazi Germany, appeared an excellent device to force the hand of the Zionist movement into renunciation of Zionist aspirations in Palestine. The basic premise of this political scheme seemed to be logical and unshakable. There was only a need to prove that the fate of the Middle East depended on Arab sympathies, and that Arab sympathies could be won by the liquidation of Zionism, and capitulation of the Zionist front.

American officials cooperated in some instances, even eagerly, with this British scheme. There is enough reason even to add that some high officials of the State Department did not necessarily need British indoctrination in order to do their utmost in turning themselves into knowing tools of British devices. The American minister in Egypt, Alexander C. Kirk, was flooding the State Department with dispatches that

> Zionism underminded the loyalty of the Arab countries to Britain and attached their sympathies to the Axis.

But Mr. Kirk had a solution for this problem. For the matter of initiating efforts for the liquidation of the Zionist program,

> the American Government is generally regarded as in the most favorable position to act.

He had even a simple device for achieving such goal: all that the American Government has to do is to dispel the convictions prevailing in Arab circles

> that the influence of American Jewry is one of the principal deterrents to a resolution of the Palestine question.

No wonder that under such political guidance the officials concerned with these matters in the State Department found no difficulty to act accordingly. They had an address to turn to. They knew that a central political authority of American Zionism and with certain limitations, of World Zionism, was established in the first months of World War II, in October, 1939. The American Emergency Committee for Zionist Affairs, composed of the American members of the Zionist World Executive and representatives of the four major groups of American Zionism, the Zionist Organization of America, Hadassah, Mizrahi and Labor Zionists was, on authority of the Zionist Congress, not only a representative body to assure unity of action in American Zionism, but also the Zionist authority empowered to act on behalf of the world Zionist movement in emergencies

when they occurred. The fact that Dr. Haim Weitzman, the President of the World Zionist Organization, arrived in the United States to lead Zionist activities with the Emergency Committee strengthened even more the authority of that Committee. It appeared therefore natural to Adolph A. Berle, Jr., Assistant Secretary of State, to address his invitation for a discussion on Zionist matters to Dr. Weitzman, who had the authority to speak for World and American Zionism alike. For some reason, Dr. Weitzman had to forego this meeting and asked Dr. Emanuel Neumann to substitute for him. The meeting was a most revealing experience. In Dr. Neumann's own words, it was "one of the most fantastic interviews I ever experienced."

Why it was so fantastic was consequently revealed in Dr. Neumann's report on this meeting, in which he wrote:

> Mr. Berle started by painting a really terrifying picture of what may happen to the *Yishuv* in Palestine if the Germans overran the Middle East and what carnage would result from a combination of Arab fury and Nazi brutality: our whole work would go up in flames; our settlers would be massacred and the remainder driven out or exiled. Should we not do something to avoid such a catastrophe? By dint of questioning I drew out what he had in mind: 'there should be prompt negotiations with Arab leaders; we should be prepared to renounce our political claims to Palestine; a large part of the *Yishuv* might be evacuated to Kenya and to Saudi Arabia under the protection of King Ibn Saud. In return, and by way of compensation for our renunciation, we might get a kind of Vatican City in Palestine after the war, and a real territory for building a Jewish nation elsewhere -- in the highlands of Abyssinia, which was a good country for white settlers.'

The mood in the State Department was therefore clear. But the British seemed to have had a misleading notion of the political fibre of the leaders of the Emergency Committee. The Zionist leaders strengthened their fight, they increased pressure. They did so not only in the best interests of Zionism, but also in what they understood as the best interests of the Alliance fighting the Nazis. They discounted the correctness of the appraisal of Arab strength, and real political sentiments, and they asserted that a strong Jewish Commonwealth is in the best interests of Great Britain and the United States alike. And what is most important, they were not too impressed by the attitude of officials, irrespectively of their importance.

The political appointees of the State Department were much more cautious in expressing their opinions on the Palestine question. They were well aware that they were not working in a political vacuum. They knew well that a growing number of Americans were adopting attitudes sympathetic to Zionist demands. The Emergency Committee did not limit itself to political contacts in Washington. A growing net of instruments for the mobilization of public opinion penetrated with the Zionist message the remotest corners of the country. The value and political impact of this activity was best illustrated by the official British intervention in regards to a dinner the American Palestine Committee had scheduled in Washington on April 30, 1941.

That this was no "small affair" in British eyes is best proven by the seriousness of the British efforts to forestall the holding of the dinner. Lord Halifax, the British Ambassador, called on Secretary of State Cordell Hull to discuss the dinner. As could have been expected, Hull refrained from promising any action. After all, he could not interfere with a private affair in which most important legislators, with Senator Wagner as chairman of the Commitee, played a leading role.

Lord Halifax did not accept that "no" for a "no" and instructed the Counsellor of the Embassy, Neville Butler, to continue pressuring the lower echelons of the State Department. Mr. Butler had a ready-made argument, so often repeated by British representatives: because Dr. Weitzman was going to be one of the speakers at the dinner, he would undoubtedly demand the immediate opening of Palestine for Jewish settlement in the event of a British victory, and thus the dinner would excite the Arabs and expose Great Britain to intensified German propaganda attacks. The man whom he contacted, Wallace Murray, the head of the Middle Eastern Division of the State Department, informed Mr. Butler that the committee was established by

> certain Zionist interests in this country . . . to influence American opinion, and was similar to or a continuation of a body by the same name founded some years ago, for the same purpose.

Dr. Silver and Dr. Goldstein with Congressman Sol Bloom (seated at right with hand raised) conferring on Palestine affairs.

All that Murray and his superior, Mr. Berle, promised to do was to play down the matter and to suggest that the President send no message to the dinner.

In this tug-of-war for the ear and sympathy of the American Administration, the American Zionist Emergency Committee did not hesitate to use the argument that the five-million-strong American Jewish Community had a valuable bargaining position in a democratic country. They also leaned heavily on the many millions of non-Jewish American citizens who were no less involved and no less sympathetic for the Zionist point of view on the future of Palestine, than were the Zionists. It was the awareness of this situation, strengthened by personal sympathy that most probably led Under-Secretary Sumner Welles, to commit the American Government to a course of action, which must, by all standards, be considered a decisive success for the Zionist cause. Almost at the very same time that Mr. Berle made his frightening presentations on the future of the *Yishuv* and suggested complete renunciation of the Zionist aims, Mr. Welles responded positively to Zionist requests that the American Government elicit from Great Britain a commitment that whatever step it will take in relation to Palestine, it will do so only after prior consultation with the American Government, and that the American Government in turn will not adopt any final decisions on Palestine without prior consultation with the Zionist leadership. To strengthen and affirm this official commitment, Dr. Neumann's memorandum on this

William Green, president of American Federation of Labor
honored by the Jewish National Fund. Also in picture Mr.
Zaritsky and Dr. I. Goldstein.

matter was sent to Mr. Welles with a covering
letter by Dr. Stephen S. Wise, the chairman
of the Emergency Committee.

With such undertaking by the American
Government and in view of the British
pressures for American acquiescence with the
final conclusions of the 1939 White Paper, mere
opposition to the White Paper was no longer
adequate. The Zionist leadership understood
that British plans would be fought only by
presenting plans as far reaching from the
Zionist point of view, as were the British plans
in their anti-Zionist aims. It was clear that
the vague term *"National Home"* was not
only open to the most contrasting interpre-
tations, but could also become a trap to
serve British devices. Zionism was in dire need
of a new formulation, or a restatement of its
aims.

It was easier to acknowledge the need for
such restatement than to find the formulation on which all Zionist forces would agree,
moreover, which had a good chance of becoming
acceptable to non-Zionists as well.

In view of recent Zionist history, this was
no easy task. For more than a decade the
Zionist movement was split over the basic
issue of whether Zionism means Jewish
Statehood, Palestine as a Jewish Commonwealth, or some amorphous National Home

for which territory and a Jewish majority were
rather of secondary importance.

In fact, this latter conception of Zionism
was rather the predominant one in the Zionist
organization. It was therefore a daring
departure from routine and accepted political
terms in the official Zionist parlance when
the chairman of the United Palestine Appeal, Dr. Abba Hillel Silver, used the platform
of the National Conference for Palestine,
January 25-26, 1941, to proclaim that

only by large colonization of (displaced)
Jews in Palestine, with the aim of its
reconstruction as a Jewish Commonwealth,
can the Jewish problem permanently be
solved.

Dr. Silver did not fail also to prescribe the
method of struggle for the attainment of this
goal: emulation of the Irish fighters for
independence, adoption of the political
methods of the Irish liberator, Daniel
O'Connell --
Agitate! Agitate! Agitate!,
and of France's revolutionary zealot Danton,
Boldness! More Boldness! And always
Boldness!

The very conception of Silver's approach
to Zionism's political tactic was sufficient
proof that he considered the United States
of America a vitally important front of Zionist
struggle and, the five million Jews the shock
troops of a general political offensive in
which the pro-Zionist sympathies have to be
utilized to the maximum.

It was fortunate that in this initial stage of
American Jewry's mobilization for Zionist aims,
Silver expressed in fact a mood which prevailed
in almost all Jewish circles in America.
Of course, opponents of such approach to
Zionist tasks and aims were not lacking. The
American front was considered decisive not
only by the proponents of the Herzlian concept
of Zionism. Dr. Judah L. Magnes, the
Chancellor of the Hebrew University, was
busy with propagating his version for the
solution of the Palestine problem through
a bi-national State, where Jewish and Arab
equality will be preserved. The *Hashomer
Hatzair* had similar notions. For some time
it appeared that Hadassah was as well rather
sympathetic to the Magnes point of view. Ben
Gurion had to devote many hours in exposing
the faults of this approach, at the Hadassah
Convention. And on the other hand, the New
Zionist Organization, the Revisionists, was
developing its own Zionist approach with all
the trimmings of faithfulness to Jabotinsky's

political concept of Jewish Statehood. Soon appeared another outgrowth of the Revisionist movement, the Palestine Liberation Committee, headed by a group of emissaries of the *Irgun Tzvai Leumi,* with Peter Bergson (Hillel Kook) as chairman.

But the Emergency Committee did not consider satisfactory the measure of Zionist unity it succeeded in achieving. The leadership of the Committee felt obliged to concentrate on efforts to assure not only a united Zionist front, but it engaged in striving for general unity of the other major forces in the American Jewish Community. For practical purposes this meant first of all the American Jewish Committee and the Jewish Labor Committee.

The problem of formulation of the Zionist program was solved with no great difficulties. The Extraordinary Zionist Conference held on May 6-11, 1942, at the Biltmore Hotel in New York City, at which 600 delegates represented the Zionist Organization of America, Hadassah, Mizrahi, and Poale Zion adopted an eight-point program to become known as *The Biltmore Program,* and to attain prominence perhaps not less than the initial proclamation of the Zionist movement, the Basle Program.

If American Zionists needed a formal, external symbol of the importance and influence they had attained in World Zionism, it was clearly demonstrated by the adoption of the new formulation of the Zionist goal on American soil, by American Zionists, with the participation of the President of the World Zionist Organization, Haim Weitzman, and the representative of the *Yishuv,* David Ben Gurion. The concluding paragraph of the Biltmore Program was intended to leave no doubt as to what Zionists understand by the term, Jewish National Home. It read as follows:

> The Conference urges that the gates of Palestine be opened; that the Jewish Agency be vested with control of immigration into Palestine and the necessary authority for upbuilding the country . . . and that Palestine be established as a Jewish Commonwealth integrated in the structure of the new democratic world.

Thus the British offensive for the liquidation of the Balfour Declaration and the Mandate was countered by the new, clear formulation of the Zionist aim.

American Zionists were fully aware of the importance of their decision. David Ben

At American Jewish Conference, 1943. From left to right: Dr. Stephen S. Wise with Judge Joseph M. Proskauer, president of the American Jewish Committee, and Henry Monsky, President of B'nai Brith.

Gurion thus formulated this change in the tasks and standing of American Zionism:

> At the meeting of the Zionist Executive in Jerusalem, I reported about the activities in America. I appraised, at this occasion, the role of the Zionist movement in America. I stated at this meeting that until the last war the American Zionist movement in America had concentrated itself on financial assistance for Eretz Israel. We should not underestimate the importance of this effort. . . . But the war has suddenly transferred the center of Zionist policy to America.

American Zionists knew well that in the American political realities a successful Zionist effort would, to a great extent, be conditioned by the measure of general Jewish support for the Zionist point of view. It is interesting that Dr. Weitzman and David Ben Gurion were much more active in these efforts for Jewish unity through negotiations with leaders of non-Zionist organizations than were the leaders of the Emergency Committee headed by Dr. Stephen Wise and Rabbi Abba Hillel Silver as co-chairmen, Dr. Neumann as the head of the public relations department, and Solomon Goldman, Louis Lipsky, Mrs. R. Jacobs and Haim Greenberg as its members. Winning the support of *B'nai Brith* posed no problem. Under the presidency of Henry Monsky, this great organization moved resolutely towards unreserved support of the Zionist point of view. It seemed, at some juncture, that the American Jewish Committee as well would subscribe to the major principles of the Biltmore Program. On June 5, 1942, Ben Gurion reached an understanding with the president of the American Jewish Committee, Maurice Wertheim, to

Zionist leaders in protest against British, 1939, White Paper on Palestine, call on British Ambassador to the U. S. Lord Lothian. Leaving the British Embassy grounds are (left to right): first row: second Rabbi Gellman, fourth Dr. Solomon Goldman, fifth-Dr. Stephen S. Wise, seventh-Dr. Israel Goldstein. In second row-in center between Dr. Goldman and Dr. Wise-Chaim Greenberg, at the right of Dr. Wise, in second row, Louis Segal.

act in common for the maintenance of Jewish rights in Palestine under the Mandate in the immediate future . . . for unrestricted immigration and large-scale colonization under a regime designed for that purpose in order that Jews may constitute a majority in Palestine and establish an autonomous community.

The success, and a success it was, did not last long: an internal revolt against that agreement resulted in a new formulation of the AJC position on Palestine. Not conforming with the principles of the Biltmore Program, it stated that the AJC approves

for Palestine an international trusteeship responsible to the United Nations for the following purposes: a) to safeguard Jewish settlement in and Jewish immigration into Palestine, and to guarantee adequate scope for future growth and development to the full extent of the economic absorptive capacity of the country . . . b) to prepare the country to become . . . a self-governing Commonwealth under a constitution and a bill of rights that will safeguard and protect these purposes and basic rights for all.

With the failure of this effort to achieve Jewish unity on the Palestine question another tactic had to be tried. The Zionist movement had behind itself such historic experience, the American Jewish Congress at the end of World War I, which created the American Jewish unity on Palestine, and thus contributed greatly to the political Zionist successes of those days. The initiative for

a conference of the national Jewish organizations to express

the judgment of American Jews along with other Jewish communities with respect to the post-war status of Jews and the up-building of Jewish Palestine

came from Henry Monsky, president of B'nai Brith. Maneuvering to have the conference postponed failed, and it took place as scheduled, in Pittsburg, on January 23-24, 1943. The basic initial aim of the Zionist movement was achieved when the conference decided to hold an American Jewish Assembly. Here again, as in the days of the American Jewish Congress, opposition arose against the word, "assembly," which could imply the stability of the representation of all American Jews. The opposition came from the American Jewish Committee. The Zionists accepted the demand, substituted "Conference" for "Assembly" and an all-representative American Jewish Conference came into being. Over two million Jews, in seventy-eight communities and fifty-eight regions in every state of the Union, including the District of Columbia, participated in the election of delegates to the Conference. It was the first democratically elected Jewish body in almost a quarter of a century.

The confidence of the American Zionist leaders in the good judgment and basic pro-Zionist sentiments of American Jewry, irrespective of the formal strength of the organized Zionist movement, proved correct. The hesitations and doubts of certain Zionist leaders, whether it was advisable to press for the adoption of the full Biltmore Program as the political platform of the entire American Jewry, proved baseless. A powerful exposition of the Zionist point of view by Dr. Silver, delivered on the second night of the Conference, the so-called "Palestine Night," at the end of August, 1943, in the Waldorf Astoria hotel in New York City, helped magnificently in turning the sentiments in favor of the Zionist formulation.

With this speech, says Dr. Samuel Margoshes, the veteran Zionist publicist, Dr. Silver has made his first real mark in Zionist history.

Out of a total of 502 delegates, only four cast dissenting votes. The Palestine resolution adopted at the Conference urged the

loyal and faithful fulfillment of the covenant entered into between the nations of the world and the Jewish people whose intent and

Dr. Chaim Weitzman addresses the Biltmore Conference, 1942.

purpose . . . was to reconstitute Palestine as the Jewish Commonwealth. ·

After demanding the suppression of the, 1939, White Paper, the Conference urged that the gates of Palestine be opened to Jewish immigration and that the Jewish Agency assumes the responsibility for Jewish colonization, so that these measures constitute

> the essential prerequisites for the attainment of a Jewish majority and for the creation of the Jewish Commonwealth . . . within the new democratic order.

Thus the entire American Jewish community stood mobilized behind the Biltmore Program. The importance of this achievement was even greater in view of the pressure by the American Administration to have the entire Conference postponed. Washington informed officially that non-compliance with its demands will result in the issuance of a joint Anglo-American statement, which will urge all citizens to shelve any public debate on the future of Palestine, in the interests of the war effort. Though the Office Committee, the executive body of the Emergency Committee, decided not to succumb to the Government pressure, it advised its representatives with Dr. Wise as their leading exponent, to intervene in Washington against such Government action.

For months the struggle against such Government call occupied the Zionist leadership. But the very fact that the Emergency Committee, the entire Jewish community, refused to be intimidated by Government pressure, was not only proof of growing political audacity and resoluteness, but also greatly strengthened the hand of those who argued for "boldness, more boldness, and always boldness."

Henry Monsky-B'nai Brith president.

The mandate was therefore acquired for pressing the Zionist cause in the name of the entire American Jewry. In view of this result of the vote at the American Jewish Conference, any dissenting view could not expect too much of a hearing. And there was certainly no danger in the utterances of those circles

which refraining from participation in the mainstream of Zionist thought and action, propagated even a more outspoken criticism of British policies and formulated in different language, more definite, their Zionist ideology.

In an advertisement published in the *New York Times,* in May, 1943, during Prime Minister Churchill's visit in the United States, the New Zionist Organization (The Revisionists) called upon Great Britain to give up the Mandate. *"Mr. Churchill, Drop the Mandate"* as the advertisement was titled, was a call that carried the opposition to Britain's policy in Palestine to its extreme.

The Zionist leadership was resolved to press incessantly for the full exploitation of its victory. It decided to do so out of its deep conviction that the path of political action it entered corresponded not only with the needs of the Jewish people and the possibilities of the hour, but also with the hopes and wishes of the *Yishuv.*

The heroic *Yishuv* in Palestine has prayerfully appealed to us to uphold its hands, exclaimed Dr. Silver, in his Conference speech, which preceded the adoption of the Palestine resolution, and he thus gave the most powerful endorsement and publicity to the partnership which linked American Jewry and the Jews of Palestine in the struggle for a Zionist solution of the Palestine problem. And that the

Yishuv was partner to the formulation of the Zionist goal, which some wanted to term "extremist" was best expressed by the chairman of the Jewish Agency Executive, David Ben Gurion, who stated that

what was termed the Zionist maximum has now become the essential minimum.

But the formulation of this "essential minimum" was no more than the essential guideline for the Zionist leadership, for the Zionist Emergency Committee. To translate it into the language, first of practical support by the American government, and, in the second and final stage, into the accepted policy on the future of Palestine, became the central task of the Emergency Council. The Council's dual chairmanship of Dr. Stephen Wise and Dr. Abba Hillel Silver, was considered a guarantee for a maximum political effort. There was a clear perception how this effort should be organized. The Emergency Council understood thoroughly that its strength was deposited with the public opinion. To win this opinion, to organize it so that it also had a voice, became a major activity of the Council, simultaneously with the intensive and recurrent political interventions in Washington. It was this public opinion, more and more outspoken in its sympathies for the Zionist goal, from which the Zionist leadership drew its mandate and its strength. Thousands, tens of thousands, hundreds of thousands were involved in this political effort.

A detailed report in the Palestine Year Book for 1944 illustrated the numerical strength of the organized Zionist movement in the United States. Zionist Organization of America -- 153,000; *Hadassah* -- 150,000; Mizrahi, *Hapoel Hamizrahi, Mizrahi* Women -- 75,000; *Poale-Zion, Zeirei-Zion,* Pioneer Women, League for Labor Palestine, *Habonim, Hehalutz,* Jewish National Workers Alliance -- 69,800; Zionist Revisionists, *Brith Trumpeldor* -- 14,700; Young Judea -- 17,000; *Bnai Zion* -- 4,200; *Hashomer Hatzair* -- 2,500. A total of 486,200 organized men and women. It became a virtual crusade, participation in which was considered a honor and privilege The Jewish Commonwealth idea fired the imagination of American Jews. The scope of this unprecedented political effort was best characterized in the words of one of its chief architects, Dr. Abba Hillel Silver, in a report on October 15, 1944, on the activities of the Emergency Council:

We circulated books, tracts, pamphlets, press releases by the thousands, by the tens of thousands, by the hundreds of thousands. We placed our literature in every key center in our country. We interviewed editors, writers, news commentators and others, who help mold public opinion. We arranged meetings throughout the country, sent speakers to tell our story and organized large and impressive conferences. A great demonstration meeting was held under our auspices in Madison Square Garden on the eve of the White Paper's effective date. It was to the non-Jewish world that we directed our attention principally, and in this we had the invaluable cooperation of the American Palestine Committee headed by that staunch friend, Senator Robert F. Wagner, and of the Christian Council for Palestine.

We placed every month a very helpful political bulletin, *Palestine,* ably edited by Mr. Louis Lipsky, in the hands of 16,000 leaders in American educational, political and religious life. To counteract the legend which had been studiously cultivated in Washington and which was accepted in the highest circles, that Palestine was a starved little country, about the size of a handkerchief, and to send people there in large numbers was to consign them to wretched poverty and starvation, we publicized in every way Dr. Lowdermilk's magnificent book, *Palestine, Land of Promise,* which has now gone through five editions in the United States and has been republished in England, and which made innumerable converts and friends for our cause. Under the auspices of our Council an impressive dinner was tendered to Dr. Lowdermilk in Washington, attended by many scientists and Government officials. This was the second important meeting which was held in our national capital the first, an all-day session, having been held under the auspices of the American Palestine Committee and the Christian Council for Palestine, attended by leading Christian laymen and clergy from all parts of the country and climaxed by an impressive dinner in the evening, addressed by the foremost men in the political and religious life of America. . . .

Extensive publicity was also given to the Jordan Valley Authority project and to the engineering studies and the important work of economic planning for irrigation,

Dr. Weitzman and Dr. Silver in London, 1945.

power and development, which are being carried on by the Commission on Palestine Surveys under the direction of Dr. Emanuel Neumann. Our purpose was clear: to dissipate the false propaganda which has been spread concerning Palestine's limited absorptive capacity as an argument for the retention of the White Paper and the curbing of immigration into Palestine.

. . . A special and successful activity was carried on among the ranks of American labor, in which we had the eager and most generous assistance of the leaders of organized labor in the United States.

. . . The Emergency Council published a very important volume, *America and Palestine,* a book of 500 pages, giving the history of America's deep and continuous interest in the Jewish National Home over a period of many years, including all important documents bearing on the subject and recording the opinions of over four hundred members of the Congress of the United States, 77 per cent of the entire body, in favor of our movement. . . .

. . . The manifold activities of the Emergency Council have been supplemented, of course, by the very effective and important Zionist propaganda which was carried on throughout the country by the Zionist Organization of America, as well as by Hadassah, the Mizrahi and the Poale Zion. The Emergency Council is no more than the political arm of these national organizations, in whose behalf and by whose authority it functions. It is not a membership body. The leaders of the Zionist Organization of America are quite naturally leaders within the Emergency Council.

. . . There were many other activities which were carried on, which because of their confidential nature cannot be publicly discussed.

Sidney Hillman, chairman of the Political Action Committee of the Congress of Industrial Organizations, intimate friend of President Roosevelt with whom he often pleaded for the cause of a Jewish Palestine.

The twenty-six members of the Emergency Council, nominated by the constituent organizations, had their hands full in translating their decisions into action. Too cumbersome to act in its plenary composition, the Zionist Emergency Council chose smaller executive organs as the Office Committee and an Administrative Committee. Until 1943 these three bodies of the Emergency Council worked under the chairmanship, respectively, of Dr. Wise, Haim Greenberg and Herman Schulman, to be later reorganized and put under the joint chairmanship of Wise and Silver. Such vast and diversified program of action as the one described by Dr. Silver necessitated an accordingly elaborate organization. Besides the central office in New York, 380 local Zionist Emergency Committees, subdivided into 76 state and regional groups gave the opportunity of active participation

Protest-one of the many scenes of protest against British policies in Palestine in suppressing so called "illegal" immigration.

in the struggle for a Jewish Commonwealth, for the widest masses of the Jewish Community. Only such a widespread organization, reaching into every corner of the United States was able to keep up a constant pressure on the Administration and on the legislative bodies. With such an organization only was it possible to have hundreds of thousands of cables flooding the White House and the offices of the legislators.

The time was approaching to put to test the effectiveness of this organization and the seriousness of the prevailing sympathies for the Zionist cause. The 1944 Presidential elections seemed to be an opportune time for such test. The Democrats and the Republicans made pro-Zionist resolutions part of their election planks. Less than a month before the national elections, President Roosevelt gave his support to the pro-Zionist paragraph in the Democratic platform stating:

I know how long and ardently the Jewish people have worked and prayed for the establishment of Palestine as a free and democratic Jewish Commonwealth. I am convinced that the American people give their support to this aim and, if re-elected, I shall help to bring about its realization.

This apparent Zionist victory became a source of an internal Zionist controversy, which had for a time, caused a serious cleavage in the united Zionist front. Contrary to the opinions of the majority of the Emergency Council, Dr. Silver thought that Zionist reliance solely on the Democratic party and the Democratic President was not only disadvantageous from the point of view of current Zionist interests, but also from the point of view of future struggles for Zionist goals, and the general standing of the American Jewish community. In Dr. Silver's opinion, the success of the Zionist cause could be assured only through winning the support of both major parties, Democrats and Republicans alike. Dr. Silver represented in fact a policy line which became a standard principle of American Zionism (and even of the entire Jewish Community) that Zionists need not identify their cause with any particular party.

This principle of bipartisan support had soon to prove its salutary importance for the Zionist cause. The occasion for such opportunity afforded itself when the time has come for a formal expression of support for the Jewish Commonwealth idea through a resolution of both Houses of Congress. The fact that the pro-Zionist resolution was introduced jointly by the Democratic and Republican Congressmen was in itself a most important achievement, as was a most important success the fact that in the Senate this resolution was jointly sponsored by the leading Senators, Robert A. Taft (Republican) and Robert F. Wagner (Democrat). Recurring interventions of the Administration impeded the adoption of the resolution. Members of the Cabinet appeared in person before the Congress committees, urging the tabling of the resolution because

without reference to the merits of these resolutions, further action on them, at this time, would be prejudicial to the successful prosecution of war.

The question of whether to accept this excuse of the Administration, or to press with full vigor for the adoption of the resolution, became a major issue within the Zionist Emergency Council itself. Led by Dr. Wise, those who argued for conforming with the Administration's demand gained the upper hand. They won a majority in support for their contention that the Administration, President Roosevelt especially, had to be given credit that they would, at some future date, fulfill their pro-Zionist promises. This majority, composed of representatives of the then administrations of the Zionist Organization of America and Hadassah, took over the formulation and execution of Zionist policy, while the two other parties, represented in the Emergency Council, Mizrahi and Poale-Zion, continued their support for Dr. Silver's policy line.

The controversy resulted in Dr. Silver's resignation from the Council. The split spread to all constituent organs of the Council throughout the country. It became the center of a general public debate. High executives of the Zionist Emergency Council, Harry L. Shapiro, Harold Manson, Abe Tuvim and Harry Steinberg resigned and helped organize a new group to serve as an instrument for promotion of the militant point of view. Under the leadership of Dr. Emanuel Neumann the American Zionist Policy Committee was organized. The Jewish press came out unreservedly in support of the policy line which was defeated. The clamor for the return to leadership of the exponent of this militant Zionism, Dr. Silver, found its expression in resolutions, letters, telegrams, which began to flood the offices of the Zionist Emergency Council.

This leadership and policy crisis in the Council was not the only development which marred the unity of purpose and action of the Zionist camp. As early as in May, 1943, the

Political Advisory Committee planning strategy for the United Nations struggle in 1947. All Zionist parties were represented in this Committee.

Jewish Agency Executive decided to establish, in Washington, a political office to be headed by Dr. Nahum Goldman and Louis Lipsky. In view of the fact that the Zionist Emergency Council decided to establish a political office in Washington, which was supposed to be "the only Zionist office for political activity in Washington," the Agency's office appeared not only as a kind of a permanent vote of non-confidence in the American Zionist leadership, but also a permanent irritant. Dr. Weitzman's assurance that the Agency's office will observe "close cooperation" with the Council could not remove the controversy. The conflict of prerogatives did not fail to become an important factor not only in the internal relationship between the American Zionist leaders, but had also its repercussions in Zionism's dealings with external factors, first of all with the American Administration.

Though this problem of dual political authorities was not removed, the Silver crisis came to an end when in July, 1945, Dr. Silver was called to become the head of the Zionist Emergency Council, and his leadership fortified by his consequent, unanimous, election. to the presidency of the Zionist Organization of America.

Developments in the theatres of war, and in the United States itself, made a closing of Zionist ranks long overdue. The war in Europe was over and the Jewish catastrophe revealed in all its horrifying details. The wretched remnants of the destroyed European Jewry lingering in camps, gave a new sense of urgency to the Zionist struggle. Reflections on the abandonment of the six million Jews who couldn't be saved because Britain kept the doors of Palestine closed, while the entire civilized world looked on and found an excuse for its moral complicity, in the mass murder, in the argument of war conditions; the accumulation

of pro-Zionist sentiment in the American public which was a result of five years of constant action by the Zionist Emergency Council, resulted in President Truman's famous letter to the British Prime Minister, Clement R. Attlee, requesting 100,000 certificates for Jewish immigrants to Palestine.

The acceptance, by the United States, of Britain's counter proposal that an Anglo-American Committee of Inquiry investigate the position of Jews in Europe as well as the situation in Palestine, opened a new chapter in the Anglo-American relations concerning Palestine, and new opportunities for American Zionist action. The United States of America was no more a friendly nation that was being asked to intervene on behalf of a just cause: it became a directly involved factor whose position was able to decide on the future of the Palestine question. Viewed from the standpoint of the previous consistent assertions of the American Administration that the 1924 treaty with Britain does not entitle America to any direct intervention in the British conduct of Palestine policies, America's consent to participation in searching for a solution to the Palestine problem cleared, beyond any doubt, this political and legal hurdle. The American government became a direct address for Zionist action; American support for Zionism assumed dimensions of a decisive resolution of the Palestine problem.

It was the good fortune of the Zionist cause that the Zionist leadership, the American Zionist Emergency Council, grasped the importance of this turning point in the fortunes of the struggle for a Jewish Commonwealth. What was needed was a clear perception of the new political conditions and a well defined goal. The importance of the Biltmore Program and its adoption by the American Jewish Conference appeared in its full historic meaning, and potential.

Jewish War Veterans protest march on Washington.

13

THE DECISIVE STRUGGLE

THE OFFICIAL AMERICAN INVOLVEMENT in searching for a solution of the Palestine problem offered new opportunities, but raised as well new exigencies. The pending Palestine resolution assumed new meaning. Passage of the resolution appeared no more as only of declaratory importance. It became clear that it could become a political document to be used in dealings with the American executive authorities, for which the opinions of the legislature had to carry weight. Under pressure of the Zionist Emergency Council, the Palestine resolution was re-introduced in Congress. The Administration's last-minute maneuvers to have again the resolution withdrawn failed this time. The attempt to stygmatize the demand for a Jewish Commonwealth as "nationalism" and "racialism" was repulsed. After the Zionist position had been stated at a hearing before the House Foreign Affairs Committee, and after a full debate on the floor of the Senate, the Resolution was adopted by an overwhelming vote, on December, 1945.

Although the resolution did not speak about a Jewish Commonwealth, its operative paragraph left no doubt that the demand that "Palestine shall be opened for the free entry of Jews into the country" . . . "so that they may freely proceed with the upbuilding of Palestine as the Jewish National Home" could have no other practical meaning. To have this ultimate goal of a Commonwealth included in the resolution without the reservations concerning the preservation of religious and civil rights of the non-Jewish population (a reservation included in the Balfour Declaration that supplied a legal argument to the entire British anti-Zionist policy), the resolution spoke of the Commonwealth in general terms stating the obvious, that all inhabitants of the country shall have equal rights.

The ensuing political developments did not leave too much time for contemplation. President Truman's demand that Britain admit 100,000 immigrants to Palestine was a good opening for the intensification of pressure on the Administration. The demand for this emergency action for lifting the ban on further Jewish immigration could have impeded the struggle for a defined political status for Palestine. But the stubbornness of British enmity towards Zionist goals, and the breach of promise to implement the report of the Anglo-American Committee of Inquiry, including the refusal to permit the entry of 100,000 immigrants to Palestine, threw open again the entire Palestine problem.

This time American Jewry was even more united than it was in the days of the struggle for the Jewish Commonwealth resolution at the American Jewish Conference. No segment of Jewish public opinion, none of the organized Jewish groups failed to demonstrate its support for the recommendations of the Anglo-American Committee of Inquiry concerning the 100,000 Jewish immigrants to Palestine.

The American Jewish Committee made its position clear, and even the Council for Judaism, which termed the demand for a Jewish Commonwealth a "racial outrage," joined the general outcry against the delays in the implementation of President Truman's demand. The camps of the Jewish displaced persons in Germany and Austria, almost all of them in territories held by American occupation forces, were a permanent reminder and indictment against the maneuvers of the British policy, and the lack of sufficient American official pressure to have Great Britain listen, at least, to the voice of humanitarian imperatives, if it wasn't ready to accept the inevitable in changing the basic policies in Palestine.

The American Zionist Emergency Council was no more ready to cooperate in any devices for further delays in the solution of the Palestine problem. On June 4, 1946, the Council, in reply to the State Department's request for comment on the Anglo-American Committee's report declared that "further consultations and comments appear meaningless, except to produce delay when immediate action is called for, and to confuse where the issue has long been altogether clear."

The American public's reaction to the procrastination in saving human beings, vegetating in camps, was not limited to the Jewish community alone. Leaders of the non-Jewish public opinion joined the struggle for opening the doors of Palestine. Thousands of university professors, leading newspapermen, clergy, leaders of communal affairs, signed petitions, participated in meetings, cabled to their Congressmen calling for immediate action. Mass demonstrations in which tens of thousands took part, marches of thousands, kept the issue alive. On July 14, 1946, thousands of Jewish war veterans, participating in a two-day march on Washington to demonstrate support for Palestine Jewry in its fight against the British policy, informed President Truman, that they are prepared

to recruit a full division of Jewish volunteers for service in the Holy Land.

These manifold activities were constantly encouraged by the direct struggle against the British rule in Palestine. The news about the fighting underground, first of the short-lived unified action of the *Haganah, Irgun* and *Lehi,* within the framework of *Tenuath Hameri,* the Rebel Movement, or separately by each of the three groups, each in its way, were featured with growing emphasis by the American press. The humanitarian motives for support of the Zionist cause were reinforced by a new element of pro-Jewish feeling, that of appreciation, often admiration for the courage, devotion, patriotism and sacrifice of the Jewish freedom fighters in Palestine. The saga of "illegal" immigration, organized in mass dimensions by the Haganah with the direct involvement of Americans, who supplied not only the financial means for the purchase of ships and their upkeep, but also experienced seafarers, created a feeling of direct partnership with the Yishuv in its historic struggle.

Amidst these new, one could say, revolutionary conditions, a political act of the British Government, in which the American Administration got itself involved, opened, in full extent, the basic discussion on the political future of Palestine. The Morrison-Grady plan, providing for the federalization of Palestine, to preserve British rule and, in final count, to make Jewish immigration dependent on Arab consent, was seized upon, by the American Zionist leadership, as an excellent opportunity to re-route the dispute over Palestine from the problem of emergency action for saving 100,000 homeless Jews to levels of political dispute about the future of Palestine and its basic, political, national status.

It was only natural that in fighting the Morrison-Grady plan, so named for its authors, Morrison, the British representative, and Grady, the American, the Zionist camp had the opportunity to return to the original formulation for the solution of the Palestine problem through the establishment of Palestine as a Jewish Commonwealth. At this very juncture, a serious split occurred, not in general Jewish ranks, but in the Zionist camp itself. At a meeting of the Jewish Agency Executive in Paris, in July, 1946, a decision was adopted to suggest a solution to the political stalemate that developed. The Jewish Agency suggested the partition of Palestine into a viable Jewish state and Arab part.

While the American Zionist Emergency Council was still straining every bit of its energy and influence for the full implementation of the Biltmore Program, Dr. Nahum Goldman conferred the partition decision of the highest Zionist Executive body to the American Government. The Truman Cabinet Committee on Palestine, composed of the Secretaries of State, War, and of the Treasury, Acheson, Stimson and Snyder, to assist him in the early consideration of the recommendations of the Anglo-American Committee of Inquiry, received the information on the Agency proposal from Dr. Nahum Goldman, who arrived on this mission from Paris. Interviewed on these meetings with members of that Presidential committee, Dr. Goldman revealed to the author, that there were some not too pleasant remarks voiced on the account of Jewish pressure on behalf of Zionist goals. In one of such generalizations a remark was made that there are in America three groups whose patriotism is not of the "clearest vintage—Jews, the Irish, and the Italians." One of the decisive conversations was held with the Secretary of War Stimson. Dr. Goldman appeared at this meeting with the president of the American Jewish Committee, Joseph M. Proskauer, whom he induced to support partition after a four-hour conversation. When Secretary of War Henry L. Stimson manifested his surprise, at the company, Proskauer remarked, "Yes, Palestine makes for strange bedfellows."

In Dr. Goldman's opinion, these conversations, with the U.S. Government, have won the Administration's support for a Jewish State in a part of Palestine. President Truman's support for the partition was, according to Dr. Goldman, reported by President Truman's press secretary, David Niles, a Jew, who, after reporting on Truman's attitude, added with excitement, in broken Yiddish: "O my mother, my mother, why didn't she live to be witness of these days." On October 8th, 1946, Dean Acheson, the Acting Secretary of State, revealed, at a press conference, that "about two

Jewish War Veterans parade down Fifth Avenue, New York, April 5, 1948 requesting the implementation of the Jewish State U. N. resolution. The banner reads: "JWV Hails the Jewish State".

months ago Dr. Nahum Goldman presented a plan calling for partition and for autonomy in immigration and economic matters in the area which would become a Jewish state."

The American Zionist front, heretofore united around the Biltmore Program of a Jewish Commonwealth in the whole of Palestine, was thrown into an uproar. The principal opposition to the very idea of giving up part of Palestine was supplemented by a legal argument that denied the Jewish Agency Executive the right to change the Biltmore Program, the official program of the Zionist movement, that only a World Zionist Congress was competent to change. Dr. Silver, the head of the Emergency Council's executive committee at that time, and president of the Zionist Organization of America, attacked the partition proposal vehemently. *New Palestine,* the official organ of the Z.O.A., wrote in October, 1946: "Whatever the decision (whether the Agency should not take part in the Bevin-planned conferences in London) it is no longer possible to avoid the conclusion that the Executive of the Jewish Agency has been led into making one tactical mistake after another. The real initial error was the mistake to abandon the Biltmore Program and to put forward a proposal for the partition of Palestine as the official proposal of the Zionist movement." The 49th National Convention of the Z.O.A. adopted a strong anti-partition resolution that stated:

The annual Convention of the Z.O.A. reaffirms the historic claims and aspirations, and the legally established rights of the Jewish people to Palestine. Their rights which have been firmly embodied in solemn inter-national covenants apply to the whole of mandated Palestine, undivided and unlimited, as the territory in which the Jewish people shall establish its national existence as a free and equal member of the family of nations. The question whether it is tactically advisable that the Jews take the initiative in suggesting partition appeared even more important than the principle itself. A partitioned Palestine now represents our maximum Zionist demands, both in London and in Washington, and in the Arab world.

Our own Government now suggests a still further compromise, not as between the Biltmore Program and partition, but as between partition and cantonization, argued Dr. Silver in his fight against the new Agency policy. The position of the Agency Executive had its defenders. Louis Lipsky, the American member of the Jewish Agency Executive, assured the delegates to the Z.O.A. convention that "as a matter of principle no member of the Agency favors partition," but he added, "we had to come with a concrete plan in this emergency as a way out of the impasse." Another defense of the partition proposal was delivered by Dr. Goldman at the convention of Hadassah. According to Dr. Goldman: "The developments of the last two years have shown that there exists no chance for the implementation of the Biltmore Program. Adherence to the Biltmore Program could mean either a demand for the continuation of the British Mandate until the Jews become a majority in Palestine, or the establishment of some other regime for the duration of the time until a Jewish majority will become a reality. Both possibilities are impossible of achieving and thus partition is the best

At the U. N. hearings. Front: Dr. Emanuel Neumann, center and Dr. Abba Hillel Silver, right. At upper left: Dr. Chaim Greenberg and upper right Dr. Nahum Goldman.

solution under the circumstances. In spite of Dr. Emanuel Neuman's appeal that the Convention does not in any way contribute to the weakening of the Biltmore Program, Hadassah adopted a resolution which endorsed the Jewish Agency's policy of 'reluctant acceptance of the principle of partition of Palestine.' "

Thus basic problems of Zionist policy confronted the 22nd Zionist Congress in December, 1946. American Zionists were again called to play a decisive role. The central issues were sharply and clearly defined. The problem of partition was only one of them. The Congress had to formulate the Zionist position regarding a new London Conference, one of the many delaying tactics of the British Government. The Congress had also thrust upon itself

Dr. Abba Hillel Silver confers with Warren Austin, chief U. S. delegate to the United Nations.

the burning problem of Jewish direct resistance to British policies in Palestine. On these basic three issues, the great majority of the American delegation supported the policy line represented by Dr. Silver and Dr. Neumann. Ultimately, this policy line won at the Congress a majority of 171 votes of Z.O.A., *Ahduth Avodah, Mizrahi,* and Revisionists, as against 154 votes which supported Dr. Weitzman and his chief American allies, Dr. Stephen S. Wise and Louis Lipsky. A resolution demanding the "establishment of Palestine as a Jewish Commonwealth," rejecting the participation in the London Conference, was accompanied by a clear expression of the majority's sentiments in favor of the struggle in Palestine, thus indirectly voicing support for the fighting underground. "The way to end resistance is to open the door to Palestine," stated Dr. Silver in his speech at the Congress. He continued, "We believe in resistance to the illegal acts of the mandatory regime in Palestine. And we shall continue to help the forces of resistance."

Speakers at a mass rally in New York's Madison Square Garden celebrating the proclamation of the Jewish Independence. From left to right: Mrs. Rose Halprin, Senator Herbert H. Lehman, Mayor William O'Dwyer, Senator Robert A. Taft, Dr. Abba Hillel Silver and Henry Morgenthau. (May 16, 1949.)

The decision to establish an American Section of the Jewish Agency for Palestine was an organizational and political expression of the great revolution which had occurred in the composition of the Zionist forces, and an acknowledgment of the leading role American Zionism had assumed after World War II. The six members of this Section, two from the Zionist Organization of America, two from *Poale-Zion* and one each from *Mizrahi* and Hadassah, under the chairmanship of Dr. Silver, were soon to assume the leading role in setting the course of Zionist policies.

Crowd outside the Washington, D. C. office of the Jewish Agency watches the Israel flag unfurled for the first time at 6:01 P. M., May 14, 1948, the moment corresponding with the termination of the British Mandate over Palestine.

American Zionism was clearly set on the course of an uninhibited, courageous struggle. Its leaders knew fully well that it was the degree of their pressure on the American Government that would determine the attitudes of the British Government, and consequently the fate of Palestine. As early as August 1, 1946, Winston S. Churchill requested that Britain "lay her mandate at the feet of the United Nations Organization and thereafter evacuate the country." And to make clear the relationship between the American intervention and this proposal he qualified it by adding, "if the United States will not come and share the burden of the Zionist cause as defined or as agreed."

These sentiments were even more clearly elaborated by the British Labor Government's Foreign Secretary, Ernest Bevin, whose intransigence and anti-Semitism were responsible for the policies of suppression in Palestine, and inhuman treatment of those who decided to force their way to Palestine. Announcing, on February 14, 1947, that Great Britain decided to take the Palestine question to the United Nations, Bevin declared:

We might have been able to do more for the Jews . . . if the bitterness of feeling which surrounds this problem of immigration had not been increased by American pressure for the immediate admission of 100,000. I do not desire to create any ill feeling with the United States, but I should have been happier if they had had regard to the fact that we were the Mandatory Power, and that we were carrying the responsibility.

The harshness of Bevin's policies in Palestine facilitated the efforts of the American Zionist Council. The New Zionist Organization and the Hebrew Committee of National Liberation, headed by Peter Bergson (Hillel Kook), had their share in opposing the British breach of faith and influencing even more the incensed American public opinion. To keep this pressure on the American Government appeared of vital importance. Dr. Silver reminded American Zionists of it on each and every occasion:

Zionist victory rally in Manhattan Center, New York, December, 1948.

It is clear that for the success of our movement, the role of the American Government will be a decisive one. It is clear, therefore, that the Zionists of America must remain fully alerted and thoroughly mobilized.

With the submission of the Palestine problem to the United Nations the need for this mobilization and its importance grew even more. It was clear that the deliberations and resolutions of the United Nations would be greatly influenced, perhaps decided, by the most powerful member of the U.N., the United States of America. It became incumbent upon the American Zionist movement to create such conditions, in the American public opinion, that the United States Government would have no choice but support the Zionist cause.

American Zionists understood well that Britain's submission of the Palestine problem to the United Nations was not at all a proof of its decision to abandon Palestine. Britain's Colonial Secretary, Arthur Creech-Jones, made clear Britain's hidden devices in a statement in the House of Commons:

Signing of Luxemburg Agreement (on German reparations.) Standing: Frank Goldman, president B'nai Brith, Jacob Blaustein, president American Jewish Committee, seated: Adolph Held, American Jewish Labor Committee, Dr. Israel Goldstein, chairman Western Hemisphere Executive of World Jewish Congress—center Abba Eban.

We are not going to the United Nations to surrender the Mandate. . . . We are . . . setting out the problem and asking for their advice as to how the Mandate has to be administered. If the Mandate cannot be implemented in its present form, we are asking how it can be amended.

The field of political maneuvering was therefore open. The wavering policy of the American Government was not reassuring at all. The Zionist Emergency Council was faced with a double task: to master maximum support for the American Section of the Jewish Agency which provided the representative leadership of the political struggle at the United Nations, and to keep on the pressure on Washington. The need for this continuing pressure was best illustrated in the first, fateful debate, at the United Nations, on the Jewish Agency's request that its representatives be given the right to present the Jewish case. Though the American representative accompanied his remarks,

Delegation visiting State Department for conference on reparations from Germany: Frank Goldman, Dr. Nahum Goldman, Jacob Blaustein, Adolph Held, Dr. Israel Goldstein.

on this matter, with a series of reservations, the basic support he gave the Agency's demand should be considered a most important achievement. The choice of the person, Dr. Abba Hillel Silver, who had to present the Jewish case, had also additional meaning for the American Zionist movement and the close partnership in the struggle for a Jewish State between American Jewry and the Palestine Yishuv. Dr. Silver stressed the special character of this cooperation in the opening remarks of his presentation on May 8, 1947, before the United Nations: "I should like to say at the outset that were Mr. David Ben Gurion, chairman of the Jewish Agency for Palestine, here this morning, he would be making the statement for the Agency." Enemies of Zionism had, of course,

First Zionist Assembly, New York, December 1953.

seized upon the occasion as an alleged proof that American citizens were pleading for another, though not yet born, state. The accusation was brushed aside and a Zionist leader remarked on that problem, "Thus it was . . . that Dr. Silver and I, citizens -- and, I hope, good citizens of the United States, sat at the Council table at Lake Success side by side with the representatives of all nations, including those of our own government; and none but our enemies and a few traitors, in our midst, raised the issue or dared to cast doubt upon our American loyalty."

Such rebuke of allegations about "dual loyalty" was most timely as the American Zionist movement had to gird itself for new encounters with the Administration. Great Britain did not give up hope that a stalemate at the United Nations would throw Palestine back into her hands, but relieved of the obligations of the Mandate. Powerful forces in the United States were also at work to have Palestine "saved from

the hands of the Jews." Most important members of President Truman's Cabinet, led by James Forrestal, the Secretary of Defense, with the unhidden sympathies of others, including Secretary of State George C. Marshall, had stretched every bit of persuasion and influence to make the United States pay heed to Arab demands. And the situation in Palestine grew more tense by the day. The underground increased the tempo and intensity of its struggle. Shiploads of "illegal immigrants" from the D.P. camps continued in their effort to outmaneuver the British blockade boats cruising in the Mediterranean. The drama of the immigrant ship, *Exodus* 1947, the former American *S.S. President Warfield* manned by many American seamen, when 4,000 immigrants were intercepted by the British Navy and forcefully returned to the D.P. camps in Germany, incensed American public opinion and caused a degree of indignation no British friend was able to mitigate.

First meeting with leading member of Soviet delegation to the United Nations General Assembly in 1947. From left: Dr. E. Neumann, Boris Smolar, chief editor of the Jewish Telegraphic Agency, S. Tzarapkin.

This was the general atmosphere on May 15, 1947, when the first Special Session of the U.N. General Assembly was closed with the appointment of an eleven-member United Nations Special Committee on Palestine (UNSCOP) to investigate the Palestine question and to make recommendations for its solution. The reports, a majority and a minority report, were published on August 31, 1947. The majority report suggested the partition of Palestine into a Jewish and Arab state to become independent on September 1, 1949; and the minority report, prepared by representatives of India, Iran and Yugoslavia, called for a federal form of state, with autonomous Jewish and Arab areas.

The partition question appeared again on the agenda. The Zionist leadership had to decide whether to support, or to fight, the UNSCOP partition scheme. At the session of the Zionist General Council (Actions Committee) which was taking place at that time in Zurich, Dr. Silver, his friends, and other opponents of partition supported the partition proposal. This was not, as Dr. Silver explained, a reversal in his position on partition. What he opposed, Dr. Silver said, is Zionist initiative to have Palestine partitioned, but such proposals, coming from external forces, "which we shall find truly reasonable and which will meet our fundamental needs and satisfy our national aspirations and sense of justice . . . our movement will be prepared . . . to give them serious consideration." The American Section of the Jewish Agency was again charged with the responsibility of representing the Zionist cause before the United Nations.

The proud statement, "We have builded a nation in Palestine. That nation now demands its independence," voiced by Dr. Silver before the United Nations, on October 2, 1947, was a fitting expression of the feelings of American Jewry, of American Zionists. But this demand had yet to be accepted. The UNSCOP report was no more than a recommendation. To make the majority report on the establishment of a Jewish State, in a part of Palestine, a resolution of the United Nations General Assembly, was still a task to be fought for. There again the weight of the United States position appeared in its full importance.

The Zionist Emergency Council faced a most delicate situation. The promise of a Jewish State which the UNSCOP report had held evoked unbounded enthusiasm in the Jewish Community. Aware that such enthusiasm could be exploited by enemies for further whittling

Part of dais at dinner given to mark Soviet support for Jewish State resolution at the U. N. From left: Andrei Gromyko, Dr. E. Neumann, Joseph Brainin, Arthur Miller.

away of what was considered pro-Jewish parts of the UNSCOP report, the Emergency Council warned the chairmen of the close to 400 Local Emergency Committees:

If the impression is created that the Jewish people regard the majority report as being in their favor, the efforts of our enemies within the U.N. further to whittle down pro-Jewish recommendations will be greatly facilitated. . . . We urge local Zionist leaders and spokesmen, as well as the local Jewish press, to refrain from making favorable comments on the recommendations and to be guided by the official attitude of our movement, which we will rush to you as soon as it has been formulated.

But the enemies of Jewish Statehood had no need for manifestations of Jewish enthusiasm to gather their forces for a last stand. When the regular U.N. General Assembly, which had to consider the UNSCOP Report, opened on September 16, 1947, reports revealed that the Secretary of State Marshall was still assuring the Arabs that the United States was maintain-

ing an open mind on the Palestine question.
The spectre of Russia winning over the Arabs,
and thus penetrating the Middle East, in case
of American unqualified support for the partition plan, became a major argument against a
Jewish State. It was the Russian decision to endorse the Zionist-backed partition that delivered a death-blow to all these arguments. In
the words of Moshe Shertok (Sharet), who led
with Silver the political struggle at the U.N.,
the Soviet move amounted to a "real miracle."
But even after this "miracle," the United
States representative, Hershel V. Johnson, stating America's support for the "majority plan
which provides for partition and immigration,"
added that the United States favors "certain
geographical modifications"—for the benefit of
the Arab part. Among these modifications, the
most dangerous was the attempt to sever the
Negev from the territory of the Jewish State.
The Emergency Council went immediately into
action. All local Emergency Councils had been
advised to flood President Truman and Acting
Secretary of State Robert A. Lovett with cables
which read:

We are distressed to learn that the United
States delegation to the United Nations is
pressing for exclusion of the large and important area of Negev from the Jewish State,
contrary to UNSCOP majority recommendations which our Government has endorsed.
Such revision would sharply reduce Jewish
area, thus curtailing ability of Jewish State
to absorb immigrants. It would also reduce
the possibility for future economic development and render the Jewish State inviable.
We must protest most vigorously against this
unwarranted stand by U.S. delegation, which
is particularly shocking in view of the fact
that it follows our Government's forthright
support of UNSCOP majority plan which
evoked general praise and satisfaction. Fur-
thermore, the present United States position
endangers the unity which has thus far prevailed in United Nations on Palestine issue.
We appeal to you to intervene immediately
so that this injustice shall not be done.

The Negev issue was also the subject of a
last-minute intervention by Dr. Weitzman. The
story of this meeting by itself adds a new dimension to the many forms of American Jewish
partnership in the struggle for Jewish Statehood. Only after a most earnest conversation,
between President Truman and his friend,
erstwhile business partner, Eddie Jacobson, had
the President agreed to talk to Dr. Weitzman,
who received a promise that the American dele-

General view of hall at dinner marking Soviet support
for Jewish State.

Monster demonstration in support of Israel, in New York,
during 1967 crisis. Over 200,000 people participated in this
demonstration.

Pittsburgh delegation attending Israel Emergency Meeting in Washington June 7, 1967, with Congressmen James G. Fulton and William S. Moorhead.

gation to the United Nations will, after all, be instructed to vote for a Jewish Negev.

The weeks which followed became a most dramatic exercise in Zionist leadership, in American tactics of political pressure and of utilization of each and every avenue of public opinion that could have influenced the White House. The members of the American Section of the Jewish Agency, the Zionist Emergency Council, and all the affiliates the Council succeeded to organize, were busy in promoting the Zionist cause. They were aware that even if American support for the majority UNSCOP Report were assured without reservation, this would not result in a qualified, two-thirds majority of the U.N. General Assembly necessary for winning international backing for the establishment of a Jewish State, in a part of Palestine. It was necessary to have the United States Government use its good offices with members of other delegations that they be induced to cast their votes for the majority UNSCOP Report. Every stone was turned, every contact was exploited, every influence employed.

Forty-eight hours before the final vote a drama of highest tension developed with last-minute meetings, telephone calls after midnight, interventions by people who never

stated publicly their sympathy for Zionism. Justice Frankfurter, Justice Murphy, Herbert Bayard Swope, former editor of the *World*, executives of the Firestone Tire and Rubber Company, Jacob Blaustein, one of the top leaders of the American Jewish Committee, people of all walks of life, of every profession, interceded for assuring a qualified majority of two-thirds for the UNSCOP majority report at the United Nations General Assembly. This was pressure of the highest degree, perhaps not in the best tradition of diplomatic politeness, but nevertheless insistent, powerful and what was most important, decisive. American Zionists can certainly only take pride in the remarks President Truman made in his own memoirs, as sorry as they could be for the personal inconvenience, if any, they had caused the President:

The facts were that not only were there pressure movements around the United Nations unlike anything that had been seen there before, but that the White House, too, was subjected to a constant barrage. I do not think that I ever had as much pressure and propaganda addressed at the White House as I had in this instance. The persistence of a few of

Reviewing stand at pro-Israel demonstration in New York, 1967.

the extreme Zionist leaders actuated by political motives and engaging in political threats disturbed and annoyed me. . . . Some were even suggesting that we pressure sovereign nations into favorable votes in the General Assembly. . . .

Whether this was pressure unwarranted or unavoidable in a case where a people's independence struggle was at stake, is a matter of appraisal. What counted was the result: a majority of 33 against 13 voted for the majority UNSCOP Report, and thus for the establishment of a Jewish State.

There was no end to the joy. The packed halls of the United Nations, the crowds which assembled at the gates and could not get entrance, the streets of New York, were the scenes of elation people seldom experience. *Shehechyanuh*, the traditional blessing, was heard on all corners, and as witnesses recollect there was all-out embracing, dancing in the streets, joy that overflowed to capacity Jewish hearts. It was as if the longings of tens of Jewish generations were suddenly coming to fruition, and here they were throwing themselves into a burst of excitement a people can live through only once.

The man who was among the first to lead American Jewry in this struggle, Dr. Abba Hillel Silver, thus summed up the feelings of the great hour:

American Jewry has deserved well at the hands of the Jewish people. History will pay homage to the role which it played in this searching and heroic hour. It rose to the occasion splendidly. It knew how to close ranks. It acted with dignity and courage. It spoke effectively to the hearts and minds of the American people and its representatives in Government, and to the responsible heads of our Government. It is generally acknowledged that what was achieved was due in a

Baltimore Zionist Organization sponsoring petition during 1967 crisis.

large measure to the magnificent labor of American Jewry.

But while the rejoicing was still echoing in the United Nations corridors, in the synagogues, in the Zionist clubs, clouds started gathering on what seemed to be the brightest horizon in 19 centuries of Jewish martyred history. The Arabs opened the fight against the United Nations resolution with fire and destruction. The Arab war against the Jewish State began before the State was proclaimed, before it was even given a name.

In the conditions that prevailed after the partition vote, the Arab aggression appeared to pose a definite danger to what was so solemnly decided upon by a two-thirds majority of the

American members of the Jewish Agency Executive

Collectors line up at the Israel Discount Bank, Ltd. in New York City to buy the Victory Coin, issued by the Bank of Israel to commemorate the Six Day War.

highest international authority. The enemies of Jewish Statehood saw a new chance for their machinations, the British Government a hope for undoing the United Nations resolution. The State Department officials seemed to have proved what they had used as their main argument, that without the armed intervention of the United States, no chance exists for the implementation of the resolution on partition, while an international force would be bound to include Russians and open the Middle East to Communist penetration. The British saw themselves already called back to execute the authority over Palestine, this time in the name of the United Nations, with a free hand for their stated, anti-Zionist policies. The Anglo-American cooperation appeared to have been restored for sabotaging the U.N. resolution. The first practical sign of this reversal of policies was given when the American Government

Mayor Robert Wagner presents Farband proclamation to the leadership of the Farband-Labor Zionist Order on the occasion of the Farband's 50th anniversary.

imposed an arms embargo on the Middle East, ostensibly to clear the United States of any suspicion of involvement in the Middle East armed conflict. In view of the fact that the Arabs had open all channels of arms supply from Great Britain, by force of treaties which had bound Britain with Arab countries, the arms embargo had only one meaning: strangling of the *Yishuv* before it was given a chance of defending itself.

The political storm was not late in coming. Ambassador Warren R. Austin, the United States representative at the United Nations, started maneuvers which were aimed at putting the Arab aggression on the same plain as the *Yishuv's* self-defense. Dr. Emanuel Neumann and Dr. Israel Goldstein, acting chairmen of the American Zionist Emergency Council, visited Washington for interventions with Government officials. Hurrying back from Palestine where he was visiting, Dr. Silver appeared, on March 5th, 1948, before the U.N. Security Council and put the central question of the implementation of the partition resolution squarely before the body where the anti-Zionist forces hoped to neutralize it or to kill it altogether. He demanded the removal of the arms embargo

> to the Jewish people of Palestine, and urged, the organization, recognition and equipment of the Jewish militia which is of greater urgency than the sending of a non-Palestinian armed force by the Security Council. The Jews of Palestine wish first and foremost to defend themselves, but their hands must not be tied.

The forebodings on the changing American position materialized. On March 19, Ambassador Austin stated at the U.N. Security Council that in view of the impossibility to implement the partition resolution by peaceful means, the Security Council should recommend to the U.N. General Assembly:

> the establishment of a United Nations trusteeship for Palestine, while the U.N. Palestine Commission should be instructed to suspend efforts for the implementation of the proposed partition plan.

It seemed for a while that all that was achieved in long years of struggle, and the U.N. resolution on the establishment of a Jewish State in part of Palestine, were in mortal danger.

Representatives of the Jewish Agency for Palestine took up the challenge. Mr. Moshe Shertok, head of Jewish Agency Political De-

Jacob Blaustein, president of the American Jewish Committee at meeting with heads of the Israel Government which resulted in agreement on status of American Jewry.

partment, acting with Dr. Silver in representing the Jewish cause before the United Nations, rejected forcefully the Austin proposal.

Dr. Silver, who spoke also in the name of American Jewry, did not refrain from a most grave warning concerning the tragic consequences American insistence on the trusteeship scheme could bring. Speaking at the Security Council, Dr. Silver left no doubt that "it should be clear to everyone that the establishment of a trusteeship by the United Nations in Palestine will not automatically insure peace in that country, and that force will have to be used to maintain that arrangement, just as it would have been necessary, to carry out the partition decision of the United Nations." Dr. Silver added,

The Jewish Agency has repeatedly been under the necessity of stating that the partition plan represented the maximum sacrifice on the part of the Jewish people beyond which it cannot go. Any proposals calling for further sacrifices will have to be imposed upon the Jewish Community of Palestine by force. . . . If the United Nations Commission is unable to carry out the mandates

which were assigned to it by the General Assembly, the Jewish People of Palestine will move forward in the spirit of that resolution and will do everything which will be dictated by considerations of national survival, as well as the considerations of justice and historic rights.

Dr. Weitzman attacked the new U. S. statement of policy, accusing the U. S. Government of submission to Arab violence. Mr. Louis Lipsky, chairman of the Executive Committtee of the American Jewish Conference, published a statement that he "refused to believe that the Austin proposal represented the considered policy of the U. S. Government." The American Jewish Committee expressed "its keen regret at the modification of our Government's position regarding Palestine," adding that the reversal in the American policy "has resulted in a loss of international prestige by the United States and has been a blow to the United Nations."

The A.J.C. statement dwelt also on the problem of the alleged reasons which related this reversal to "security problems" of the United States. It declared that the Committee saw nothing to indicate that partition could affect ad-

Israel's Chief Rabbi I. Unterman visiting New York.

versely "the security of the United States which we, together with all American citizens, will always regard as paramount."

Frank Goldman, president of *Bnai Brith*, called the Austin statement "contrary to overwhelming American public opinion." Only the American Council for Judaism, through its president, Lessing J. Rosenwald, supported the American action because "under the circumstances the United States could take no other action." . . . Dr. Emanuel Neumann then the President of the Zionist Organization of America, warned that the Jews would not "tamely submit to any new solution" and that "overwhelming military force" will be necessary to deprive them of their independence "under the guise of trusteeship, or any other guise."

Though, formally, the battle-front was the United Nations, it was clear to everybody that the real target for bringing about a change in the American attitude was the United States Government. American Jewry had again to play the decisive role. The American Zionist Emergency Council was girding for this new activity at the moment when the decision on the arms embargo became known. On Febru-

Rabbi Eliezer Silver, Rabbi Blumenfeld, head of the Rabbinic Court in Tel-Aviv and the Boyaner Rebbe at convention of Agudath Israel.

ary 15th and 16th a conference of the Emergency Committees throughout the country assembled in Washington. Telegrams, letters. in the hundreds of thousands flooded official Washington; rallies were held throughout the country; ministers, mayors, labor, civil and veteran organizations were called to intervene. Demonstrations of unprecedented dimensions were organized in New York, Chicago, Boston, Los Angeles, and many other communities, large and small. The Jewish War Veterans occupied a central role in this mass action. A National Day of Prayer and Mobilization was held on April 8th with the cooperation of religious bodies. Special prayer services were held in thousands of synagogues and approximately one million postal cards were mailed to Washington by the worshippers. The Labor Unions extended their full support. The American Federation of Labor and the Congress of Industrial Organizations joined the campaign against the Goverment policies, and the Jewish Trade Union Council was instrumental in organizing work stoppages, often joined by employers. The American Association for the United Nations was drawn into action against the attempt to undermine a U.N. resolution, which could endanger the entire concept of the United Nations and its authority.

All these actions were excellently synchronized with the developments on the Palestine front. The Jewish Agency under Ben Gurion's leadership led the defense of the *Yishuv* and worked feverishly towards the implementation of the U.N. resolution, without regard to the machinations at the United Nations, and the Anglo-American cooperation. On the very eve of the date, set for the termination of the British Mandate over Palestine, May 14, 1948, a last-minute effort was made by the United States Government to prevent the proclamation of Jewish Statehood. The State Department suggested a new conciliatory Arab-Israel conference. Even a special plane was to be put at the disposal of Mr. Shertok to fly to Palestine and influence the Jewish Agency Executive to postpone, for some time, the final steps.

A dramatic meeting of the Jewish Agency, American Section, took place. Among the many historic problems this group had dealt with, this was to be perhaps the most fateful. The State Department's suggestion was accompanied by explicit threats. There had been hints of extending the arms embargo into a blockade, of interference with money-raising for Palestine, and there was, of course, the specter of a deep rift with a friendly power, which with all

American Jewish Committee reception for Premier Eshkol during latter's visit in the United States, 1964.

the turn-abouts had helped so much the Zionist cause.

The dramatic discussion that took place at that meeting is in itself a chapter of Zionist history and thinking. When the vote was taken, two were for complying with the request of the American Government, Moshe Shertok and Dr. Nahum Goldman, while the rest, Dr. Silver, Dr. Neumann representing the Zionist Organization of America; Mrs. Rose Halperin of Hadassah, and Rabbi Zev Gold of *Mizrahi,* voted against. Dr. Haim Greenberg, the representative of *Poale-Zion* was away on Zionist business and did not participate in the historic meeting. Whether a different decision of the American Section of the Jewish Agency would have really influenced decisively the events in Palestine, whether the Jewish Agency Execu-

tive, the *Vaad-Leumi,* the *Yishuv* already in the throes of war with the Arab aggressors and organized as a State for all practical purposes, but for the formal proclamation, would have heeded the American decision, is one of those hypothetical questions, which have no bearing on political history. But, as it was, the affirmative decision of the representatives of American Zionism, who spoke actually for American Jewry, was a most encouraging act, which gave the *Yishuv* the comforting feeling of a mighty *hinterland,* ready to stand by them through thick and thin, for better and for worse. And thus, when the United States delegation was girding itself for pressing its trusteeship proposal at a meeting at the United Nations, on May 14, at 4 P.M., the news broke that the National Council of Palestine Jewry had proclaimed a

Jewish State, to be called Israel. Within eleven minutes, this state was recognized *de facto* by the President of the United States, Harry S. Truman. The U.S. policy maneuvers at the United Nations appeared senseless.

The *Salute to Israel* demonstrations throughout the country, the largest Jewish demonstrations ever held, were not considered "victory parades" to be followed by a general demobilization. The Zionist Emergency Council knew well that its services were still to be needed. The arms embargo was still in force, Israel was facing the invading armies of six Arab states, and the needs of the immigration that started flowing through the open gates of the Jewish State were staggering. Soon was added another reason for the continuation of Zionist alertness and wide-flung emergency activities. The appointment of the United Nations mediator indicated clearly that the solution of the Palestine problem in the form of the U. N. Palestine partition resolution was not yet the last word in the political fortunes of Palestine. And when the mediator, Count Folke Bernadotte, submitted his "mediation" report, nobody could doubt anymore that "mediation" was another way of undoing the U.N. resolution after the trusteeship device had failed.

The outstanding features of the Bernadotte plan, the severance of the Negev from the Jewish State and the incorporation of Jerusalem into the Arab part of Palestine, were indicative of the general tenor and aim of that report.

The struggle had to start all over. It should be said to the credit of the American Zionist Council, of the masses of the Jews in America, that they did not hesitate to seize upon the special political conditions prevailing in America. Nineteen forty-eight was a presidential election year. The principle of bi-partisanship, in efforts for securing American support for the Zionist cause, renewed by Dr. Silver, was already an indisputable precept of Zionist policy. Pledges of support for the territorial integrity of Israel and of economic aid were included in the election planks of both major political parties, the Democratic and the Republican alike.

In the midst of these political activities the Council was suddenly faced with an emergency situation: the assassination of Count Bernadotte opened all the floodgates of anti-Zionism. The young state was in danger of being castigated as a "nest of assassins." The Council sprang into action. It took up the challenge. A devastating analysis of the Bernadotte report was published, and was widely circulated. Full-page advertisements (one of the innovations in involving public opinion, the initiation of which was claimed by a recurring practitioner in the use of this instrument, the Hebrew Committtee of National Liberation) were published in leading papers throughout the country. The title of that advertisement, *Another Reversal -- Another Betrayal*, spoke for itself. A memorandum of the Israeli Delegation to the United Nations, "Importance of the Negev to the State of Israel," received nation-wide circulation.

Zionist veterans of 40 year standing meet at Zionist Organization of America, 1946, Convention.

B'NAI B'RITH CONVENTION IN ISRAEL

M. Sidney Hellenbrand, Vice-President, in the chair at the opening of the B'nai B'rith Convention. On his left: Mr. Label Katz, the retiring International President, Chief Rabbi Unterman and Dr. Dov Joseph, the Minister of Justice. On his right: Mr. Philip M. Klutznick, the Hon. President; Mrs. A. Rosenblum, President of B'nai B'rith Women; Mr. Mordecai Ish-Shalom, Mayor of Jerusalem; Dr. Y. Mazur, President of the Israel District of B'nai B'rith; Mr. Igal Allon, the Minister of Labor; Mr. Billy B. Goldberg, member of the Board of Governors; and Mr. Aryeh Pincus, Treasurer of the Jewish Agency.

The victorious battles of Israel's Army, the decisive factor in all developments, were well supported by the American Jewish political and practical assistance. The on-and-off military operations, when Israel fought off successfully the Arab onslaught, substantiated American Zionist assertions that the Jewish State would not need, for its survival, foreign military assistance. The warnings of the anti-Zionists in the State Department that there was danger of a worldwide conflagration to be caused by war actions in Palestine proved baseless. Thus the pressure for *de iure* recognition of Israel by the United States, and the admittance of Israel to the United Nations were only a logical sequence. It appeared that there was no more need for emergency action in behalf of Israel, and of course, no more need for the great apparatus which the American Zionist Emergency Council had built over the decade of its existence. The American Zionists were filled with pride of the role they fulfilled in the final, decisive stage of the struggle for the realization of a centuries-old dream, the dream of sixty generations of a martyred people. They seemed to have anticipated the dispute that was to develop concerning the importance and decisiveness of the political struggle they had led, as against the military struggle of the Yishuv that was so magnificently victorious. A Zionist leader tried to resolve this dispute in the following words:

Israel reborn has indicated its right to nationhood by the incredible valor of its sons, by their self-immolation and their prowess on the field of battle. Without their military triumphs, the political victory would have been fruitless and evanescent. But without the political victory and the moral sanction of the world which it conferred, Israel's War of Independence would never have been fought and won.

Unfortunately the achievement of the basic aim of Zionism was not matched by a well-thought-over program concerning the future of the Zionist movement after its aim would have been fulfilled. It seems that the success had surpassed the expectations, that the Zionist movement was still geared for a long struggle, when it suddenly saw itself at the end of this struggle, facing a completely new situation, with new tasks thrust upon itself.

American Zionist leadership did not shirk its responsibility and began to formulate a Zionist program for the era of Jewish Statehood. Representative of this understanding of a need for a new approach was the presidential address of Dr. Neumann at the annual Convention of the Zionist Organization of America, on July 3, 1948, in Pittsburgh, Pa. Dr. Neumann posed the basic question, "What shall be the future of the World Zionist movement, its aims and activities and above all, its relationship to the Republic of Israel?" Answering this basic question, Dr. Neumann formulated the concept of political separation:

If there is a Jewish State asserting its sovereign rights, then under universally accepted rules and practices, none but the citizens of that State are entitled to speak and act on

Merger convention of Mizrachi with Hapoel Hamizrachi. Fourth from right is the Mizrachi-Hapoel Hamizrachi leader, Israel Minister of Interior Ch.M. Shapiro, at his left, Mordecai Kirschblum, member of the Jewish Agency Executive.

its behalf and represent it politically to the outside world. If that is so, then the first principle which we must accept without reservation is that of a definitive political separation between the Jews of the world and the Republic of Israel. The separation must be clean-cut and unequivocal. We must hereafter pursue a strict policy of non-intervention in the political life of Israel, a matter which now becomes the exclusive prerogative of its own citizens, both Jew and Arab -- the Israelis.

Outside the province of political separation a whole series of tasks were foreseen by American Zionist leaders for the Zionist movement: To facilitate Jewish immigration, to provide training for *Halutizm,* to assist in their successful settlement, and to help promote an economic development of Israel so that it may absorb the new immigrants most rapidly. Special attention was paid in this program to Zionism's cultural task in the Diaspora, since Zionism has had its responsibility in this field, and "there is no other organization in Jewish life which by virtue of historic development is better equipped to initiate and develop a greater movement for Jewish Hebraic revival."

Developments in the mutual relationship between American Zionism and the Israel Government brought into being problems which were, at the final analysis, to contribute to the decline of the Zionist movement in America. The removal of the Zionist leadership from positions of influence in providing funds for Israel proved in time to be the turning point in the fortunes of the American Zionist movement. With the political struggle over and with this basic task of American Jewry in supporting Israel removed from the overwhelming influence of the Zionist movement, Zionism appeared to have lost a great deal of its influence. It appeared in the eyes of American Jewry as a secondary force. This change, accomplished with the blessing of the Israel Government, delivered a serious blow to the American Zionist movement. With the centrality of Israel growing in evidence, in American Jewish life, the word coming from Israel appeared supreme law in appraising the importance, and actual relevance, of the Zionist movement.

The derisive remarks by Israel's Prime Minister David Ben-Gurion about American Zionists, followed by vehement attacks on the entire concept of Zionism, shocked American Zionist leaders. It weakened considerably the sense of belonging to the Zionist movement among the masses of American Zionists, who, only a year or two before, were almost standing in line to become members in the great fraternity of fighters for a Jewish State. Soon these measures, taken against American Zionism, were supplemented by statements of principle, for the elevation of direct cooperation of the Israel Government with non-Zionists, and non-Zionist organizations, to a status of an ideological turning point.

On August 23, 1950, Israel's Prime Minister, David Ben Gurion, published in response to a request of the president of the American Jewish Committee, Jacob Blaustein, a statement that:

the Jews of the United States, as a community and as individuals, have only one political attachment and that is to the United States of America. They own no political allegiance to Israel. . . . The Government and the people of Israel fully respect the right and integrity of the Jewish communities in other countries to develop their own mode of life and their indigenous social, economic and cultural institutions in accordance with their own needs and aspirations. Any weakening of American Jewry, and disruption of its communal life, any lowering of its status, is a definite loss to the Jews everywhere and to Israel in particular.

According to a prearranged procedure, Mr. Blaustein followed Ben Gurion's statement with a declaration of his own in which he elaborated ideological concepts of the American Jewish Committee. And though Zionists were perhaps ready to subscribe to some observations of these statements, the very fact that the American Jewish Committee was accorded the authority of a representative of American Jewry, was considered a major blow to the American Zionist movement.

In this context mention should also be made of the growing involvement of Synagogue and Rabbinical organizations in pro-Israel activities. Israel ascended in their midst to a position of centrality and growing attachment which became an integral part of their programming and day to day work.

The preponderance of American Zionism in representing American Jewry's pro-Israel sentiments had been further curtailed when a new political body was called into being for the exclusive purpose of representing these sentiments. The President's conference, in which presidents of nineteen, and subsequently, twenty-four major Jewish organizations participated, called into being by the President of the World Zionist Organization, Dr. Nahum Goldman, in 1954, substituted in fact the functions of the American Zionist Council. The fact that the Zionist Council acquiesced to become one of the major Jewish organizations, that participate in the President's Conference, was a formal admission that American Zionism was abdicating its political prerogatives as the exponent of American Jewry's interest in the security and well-being of Israel. The transforma-

ZOA 70 jubilee convention in Israel pilgrimage to the Herzl Tomb. From left: Rabbi Joseph S. Shubow, Jacques Torczyner, Abraham Goodman, Mortimer May and Leon Ilutovich.

tion of the President's Conference into the Conference of Major American Jewish Organizations implemented by its first chairman, Philip Klutznick, was a further step in reinforcing the stability and standing of this new Jewish American body in its role of main pleader on behalf of Israel. But these developments have not discouraged American Zionists. They continue to consider themselves the center and vanguard of pro-Israel sentiments in America, committed to its support without reservation, wholeheartedly.

As the situation developed, American Jewish cooperation in the upbuilding of the State of Israel was to a great extent removed from the prerogatives of the Zionist movement and became the concern of almost the entire organized American Jewry. The two basic functions in American Jewry's partnership in the development of Israel, financial support and political backing, ceased to be a monopoly of the Zionist movement. The fact that within the general American Jewish instruments in support for Israel, Zionists have played and play often a leading role did not influence much the outlook of the basic change that occurred in American Jewish-Israel partnership.

This partnership assumed new dimensions and new meaning in the days preceding the Six Day War and afterwards. The mortal danger which Israel faced at the hands of the Arab military might set for attack evoked in American Jewry emotions of unexpected intensity. American Jewry, almost without distinction of

organizational allegiance rose without reservations for the cause of Israel's safety. The outpouring of financial generosity that amounted to over 200 million dollars in one month was only one aspect of this manifestation of brotherly love. American Jews became aware that they are linked with Israel by mutual destiny as well. The demonstrations, the volunteers waiting for their turn to reach Israel, the craving for some action in defense of Israel surpassed anything known in American Jewry's decades-long involvement in the strugggle for Jewish national redemption and for the preservation of the State of Israel. Thousands, tens of thousands, perhaps hundreds of thousands of American Jews were ready to join their personal fortunes with those of their brethren in Israel, who were threatened with total annihilation.

American Jewry demonstrated that the principle of the *oneness of the Jewish people* is not a theoretical concept, but a practical category that can result in action and sacrifice. It was only a recognition of this revelation, of a political and spiritual fact, when Israel's leaders acknowledged that the attitude of American Jewry, and other Jewish communities as well, have forged new bonds between Israel and world Jewry, and proved that Israel is not alone, that it has partners in its struggle for survival.

Hadassah convention in Miami Beach-general view.

Mizrachi Women President Mrs. Agatha Leifer, second from left, presents JNF grove citation to Mrs. Pearl Plesser.

PART FIVE

14

RESOURCES FOR ISRAEL

THE PIPELINE OF FINANCIAL SUPPORT

THE POLITICAL BATTLES fought by American Zionism for the rebirth of the Jewish State have never earned the measure of renown and appreciation as have the many forms of American financial support for the cause of a Jewish Palestine. The reasons for such often unintentional misrepresentation were many: Financial generosity appeared to be a natural expression of American interest in the implementation of a national cause. The legendary "Uncle Sam" who helps everybody in need seemed to have played his role for the Zionist cause as well. It appeared only natural that the country of manifest wealth should bestow of the bounty accumulated in the hands of the Jewish community to a cause which carried, at one and the same time, the double image of charity for brethren in need, and of a national redemption movement for which almost every Jew seemed to have sentimental attachment.

Given such a broad framework of reference, financial support for Palestine, for the Jewish settlers in the land of their forefathers, was not necessarily identical with support for Zionism, for the Zionist idea in its classical, historical meaning. Viewing the history of American Jewry's financial support for Palestine from a vantage point of over half a century, one cannot avoid the conclusion, that at certain junctures in the history of the pro-Palestine efforts, financial support for the Yishuv came from circles which preferred to present their interest in the Jewish return to Zion as a purely philanthropic endeavor devoid of any national, political meaning.

It was in this non-political interest in Jewish activities for the revival of a Jewish community in Palestine that the very beginnings of American Jewish help for Jews living in Palestine, were rooted. As early as in 1759, Moses Mallon, the first "meshulach" (emissary), arrived from Palestine in the United States to collect funds for the Halukka groups. Moses Mallon was followed by Haim Isaac Karigel in 1771 and by Samuel Cohen in 1775.

The haphazard fund-raising system had soon to be replaced by an organized effort. In 1853 the North American Relief Society for Indigent Jews of Palestine was incorporated. It was soon followed by the New York Society for the Relief of the Poor in Palestine. As could have been expected, the American support was directed primarily to Jews from America who joined the Guardians of the Walls in the Holy City of Jerusalem. A contemporary chronicler stated proudly that the 485 persons who comprised the American *Kolel* were granted an income halfway adequate for decent living.

These Americans raised the flag of revolt against the conditions prevailing among the old settlers. To make sure that funds collected in America would really be put to their intended use, they organized an *"American Assemblage"* to receive these funds. And they meant business. They threatened to stop paying taxes to the City Elders of Jerusalem if the latter would not accede to their demands concerning the distribution of funds. As a consequence, a democratic election of a *Halukka* Council was forced upon the Halukka settlers, and modern forms of fund-administration were introduced. A representative of the new Council was sent to New York. How this unconventional action was viewed by the Jewish community of Jerusalem is best indicated in the name it was given in the first Hebrew newspaper, published in Jerusalem, *Havatzelet*: "The American Revolt."

But these forms of support for American Jewish settlers in Palestine were soon to be replaced by a more organized and more serious financial effort. From among the *Halukka* settlers who lived only on alms came the first group to try agricultural development of the

Americans salute Israel: Veterans of the American Jewish Legion in World War I, (*at right*), and American Veterans who fought in Israel's War of Independence, in 1948, (*at left*), parading with placards indicating their identity.

Women's dining room in the Nathan Straus Soup Kitchen in Jerusalem.

country. Together with the wave of Jewish immigrants brought by the *Bilu* movement and the Baron Rothschild colonization they changed the entire composition of the Jewish community in Palestine. Financial assistance was necessary for the beginnings of a modern Jewish educational system, for economic absorption, for the development of a national economy that could begin to dream of self-support.

In the realm of this financial support an early American philanthropist, Judah Touro, pioneered a project which had, after decades, assumed proportions of a nationwide, decisive importance. The $60,000 trust fund left by Touro provided for the building of cheap housing in Jerusalem outside the Walls of the Old City. It was a prototype of the *shikunim*, the housing projects, which became the stand-

Men's dining room in the Nathan Straus Soup Kitchen in Jerusalem.

ard form for the solution of Israel's housing problems with the establishment of the State, and the beginning of mass immigration. Pioneering in providing for the needs of Jewish settlers in Palestine, Touro's trust fund accomplished another function—it opened a new era in the history of the Jewish settlement in Jerusalem by extending its area beyond the closed confines of the ancient walls, with all the revolutionary changes that such expansion has breathed into the life of the growing, regenerating Jewish Community in Palestine.

This individual gift of Touro did not remain an exception. Marks Nathan of Chicago, Moses Alexander and Moses Vodner, both of New York, followed suit by building fifty and twenty houses each, respectively. With the building of houses went growing interest in employment possibilities and care for social problems. Nathan Straus, the well-known philanthropist, established in Jerusalem workshops for the training of unskilled persons, Bnai Brith founded a trade school in Safed, and Jacob H. Schiff donated $100,000 for a Jewish Institute for Technical Education in Haifa. A scholarship fund was established to enable several young men, sons of early settlers, to go to California to complete their agricultural training which had begun on their fathers' land in Palestine. The Agricultural Experimental Station in Athlit was established with help from America after its founder, Aaron Aarohnson, succeeded in gaining the active support of Julius Rosenwald, Nathan Straus, Jacob Schiff, and others. As in housing, this support was given with an eye for some much wider horizons in Palestine's development and American-Palestine cooperation. The United States Department of Agriculture took an eager interest in the Athlit Experimental Station. Dry farming, the development of the semi-arid regions of the Western parts of the United States, were problems similar to those faced by Palestine's agriculturists. Aarohnson's experiments with cross-fertilization of the wild wheat discovered by Aarohnson in Palestine, together with experiments in fruit plantations, were keenly followed by American experts. A Department of Agriculture publication of those days reveals that

> between the Department and the station at Athlit a system of plant exchanges has been established, probably to the advantage of both, Palestine and America.

Medical care to relieve Jewish women of Jerusalem from resorting to the English Missionary Hospital, and to look after the general health of pupils in nineteen schools in Jerusalem, was provided due to the support of benefactors in Chicago and Pittsburgh. Nathan Straus financed food distribution to needy and introduced milk stations for babies.

Thus American financial assistance was flowing to various sectors in the old Jewish Community of Palestine. Education, acquisition of practical skills, social care were helped in the initial attempts to lay foundations for a nation on its march towards redemption. So well-rounded was this effort and the American support for it, that even beginnings for some original art were not missing. The founder of the Jewish Museum and art school in Jerusalem, *Bezalel*, Boris Schatz, found in America support for his pioneering work and a market for the products of his school whose imprint of Jewish artistic creativity made them welcome decorations in leading American Jewish homes.

The outbreak of World War I made these forms of assistance to the Jewish Community in Palestine inadequate. The policies of the Turkish authorities jeopardized the very basis of existence of the close to 80,000 Jews, who lived, at that time, in Palestine. Conditions resulting directly from the war were only partially responsible for the grave economic crisis that overtook the early *Yishuv*. Doubts in the political reliability of the minorities under Turkish rule were soon replaced by direct suspicions concerning the political aims and activities of the Jews in Palestine. Mass expulsions from the country, relocation of Jews into the interior of the country, together with the disruption of normal economic activities that resulted from war conditions, put tens of thousands of Jews at the mercy of charitable assistance, that had one main source to come from, the United States.

In this hour of need and mortal danger to the existence of the Yishuv, American Jewry rose to heights of national responsibility. In the history of Zionism this was the first major intervention of American Zionists as a decisive factor in molding the forms of material partnership in the movement toward Jewish national redemption. There is certainly no exaggeration in the evaluation of this effort by one of the leading historians of the Zionist movement, Dr. Alex Bein:

> From the day the war broke out, Palestine had appealed to America for help. America was at that time the only country which, through its political and financial position, was able to save Palestine, permanently, from going under. . . . But for the Zionist Provisional Committee of America (in fact, the

Work room for unskilled labor established by the Nathan Straus Foundation in Jerusalem.

Provisional Executive Committee for General Zionist Affairs)—which never declared war on Turkey throughout the First World War—the *Yishuv* would assuredly have been destroyed.

As could have been expected, emergency action preceded an orderly, well-organized financial effort. As in the beginnings of organized Zionism in America, Chicago had set the pattern. A group of Zionists in Chicago organized a campaign under the name, "Bread for Palestine" and achieved in a one-time appeal, on the Day of Atonement, in an orthodox synagogue, an amount of $15,000. Collection of various goods followed. A Chicago Zionist, H. Levin, had put at the disposal of the campaign a large warehouse to store the donated goods. Individual donors tried to set an exam-

Interior of Soup Kitchen in Jerusalem supported by American funds.

of individual Jews in the war zone by transferring to their destination sums provided by American relatives. Within months after the outbreak of the war, the Provisional Executive Committee for General Zionist Affairs was able to state that

> there was then no international Zionist budget, the only known agency for financial support for Palestine was the American Organization.

Fortunately, the Zionists did not remain the sole agency for support of the Yishuv in Palestine. In addition to individual donors who were not necessarily members of organized Zionist groups, the American Jewish Committee manifested a deep sense of Jewish solidarity towards the Jewish Community in Palestine. The Zionists did not remain wanting in

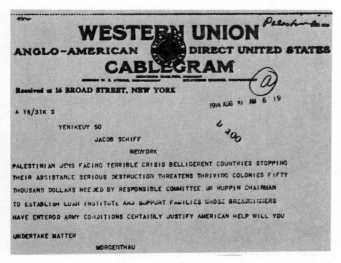

Historical cable that brought about the establishment of the Joint.

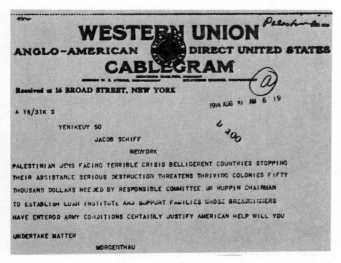

Slip of first Agency of the Jewish Colonial Trust in the U. S. at the turn of the century.

ple for giving. Julius Rosenwald subscribed a thousand dollars monthly for the duration of the war. After making such pledge in November, 1914, he followed it with another, much more substantial pledge to match ten per cent of the total amount raised in the entire country, provided this did not exceed ten million dollars.

The amount of funds needed was completely out of proportion to anything the American Zionists had achieved, or even envisaged up to that time. But it seems that the dire need of the Palestine settler goaded American Zionists into a financial effort of which they had hardly believed themselves capable. An Emergency Fund replaced sums hitherto collected in Europe, as well as in America, for the maintenance of schools in Palestine and Zionist enterprises in the colonies and cities. The establishment of the Provisional Executive Committee for General Zionist Affairs with Louis Brandeis as its head, gave new impetus to the Zionist financial effort. Up to May 31, 1915, a sum of close to $350,000 was disbursed by the Committee in Palestine.

The Emergency Fund was soon to be transferred to the Palestine Restoration Fund. The collections, which were, at first, measured in the tens of thousands, rose soon to over a million and a half. The Fund established a special service for individuals concerned with the fate

acknowledging the American Jewish Committee's share in the Palestine relief efforts. An editorial in *The Maccabean* (August, 1914), the organ of the Federation of American Zionists, gave the American Jewish Committee full credit in these words:

> In its work of relief (for Palestine) the Zionists will cooperate to the fullest extent of their powers. The American Jewish Com-

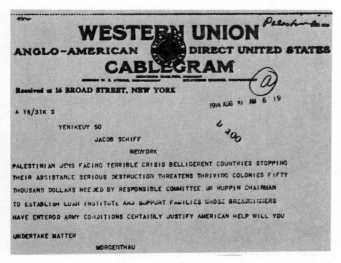

Report on Nathan Straus' work in Palestine, prepared by the U. S. Consul in Jerusalem.

mittee may not share our Zionist views, but in action it comes very close to sympathy and cooperation in our practical work. We accept its readiness to contribute to Palestine relief as an indication of its sympathy with that work, and we hope that in whatever effort it may be called upon to make, Palestine also shall be accorded equal rights.

Though this all-out, unreserved hope for wholehearted support of the Committee for Zionism's practical efforts in Palestine, was to be put, in later years, to test, the American Jewish Committee's cooperation, was, at that time, considered a most important asset in the relief work for Palestine. Indeed, the need for

relief was most urgent. Wrote *The Maccabean*:

> We must send from here coffee, tea, flour, potatoes, petroleum, rice and other staples, or the Jewish population, as well as the Arabian population, will starve.

The alarming news of this situation reached America through various sources, Zionist and non-Zionist alike. The United States ambassador in Turkey, Henry Morgenthau, alarmed that a "generation's work was menaced with extinction," and the Zionist Bureau in Haifa sent urgent calls for help for combating the danger that the achievements of Zionist work of an almost entire generation might be erased.

Founders of the Joint, (seated left to right): Felix M. Warburg, chairman, Louis Marshall, Albert Lucas, secretary, Mrs. F. Friedman official stenographer, Boris D. Bogen executive director, Leon Sanders, Harry Fischel, Sholem Asch, Alexander Kahn, Jacob Milch, Miss Harriet E. Lowenstein, Colonel Moses Schoenberg, Aaron Teitelbaum, M. Z. Margolis, Israel Friedlander, Paul Baerwald, Julius Levy, Peter Wiernik, Meyer Gillis, Harry Cutler, Cyrus Adler, Arthur Lehman, Jacob H. Schiff; Standing left to right: Herbert H. Lehman, Abraham Zucker, Isidore Herschfield, Meyer Berlin, Stanley Bero, Louis Topkis, Morris Engelman.

The first "visiting nurses", the pathbreakers for Hadassah activities in Palestine.

The dimension of the need and the increase in the numbers of needy, after economic calamity overtook the Jewish Communities in the war zones of Europe as well, resulted in a strenuous, though organizationally diffuse effort for general Jewish relief work. This emotional mass response of American Jewry to the needs of suffering Jews overseas, was, no doubt, a reflection of the general mood of the country. The relief work done for war torn areas of Western Europe under the leadership of Herbert Hoover, made the Jewish relief effort a component of the general mood of the country. As could have been expected, various groups in the Jewish Community tried to set up their own relief organizations. The orthodox groups organized the Central Relief Committee; the Jewish labor groups, including the *Poale-Zion*, called into being the People's Relief Committee; a third relief organization, mainly under the influence of the American Jewish Committee, The American Jewish Relief Committee succeeded in getting the support of the well-to-do Jewish circles and thus became the most substantial Jewish relief agency.

Fortunately, this duplication of effort was soon overcome. In November, 1914, the three relief organizations united their forces and established the American Jewish Joint Distribution Committee, the central Jewish relief agency that was destined to prevail for over half a century and to become a major lifeline that saved millions of Jews the world over from want, hunger and disease.

It would be an over-simplification to say that this unification of Jewish relief efforts in America came to pass without obstacles to overcome, and hurdles to remove. Though the initiative for uniting the relief efforts came from the Provisional Executive Committee for General Zionist Affairs, under the personal leadership of the Committee's chairman, Louis D.

Brandeis, the Zionists had to sacrifice their rights to identity of their relief work to have such unity of relief action assured. Brandeis, Lipsky and other Zionist leaders hardly foresaw that what was happening then, in the coordination of financial efforts for Palestine, would repeat itself many times in the future; that by giving up Zionist prerogatives and giving in to non-Zionist pressures, they were setting a pattern which was destined, some three decades later, to become an important factor in devising methods for providing funds for Palestine, and as a consequence, in the fortunes of the American Zionist movement. The very name of the united relief organization "Ameri-

Felix M. Warburg.

can Jewish Relief Committee" was very much opposed by the Zionists as it meant adopting the name of the American Jewish Committee for relief work conducted by the entire American Jewish community. But the Zionists, realizing the urgency for relief funds, gave in. Even the Zionist demand that the Emergency Fund, the Zionist movement, be recognized as the body responsible for the work in Palestine, met with stubborn resistance. In his appraisal of the fateful developments of those days wrote Lipsky: "Tacitly we agreed to leave the control of the American Jewish Relief Committee to the leaders of philanthropy"—and he added sadly "this was one of our earliest mistakes." The Zionist leaders were so willing to compromise that even when the *Vulcan* was sent to Palestine with food for the *Yishuv*, it did not

The first Jewish labor group in Herzliah.

fly the Zionist flag, "although the supplies have been gathered chiefly by Zionists."

The fact that the American Jewish Relief Committee had lost its identity and became part of the American Jewish Joint Distribution Committee was no consolation as, basically, the name of the American Jewish Committee was preserved in its entirety. The relative successes of the new fund together with the pressure of the relief needs muted the unpleasant awareness of what had happened. By the end of 1916 the Joint had collected six million dollars, and by the end of 1917 over ten million dollars. The news from Palestine made it clear beyond doubt that the assistance coming from American sources was more than relief, it was vir-

The beginnings of Herzliah founded by the Zion Commonwealth.

Yablonner Chassidim, followers of the Rebbe of Yablon who were supported by the Zion Commonwealth in their first steps in establishing an agricultural settlement in Palestine.

Keren Hayessod delegation to the U. S. which arrived in November, 1921. From left to right: Vladimir Jabotinsky, Nahum Sokolov, Prof. Otto Warburg, Dr. Alexander Goldstein.

tually a lifeline that saved the Yishuv from starvation. The American Consul in Jerusalem, Otis A. Glazebrook, reported in July, 1916:

All sources of assistance were stopped and replaced by the only possible remittances which are the remittances from the Joint Distribution Committee. No wonder that the disinherited ones have been looking to the American relief as their only bright star.

The American consul had exact figures concerning those in need of assistance. Out of a Jewish population, which according to Glazebrook, numbered about 82,000, only 18,000 were able to support themselves, without recourse to help from the Committees in charge of the distribution of money from America.

Management and staff of Zion Commonwealth—in center fourth from left Solomon J. Weinstein, head of the corporation in 1926. Photo taken in Jerusalem.

Support coming from the Joint was far from satisfactory from the Zionist point of view. As a relief organization, the Joint was concerned with prevention of starvation which was threatening the Jewish community of Palestine. The Zionists on the other hand were concerned not only with survival -- they were concerned with the preservation, and even, if possible, development of the Zionist institutions and enterprises which had risen in Palestine within the preceding three decades. Preparations were made for the organization of a corporation with a capital stock of one million dollars for the purpose of maintaining the Jewish settlements and for developing economic resources in Palestine on a business basis. Close attention was paid to various aspects of life of the *Yishuv* with a view to the future. Plans were drawn up for medical care that had to rid the country of malaria and thus to prepare it for absorption of new im-

Signing of agreement for the establishment of the United Jewish Appeal, November, 1938. Seated from left to right: William Rosenwald, acting for National coordinating Committee (later National Refugee Service), Rabbi Abba Hillel Silver for the United Palestine Appeal, and Rabbi Jonah B. Wise, for the Joint Distribution Committee.

THE NEW YORK TIMES, WEDNESDAY, JANUARY 11, 1939.

THREE GROUPS JOIN TO AID PERSECUTED

GOAL MAY BE $9,000,000

Plan Is Revealed at Clothing Men's Tribute to Hillman— Mayor Assails Oppressors

An unprecedented campaign for the victims of European oppression, which will unite for the first time the three major Jewish fund-raising organizations in the United States, has been decided upon and will soon be announced in detail, it was learned last night.

The decision became known at a dinner of the clothing industry to Sidney Hillman, president of the Amalgamated Clothing Workers of America, at the Hotel Commodore. It was mentioned in a telegram to Abraham Landau, the chairman, from Edward M. M. Warburg, which read:

"Regret that at last minute cannot be with you. I am sure your group realizes that it is the first in the field, since it is the first Jewish Joint Distribution Commit-

tee, the United Palestine Appeal and the National Coordinating Committee for Aid to Refugees and Emigrants Coming from Germany have unified their campaign.

"Therefore the results of your efforts tonight and in the next few weeks will set the pace for the whole campaign. We must all forget past standards of giving and realize that in the effort to raise $9,000,000 in Greater New York to meet the terrific demands that have fallen upon the shoulders of these three organizations, we are not asking for contributions but rather for the investment of money toward maintaining those standards which we, not only as Jews but as Americans, hold indispensable."

Federation to Aid Drive

Mr. Warburg was chairman of the Greater New York drive of the Joint Distribution Committee last year. The committee and the United Palestine Appeal conducted a single drive three years ago, but the experiment was not repeated and the "rivalry" between the two has frequently been discussed.

The Joint Distribution Committee conducts relief work for the persecuted in all Central and Eastern Europe. The United Palestine Appeal has been primarily concerned with the settlement of refugees from those countries. The third major group to figure in the new set-up was not the coordinating committee mentioned in the tele-

gram—it is a comparatively new body. The third participant will be the Federation for the Support of Jewish Philanthropic Societies, regarded as one of the most efficient fund-raising bodies for purely local relief in the United States.

But the federation, it was explained, will not share in the proceeds of the joint drive. They will be divided among the J. D. C., the U. P. A. and the Coordinating Committee, according to a scale to be set up. The federation will only supply the fund-raising machinery.

Leading personalities in Jewish life, including leaders who have differed on various questions, will be brought together by the great need that led to the decision to unite. Rabbi Abba Hillel Silver and Rabbi Stephen S. Wise are high in the leadership of the U. P. A., Rabbi Jonah B. Wise is national campaign chairman of the J. D. C.

Mayor Denounces Reich

Another strongly worded attack on the Hitler regime by Mayor La Guardia, a disavowal of communism by Mr. Hillman, often referred to as a "Red," and the pledging of funds by those present were other features of the dinner.

"Perhaps I have mislearned the entire lesson of history," the Mayor said, "but I am convinced that children who, under compulsion of governments, are separated from their parents, will live to see the day when that government is totally dstroyed."

The news story on the establishment of the United Jewish Appeal.

David Ben Gurion in conference with Edward M. Warburg.

Dr. Abba Hillel Silver (right) and Edward M. Warburg in demonstration of friendship at one of the UJA conferences.

migrants; and blueprints for industrial enterprises were put on the drawing boards to make a sizable immigration feasible from the point of view of the economic absorption capacities of the country.

The end of the war, the signing of the Peace Treaty, the confirmation of the Balfour Declaration produced new problems for financing and carrying out a program of building a Jewish Palestine of completely different dimensions. The problem was no longer the rescue of Palestine Jewry from starvation, but the development of the absorptive capacity of Palestine to enable it to become a haven for hundreds of thousands, of millions of Jews.

How the necessary funds should be secured became for some time the major, the central,

preoccupation of the Zionist leadership. In one of his many statements concerning the new era of redemption Palestine was facing, Brandeis tried to impress the Zionists that a successful financial effort cannot be based on the support of individuals only, be their financial resources great as they might be.

It must be the support of the million -- not of the few generous, philanthropic millionaires.

Brandeis was definitely disappointed in the degree of the American Zionist response to the calls for financial support of the Zionist constructive effort in Palestine. At the London Conference of July 1920, he gave clear expression to his disappointment.

So far as money goes, he stated, America,

Dr. Weitzmann on one day visit, on Jewish Day, at Chicago's Century of Progress Fair in 1933. At Dr. Weitzmann's **right** Meyer Weisgal, the organizer of that Jewish Day.

The contract for participation by the Jewish Palestine Pavilion in the World's Fair of 1939 in New York is signed. The signatures were affixed by Dr. Chaim Weizmann, (seated left), President of the Jewish Agency for Palestine, and Grover Whalen (seated next to Dr. Weizmann), president of the Fair corporation. Others in the photograph are: seated, left to right: Rabbi Stephen S. Wise; Mrs. Moses P. Epstein; Dr. Israel Goldstein, Chairman of the Board, Palestine Pavilion; standing: Joseph Schlossberg, Louis Lipsky, Jacob Fishman, Jacob Sincoff, Pierre Van Passen; Samuel Blitz, Mendel N. Fisher, Edward A. Norman, and Meyer W. Weisgal, Director General of the Palestine Pavilion.

including of course Canada, has in the last two and one-half years contributed the money with which Palestine has been kept going. But we have not done anything else. All that we have done practically in this time is to pay the living expenses of the administration. And we have done it with very great difficulty.

This difficulty had to be removed by all means if the Zionist movement had to seize on the opportunity afforded by the political victory it had achieved. The *Keren Hayessod,*

the Foundation Fund, had to be the answer. It had to put the support for Zionist work in Palestine on a basis completely different from everything Zionists, and for that matter Jews, in general, were used to. Millions, tens of millions, were a necessity -- and they had to come within the brief period of a few years, if they had to help in quickening the pace of the Zionists' upbuilding work in Palestine, which appeared as the most important step for exploiting the opportunities created by the Balfour Declaration.

Representatives to the U. S. Occupational Forces in Germany sign agreement with representatives of the Joint and the DP's on American assistance to the remnants of European Jewry clamoring to emigrate to Palestine.

In the terms of those days -- the plans were grandiose. The initiators and planners of *Keren Hayessod* spoke about an amount of *L* 25 million, that amounted, at the time, to $100 million, to be collected within five years. To raise such sums they envisaged a general taxation of Jews the world over, a general payment of a tenth of the annual income, the revival of our ancient tithe.

It is clear that American Jewry was considered the primary source of such funds. Such hopes were dictated not only by the economic destruction of the major Jewish centers in Europe, they were based on the affluence of the American society, and American Jewry within it. It is hard to judge, from the perspective of almost half a century, whether unity in Zionist ranks would have assured success for the initial plans of *Keren Hayessod*, the Palestine Foundation Fund. The figures achieved were far from encouraging, anyway, from the point of view of the needs and

President Eisenhower admires ancient Israel clay lamp presented by William Rosenwald, General Chairman of the UJA, 1955-57, in appreciation of his compassionate treatment of Jewish D. P. while Allied Supreme Commander. Next to the President Rabbi Herbert A. Friedman, UJA Executive Vice-chairman.

expectations. Though enormous when compared with everything achieved, in this field, in previous years when the accomplishments of the Keren Hayessod were almost beyond comprehension, they failed to supply the funds necessary for a grand-scale Zionist reconstruction program in Palestine. The political situation in Palestine dictated speed, as speed was of vital essence in view of the gathering anti-Zionist clouds on the Palestine political horizon.

The three and a half million pledged in the first year since *Keren Hayessod* was established in America in June, 1921, were certainly a most glorious accomplishment for those who stood at the helms of *Keren Hayessod*, S. Untermeyer its president, Emanuel Neumann its first national director, Louis Lipsky, the head of the Zionist Organization, and Meyer Weisgal, who as editor of the New Palestine was most effective in the promotion of Keren Hayessod affairs. But still it was far from what was needed, if not actually expected.

The President of the World Zionist Organization, Dr. Haim Weitzman who was shuttling between the two continents for the annual Keren Hayessod campaigns, did not change, basically, the tempo and dimensions of giving. It is again immaterial, from the point of view of reviewing the factual history of American Jewish contribution for the rebuilding of a Jewish Palestine, whether the adoption of some of Brandeis' ideas concerning the financing of the Zionist work would have accelerated and raised the standards of giving and thus supplied greater funds for Zionist work. The fact remains that world Jewry missed the historical hour, and American Jewry with all its fabulous generosity did not, essentially, do much better.

The collection for Palestine work during one month equaled to rather less than two cents per Jew in the United States, the *Jewish Day* stated wrily.

Such appraisal of American Jewry's financial contribution to Zionist work in Palestine was not an opinion popularly acknowledged. Compared with the response of Jewish Communities in other countries, American Jewish contributions stood out as an example of unprecedented generosity, of which American Zionist leaders were proud. In fact, in the light of the staggering need, these amounts, small as they were, had become the main source of sustenance of the Zionist work in Palestine. In the overall Zionist budget the funds supplied by America represented well over fifty per cent of the income from the entire Zionist movement, and at times as much as seventy per cent of the general income of Keren Hayessod.

Raising the degree of generosity was not the sole problem of the American *Keren Hayessod* leadership, and for that purpose, of the leadership of American Zionism. *Keren Hayessod* was by no means the sole agency for mobilizing American Jewry's financial support for Zionist reconstruction work in Palestine. *Keren Kayemeth* -- the Jewish National Fund, was already well established when the Foundation Fund appealed, for the first time, for the support of American Jewry. In addition, the J.N.F., the Hebrew University and *Mizrahi* were conducting separate campaigns for their specific projects. Unification of these campaigns under one overall agency, with, in advance approved, percentages in the income of the united campaign, seemed to be the best solution. Irrrespectively of this division, the financial support for Zionist causes was threatened by a diversion, which only a new vision of Zionist unity and goals was able to overcome. In this spirit, and in these circumstances, the United Palestine Appeal was established in 1925. Dr. Emanuel Neumann took upon himself the practical leadership of

Planning the establishment of the Weitzmann Institute of Science, Members of the Scientific Planning Committee with Meyer Weisgal, Herman Mark, David Rittenberg, Chaim L. Pekerski, Joseph Cohn and others.

the U.P.A. as chairman of the Executive, after he succeeded in persuading Dr. Stephen Wise to accept the general chairmanship, and thus brought back to active Zionist work one of the acknowledged top leaders of American Zionism, who preserved a kind of a self-exile from the Zionist Organization of America after siding with Brandeis in the 1921 Weitzman-Brandeis rift. But even with this closing of the ranks, the overall goal for the year 1925-1926

The Founders Dinner for the Weitzmann Institute of Science, November 27, 1945. Dr. Weitzmann and leaders of science throughout the country participated.

Dr. Joseph Schwartz, Henry Morgenthau, Jr. and Henry Montor—the three responsible for the unprecedented upsurge in collection of funds for Israel.

Great moment in the history of the United Jewish Appeal: in December 1945 representatives of America's Jewish Communities met at Atlantic City to endorse the proposal of the UJA executive vice-chairman Henry Montor, to raise $100 million for the newly liberated Jews of Europe and their settlement in Palestine. The $100 million goal, the first ever adopted by American Jewry, was surpassed as American Jews responded quickly and most generously.

Shown in the photo is Joint Distribution Committee chairman Paul Baerwald speaking in favor of the proposal. Other noted leaders on the platform include William Rosenwald of the National Refugee Service, Rabbi Jonah B. Wise, UJA National Chairman, Edward M. Warburg of the Joint Distribution Committee, Rabbi James G. Heller, UJA National Chairman representing the United Israel Appeal, Dr. Abraham Granot of Israel, Chairman of the Jewish National Fund, Edwin S. Rosenberg representing New York UJA, Rabbi Stephen S. Wise and Judge Morris Rothenberg of the United Israel Appeal.

— 15 —

Regenfallrohr	Rain-water Pipe	מרזב
Verbindungsstelle	Joint	משק
Wulst [Blei Wulst]	Wiped Joint	משק ארוח
Messing	Brass	נחשת קלל
Setzung	Settling	נחותה
Werg	Picked Oakum	נעורת
Zweig	Branch	סעיף
	Vent Branch	סעיף אויר
	Waste Branch	סעיף דלוחים
	Soil Branch	סעיף שופכים
Waschbecken	Laundry Tray	עריבת כביסה
Verstemmt	Calked	סתום
Pissoir becken	Urinal	עביט
Pissoir stand	Urinal Stall	עביט עמוד
Revisionsoffnung	Inspection Eye	עין בודקה
Gezogenes Blei	Drawn Lead	עופרת משוכה *
Stöpsel	Plug	פקק
Shraubstöpsel	Screw plug	פקק בורגי
Selbstreinigung	Scouring action	פעולת התנקות
Oberlicht	Skylight	צוהר
Luftungsrohr	Vent Stack	צנור אויר
Canalizationsrohr	Sewer Pipe	צנור ביוב
	Waste Stack	צנור דלוחים
Überlaüf	Overflow Pipe	צנור הגלישה
Schlanglrohr	Pipe Coil	צנור סליל
	Soil Stack	צנור שופכים
Fördermenge	Capacity of Pipe	קבול הצנור
Küchenausgüss	Kitchen Sink	קערת מטבח
	Flanged end	קצה אגפי
Rohrverbindung	Service Connection	קשור שרות *
Lüftung	Ventilation	אוורור, רווח
Lüften	To ventilate	רוח, אורר
Lüfter	Ventilator	רוחן, אוורורה
Löthen	To solder	רתך
Muffe	Socket, Bell, Hub.	שקע

Page from dictionary of technical terms for sewage building purposes prepared for the first all-Jewish city, Tel-Aviv, by American engineer Philip Thau. Dictionary was mimeographed.

אויפרוף

צו די

אידישע ארבייטער און פאָלקס מאַסען פון אַמעריקא

פון דעם

געווערקשאַפטען קאַמפיין קאָמיטעט

פאר די

ארגאַניזירטע אידישע ארבייטער פון פאַלעסטינא

United Hebrew Trades Drive

FOR THE

Organized Jewish Workers of Palestine

175 East Broadway, New York

MAX PINE, Chairman MAX ZUCKERMAN, Treasurer

First appeal of American Jewish organized labor for support of Histadruth.

President Truman receives UJA delegation of Hon. Herbert H. Lehman, Mrs. David Rosenwald Levy, Chairman of the National UJA Women's Division and Henry Morgenthau, Jr. UJA General Chairman who came to express thanks of American Jewry for U. S. help in D. P. crisis.

was set at no more than $5-million, an indication that the sights of giving were not set in those days, too high.

This goal, though modest, at least by today's standards, was faced with serious obstacles. Colonization of Palestine and support for the *Yishuv* were exposed to a competitive undertaking. The Soviet scheme for settling Russian Jews in the Crimea attracted a most surprising array of forces. And though the official language of the Crimea plan enthusiasts carefully avoided drawing any conclusions as to the continuous validity of the Palestine colonization, there was no secret that many non-Zionists seized upon the Crimea plan more out

of ingrained opposition to Zionism than due to a belief that the Crimea plan would indeed solve problems of Russian Jewry. So great was this desire to harm Zionism financially and ideologically, that even the fact that the support for the Crimea plan meant indirect strengthening of the Communist regime, did not hold back some foresworn capitalists of the Jewish faith from supporting the Crimea plan.

It seems that even with the support of the many of the Jewish philanthropists, the enthusiasts of the Crimea plan could not have ignored the appeal of the Zionist idea in the wide circles of the American Jewish community. The Philadelphia conference on

David Ben Gurion presents to President Truman an antique bronze Menorah in honor of Truman's sixty seventh birthday.

Crimea, held in the year in which the United Palestine Appeal was organized, did not fail to resolve that

it regards it as self-evident that American Jewry whenever called upon is prepared generously to support the work of Jewish resettlement in Palestine. It is persuaded that through the Jewish Agency and other instruments, the Jews of America will always give adequately and generously of their strength and substance to the performance of this great and historic task.

The fact that the Crimea plan appeared at the very time when the hopes for the inclusion of American non-Zionists in the extended Jewish Agency ran very high, prevented a serious flare-up of the controversy between Zionists and the non-Zionists. Many of the most influential among the latter, actually favored the Crimea plan while continuing to profess interest in supporting practical work in Palestine. Under Dr. Weitzman's prodding, negotiations for an agreement on a joint fund-

Leaders of American voluntary overseas agencies honored President John F. Kennedy for his "vigorous championship of constructive assistance to the needy abroad", at a White House ceremony. An illuminated scroll was presented by Rabbi Herbert A. Friedman, Executive Vice Chairman of the UJA in behalf of the Catholic Relief Services, Church World Service, United Jewish Appeal, American Friends Service Committee, CARE, Lutheran World Relief and the American Council of Voluntary Agencies for Foreign Service. Joseph Meyerhoff, United Jewish Appeal General Chairman, is seen standing behind the scroll with leaders of other agencies.

raising effort were conducted continuously. In 1930 these negotiations were concluded with an agreement by which the Allied Jewish Campaign was established.

The goal set for the A.J.C. (Allied Jewish Campaign) appears today rather modest, but by the standards of the thirties, six million dollars, for the year 1930, appeared a considerable amount. The Zionists' agreement to a division of the income from the campaign indicated an unusual desire for a united Jewish financial effort. In spite of the fact that the Palestine

Emergency Fund, proclaimed in the aftermath of the August, 1929, anti-Jewish Arab disturbances, brought within weeks $2,600,000, the Zionists agreed to a division of the six million dollars at a ratio of $2.5 million for Palestine, and $3.5 million for Jewish relief purposes outside Palestine. Felix M. Warburg, who served as chairman of the Allied Jewish Campaign gave expression to the prevailing sentiments by stating:

Blending of effort for our people in Eastern Europe and for the promotion of the program of the Jewish Agency for Palestine will bring a measure of harmony and cooperation which will serve not only these two great causes, but which will lead toward a lasting and permanent unity in American-Jewish efforts.

The Zionist consent for such joint fund-raising effort was dictated mostly by political considerations. The world Zionist leadership was interested in manifesting Jewish unity in support of the Jewish Agency, even if this had to be achieved at the expense of financial sacrifices. But the hoped for salutary results of such united fund-raising were slow in coming. The unity of purpose was rather lagging on each level of the united campaign. In a campaign letter sent to the workers of the Allied Jewish Campaign, Palestine was completely omitted and many other instances of conduct by some leading non-Zionist gave ample proof that the unity of purpose was rather a myth of which Zionist interests were the first and foremost victim. For Zionists the unity of financial action became an illusion. They had to draw conclusions. The

Allied Jewish Campaign ceased to exist. In explaining the initiation of a separate campaign, the Joint Distribution Committee used arguments diametrically opposed to those which had to affirm the wisdom, national merits and financial advantages of a united campaign. One of these statements asserted that one of the advantages of separate campaigns was that both the Joint Distribution Committee and the American Palestine Campaign would be free to intensify their special appeals and could enlist in their particular efforts additional supporters for their respective programs.

This organizational bickering and financial controversies as well as the striving for fund-raising unity were not a passing phenomenon. Once the attempt for united fund-raising was made, the leading forces in Jewish giving tried time and again to find a common denominator which would permit the renewal of cooperation. The real reason behind these efforts was mainly financial as both sides, Zionists and non-Zionists, could hardly register results which they would consider satisfying.

Young UJA leaders fly on study mission to Israel.

Mrs. Rose Halprin, Chairman of the Jewish Agency—American Section, receives testimonial from Monroe Goldwater, New York UJA Chairman, in tribute for Agency's Program in Israel, on occasion of its 35th anniversary.

In the period between October 1, 1925 and May 31, 1930, the United Palestine Appeal registered an income of over twelve million dollars out of which close to $9 million were remitted to Palestine. At one time, in 1934-35, a joint drive of the J. D. C. and the Jewish Agency brought less than two million dollars. The reasons were obvious -- the economic slump which enveloped the United States in the thirties made fund-raising a most arduous undertaking. The ideological differences between the Joint Distribution Committee and the United Palestine Appeal concerning the relative priority of helping needy Jews in the countries of their residence, as against stimulating emigration to Palestine, were present even in the days of cooperation between the two fund raising institutions.

Food articles ready for shipment to Israel, immediately after the establishment of the State.

The UJA campaign slogan in 1957 displayed at luncheon meeting of the Appeal.

October 1957 UJA Study Mission at meeting with members of Israel's Government. Morris W. Berinstein, General Chairman of UJA addresses meeting.

The advent of Nazism and the initial conquests of foreign territories by Germany have created a completely new situation for the agencies collecting funds for overseas needs. Even non-Zionists had to acknowledge the leading role of Palestine as a haven for the persecuted Jews of Central and East Europe. But at the same time circumstances had also complicated the fund-raising problem as a need arose to assist Jewish refugees from Europe who started flowing into America as well. The United Service for New Americans (U.S.N.A.) and the New York Association for New Americans (N.Y.A.N.A.) became new pretenders to a share in the receipts of charitable collections. The Council of Jewish Federations and Welfare Funds, responsible for fund-raising in the respective communities, came under pressure of its constituents who demanded a coordination of efforts between the United Palestine Appeal and the Joint Distribution Committee. William Shroder, President of the Council, in 1939 expressed this growing desire for fund-raising unity in the following words:

This request (for a fair agreement) was based on a desire to avoid friction arising from competition for funds in welfare fund cities . . . this request was based (even more) on the belief that a fair agreement would produce maximum giving.

The Zionists, the United Palestine Appeal, had to abide with the desire of the Jewish community. The initiated negotiations resulted in an agreement exceeding the mere setting of the percentage ratio in the distribution of funds. The United Jewish Appeal, the name adopted for the joint fund-raising campaign, established a unified procedure of campaigning, a co-ordinated organizational set-up, and laid the foundations for what had to become a most potent instrument of a united American Jewish financial effort for all the needs of Jewish national and philanthropic tasks. The agreement which established the United Jewish Appeal was signed by William Rosenwald, representing the National Coordinating Committee for Aid to Refugees and Emigrants coming from Germany, Rabbi Abba Hillel Silver representing the United Palestine Appeal and Rabbi Jonah B. Wise, representing the American Jewish Joint Distribution Committee.

With the will of the community implemented, the many differences inherent in the basic philosophies of the partners on the

First University Students Study Mission of the United Jewish Appeal before leaving for two months survey of Jewish life in Europe and Israel. Mission members came from 18 different communities and represented 21 colleges and universities.

The late Mrs. Adele Rosenwald-Levy who organized the Women's Division of the UJA in 1946 and served as its first chairman.

new financial structure were not removed. Only one year after the signing of the agreement, the united appeal became disunited. The seesaw changes in the mutual relationship between the U.P.A. and the J.D.C. persisted. Only in 1945, after six years of an uneasy cooperation that was terminated several times, did the U.J.A. achieve stability, though the basic principle of renegotiating the agreement each year persisted for another eight years, until 1953, when the agreement was concluded, for the first time, for five years.

Many factors contributed to the firming up of the U.J.A. structure. These had to be found not only in the growing pressure of the Council of Jewish Federations and Welfare Boards, the growing needs of overseas Jewish communities, the rising fervor of national commitment to the needs of Palestine, but also in the American Government's action which established the President's War Relief Control Board. The united fund-raising heralded a revolution in American Jewish awareness of its Jewish obligations, that remained unique in the history of Jewish communities and of voluntary giving in general. And though many important Jewish leaders considered and still consider this volume of contributing inadequate, as compared with the measure of affluence of the American Jewish community, it has broken all precedences as far as the overall gross amount collected and the number of contributors were concerned.

Meeting for the proclamation of the Israel Emergency Fund, 1967: In first row, from left: Edward Ginsberg, UJA Associate General chairman, Aryeh Pincus, Chairman of Jewish Agency Executive in Jerusalem, Max Fisher, UJA General chairman, Pinhas Sapir, Israel's Finance Minister, Rabbi Herbert A. Friedman, UJA Executive Vice-Chairman, standing between Mr. Fisher and Sapir—Dewey Stone, Chairman United Israel Appeal.

Knocked down sign, pierced by Syrian bullets, at the entrance to kibbutz Gadot, one of the main targets of Syrian guns on the Golan Heights. As many other such signs at new settlements this too marks that the settlement was built with the assistance of the United Jewish Appeal-United Israel Appeal.

Rabbi Herbert A. Friedman, UJA executive Vice-Chairman (first at left), Edward Ginsberg, of Cleveland, Associate General Chairman of UJA (Mr. Ginsberg was since elected General Chairman) (at right) Leonard D. Bell, Chairman Young Leadership pointing at map at one of their stops on their study mission during June, 1967, crisis.

From close to $35 million in 1945, collected through the Welfare Funds, this amount rose to $135,564,000 in 1948. This unparalleled increase in the funds raised has vindicated the contention of the Zionist partners in the united fund-raising, that it was Palestine, Zionist efforts for an independent Jewish State, that had the maximum appeal to American Jews and were the most potent factor in stirring their hearts and in opening their purses. Such development was important not only from the point of view of general contributing for the rising needs overseas. It was most important in resolving the never ending dispute to what percentage in the moneys raised through

the welfare funds, through the United Jewish Appeal, was the United Palestine Appeal entitled for the needs of Jewish Palestine.

The 1948 emotion-packed statement of the General Chairman of the U.J.A., Henry Morgenthau, that the Jewish communities in America must wait with their local needs and acknowledge the preference of the pressing needs abroad, of the new State of Israel, and the hundreds of thousands of immigrants flocking to its shores, was well based on the general moods of the Jewish donors. Morgenthau knew well that he was speaking the mind of those donors, big and small, who understood that they had to forego, for the

Mass rally for the Israel Emergency Fund in Cleveland.

time being, the local needs for hospitals, centers, building development and various civic affairs, for the benefit of Israel. It was the appeal of the Israeli cause that made people double and triple their gifts to the U.J.A. with the obvious intent that the greater part of this revenue be allocated for the needs of the U.P.A., which was renamed the United Israel Appeal.

The obvious victory of the Zionist sentiment in the field of financial support for Zionist goals did not prevent a development that opened a completely new era in direct involvement of organized Zionism and Zionist prerogatives within the framework of the United Jewish Appeal. Paradoxically, the very success of the Zionist movement in attracting almost the entire American Jewish Community to the cause of Zionist realization in Palestine, gave rise to a contention that this general pro-Israel sympathy should find its expression in an organization of pro-Israel support that would be wider than the one represented by the organized Zionist movement.

The fact that the United Palestine Appeal was under the control of the Zionist movement, and especially since 1927 of the Zionist Organization of America, became the prime target of attack. In October 1948, a statement was published in the name of

80 Jewish Community Leaders representing over 30 major welfare funds, who constituted themselves as the Committee of Contributors and Workers of the U.P.A. and resolved to,

a) reorganize the United Palestine Appeal as a self-governing body with full power of action over disbursements in the U.S., and with the Jewish Agency in Jerusalem retaining full control of expenditures in Israel;

b) give the Welfare Funds a fifty percent representation on the reconstituted United Palestine Appeal.

The other parts of that statement left no doubt that this was an attempt to wrest from the Zionist movement, primarily from the Z.O.A., the control of the funds collected in America for the needs in Israel. The clear-cut support of the Israel Government given to this "palace revolution," the reluctance of the Z.O.A. leadership to contend the wishes of the Israel Government and the partly tacit and partly open support of this change by other Zionist groups prejudiced the outcome of this contest. Fund-raising for Israel ceased to be a Zionist affair. With this change the American Zionist movement reached a turning point in its fortunes. For the second time in its history, after over three decades, the Zionist movement gave up its title of provider for the needs of the reconstruction work in Israel. Together with the changes in the construction, standing, and functions of the Zionist movement which the establishment of the State made unavoidable, relinquishing the control over funds was bound to relegate the Zionist movement from its position of strength and independence into that of a partner whose fortunes were determined in a center that was not always

Hulah marshes under cultivation after they were drained by the Jewish National Fund.

especially friendly and cooperative, the State of Israel and its government.

There is no doubt that Zionist leadership bore, at least partly, responsibility for these developments. Organized Zionists failed to penetrate the Welfare Funds, and what was even worse, they failed to give those active in the Welfare Funds the feeling of partnership in the realization of Zionist goals. Speaking at the World Zionist Congress in 1951, Rudolph Sonnenborn, at that time national chairman of the United Palestine Appeal, warned of the consequences of such Zionist policy:

While the bulk of our money comes from

Mr. Joseph Soldinger, 82, Mrs. Jennie Witt, 82, and Mrs. Emma Wertheimer, 72, residents at Drexel Home, a Jewish Federation institution for the aged, hand over a check for $1,100 collected at the institution. Accepting the check is James P. Rice (right), executive director of the Combined Jewish Appeal and the Jewish Federation of Metropolitan Chicago.

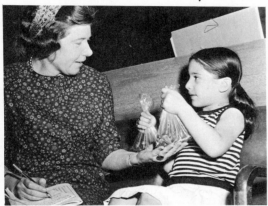

Dorothy S. Byrd, a reporter for the Evening Bulletin, chats with seven-year-old Amy Wolgin, daughter of Mr. and Mrs. Norman Wolgin, who turned in two large bags filled with pennies for the Israel Emergency Fund.

Welfare Funds we continue to abuse them and reject them. If we Zionists are not among the top leadership of the Welfare Funds we alone are to blame because in our preoccupation with other matters we have not given time and energy, not taken our rightful place in the development of these Welfare Funds.

How best to organize the mutual relationship between the U.J.A. on one side and the United Israel Appeal with the recipient of these funds, the Jewish Agency on the other, continued to preoccupy Zionist and general

Donors for the Israle Emergency Fund in Philadelphia wait in line to give their share in support of Israel, at the front desk at the offices of the Federation of Jewish Agencies.

American Jewish leadership for over a decade and a half. Legal entities have been initiated and disbanded. The year 1966 marked the most recent phase in this development. The Jewish Agency for Israel, Inc., and the United Israel Appeal merged into "an overall Israel philanthropic group" to be known as United Israel Appeal, Inc. The list of speakers at the meeting marking this occasion symbolized the measure of unity American Jewry has achieved in its assistance for Israel. In included: Mrs. Rose Halprin, chairman of the Jewish Agency, American Section, Dewey D. Stone, chairman of the United Israel Appeal, Inc., Dr. Emanuel Neumann, member of the Jewish Agency

At the 1950 Jerusalem Conference at which the Israel Bond drive was planned.

Ships of the fledgling Israel Navy visit the United States to dramatize the inauguration of the Israel Bond drive.

Parade up lower Broadway for Prime Minister Ben Gurion in May, 1951, when he came to launch the Israel Bond drive.

Executive, Rabbi Herbert A. Friedman, executive vice-chairman of the United Jewish Appeal and Irving Kane, chairman of the Overseas Committee of the Council of Jewish Federations and Welfare Funds.

The philanthropic instruments for providing funds for the upbuilding of the State, absorption of the masses of immigrants and development of Israel's economy proved insufficient. The first year of Israel's existence proved that the staggering task of building a nation could no longer rely on U.J.A. support alone. New forms had to be found for financing the reconstruction of the State. Philanthropy appeared no longer adequate for the new dimensions of the state-building tasks. Again a new leaf had to be taken out from the legacy of the immortal Herzl. The great idea of a national loan became a living reality.

Conceived and proclaimed by Israel's Prime Minister David Ben-Gurion, it was put before the scrutinizing eyes and minds of American Jewry. Nobody even pretended that American Jewry would be only one of the partners in the great scheme of a national loan. It was clear and it was so stated, that American Jewry is the prime, central, and decisive component of such undertaking. And this time, the entire American Jewish community was to become directly involved in the organizational and financial developments of this effort. A conference convened in Jerusalem brought together Zionists and non-Zionists for a serious consideration of the ways and means that could provide Israel with the billion dollars, the minimum estimated amount, for assuring a planned development of the new State. The fifty American Jewish leaders assembled in Jerusalem, in the summer of 1950, adopted a decision to accept the challenge of the Israeli Government. The one billion dollars had to come from four sources: philanthropy, loans, private investments and American Government aid.

The pace of implementation of the new program was rather swift. Seven weeks after the Jerusalem Conference, an Inaugural National Planning Conference for Israel and Jewish Rehabilitation was assembled in Washington. 1,102 delegates were on hand. The most representative communal and organizational assemblage in American Jewish history came into being. Each and every community and every organization wanted to participate in the steering committee. And though a 280 persons-strong committee could have had hardly pretended to really be able to steer, the goal was set in advance and the enthusiasm seemed to be waiting for exploitation. The practical results seemed to have fallen short of expectations: fifty million dollars in emergency cash and five million dollars in community checks which were donated at the monster banquet in the National Guard Armory, were no doubt a most encouraging demonstration of the strength of Israel's appeal, but were not a demonstration of promise for the future of sales of the Israel Bonds. The fact that this was really a loan, an interest paying bond, did not penetrate easily the minds of the American Jewish Community. In general terms, the Israel Bonds were considered a new form of fund-raising. Many saw in it a new fund-raising device, a kind of a "gimmick" which had to increase the flow of funds to Israel, under the pretext of investment.

When the Israel Bonds were officially and formally launched in May, 1951, through the American Financial and Development Corporation for Israel, the very term, "campaign," which symbolized philanthropic fund-raising, was not abandoned. No wonder that the first years of the Israel Bonds were years of mis-understandings and even controversy between the U.J.A. and the Israel Bonds organization. Even a coordinating committee of representatives of the Israel Bonds, U.J.A., the Jewish Agency and the Israel Embassy could not accomplish a quick enough solution to the inherent problems of competition between the two major arms of American financial support for Israel. The volume of funds raised from the two sources, in the first year of the Israel Bonds existence, demonstrated that American Jewry treated U.J.A. and

Triplets give the money they had saved for the Father's Day gift to a volunteer worker for the Israel Emergency Fund of the United Jewish Federation of Pittsburgh.

Israel Bonds as almost equally important. The U.J.A. produced forty-eight million dollars and the Israel Bonds thirty-seven million dollars. The changes in the composition of the leadership of the two institutions to which was attributed the smoothing out of the mutual relations between U.J.A. and the Israel Bonds were only partly instrumental in clearing the public atmosphere surrounding work for the Israel Bonds and U.J.A. Time has again proved to be the most important factor. With each passing year the non-philanthropic character of Israel Bonds grew in evidence. The Israel Government proved itself a trustworthy recipient of credit. The payments of interest, the convertability of the bonds into Israel currency in Israel, and finally the redemption of the first Independence Bonds have proven that the Israel Bonds have really nothing in common with philanthropic fund-raising. Thus were finally overcome the apprehensions that Israel Bonds would in fact infringe on the U.J.A. campaigns. The over one billion dollars ($1,073,000,000) American Jewry has invested in the Israel economy through Israel Bonds in the 16 years of the Bonds existence till September 1967, and the over $1 billion the U.J.A. has supplied in the same period for the basic needs of immigration and colonization of over a million new immigrants, were a fitting new chapter of American Jewry's contribution to the solution of Israel's financial and economic problems. Whether this was a contribution corresponding with the financial capabilities of American Jewry is more a moral and national question than a matter of practical evaluation. It is true that a cautious estimate would prove that with all the unprecedented generosity of American Jews, they do not give annually for pro-Israel

Beginnings of one of the settlements built on Zion Commonwealth land.

financial instruments more than an average of ten dollars per person, as one could well consider Dr. Leo Keyserling's (President Truman's economic advisor) assertion that compared with what American Jews are spending annually for drinks, their investment in Israel bonds does not reach even fifteen per cent of that expenditure. But with all these qualifications no doubt remains that the more than two billion dollars that American Jews have put at the disposal of the Israel economy since the establishment of the State, were a most important, if not decisive factor in the development of Israel and the state its economy has achieved.

But viewing the measure of American Jewish financial support for the needs of Israel one cannot limit himself to registering only the two major arms of this support. The Jewish National Fund, for some years, since the presidency of Dr. Israel Goldstein, an equal partner with the Foundation Fund, in the United Palestine Appeal, channeled tens of millions of dollars to Palestine, and later to Israel. Almost two decades before the establishment of the Foundation Fund, the Jewish National Fund initiated an effort to educate American Jews for permanent planned donations to a Jewish Palestine. From $8,000 a year in 1908, the amount raised annually by J.N.F. rose to millions. In 1946 alone, on one occasion, J.N.F. cabled five million dollars to the J.N.F. headquarters in Jerusalem for new land purchases. Whatever land purchases the J.N.F. succeeded in transacting in the years preceding the establishment of the State, the contribution of the J.N.F. in America was most important. In the year of the establish-

ment of the State it reached the amount of twenty-five million dollars, and since then an additional twenty million dollars. Whatever the statistical facts pertaining to the J.N.F. funds are, the importance of this first financial instrument of the Zionist movement cannot be appraised in terms of dollars and cents. Those first Zionists who ventured to collect money for J.N.F. on the High Holidays, on weddings and bar mitzvahs, in cemeteries, those who braved rain and cold on the Flower days and Flag days, those who joined the planting groups, and who were never tired of visiting the blue-white J.N.F. box-owners, whose number rose from some odd thousands to a quarter of a million, this anonymous legion of Zion-lovers, were among the most important proponents of Zionist education in America. It was the J.N.F. that renewed and strengthened the bonds between the land of Israel and the people of Israel; it was the J.N.F. that accompanied the planting of each tree in the holy soil with planting a corresponding seed in a Jewish heart in America that bloomed and bore fruit in the decisive days of the struggle for the state and of creating funds for its reconstruction.

These major channels of support of Israel never had a monopoly. The *Mizrahi* Fund started early in its fund-raising campaign for religious institutions in Palestine. The labor movement tried to provide funds for the Palestine Jewish Labor organizations even before the establishment of the National Labor Committee for Palestine from which the *Histadruth* campaign evolved. As in the case of other funds centered on Palestine this fund grew in time, in geometrical proportions, from $51,165 in 1924 to $1,178,257 in 1943-1944, and over three million in 1965. It reached a total of over eighty million dollars at the end of 1967, in the 44 years of its existence. The Hebrew University in Jerusalem enjoyed special favor with the American Jews. The priority of concern with funds for the Hebrew University was underlined on every occasion and in a most conspicuous way by Dr. Weitzman, who proclaimed the collection of funds for the University as one of the two major goals of his American visit in 1921, the first of these goals being the establishment of the Foundation Fund. In time other institutions of higher learning looked also to American Jewry for funds. A group supporting the Haifa Technion whose origins precede World War I, developed into the American Technion Society which supplies an important part of the budget of the only Israel higher school of technical education; the Tel Aviv University draws part of its financial support from America, and the Bar-Ilan University is completely American-sponsored. The Weitzman Institute of Science had and has in American Jewry its main supporter to the tune of millions of dollars, provided through the American Committee for the Weitzman Institute of Science here, led by Abraham Feinberg as President and Joseph Brajnin as executive Vice-President. It is certainly no accident that the initiator of this great venture in scientific endeavor is an American Zionist, Meyer Weisgal, whose services for the Zionist cause range over a period of almost half a century, encompassing many positions, from editing the Zionist magazine to the contribution in the wording of the Biltmore Program.

Besides these major educational institutions there is a host of schools of more modest standing, which are of major importance for the development of the country, and completely American-sponsored, or American-supported. The latest development in this field is the organized effort to have American Jews sponsor the building of high schools in Israel. Within a brief period of two to three years millions of dollars have been donated and high schools opened to contribute to the solution of one of Israel's most acute problems of educational and cultural elevation of the

October 1951—Albert Einstein purchases the 200,000 Israel Bonds from Yael Sharett, daughter of Israel's Foreign Minister, Moshe Sharett. A special Israel Bond scroll designed by famous artist Arthur Szyk is presented to Einstein by Rudolf G. Sonnenborn, present of the Israel Bond Organization at the Princeton home of the famous scientist.

children of new immigrants, with all the results such elevation implies for the integration of the immigrant groups from various countries of origin, and for the cultural standards of the country. This special arm of the U.J.A., the Israel Education Fund established in 1962, has succeeded to draw new vigorous support for Israel's needs. In this category mention should also be made of a unique experiment of establishing a high school in Israel for American youth sponsored by the Zionist Organization of America.

There is almost no major or minor Jewish organization or institution in the United States which does not provide for some needs of the complicated fabric of Israel life. Pioneer Women with its many institutions in towns and villages in Israel has written a glorious chapter in providing for the needs

of the working woman. Child care, homes for halutzot, exemplary economic enterprises geared to the needs of the women, in all parts of Israel, bear witness what this organization of about 50,000 American women has accomplished. The National Council of Jewish Women, *Mizrahi* Women, Women's League for Israel, *Agudath Israel*, Rabbinical organizations, *Yeshivoth*, The Palestine Endowment Fund, and charitable institutions of all kinds have in Israel institutions they have established on their own, or serve as important supporters for already existing institutions. The saying about a "thousand bonds" linking American Jews in terms of financial cooperation with Israel institutions is not just a phrase, it is a most truthful expression of a state of affairs that must amaze an observer and elate a friend. Long before the famous Fulbright scholarships

Leaders of UJA and Israel Bonds at the Jerusalem Economic Conference in October, 1953, meet with Prime Minister Ben Gurion. Left to right: Dr. Joseph J. Schwartz, UJA Executive Vice-Chairman; Julian B. Venetzky, Israel Bond Executive Committee Chairman; Edward M. Warburg, UJA General Chairman; Henry Montor, Israel Bond Vice President, David Ben Gurion, Samuel Rothberg, Israel Bond Special Sales Chairman, and Morris W. Berinstein, UJA National Chairman.

came into being American Jews have promoted scholarships to Israeli students in this country, or provided such scholarships to needy students in Israel. The American-Israel Cultural Foundation alone has provided, within ten years of its existence 1,634 scholarships for artistically endowed Israelis, many of whom have already attained outstanding positions in the international world of art and music. And these scholarships are given over and above a wide-flung program of support for Israel's art which this Foundation started to assist decades ago, when it still was known under the name of its initiator, "The Norman Fund."

In the years of this Fund's existence millions of dollars have gone from the United States into Israel to establish music schools, art studios, promote Israel's art life and thus contributed considerably to making Israel an island of culture in the entire area, a virtual mecca for artists from all over the world. A special chapter in these manifold forms of support for Israel was written when the first Israel currency was printed in the United States, after the legal tangle was solved by a group of lawyers headed by Maurice Bookstein. And much will certainly yet be said about the separate account set up with a major New York bank after Israel has been removed from the sterling bloc.

Among these many forms of support given to Israel by American Jewry, one stands out by its dimensions and importance: it is the work which Hadassah, the Zionist Women Organization, is doing in *Eretz Israel* for over half a century. From an organizing meeting on Feb. 24, 1912, in the Vestry Room of Temple

Israel Bond delegates to the Jerusalem Conference in October, 1953, are greeted at Lydda Airport.

Dr. Abba Hillel Silver, Chairman of the Board of Governors, receives a Trustee pin for his purchase of $10,000 in Israel Bonds from Dr. Schwartz at the inaugural Bond Conference in February, 1956.

Emanu-El in New York, at which a goal was adopted to organize 300 Daughters of Zion for Zionist work, to over 300,000 members half a century later, Hadassah has a history that certainly surpasses imagination and the wildest dreams. And certainly not less fantastic is the growth, in financial terms, from a budget of $4,000 in 1913, to over ten million dollars of the annual Hadassah budget of the sixties. In fact, Hadassah medical services in *Eretz Israel* were more extensive than those supported by the budget of the Department of Health of the British Mandatory Government in Palestine. In 1930 the Hadassah budget in Palestine amounted to about 110,000 pounds ($440,000) while the entire Government budget for its Department of Health reached only 108,000 pounds. The permanent Mandate Commission of the Council of the League of Nations remarked in its report that

The commission expresses appreciation of the important contribution of Hadassah toward public health in Palestine. This contribution is important not only professionally but socially and politically as well, in view of its rendering service to all sections of the population.

What these millions, human zeal, and national Jewish commitment have done in Israel through medical services, institutions of social care, support of Youth Aliyah was best described in the congratulatory message,

Israel's Prime Minister Levi Eshkol sent to the 52nd convention of Hadassah, in Boston, August, 1966:

The name of Hadassah is written large across the panorama of modern Israel, bearing testimony to the magnificent record of creative achievement and inspired endeavor, which has consistently characterized your movement from its inception.

These numerous philanthropic or public outlets and avenues of financial support for the upbuilding of Jewish Palestine, and later of Israel, were fortunately only one aspect of American Jewish financial involvement in the development of Israel. Decades before

the formalization of the policies for the promotion of private investments in Israel, the idea of such economic cooperation in the development of Israel's economy, was not only theoretically acknowledged, but implemented as well. National conventions of the Zionist groups almost half a century ago repeated resolutions which called

to collect data regarding investment possibilities, encourage and foster interest of American Jews to organize and develop Palestine enterprises; introduce Palestine products to American markets.

The great controversy between Weitzman and Brandeis centered, to some extent, on

Miami Beach, 1957—(left to right): George Jessel, Eddie Cantor and Jack Benny mark the sale of $20,000,000 in Israel Bonds in honor of Cantor's sixty-fifth birthday.

Senator John F. Kennedy appears at an Israel Bond meeting in Philadelphia in 1960, several days prior to his election as President of the United States. At the podium, Mrs. Arnold D. Cohen who presided at the meeting. At the right Mrs. David L. Lawrence, wife of the Governor of Pennsylvania.

Houston, 1959—President Lyndon B. Johnson, who at that time was Senate Majority Leader, is the guest of honor at an Israel Bond dinner. Shown (left to right) are: Joe Weingarten of Houston, Philip M. Klutznick, International President of B'nai B'rith, Mr. Johnson, and Israel Consul Moshe Leshem.

the dispute about the advantages of private investments for the development of Israel's economy.

Though the idea of investments was not on the winning side, the very dispute stressed its importance and gave birth to the first major American Jewish investment effort in Palestine, the Palestine Economic Corporation (Israel Economic Corporation). The character of this enterprise was well defined in its statute which stated that it is

an instrument through which American Jews and others who may be interested, may give material aid on a strictly business basis to productive Palestinian enterprises and thereby further the economic development of the Holy Land and the re-settlement there of an increasing number of Jews.

Throughout the four decades since its inception, the Palestine Economic Corporation operated through subsidiary companies and through direct investments in basic industrial enterprises such as the Palestine Electric Company, Palestine Potash Company, Palestine Water Company, Bayside Land Corporation, banks, hotels. Tens of millions of dollars have flowed into the Palestine economy through the P.E.C. and many a basic enterprise was either established in its entirety with P.E.C. capital, or with P.E.C. capital as a promoting factor. Though it did not fulfill expectations nurtured by its organizers, the Palestine Economic Corp. (Israel Economic Corporation) has put its imprint on Jewish Palestine's economy.

Another major investor in Israel's economy is *Ampal* -- the American Palestine Trading Corporation, organized in 1941 under the auspices of the cooperative sector of the Palestine economy. *Ampal's* prime purpose was to

provide a financial and commercial instrumentality in the United States in order to assist, financially and commercially, the economic enterprises in Palestine . . . The corporation does not propose to set up, in Palestine, agencies of its own but rather to cooperate with those now in existence.

September, 1961, Foreign Minister Golda Meir presents to Mrs. Eleanor Roosevelt a plaque of Israel stamps in recognition of her dedicated services in behalf of Israel and Israel Bonds.

From an initial capital of $1,600 in 1941 Ampal assets, in 1966, exceeded eighty million dollars.

These major companies devoted to American investment activities in Israel are supplemented by a whole series of individual or group investments which have brought to Israel hundreds of millions of dollars, and helped establish new industries as well as develop and extend existing ones. There is almost no private or cooperative enterprise in Israel in which American capital is not involved in some form. Promoted by official Israeli Government efforts as the Israel Investment Center, which was preceded by a similar institution under Jewish Agency auspices, by the Rassco Israel Corporation, by the American-Israel Chamber of Commerce and Industry, by enterprises which base their activities on the conversion of Israel bonds, the pace of

Philadelphia, May, 1961: Prime Minister Ben Gurion addresses a meeting of the national Board of Governors of the Israel Bond Organization, celebrating the tenth anniversary of the Israel Bonds. Shown on the dais (left to right) are: Samuel H. Daroff of Philadelphia, Samuel Rothberg, National Campaign Chairman of the Israel Bond Organization, Israel Ambassador Abraham Harman, Abraham Feinberg, Israel Bond President, Colonel Jacob M. Arvey of Chicago, Dr. Joseph J. Schwartz, Vice President, Mrs. Jan Peerce, Chairman of the Bond's Women's Division and Ira Guilden, National Chairman.

American private investments in the Israel economy varies at particular times, but keeps up a steady flow of many millions of dollars which help expand Israel's economy, raise the productivity of its industries, increase Israel's gross national product. In 1959 alone, for instance, private investments from the United States channelled through the Israel Investment Center reached an amount close to forty million dollars.

When, at the inception of the State of Israel, high hopes were linked with private investment, nobody knew whether the time was yet ripe for a real response by American Jewry. The hopes have been high, indeed. *Palestine Reports* a publication of the United Palestine Appeal, has best illustrated these hopes in its February, 1949, issue, when it carried a

lengthy article entitled "Gift dollars versus investment dollars":

The gift dollar will have to be joined by the investment dollar, stated the article and elaborated:

In our administration of campaigns for voluntary contributions . . . . we should avoid building up the myth that Israel is an almost permanent relief recipient . . .

On the other hand, in the investment campaigns we should likewise refrain from campaign isolationism and avoid spreading a psychology of 'colonization' among the prospective clients. Investment organizations should not stir up expectations of exaggerated profits, but should make it rather abundantly clear that Israel's economy is a profit economy only to the extent to which

Prime Minister and Mrs. Eshkol are honored at Israel Bond Board of Governors meeting, New York, June, 1964: Seated left to right—Samuel Rothberg, the Prime Minister and Mrs. Eshkol, Dr. Joseph J. Schwartz, and Adolph Kiesler, dean of the Denver Jewish Community; Standing (left to right): Louis H. Boyar, Chairman of the Israel Bond Board of Governors, and Abraham Feinberg.

the security and daily needs of a growing population allow individual profits.

The awareness of this special situation and the special conditions of profitability of private investments in Israel remained a permanent component of considerations by those who have decided to invest their dollars in Israel's economy. But even with this reservation those who promote private investments in Israel could well point not only to the financial advantages derived from investments in Israel, but also to the fact, that while American investments in many countries, "went down the drain," in business recessions or political upheavals, no such fate has met

investments in Israel. In terms of investment security, Israel remained one of the safest countries.

Thus philanthropy and private enterprise have joined hands in the unprecedented dimensions of American Jewish support for a Jewish Palestine, for Israel. This is as unique as it is unprecedented. It has set new standards of philanthropic giving not only in the American Jewish community, but in American life as well. It manifested tangibly the unchanging bonds between the Zionist dream implemented and almost all sections of American Jewry. It has elevated American

Minister of Agriculture H. Gevati pins the Tsur Nathan emblem on the flag of this new settlement established in a strategic border area by the Jewish National Fund in cooperation with the Ministry of Defense.

Golden Book presentations at Farband JNF Conference.

Jewish affluence to the heights of human responsibility for fellow men, it has manifested, in this tangible field, the truth of Jewish nationhood, of the age-old Jewish maxim that Jews are responsible for each other, that the tradition of *tzedaka* instilled for thousands of years in Jewish hearts bore fruit so remarkably beneficial to the renewal of Jewish Statehood. The roads, housing projects, industries built with the help of Israel Bonds, those signs at the entrances to many settlements in

Israel such as those which say "built with the assistance of the United Jewish Appeal" are only an insignificant illustration of what American Jewish financial help has done to have Israel restored, its economy strengthened, over a million of its immigrants absorbed, its youth educated, its cultural life elevated. Without taxes, without the force of government institutions, American Jewry has channelled billions of dollars into Jewish Palestine over a period of seven decades. It can well say that it was a willing and faithful partner of building Israel's future on sound economic foundations.

August, 1957—Baron Edmond de Rothschild (center) President of the Israel Bond drive for Europe, is shown at New York headquarters of the Israel Bond Organization with Abraham Feinberg, President (left) and Dr. Joseph J. Schwartz, Vice President.

One of several booths to promote Israel Bonds sales during recent Middle East crisis set up by the Pittsburgh Council of Bna'i Brith.

Brooklynites at ZOA Metropolitan Bond Conference. In front, first, on left, Harold Carmely, at right, Judge Albert Shanzer.

At the conference of the Histradruth campaign.

Leaders of American Labor meet with Histadruth representative: Louis Hollander, vice-president, Amalgamated Clothing Workers of America (left), Louis Stulberg, International Ladies Garment Workers Union president, and Zev Haring, Histadruth spokesman.

Pinhas Sapir, Israel's Minister of Finance addresses Ampal's Board of Directors meeting in Israel.

JNF entertainers from Israel bring message of Israel to Jewish summer camps throughout the United States.

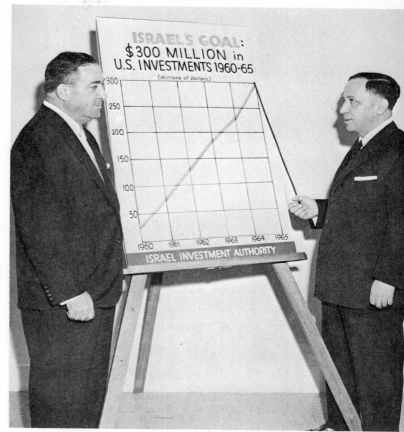

March, 1960—Aryeh Manor Israel Economic Minister to the U. S., points to industrialist Joseph Mazer, to steps by which Israel hopes to attract $300 million worth of U. S. investment by 1965.

David Dubinsky (left) hands Histadruth treasurer Yehoshua Levy a check of $427,500, proceeds of Amun Housing venture of the 1950's as Dr. Sol Stein (center) national director of the National Committee for Labor Israel, looks on.

Pioneer Women confer on ways and means to aid Histadruth drive. Shirley Bogen, national Histadruth chairman of Pioneer Women, speaking. Seated are Amos Eiran, Israel Labor attache in Washington, Rose Kaufman, Pauline Berkowitz, Clara Leff, Blanche Fine and Lois Bloomberg.

Joseph Schlossberg, 91-year old dean of American Jewish labor, after re-election as President of the National Committee for Labor Israel. He is shown seated at Oneg Shabbat with Israel Stolarsky, associate director of the Histadruth Campaign, standing at his side.

President of Farband honored (from left): Hanan Yarden, Samuel Bonechek, Mrs. Gnendl Bonchek.

American Histadruth Center in Israel.

Albert Einstein presented with certificate of inscription in JNF Golden Book. At left Dr. E. Neumann, Prof. Einstein, Rabbi Zev Gold, Miss Henrietta Szold, Joseph Weiss, treasurer of the JNF. Photo taken in 1929.

Dr. Abba Hillel Silver and Mrs. Silver are greeted at the entrance to the ZOA Agricultural High School in Israel, Kfar Silver.

The first 1964 shipment of Jaffa oranges, arrives at the port of New York. Left, Dr. Max Leron, Israel Trade Commissioner in the U. S.

Structures nearing completion at Kiryat Segal on the outskirts of Tel-Aviv, named in memory of Louis Segal, late secretary general of the Farband Labor Zionist Order.

The Chief Rabbis of Israel and Holland join in a prayer at rededication of the reconstructed interior of the Leeuwardeh Synagogue in the Kraushar Synagogue of Mizrachi Women's Children's Village in Raanana, Israel.

American trade unionists pause for a picture during hectic three-week seminar that took them to the borders of Israel.

Students at work at the Bar-Ilan University.

Honor Roll plaque in the ZOA House in Tel-Aviv.

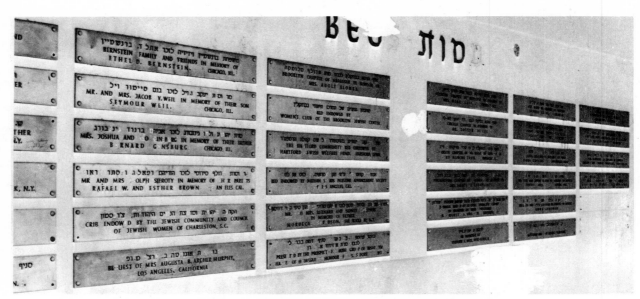

Plaques indicating Hadassah hospital facilities endowed by Americans.

Hadassah Hospital in Haifa.

First Hadassah Nurses Settlement in Jerus

Dr. Judah L. Magnes (right) receives one of the first two honorary degrees to have been awarded by the Hebrew University, July, 1947.

Hebrew University High School, built by the National Council of Jewish Women, in Jerusalem, at a practice teaching center for the John Dewey School of Education, which the NCJW has supported for nearly two decades.

President Johnson receives Fellowship Award in the name of the late President Kennedy at the Weitzmann Institute dinner. To his left—Abraham Feinberg and Dewey Stone.

177 college and university students taking off for One-Year Study Program at the Hebrew University, conducted by the American Friends of the Hebrew University.

A. Feinberg receiving honorary fellowship at the Weitzman Institute.

Dewey Stone addressing guests at opening of Stone Administration Building at the Weitzman Institute.

American youth group attending Winter Institute in Israel, studies antiquities at Ashkelon.

John F. Kennedy Memorial in Israel dedicated by the
Jewish National Fund on July 4th, 1966.

Participating in the dedication ceremony of the Kennedy Memorial left to right: U. S. Ambassador Barbour, Premier
Eshkol, Chief Justice Warren, Herman L. Weisman, Dr. Milton Aron.

Youthful American educators gather for orientation before leaving for a Study Program in Israel sponsored in cooperation with the Association of Hebrew Teachers' Colleges.

Jewish National Fund Jerusalem Banner Award celebration, introduced many years before the liberation of Old Jerusalem. A growing number of schools are participating in the celebrations.

יצחק בן־צבי (ניו־יורק) אל ויקטור יעקבסון (קופנהאגן): על ראשית תנועת "החלוץ" בארצות הברית,
ו' טבת תרע"ז / 31 דצמבר 1916
Izhak Ben-Zvi (New York) to Victor Jacobson (Copenhagen): On the beginnings of "He-Chaluts" in
the U.S.A., 31 December 1916.

Yitzhak Ben-Zvi letter on the beginnings of He-Halutz in the U. S. December 31, 1916, written during the future
Israel President's stay in New-York.

At top—Drilling tower in Negev; center—Sign on drilling
site which includes the American-Israel Petroleum Corporation
and the group of American investors Samuel Friedland and
Max Horwitz;—Mr. Eshkol turns pipeline tap.

The Monsanto Chemical Works in Ashdod—U. S. major industrial concern establishes factory in Israel.

Architects' rendering of the Harry S. Truman Center for the Advancement of Peace to be erected on the Hebrew University campus, on Mount Scopus.

American Committee shipment of medical supplies to the National Sick Fund in Israel.

The America-Israel Culture House in New York.

Arthur Rubinstein and Mayor John V. Lindsay join in a lively hora at the dinner given by the America-Israel Cultural Foundation in honor of Mr. Rubinstein.

Launching sale of an Israel product in Philadelphia. This time it is a Shalom blade.

15

MANPOWER AND BRAINPOWER

THE FLOW of American Jewish funds for Zionist work in Palestine was never separated from the awareness that Palestine would never be Jewish without personal commitment of Zionists to go there and settle. The fact that the American *Kolel,* the American community among the *Haluka* Jews in Jerusalem, was the most numerous is only a small detail in case. Forms of colonization, character of settlers, dimensions of immigration were foremost in the minds of American Zionists. The reason why this did not result in practical acts of American mass immigration to *Eretz Israel* before the establishment of the State and thereafter, would have to be sought in the complex of sociological, economic and -- only in the last instance -- Jewish national circumstances that have determined the dimensions of *aliyah* from each country, in every particular period of time.

The beginning of American Zionism seemed to be most promising in this respect. In fact, the early years of American Zionism seemed to augur a much greater American Zionist involvement in the actual settlement of Palestine than raising the funds for such settlement. The *Hovevei Zion* Society, one of the first Zionist societies in New York, established before the first Zionist Congress, was organized with the express intention of working for the settlement of its members in the Holy Land. The delegation this Society sent to Palestine consisted of two gentlemen, Adam Rosenberg who represented later American Zionists at the First Zionist Congress, and Meyer London, an East Side *matzoh* baker, who made practical preparations for the liquidation of his business and emigration to Palestine.

Though their effort to buy land for colonization fell through -- the idea of American Jews settling in Palestine continued to agitate American Zionists. Imbued with the spirit of American initiative and economic success, American Zionists considered themselves a most useful element in the settlement of Palestine. *The Maccabean* promoted these ideas enthusiastically. A Zionist writer who visited Palestine had a ready-made formula for American Zionist personal involvement in building a Jewish Palestine:

If I were to divide the work for Palestine, he wrote, I should assign the buying of land to the Russian Jews, and the establishing of industries to the American Jews.

This was not sheer advice without proper argumentation.

American Jews, he continued, have the command of greater funds, have learned to organize larger trades and industries, and they moreover know the secret of 'cast thy bread upon the waters, for in many days thou wilt find it again.' It is for them to make the experiment of introducing trades and industries into Palestine, and wait for results. And that their endeavors in that direction will be crowned with success, I do not have the slightest doubt.

A. S. Waldstein, the author of these remarks was not the only one to make such statements. Another writer, Helena H. Cohn, already had a report on the success of the American settlers in Palestine -- and of course, words of praise for the contribution American Jewish women were making towards the success of the Jewish settlements.

These immigrants from America, she wrote, have imbibed the typical American qualities -- a quick and practical intelligence, cleverness in business, initiative and understanding for the moral and aesthetical values of a well-kept household. Thanks to certain peculiarities of American life they have accustomed themselves to manufacturing many of the things which they want for everyday use and to make their surroundings as pleasant as can be. It is especially the American woman, having gone through the school of American life, that can be held up as an example of a competent house keeper. . . . There is another quality that makes the settler from America a valuable acquisition for Palestine -- his pecuniary circumstances. Their capital can be called small or modest only from the American point of view, while it is about four times larger than that of a family on the same social level in Europe. . . . Compared with the capital of laborers and colonists from East and West Europe, it is rather large. . . . The American Jewish emigration to Palestine will comprise a smaller percentage of unfit elements than that of any other country.

But it seems that the number of American Zionists ready to settle in Palestine appeared to the author rather limited.

Every American Zionist who gives up the greater economic advantages of America to come to Palestine to help with the work of colonization does always become a useful member of the young Jewish community. Unfortunately, such strong characters are but rare and the number of people who combine with high idealism, courage, strength and intelligence is but limited.

And limited it was indeed, though not non-existent as is the generally prevailing opinion.

But these limited dimensions of emigration to Palestine should not be identified with lack of initiative and original thought as far as forms and ways of settling in Palestine are concerned. The idea of *halutziut*, of pioneering, the first *Hehalutz* movement came into being on the New Continent as early as 1909. In that year, a *Hehalutz* movement was organized with 400 members, though when it came to personal commitment only four actually emigrated to Palestine. Among them was Eliezer Yaffe of the Agricultural College in Woodbine, who organized as well the *Haikar Hatzair*, the Young Farmer, and who became later the ideological

Assembling Jeep chasis at the Kaiser-Frazer automotive facility in Haifa. Kaizer-Frazer (Kaiser-Ilin) is one of more than 200 Israel based plants in which, by 1960, over $130,000,000 of U. S. private capital has participated in the development of Israel's economy.

father of the *Moshav Ovdim* movement, a cooperative form of agricultural settlement, the most accepted form in today's Israel. But it would be crass injustice to judge the American *Hehalutz* movement by that pathetically small figure of four olim it produced in 1911. They were among the nuclei of the volunteer movement to the Jewish Legion in America, from which later emanated close to 2,000 potential *halutzim* who were ready to settle in Palestine after the war was over. David Ben Gurion acknowledged this fact, writing:

> Perhaps not all of you know that the first *aliyah* in mass after the Balfour Declaration, came not from Russia or Poland or Galicia, from nowhere in Europe, but from America.

The late President of Israel, Itzhak Ben Zvi, wrote about *immigration in khaki,* which

> became a very popular slogan in the United States.

It was not their fault that they were not able to fulfill their dream. Seventy per cent of the American Jewish Battalion stated their desire to settle in Palestine. Only because of the lack of understanding and support of the Zionist authorities did a mere 530 out of 1200 finally remain in Palestine.

The *Hehalutz* movement and the *Moshav Ovdim* idea, originated in the mind of an *oleh* from America, were not the only contributions of American Zionists to the process of growth of the *Yishuv* in Palestine, in its early days. Almost simultaneously with the establishment of the first communal settlements in Palestine, when the *kibbutz* was born, American Zionists conceived a different form of settlement, adapted to the American way of life, the ideas of private initiative and individual ownership. Simon Goldman, a businessman from St. Louis, initiated a bold and ingenious idea to attract individual American Jews to settlement in Palestine. The name he chose was to express the character of the idea, *ahuza* -- possession. That this was not a fancy born in the mind of an idealistic individual was proven not only by the serious opposition the *ahuza* idea encountered at national conventions of the Federation of American Zionists, but by the practical acceptance of that concept throughout the United States and Canada. Though leading Zionists criticized the plan as a political heresy and a manifestation of acceptance of the idea of practical Zionism, the *ahuza* idea assumed

A sign at the entrance to an all American kibbutz in the Galilee. It reads: "The path to the goal for American pioneers". The second line is a quotation from Ezekiel 34:14: "Upon the high mountains of Israel shall their fold be".

dimensions of a nationwide movement. Proclaimed in 1907, it had within four years groups in St. Louis, New York, Chicago, Cleveland, Pittsburgh, Philadelphia, Toronto, Winnipeg. In some cities this movement had to establish additional groups A, B, and C, as the number of interested grew, while according to the plan, an *ahuza* group could not accommodate more members than a modest agricultural, self-supporting settlement could contain. The 250 families which were organized in the *ahuza* groups proved the seriousness of their intentions by providing funds that had, in these initial years, accrued a capital of over $500,000.

This was not merely a plan. Simon Goldman himself liquidated his business in St. Louis and established the settlement Poriah in Galilee, and groups of other *ahuza* members moved as well to link their future with the slowly growing *Yishuv.* The attractiveness of the *ahuza* was of course anchored in the desire to settle in *Eretz Israel,* but there is no doubt that its practical aspects played a most important role as well. Its most important feature was the fact that people with limited means could become members. The plan provided for groups of about fifty who had to subscribe for a minimum of seven shares a person, at $200 a share, payable in weekly or monthly installments, in the course of seven years. For special cases this period could have been prolonged to ten years. The sum of $1,400 thus invested could secure an estate of 16 acres, 14.5 under cultivation, planted with fruit trees, and 1.5 acres reserved for house, barn and garden. For the buildings, furniture, implements and live stock, the settler was required to have another $1,000. As soon as the treasurer had $500, he was supposed to remit it to the Anglo-Palestine Bank in Jaffa, and when a sum sufficient to pay for two acres had accrued in

Prime Minister Eshkol addresses UJA's fifth annual Young Leadership Mission in Jerusalem.

the bank, on each share subscribed for, the Palestine Office was requested to buy the land for the group.

Thus the first part of the *ahuza* plan was considered accomplished. The second stage encompassed the hiring by the Palestine Office of the Zionist Organization of an expert to manage and develop the *ahuza* estate. According to plan, the payments of the first three years had to buy the land needed. Within ten years, the colony was supposed to be ready to receive settlers and provide them with a livelihood. It was calculated that the income from 14.5 acres of fruit-bearing trees should yield $380 annually, an amount considered sufficient, in those days, for a family of four to make a modest, but decent living. The plan was no pure capitalistic enterprise: there was a provision enabling a settler who could not save the $1,000 for buildings to become a member of the colony under the condition that he would repay this amount in time, through his income from employment, preferably in the colony, or through the income from the estate itself.

Interestingly, the *Ahuza* groups did not try to concentrate on the coastal area of Palestine. Poriah was established in Galilee, and the five other *Ahuza* associations which purchased land, selected the area between Haifa and the Valley of Jezreel. Only a few decided to build their colony on the coastal plain, which later became the major center of Jewish settlement. It seems that those early American settlers had a rather clear vision of the real needs of the country, as far as the proper territorial division of Jewish settlement of the country was concerned. And so attractive was this idea of *ahuza* that it soon spread to Germany and Russia, giving rise to

what appeared, at that time, relatively serious efforts of settling Palestine through individual initiative and group cooperation.

That this was not an isolated expression of American interest in practical contribution to the settlement of Palestine was soon to be proven by a new initiative in the field of settlement in Palestine. This was the Zion Commonwealth that concentrated on urban settlement. Its organizational basis was rather national and not local in scope as was the *ahuza* movement. It provided for individual holdings of about two and one half acres, which were to suffice for a homestead. Such holding represented a single share certificate. Members who intended to engage in farming were expected to purchase at least ten certificates. Imbued with the ideas of progress, Zion Commonwealth tried to find some kind of a compromise between private ownership of land and the principles of communal land-holding. Ten per cent of the land had to be kept as an unalienable communal estate, to be leased but not sold, on which was to be built the city, town or industrial district of the community. From the communal land the members were supposed to draw rent and profit. Because Zion Commonwealth membership was not necessarily conditioned by personal commitment through settling in Palestine, opponents of the idea coined a term, "real estate colonization," to express reservations concerning a plan that envisaged profits out of an investment in *Eretz Israel*. But such remarks, meant to be somewhat derogatory, did not impair wide acceptance of the idea of owning land in Palestine. Close to ten thousand individual purchases were made from Zion Commonwealth, which at one time had more land redeemed than had the Jewish National Fund. Some of the purchases were of the most far-reaching importance for the future development of the *Yishuv*, the economic and strategic interests of the future Jewish State.

whatever and wherever we bought, we always had our eyes open on the strategic location of the tract,

stated Solomon Weinstein, the last president of Zion Commonwealth, who followed in the footsteps of the founder and initiator of this form of American Jewish personal involvement in the Zionist work in Palestine, Judge Bernard Rosenblatt.

Members of UJA mission in Israel.

On the 36,000 redeemed acres of land, such flourishing Jewish settlements were established as Herzlia, Afule, Balfouria. But the greatest pride of Zion Commonwealth land redemption actions was the purchase of the entire coastal plain from Haifa almost to Acco, which became the center of Palestine's industrial development, and a major source of its economic strength. The fact that Zion Commonwealth, one of the institutions of the Zionist Organization of America, encountered, at one period of its activities, financial difficulties and became a target of vehement criticism by opponents of the then ZOA administration, does not impair the fact of its importance in the process of growth of the Jewish settlement in Palestine.

As important as these colonization activities of American Zionists were, they were a far cry from the implementation of the clear vision about the manpower needs of Palestine if it really had, some day, to become a Jewish State. More than in any other territorial Zionist organization has the awareness of the imperative need of a mass immigration to Palestine been present in the minds of leading American Zionists. The foremost leader of American Zionism between 1914 and 1920, Louis D. Brandeis, whose stature and influence never actually faded from the Zionist scene, considered a mass immigration the most important, most pressing and urgent task of the Zionist movement. At the London Conference

of July, 1920, which had assumed the proportions of a major milestone in the fortunes of American and world Zionism alike, Brandeis repeated an opinion he expounded frequently before that

> the most urgent Zionist task is to populate Palestine, within a comparatively short time, with a prepondering body of manly, self-supporting Jews.

Brandeis did not hide this conception of Zionism from non-Zionists, for whom such dimensions of Zionist action appeared shocking and outrageous. Louis Marshall, the most outstanding leader of the American Jewish Committee, reported on a discussion he held with Brandeis in September, 1919, in which Brandeis expressed his opinion that Palestine could support a large population.

> He several times spoke of six million people,

asserted Marshall. In view of such conceptions of Zionist practical action, it would be only natural to assume that Brandeis also gave thought to the sources of manpower that had to populate Palestine in a quickened tempo. The developments within the Zionist movement blocked any search for a practical way to organize such mass emigration to Palestine.

Brandeis' removal from Zionist leadership and the express opposition of those who occupied the positions at the helm of the Zionist movement to mass *aliyah*, made the entire scheme immaterial. Whether American Zionists would have joined, by personal commitment, in such emigration is a question nobody can answer. Though there is good reason to assume that even enthusiasts of such mass emigration looked rather at the East European Jewry as the foremost reservoir of Zionist manpower, no doubt can prevail that in the process of such enormous population transfer in the name of Zionist ideals and goals, considerable numbers of American Zionists would have been carried away by the enthusiasm of the great drama of movement of millions and by the prospects for immigrants, equipped with skills, such rapidly growing Jewish community would have required.

It seems that even the limited tempo of emigration to Palestine did not involve a number of Americans that many would have liked to have seen. Though the term, *aliyah from the West,* was not yet coined and its importance not yet urgently felt, immigrants from America were considered a special, most useful breed.

Unfortunately, the *aliyah in khaki* did not have a sequence which could have satisfied the hopes those legionnaires instilled in the *Yishuv*. The absence of considerable numbers of immigrants from America gave rise to some profound Zionist contemplation. M. Sheinkin, one of the leading personalities of the *Yishuv*, dealt extensively with this problem in the August 4, 1922, issue of *New Palestine*, when he wrote:

> If the American Jews should cling to their present belief that there are necessary in Palestine only those Jews who suffer persecution and hunger, and consequently American Jews are not needed in Palestine, their duty to Palestine consisting in supplying the money, then Zionism in America assumes the aspect of mere charity for our poor unfortunate brethren, a kind of relief, a luxury charity. The bitter truth of this assertion can be substantiated by all those who are working so earnestly to gather funds for *Keren Hayessod* . . . The supposition that Jews living in peace and freedom have no need for Palestine leads to the psychological absurdity concerning Zionism, that in proportion to the liberty-and-peace the Jews enjoy in a given country, Zionism must lose its active aspects and become a matter of charity. In other words, Zionism must draw its spiritual sustenance and its human material from Jewish misfortune, persecution and suffering. If the Jews for Palestine are to come solely from the poor and bankrupt European countries, then the land cannot be built up.

American Zionists were well aware of this state of affairs as far as a personal commitment to Zionism, by settling in Palestine, was concerned. Some tried to draw consolation from the fact that the much praised higher volume of personal commitment in Eastern Europe was conditioned more by unbearable local conditions than by sheer idealism and Zionist zeal. But some have tried to penetrate deeper into the intricate causes that made a diatribe as Sheinkin's possible. American Zionism, American Zionist leaders, the type of education American Zionists were given, were blamed. *New Palestine*, in the Editor's Note, admitted,

> We must remember that the American boy and girl did not learn Zionism as an ideal as did the European. He learned it as a campaign for money. Zionism was something his mother went to teas to talk about, something his father was continually being pestered about to donate money to.

> *Dedicated to*
> THE CHALUTZIM OF AMERICA
> *Those who came,*
> *are coming,*
> *and will come.*
> KIBBUTZ SASA.

Opening page of pamphlet on the American kibbutz Sasa.

Indeed, the financial needs of the Zionist movement led to many distortions of the real Zionist obligations in America no less than in any other country. The slogan of the World Zionist leaders. "You give us the tools and we will do the job," had to have its results. The total concentration of this world Zionist leadership on American generosity could hardly have had American Zionists educated to personal Zionist commitment. There was also another factor that should be accounted for: the immigration restrictions of the Mandatory government precluded any sizeable immigration to Palestine, in the distribution of the few thousand available certificates consideration had to be given to priorities that could not favor American immigrants, who were neither in danger nor in need.

In spite of these many objective and subjective obstacles in the efforts for the promotion of emigration from America, the American Zionist leaders did not forego their duty to encourage aliyah and even to create formal instruments for its promotion. The annals of national conventions of the ZOA, of Mizrahi, of Labor Zionists, are full of resolutions calling Zionists to emigrate to Palestine. A resolution of the 25th annual Convention of the ZOA

> recognizes the importance of the formation of groups of American Jews for the purpose of settling in Palestine, and particularly along agricultural lines.

The second paragraph of this resolution stated that

> the convention therefore recommends that the incoming National Executive Committee should encourage this movement and give its full-hearted support to it.

Group of Hassidim before their departure from the U. S. for permanent settlement in Israel.

Records of the Palestine department of the ZOA and similar departments of the smaller Zionist groups indicate that these resolutions were not only taken seriously but were also meeting some degree of response, limited as it was. Indicative of the dimensions of these practical efforts in the field of Zionist personal realization was, for instance, a report of the Palestine Department on 202 inquiries of prospective settlers and the processing of "175 applications of *aliyah* from young men and women" in the period between November 1929 and June 1930. The same report added that an average of 150 inquiries reached the department weekly concerning land purchases in Palestine and immigration.

It seems that economic conditions had their bearing on the degree of American Jewish interest in emigrating to Palestine. The fact that during the great Depression, in the early Thirties, the number of American *olim* was tripled and reached close to 1,500 in one year, was certainly evidence that American Jewry was no exception in the inner logics, on aliyah, of the Jewish community in a given country.

Zionist leaders seized on this development most eagerly. Louis Lipsky published a vigorous call for *aliyah*, for American *halutzim*, and many leaders were convinced that American Zionism was on the threshold of a new era when it will supply not only financial resources but manpower as well for the Zionist creation in Palestine. In that hour of rising expectations, these leaders revealed their innermost but frustrated feelings of envy that European Zionists and not Americans were supplying the human material for Zionism and were receiving all the praise and admiration such effort was bringing. The editor's note in one of the *New Palestine* issues of 1930 was in this respect a most interesting document. Under the heading *The American Halutz,* he wrote:

Gradually there is seeping into the life of Jewish Palestine a new type of chalutz: the American. American young men and women are taking their place beside the European halutz. The European *halutz* movement had its vanguard. They are heroes about whom songs are sung now . . . Now the American *halutz* has a vanguard, too. It is time that songs are being sung about him. No one seems to realize or believe that he is really here. For it is true that he is a queer assortment, a different race altogether than the European pioneer.

The author closes with a clarion call of profound hope:

When the American Youth gets the tidings which its vanguard is searching out, the American *halutz* will come.

He did not come, at least not in numbers, to imprint his special mark on the *Yishuv.* Before the tidings could reach the American Jewish youth, Palestine was again in the center of a rescue operation that demanded that every certificate be given to those for whom *aliyah* was identical with rescue from the hands of Hitler. For those who looked for explanations, if not for excuses for explaining the lack of American *aliyah,* the political situation in Europe was an excellent argument.

And so the *Fifth Aliyah,* with its 5,190 American *olim* with 845 settled tourists made up only 2.2 per cent of that immigration wave that brought to Palestine 278,000 persons. This was far from reaching, in percentages, the figure of American *olim* which the *fourth Aliyah* had registered, when 3,299 American *olim* reached roughly 4 per cent of that *Aliyah.* The majority of these American *olim* settled in the colonies based on American initiative, in Raanana and Herzliyah, with some of them concentrating in Tel-Aviv, while only 5 per cent, members of the *Halutz,* joined agricultural settlements. Compared with the *Third Aliyah* (1,071) *olim* from America) the *Fourth Aliyah* was three times larger, though in percentages it reached no more than 4 per cent of that wave of aliyah that came from a Europe of a deteriorating economic situation and from among those escaping from the anti-Semitism of the Polish government.

But the hopes for a halutz movement in America were not completely frustrated. The Thirties witnessed the first serious attempts in organizing and actually preparing *halutzim* for life in Palestine. The *Hashomar Hatzair* succeeded within one year after the start of its activities in America, in 1930, to send a group of olim. Soon they were no longer the only Zionist youth movement concerned with actual aliyah. *Habonim, Bnei Akiva, Hashomer Hadati,* a religious group and later, in a more modest way, *Betar,* began to stress *aliyah* in their education program. Though all these youth movements had not produced considerable numbers of olim, they kept alive the awareness that alijah is a central problem of Zionist ideology. Even in their small numbers they contributed to the establishment of a series of settlements which, at least, symbolized practical, personal involvement of American Zionism in Zionist realization. In the *kibbutz* movement alone, close to 2,500 are former members of the American *Halutz.* Of the 27 Anglo-Saxon settlements, 16 were founded or co-founded by Americans and five others have a considerable percentage of Americans. These Americans are to be found in every corner of the country, literally from Dan to Eilat. Avihail, Barkai, Beit Heruth, Ein Hashofet, Ein Dor, Gal-On, Gesher-Haziv, Hasolelim, Hatzor, Hazorea, Kfar Blum, Kfar Menahem, Kisufim, Maayan Barukh, Nahshon Orot, Ramat Yohanan, Sasa, Shluhot, Timorim, Urim are known in Israel as the "American settlements," as are Beer-Tuvia and Gan-Yavneh though there are many other communal settlements with considerable numbers of Americans who had decided that integration with aliyot from other countries is much more desirable than separation according to countries of origin.

A special chapter in these aliyah efforts was written after World War II. Centers of practical training were established in Whitestone, Cream Ridge in New Jersey, Poughkeepsie, New York, and San Bernardino, California. As a result, the number of *Halutzim* instantly rose and reached over one thousand in one year.

Agricultural training and settlement were no longer the only goals. The need for people with skills became urgent. A special office under the name of Land and Labor was organized. Through this office came the Americans who participated in manning ships with illegal immigrants, while some Americans themselves joined illegal groups to enter Palestine. With the approaching decisive struggle for Palestine, there began the mobilization of manpower for the Israeli armed forces in the making, for the *Haganah.* And though only part (370) of the volunteers of *Mahal* (Volunteers from Abroad) settled in Israel after

Group of American youth leaves for Israel to participate in the Summer-in Kibbutz Program of the Jewish Agency.

the War of Independence, they followed faithfully in the footsteps of their predecessors from the Jewish Legion of World War I, who came also to fight and remained to continue to build what their battles had brought to being.

The establishment of the State did not result in an appreciable change in the dimensions of *aliyah* from America. In strict figures, the number of American *olim* was rather on the decline. During the first twelve years of Israel's existence, only 3,172 *olim* settled in the country, and 1,483 tourists decided to stay permanently. Together with other Americans, 2,400 in number, who had in various ways and circumstances settled in Israel, the overall number of Americans who settled in Israel between 1948-1960 reached 7.595. In this overall figure are included *olim* of all categories. Among these are the investors-*olim,* the middle-class *olim,* the golden-age *olim, the hassidic-olim.*

But it would be an injustice to judge American contribution (besides the unprecedented financial help) towards the development of a Jewish Palestine and later of Israel, only by the number of persons from America who settled in Israel. American contribution in terms of man and brainpower was of sometimes decisive dimensions. The first two American "visiting nurses," who arrived in Israel in 1912 became the nucleus of Hadassah medical services in *Eretz Israel,* which absolved Jewish mothers from the need of seeking medical assistance at Christian missionary infirmaries; the American Zionist Medical Unit, later the Hadassah Medical Unit, consisting initially of 44 and later close to 400 medical personnel,

Summer campers from Detroit enjoy their time in Kfar Hayarok, Israel.

complete with physicians, hygiene engineers, nurses, laid the foundation for the entire health system in the country, and prepared it for absorption of the Jewish immigration. This medical help was no exception. Though medical care was foremost in the minds of American Zionists, particularly Brandeis, who considered eradication of malaria a basic condition for a successful settlement effort, it was not the only form of American Jewish initiative for the development of a Jewish Palestine. It was no hollow phrase when, at the end of World War I, *The Maccabean* thus defined American Jewry's readiness to serve any need that might arise in building a Jewish Palestine:

> We are making Jewish life transposable to those places where service may be rendered and where the needs of Jewish life require protection and building up. The same principle applied elsewhere produced the Jewish Legion. It produced the Zionist Transfer Bureau. It will produce, when the need develops, the Zionist Engineering Corps. It will produce the Labor Army.

This was not merely a project. Details were elaborated. A Pioneer Industrial Army was proposed for

> service behind the British lines for the purpose of reconstructing the war-ridden districts of Judea.

Judge Bernard A. Rosenblatt, who suggested the project, spoke about an enlistment for two years as soldier-workers. The plan envisaged military discipline in units of this Pioneer Industrial Army, whose

> subject matter and plan of work would be industrial,

and which should work only on lands belonging or purchased by the Jewish National Fund and the Zion Commonwealth.

In line with these ideas which were basically implemented in the *Gdud Avoda* (Workers Battalion), the Zionist Society of Engineers, organized in 1917, set as its purpose:

> To utilize the technical knowledge and training of Jewish engineers and scientists; to make a survey of the national resources of Palestine; to plan and aid the upbuilding of Palestine along scientific lines; to project and develop the possible industries in Palestine.

This concentration on the scientific and industrial development in Palestine was no accident. American Zionists understood that mass immigration and the absorption of immigrant masses could not be accomplished by concentration on agriculture alone. Such thinking was in line with the central Zionist concern of the then Zionist leadership, that mass immigration was the surest way to full exploitation of the political gains.

This special emphasis on industrialization of Palestine as the means for increasing its absorption capacities never obscured the importance of augmenting the land reserves for Jewish colonization. These were American Zionists who organized, in 1934, a chartered company for the development of Trans-Jordan with an initial capital of $1,000,000 after the American representative in the World Zionist Executive, Dr. Emanuel Neumann initialed an agreement with Abdallah, the ruler of Palestine on the left bank of the Jordan. And the contribution of the Palestine Economic Corporation, the practical, economic enterprise initiated by the Brandeis group for the economic development of the country exceeded by far, in dimensions and practical impact on the development of Jewish Palestine, everything any private enterprise could claim in almost any other country.

This approach to the industrialization of Palestine caused American Zionists to give fullhearted practical support to Ruthenberg's plans of electrification of Palestine, to Novomiesky's plan for exploiting the chemical treasures of the Dead Sea, to building smaller industries, among which an artificial tooth factory and a silk factory built by Americans served for many years as an example of success and potent argument for the advantages of industry building.

Among these many American contributions to the development of a Jewish Palestine, one stands out in its full importance today even more than some three decades ago: the big project of irrigating Israel's wastelands in the Negev was conceived, planned and worked out in all technical details on American soil, by American experts, on the initiative of an American Zionist leader, Dr. Emanuel Neumann. The Jordan Valley Authority, thus named and modeled after the American Tennessee Valley Authority, was conceived as a practical scheme for the exploitation of the Jordan waters for the fructification of Israel's barren soil. The plan served as an important element in the political field when there was need to dispel the doubts of American government circles whether Palestine could contribute to the solution of the emigration problems of Jews who had to be saved and removed from countries of their birth. The plan as prepared by the American soil expert, Walter Clay Lowdermilk, envisaged possibilities of settlement for millions of Jews. The then popular joke in American circles that Palestine will become a land "flowing with Lowdermilk and honey," was a fine illustration of the expectations attached to this plan. The water-carrier, Israel's pride in development planning, the Johnston plan for the distribution of the Jordan waters between Israel and the Arab countries, had their origin in American Zionist initiative, thought and practical planning.

In reviewing the American Zionist thought and actions for the development of a Jewish Palestine, one is amazed at the multiplicity and overall character of these plans and actions: when the Federation of American Zionists was hardly five years old, its National Convention adopted a resolution calling for a permanent traveling exhibit of Palestine's products to spur the sale of these products, with all the results such growth of Palestine exports could bring. *The Maccabean* conducted a campaign for the promotion of sales of Israel's products. In a somewhat lighter vein, *The Maccabean* of June, 1904, wrote:

> Well, drink as you will—it is your concern —the Carmel Wine Company is justified in hoisting the Jewish flag over its enterprise and teaches a new reading of an old political proverb: Instead of saying, "Trade follows flag," it is earnestly drawing the flag in the wake of trade.

In the best fashion of today's public relations experts, these Zionist dreamers succeeded in infiltrating with their ideas the general press as well. *The New York Post* of the same date

First contingent of U. S. students at Kennedy Airport before departure for Israel to study at the Mollie Goodman Academic High School established by the Zionist Organization of America. In center: Boris Shteinshleifer, Mrs. Abraham Goodman, Abraham Goodman.

drew a most promising picture of Palestine's commercial potential, writing:

> Now that the attention of the great nations of the world is being directed, for commercial reasons, more and more to the East, Palestine again becomes important. It is in the great land routes of travel. . . . A development of this character would rehabilitate the entire country, and would probably hasten the time when 'the lost sheep of the house of Israel' would again be gathered together in realization of the dreams of the ardent Zionists.

These dreams of ardent Zionists were never confined to one particular aspect of the reconstruction of a Jewish state. What is most amazing in American Zionist practical efforts for a Jewish Palestine is their all-embracing character, their real state, economy and nation-building scope. The fact that these efforts have in time encompassed non-Zionists is only a proof of the success of the Zionist educational vision and a confirmation of the thesis that Zionism has expressed the real sentiments of a vast majority of American Jewry. And what was true in the pre-State days became even more evident since the establishment of Israel. Even on such a minor problem of proper functioning of a State as the mail service, American Jewish assistance kept open Israel's contacts with the world before it was admitted to the International Postal Union. Using a provision in the American law that permits organizing private mail service, such service was made available for Israel in the crucial days of its birth. American know-how served and serves Israel's most important needs in every field of industry, agriculture, communication, social welfare and scientific progress. To enumerate in detail

New York social workers honor Jewish Agency aliyah and absorption workers in Israel.

this entire contribution would amount to a review of a considerable portion of Israel's achievements in the years of its independence.

But these American Jewish contributions to the upbuilding of Israel could hardly be a substitute for the growing need for immigrants from America. The growing emphasis of official Zionist policy on *aliyah* as the most important Zionist duty does not seem to have had any considerable impact on American Jews, neither for that matter on American Zionists. It seems that laws of emigration are much harder to change than to have people made ready for the supreme sacrifice, the sacrifice of their lives in defense of an idea.

American Jewish contribution in the military struggle for a Jewish Palestine in both World Wars serves as the best illustration of such thesis. Fourteen thousand immigrants from the United States and Canada within 19 years of Israel's existence, as important as their settlement in Israel might be, are a far cry from the expectations and needs of a normally developing and growing Jewish State. In this field of becoming a source of manpower for a Jewish Palestine, American Zionism has to admit its historic failure. The commendable efforts of the Jewish Agency, American Section, in promoting *aliyah*, the special organs established for that purpose have not changed materially the situation. PATWA, *Shnat Sherut*, excursions, work-study groups which bring, annually, thousands of Americans to Israel, for various periods of time, have not resulted in an appreciable growth of *aliyah* from America. And though an objective analysis of this state of affairs could well prove that in view of the prevailing circumstances, American Zionists, American Jews, were and are not different from any other Jewish community, nothing could do away with the fact that the great promise American Zionism has held, and

so magnificently fulfilled in so many fields, remains wanting in the field of *aliyah*. It is a fact that some American Zionist groups were reluctant, even programmatically, to include *aliyah* in their program, and those who have overcome inhibitions in the field of *aliyah* have not yet proven that they also can perform.

The Six Day War reopened the discussion on *aliyah* from America. The thousands who volunteered to go to Israel raised new hopes. The need for new settlers became most pressing. The awareness that the United States Jewry is the major reservoir for *aliyah* grew in intensity. American Jews, who have so magnificently responded in Israel's hour of danger and shared so proudly in Israel's finest hour of victory, understand now more than ever, that what they are called for is helping to increase Israel's human potential.

This awareness of the new duties and obligations of American Jews, American Zionists, in the field of *aliyah* has found expression in practical measures and statements of principle. Indicative of this new era is the statement made by Mrs. Rose L. Halprin, chairman of the Jewish Agency, American section:

The key word in Israel today is *aliyah*. It dominates the thinking of the whole country and of all who are concerned for its future. The country is exuberant about the response of the Jews of the world to the war crisis; it is exultant as it absorbs the six thousand volunteers who dropped their normal ways of life to rush to Israel to help in any way possible.

But, and this point of view I conveyed to the Prime Minister and other leaders in Israel, the outpouring of volunteers, which is still going on, does not mean a mass *aliyah* tomorrow from the countries of the west. It does give a new hope to Israel's need and for western *aliyah*.

The potential *aliyah* from the United States will be a well educated and thoroughly professionalized group. This group has tremendous potential for Israel only if it is successfully absorbed. But their very professionalization presents problems. A similar group of well educated and professionalized Israeli youth is being trained in its universities. These groups must be coordinated, and not competitive.

This rather sober appraisal concerning the future of *aliyah* from the United States expresses truthfully the situation. The breakthrough has yet to come. And there is justifiable hope that indeed, it will come.

Masthead of the AACI's bulletin.

Prime Minister Levi Eshkol addresses the 15th annual Convention of the Association of Americans and Canadians in Israel.

American volunteer after Six Day War, at work.

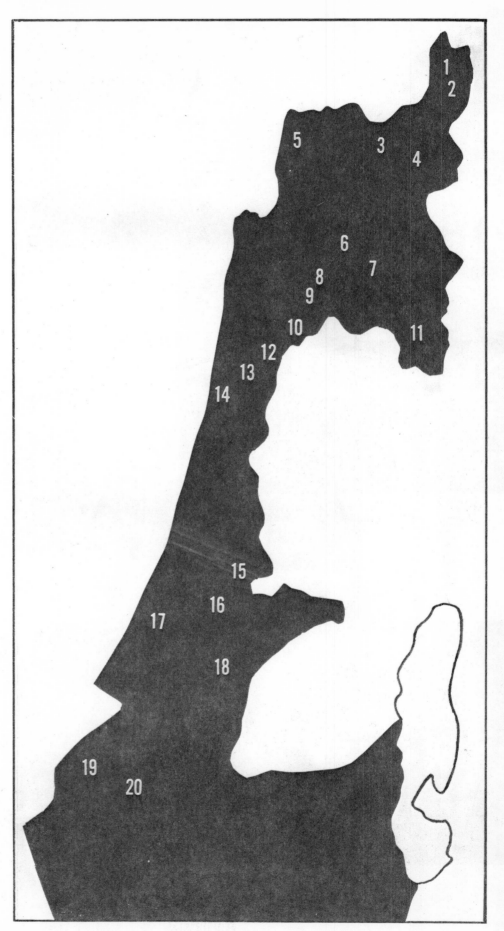

¹Kfar Blum

²Yiftach

³Sasa

⁴Hatzor

⁵Gesher Haziv

⁶Hasolelim

⁷Ein Dor

⁸Hazorea

⁹Ein Hashofet

¹⁰Barkai

¹¹Shluchoth

¹²Beth Hazon

¹³Beth Herouth

¹⁴Avichail

¹⁵Nachshon

¹⁶Kfar Menachem

¹⁷Oroth

¹⁸Galon

¹⁹Kissufim

²⁰Urim

Map showing settlements established by Americans, through the initiative of olim from the United States, or with a considerable percentage of American olim.

PART SIX

16

FROM THE LEGION TO MAHAL

THE MACCABEAN SPIRIT REKINDLED

UNLIKE THE DAYS of the first blossoming of the Zionist spirit in Europe, dreams of liberation of Palestine by military means were an integral part of American Zionism from its inception. Among the first Zionist societies, the name *Zion Hamezuyeneth* (Zion armed) was not unique. It was perhaps no less characteristic of the real spirit which dominated the early American Zionists than such names as *Hovevey Zion, Ohavei Zion,* or *Dorshei Zion.* The first large Zionist group which came into being in Chicago bore the name "Knights of Zion." They were "knights," not only by name, but they wore uniforms, indulged in military exercises, and paraded their military preparedness on every possible occasion. Their chapters were called "Gates," for the distinction of organizational units, gates that would be leading the "knights" to Zion.

Chicago, cradle of American and Midwestern Zionism, was not an exception. Documents of Zionist history at the turn of the century indicate clearly that this "military" trait of American Zionists proved a trend with which the leaders of the Federation of American Zionists had to deal. The report on the Cleveland Convention of 1903 stresses the fact that

> it (the Convention) has also taken no decisive action on the formation of Guard and military societies, which seem attractive to many young men.

This rather laconic report on a subject which must have attracted considerable attention among the delegates, remained unfinished business requiring the continuous concern of the Zionist leadership. Louis Lipsky, the editor of *The Maccabean,* felt it mandatory to use his pen for fighting these military conceptions of the dreamers of Zion. In the article in which he praised and enumerated all the virtues of the Boys Brigade, he considered it imperative to deal with this subject as well.

> The writer looks upon the formation of mature or adult Jewish regiments, or "Zion Conquerors," as absurd, Lipsky stated.

His aim was clear: to discourage any fancy ideas that American Zionists could entertain in preparing the liberation of Palestine through the force of arms. It seems that Lipsky's discouraging tone, voiced in the official organ of the Federation and thus presumably expressing the official position of the Zionist leadership, was not very influential. The *Maccabean* of February, 1904, stated that at a Zionist Convention,

> the Zion Guard, a Hebrew military organization of New Haven attended in body. An exhibition of military drill was given, and it was well done.

Such militancy seemed to have been well attuned to the existing moods of the new Jewish immigration. Many of the immigrants from Russia were reared in concepts of the Russian revolutionary movements, and the immigrants from Austro-Hungary bore the spirit of national liberation movements in which the force of arms appeared as a natural—most often the only—means of the realization of their ideals. On occasions they manifested this militancy, and not only in parades. In those days of anti-Semitic outbreaks, there was little reliance on police protection and intervention. When a funeral procession for Rabbi Jacob Joseph which crowded the streets from curb to curb was showered with screws, bolts and nuts by workers of the R. Hoe and Company, manufacturers of printing presses, the mourners did not wait for police intervention but burst into the place, swept through the floors of the factory building and settled accounts with the pogromists.

At approximately the same time, American Zionists had occasion to prove their trust in self-defense tactics when they were called to manifest their support for the self-defense organized by Russian Jews after the Kishenev pogrom. Although basically engaged in collecting funds for the self-defense program of Jews in Russia, they were far from being content with mere financial support. There was talk

Peter (Pinhas) Ruttenberg at the time when the American Jewish Legion was organized.

about the idea of self-defense in general, the method of achieving goals through putting arms and ammunition into the hands of Jews. The *fighting Jew became a reality,* his importance for Jewish survival an undisputed necessity.

But as in the case of the Boys Brigades, this trend in American Zionism came to an abrupt end. With the ascendency of "practical Zionism," American Zionism could not avoid the gradual relegation of strict Zionist political thinking into a secondary position. In an atmosphere of lesser emphasis on the political character of Zionism, the sympathy for military forms of Zionist expression became less and less evident. The process of Americanization, no doubt, played its role as well. Those immigrants from Austria, who liked to don uniforms and parade on the Kaiser's birthday before the Ambassador of the Austro-Hungarian monarchy, forgot their allegiance for their old country and were gradually submerged into the stream of the American way of life and succumbed to the "pressure cooker" of American integration.

The outbreak of World War I soon proved that there were still old hidden military dreams of liberating Palestine by force of arms. But

between the release of these hidden cravings and the circumstances which could have promoted such release, a most serious obstacle prevailed: the lines drawn between the belligerents were not too conducive to a clear Jewish military commitment. The Allied powers, for whom the United States harbored deep, undisguised sympathies, had in their camp a State whose very mention caused only anger among the Jewish masses. Russia's participation in the Grand Alliance made the entire cause of the Allies anathema to American Jews. If there was any desire for active participation in the war, it was a wish to contribute in some way, any way, to the defeat of the pogromist Czarist regime in Russia.

This was the mood of American Jewry when the first news arrived that somewhere in Egypt a Jewish military corps was being organized to fight on the side of the Allies. Communications in those days were comparatively primitive even under normal conditions, and war disrupted even more the routine flow of information. When the first news of Jabotinsky's and Trumpeldor's efforts for the organization of a Jewish Legion reached America, their credibility was strongly questioned by the Zionist press. *The Maccabean* of May, 1915, disputed the news and stated in a headline, unequivocally, "No Jewish legion to conquer Palestine." This was followed by a statement that

a cable report emanated from London the last week of April, stating that there was being formed a legion of Jewish volunteers to join the Allies in their attempt against Turkey and that the legion was being supported by Luigi Luzatti, Leib Brodsky and Baron Edmund de Rothschild. The Provisional Zionist Committee has received a categorical denial of the truth of this report.

But *The Maccabean* was not satisfied with this denial. In a manner which we would hardly understand today, *The Maccabean* took to task those Jewish newspapers which "dared to publish this information."

It is an indication of the chaos which reigns in Jewish affairs that responsible Jewish newspapers will print from time to time reports of Jewish activity in the political field, which if true, should be unreported, and which if untrue can do the greatest injury to the Jewish cause.

The chief culprit was *Der Tag* (The Day) according to *The Maccabean,* and it was accused of finding this information in . . . its own archives, and of augmenting its guilt by mentioning Jabotinsky's action in one breath with the name of the Zionist Organization. After such reprimand came the categorical statement that

> there are no Jewish Legions to fight with the Allies against Turkey. The Zionist Organization has nothing to do with a scheme conceived by one of its own irresponsible firebrands who, as a member of the Zionist organization, has been guilty of an absurdity as well as of a disloyal act. Responsible newspapermen know better than to give credence to every wild report that comes to them in time of war.

To fight and discredit the Jewish Legion idea seemed to have been of such urgency that the *Maccabean* continued its attack because

> there was no sense in offering England the cooperation of a few hundred, undisciplined, unorganized Jews in Alexandria, for England could not consider the offer of such service of any consequence.

The complaint of the official Zionist organ against the Yiddish press was in fact a crass exaggeration. Notwithstanding its duty of reporting news, even if it was unpleasant for the editors, the editorial pages of the majority of Yiddish papers were in complete agreement with the policy of *The Maccabean* concerning the Jewish Legion idea. The *Jewish Daily News, The Tageblatt,* pointed to the political risks involved and branded the Legion movement a

> piece of folly that would neither shed glory on the Jewish people nor bring practical benefit to the Zionist movement.

Die Wahrheit, the only Yiddish paper which dared to support the Legion, lost thousands of readers within a period of weeks. There was no doubt that opponents of Jewish military participation on the Allies' side were an overwhelming majority among the nearly four million American Jews.

It was into such political atmosphere that an envoy of the Legion idea arrived in the United States. The man designated to initiate the struggle for that idea was not the type to be discouraged by being in the minority. Pinhas Ruthenberg, or as he still called himself, Piotr, was no novice to a serious political fight. He came to the United States with the reputation of a fighting revolutionary leader. His services to the Russian revolutionary movement were common knowledge. His hatred of

Young legionnaires from the U. S.

the Czarist regime and his leadership in the fighting arm of the Russian Social Revolutionaries brought him fame and respect among the oppressed. To be in a minority, especially a negligible minority, was for Ruthenberg only a challenge. The fact that he, who had fought the Czarist regime, now sided with those who argued for Jewish military participation on the side of the Allies, which meant on the side of Russia as well, was supporting the Jewish Legion idea, should have served as a sufficient argument for the Americans hostile to Czarist Russia. After all, Ruthenberg had more authority in this area than the editors of the Jewish press and the kibitzers of the East Side cafes.

It is therefore somewhat difficult to understand why Ruthenberg did not keep his part of the agreement made with Jabotinsky concerning the struggle for the Jewish Legion idea in America.

According to this agreement, the two men arrived at three basic conclusions,

(1) that a Jewish Legion is the need of the hour;

(2) that alignment with the British war effort held the best promise for Zionist aspirations and

American legionnaires at the Jewish Soldiers Home in Jerusalem.

(3) that the two had to divide geographically the areas of their activity for the Legion, i.e., Jabotinsky was to work on it in Europe, Ruthenberg in America.

The "deal" reached at Brindisi in April, 1915, materialized only on its European end. On the other, in America, political considerations other than the ones agreed upon in Brindisi, prevailed.

The reasons for Ruthenberg's new attitude to the Legion idea were not related to his personal convictions. Ruthenberg did not change his mind upon confrontation with American realities. A brochure which he wrote on the pressing problems that face Jewry in the war, presented the Jewish Legion idea as one of the central tasks of the times. But this part of the brochure never saw light. The reason: Ruthenberg's political friends thought that the Jewish Legion idea was not worthy of priority and certainly not exclusively vis a vis all other problems of those days. By the force of basic ideological considerations, Ruthenberg found his political home in America with the Poale-Zion. Within this Zionist group Ruthenberg found affinity, understanding and

political admiration. After all they were still talking about a political revolutionary movement, about social revolution and Ruthenberg had already behind him accomplished facts of that nature. They did not discount the Jewish Legion idea; neither had they tried to question its validity or importance. What they questioned was the timeliness of that idea's implementation. The considerations for such position were many; there was first of all the general attitude towards the cause of the Allies. The leadership of *Poale-Zion* was torn by the internal dispute between the supporters of the Allies' cause and those who could not divest this cause from the historic accounting Jews had had with progromist Czarist Russia. And the Russia-haters held overwhelmingly the upper hand.

To support the idea of a Jewish Legion, fighting on the Allies' side, would have meant the end of *Poale-Zion* as a unified, political group. For a political party bound on self-preservation, this consideration alone appeared convincing enough to prevail upon Ruthenberg to exclude the Legion idea from his programmatic brochure. But this was not the only consideration to *Poale-Zionists,* and with them to Ruthenberg. As later publications reported, and among them the memoirs of one of the central figures of American *Poale-Zionism,* Baruch Zuckerman, tasks other than the Legion appeared, at that time, more pressing, more important.

American Jewry was in the midst of the struggle for a Jewish representative body, for the Jewish Congress, as well as for an adequate response to the needs of Jewish communities that suffered as a result of the war. Whether preoccupation with organizational problems of American Jewry and problems of relief work for needy Jewish brethren really justified a hands off policy concerning the Legion idea is a matter of opinion. The fact remained that the center of early Legion propaganda, which was supposed to rise on the American soil, never came into being. The official policy adopted by the Greater Actions Committee of the World Zionist Organization in the summer of 1915, remained the determining factor in the attitude of American Zionists towards the Legion idea. This policy was clear and definitive: the Legion is an abortive idea and all it can accomplish is to destroy Zionism utterly. The debate in that highest Zionist body pointed out that Germany, the Central Powers with which Turkey was allied, will win the war, and that Turkey will never leave Palestine. The formal resolution called upon Zionists everywhere to oppose the Legion propaganda. To support it meant a breach of Zionist discipline in times as crucial as times of war, and supreme trial in world affairs.

Thus America remained, in the early years of the war, basically outside the stream of that part of Zionist activity that was concerned with the Jewish Legion. The fact that America was not a belligerent, that it preserved its neutrality, at least, formally, for almost three years, since the outbreak of the war, played no doubt an important role in the fortunes of what could be defined as the dormant American Jewish sympathy for the Jewish Legion idea.

The change in this American Zionist attitude towards the Legion had to wait for political developments which transformed completely the Zionist outlook on the problems of Zionist policies during the war. With the war wearing on, the resolution of the Greater Actions Committee was wearing off. Conditions of war affected the authority of that highest Zionist body. Losing contact with Zionist territorial organizations, it lost authority as well. The illusory policy of neutrality in the world conflict was discarded not only by Vladimir Jabotinsky "the firebrand." Zionist leaders of highest standing, entire territorial sections of the Zionist movement decided that if there is any hope for Zionist gains during and after the war, it is the abandonment of neutrality that can make the Zionist movement a political factor. The negotiations between the Zionist Federation of England and the British War Cabinet, the involvement of American Zionists in these negotiations were no more secret at the end of 1916, and beginning of 1917. American Zionists knew where the sympathies of their movement lay.

The American entry into the war delivered the death blow to the theories of neutrality, whatever their reasons and origins were. British recruiting missions opened their offices all over the country. It was in this general atmosphere that the news broke about the decision of the British War Cabinet to establish Jewish military units with their Jewish insignia, with Jewish officers in command, with Hebrew as the language of command. The American Jews learned with pride that similarly to the role they played in the political negotiations, their standing was used as a potent factor in convincing the British government that the establishment of the Jewish Legion will be helpful in assuring the sympathies of American Jewry

Jewish Legion volunteers from the U. S., Canada, Argentina at the Wailing Wall.

for the Allies' cause. In one of the conversations between Jabotinsky and British officials, this argument was quoted explicitly:

There is only one thing a Jew loves more than he hates the Russian regime—Palestine! Only through a great love can you forget a great hatred—not otherwise. Does that mean that if the British government issued a manifesto in favor of Zionism—then . . . ?

Then the American Jews would say: Fine, but what is a manifesto without facts? At the beginning of the war a term was created, 'scrap of paper'—and this term has become sadly popular. A manifesto—certainly; but you must have facts, besides.

What do you mean by facts?

A Jewish Corps which should participate in the conquest of Palestine.

When in August, 1917, the British government finally approved the Jewish Legion, officially named The Jewish Regiment, young American Jews had reason to be stirred. They saw a goal, a defined instrument for the implementation of their professed love for Zion. The insignia of the Legionaires, a *menorah* with the Hebrew word *Kadimah* (which means both "forward," and "eastward") and a blue-white mark on the collar added only excitement to the already stirred youngsters. Within three months came the political commitment for the support of Zionist aspirations: The Balfour Declaration, whose implications were, at that time, much more overestimated than at any later date.

Colonel John H. Patterson, D.S.O.

Thus the recruitment campaign for American volunteers started almost spontaneously. Of course, organized Zionists formed the backbone. Members of the existing *Hehalutz* organization were the most logical and natural candidates to lead the stream of volunteers for the Legion. The enthusiasm surpassed the slim ranks of the *Hehalutz*, whose membership did not reach even five hundred. The volunteers came in the hundreds, every week. New York was leading but was by no means the only city that enjoyed this outpouring of Jewish patriotism. Boston, Chicago, Detroit followed suit with even greater excitement, since the cities were smaller and the Jewish communities more tangible and more compact. Meetings for the Legion were attended by thousands. Those who volunteered assisted in the recruiting campaign, and in the forefront were the recognized leaders of the Zionist movement. The big cities of America were turned into a kind of sprawling "Hyde Park," where street corners were turned into meeting places; trucks bedecked with American and Jewish flags frequented the street corners especially at lunch time, when thousands of Jews appeared for their lunch break. An already enlisted volunteer would deliver a fiery speech, calling his enthusiastic listeners to follow his example. Not infrequently would a new volunteer board the truck, raise his hand, and deliver his oath of joining the Legion.

The establishment of the office for volunteers by the Zionist administration coincided with the quite advanced stage of recruitment for the Legion. The head of the British-Canadian Recruiting Mission in New York, Colonel F. C. Jameson, had his job done by hundreds of Zionists. Each and every Zionist, and many who were not members of the organization, did their best to support the recruitment. Those who could not join intensified by their enthusiasm the atmosphere of elation, which in turn encouraged the young, and the not-so-young, to volunteer. There were youngsters under eighteen who lied about their age in order to be accepted, and there were enthusiasts who did not hestitate to jeopardize their positions, separate themselves from their families, give up their careers. There was J. Cooper, who gave up his Sheriff's badge in Connecticut; there was a Rosenberg who gave up a flourishing business in Philadelphia and met no opposition from his wife and seven children; there was Joseph Cohen, a Fellow of Columbia University and graduate of the University of Cambridge; Gershon Agronsky, managing editor of *Das Yiddische Volk*, who in the words of his fellow editor of the paper,

> upheld the prestige of newspapermen by passing the medical examination as physically qualified to enter the aviation corps;

the two Brajnin brothers, Moshe and Joseph, the sons of the revered Hebrew writer, Rueven Brajnin; Jacob Goodman, Louis Fischer, Morris Speiser, L. Bunin, Elias Gilner, Judah Lapson, Moshe Rivlin, Dr. Ravid, Dr. J. L. Gordon, Dr. Abrahami, Fred Mallet and many others responded until their over-all number reached about 6,500, a number completely sufficient for organizing a military unit of brigade strength.

The American recruiting campaign was not free of national demands the British High Commissioner and Ambassador to Washington, Lord Reading, had no difficulty to accept. The pattern was already set in London. The British representative in America had no reason to reject conditions which were already accepted in Great Britain. The British consul in New York served as intermediary. As formulated, these condition demanded that

(a) the American Jewish volunteers be incorporated into the Jewish Legion, and not be dispersed among the various battalions of the British army;

(b) the Jewish Legion be dispatched only to the Palestinian front;

(c) the language of command be Hebrew;

(d) the Legion be accorded insignia which will leave no doubt that this is a Jewish unit.

What is amazing in this final stage of implementation of the Legion idea was the silence of Ruthenberg. The man who was supposed to spearhead the drive for the Jewish Legion did not seize upon the opportunity that afforded itself after the initial obstacles were removed. After a period of close cooperation with the two leading Palestinians, David Ben Gurion and Yitzhak Ben Zvi, who arrived in America almost at the same time as Ruthenberg, after a period of intensive activity for the propagation of the idea of the American Jewish Congress, Ruthenberg was seized completely with the idea of the electrification of Palestine, leaving to his two friends from Palestine the initiative in support of the Legion idea, as belatedly as their open and clear support had come.

In fact there was no need for too much fight for the Legion idea. Even the front of the opponents of Zionism witnessed serious cracks in relation to the Legion idea. And the majority of the American Jews, Zionists and non-Zionists, supported enthusiastically the Legion. "From sources wholly dissociated from Zionist influence, words of commendation and praise have been received for the young," reported the press. Although the membership figures of the Federation of American Zionists, together with the other already active ideological Zionist groups, hardly surpassed ten thousand, many more Jews used to appear at many of the meetings called in support of the Legion and almost that many volunteered for service in the Legion.

The Jewish Legion idea sparked a veritable mass movement among American Jews, the like of which only real turning points in the history of nations can create. As in the days

A religious service in the field.

of opposition to the Legion idea, the press, particularly the Zionist press, mirrored the real mood of the Jewish masses. There was no limit to the demonstrations of pride and joy. Zionism in action—this was the phrase used in appraisals of the importance of the Legion. An editorial in *The Maccabean* stated:

Everyone who knows what national interest means appreciates the great value of Jewish Military Units. . . . To be part of the army is to be part of the first Jewish Army since the death of *Bar Kokhba* and *Bethar,* the first army proudly to carry the rejuvenated Jewish flag, the first army to be led by Jewish officers. . . . These Jewish Military Units may open up for us other national opportunities of which it may be premature to speak, but anyone who hesitates to support the enterprise shows by hesitation a lack of understanding of Jewish national needs. He lacks the national instinct. He is unable to appreciate the fact that the Restoration of the Jews will be brought about only by physical and material readiness to enter any of the many doors that may be opened for our return.

The Zionist leadership drew other conclusions as well from the establishment of Jewish units. It considered these units a most decisive, a definitive argument in the decades-long dispute whether Jews are a nation or only a religious denomination. Concerning this dispute, *The Maccabean* wrote:

When a Jewish Battalion leaves for the Palestine front from New York, of what earthly use is it to declare that the Jewish people are only a religious denomination?

Insignia of the Judeans—the Menorah with the inscription Kadimah (Forward) and the Mogen David on the armpatch.

From the Legion, the American Zionists drew not only political and ideological conclusions. They saw in it an instrument for moral encouragement:

It is a sign of health that Jewish manhood has responded to the call. There is to be one place where if Jewish blood is to be shed, it shall be placed to the credit of the Jewish people. And if there are to be heroes, it is of value to know that there were some heroes living in our day, Jewish heroes who offered their lives for the homeland of the Jewish people.

Such was the response to the opportunity given for serving the Zionist idea. The fact that such enthusiasm produced only some six thousand or so volunteers should be ascribed to two basic conditions: only non-American citizen were able to enlist, as citizens were liable for the general war draft, and that only a few months were devoted to the entire recruiting campaign which started in earnest less than a year prior to the end of the war.

In spite of these limitations, the impression created by the recruiting campaign was such that the entire American Jewish community was thrown into an outburst of enthusiasm no skeptic could dispute. As soon as a group of some two hundred volunteers assembled, they were loosely organized into a unit and sent off to the training camp in Windsor, Canada, to prepare for transportation to England, and later, to Palestine. After the first such group of 200 left for Canada, transports followed at intervals of some three to four weeks each. Some of these groups comprised as many as 500.

Before leaving they had to undergo the ritual of banquets, farewell parties, honor parades and listening to speeches. The Zionist Lunch Club of New York was kept busy with arranging parties. The Hotel Imperial never witnessed such throngs of enthusiastic young people, who were carrying away with their enthusiasm the renowned leaders of the Zionist movement, like Louis Lipsky, Shmaryahu Levin, Nahman Syrkin, none of whom ever missed an occasion to address the young volunteers. The members of the Club fought ardently to be given the honor of playing host at these banquets, and delivering a speech at such occasion was considered a most momentous achievement. The speech-making was multilingual, English, Yiddish, Hebrew and even French, for stressing the fact that Jews are joining the cause of the Allies, and especially Britain's closest ally, France.

The Zionist Federation opened a central bureau in New York for the purpose of carrying on an active recruiting campaign. A special organizer was put in charge of the drive. The office was open for consultation on personal problems for those who had to make arrangements concerning their local current obligations, insurance, and any form of assistance required. Recruits who wanted it were given a kit with basic utensils and some clothing they could use even after donning the military uniform.

The parades became soon a landmark of Jewish life in New York. Following the ban-

Vladimir Jabotinsky.

the recruits gathered at the offices of the British Recruiting Mission to say farewell to their dear ones, friends and fellow Zionists. When the group sailed away from the Fall River Line Pier, it was carrying a blue and white flag presented by the Zionist Council of Greater New York.

The recruitment in Canada was made much easier due to the decision of the Canadian military authorities which permitted young Canadian Jews called into service under the Conscription Law to apply for transfer to the Jewish Battalion for service on the Palestinian front. The significance of this decision was stressed by the fact that members of the American contingent (the Third) were assigned to recruiting duty for the Jewish Battalion. Quartermaster Sergeant Gershon Agronsky (Agron, subsequently the founder and editor of the first and only English daily in Palestine and Israel, and mayor of Jerusalem), Sergeant Moses Brajnin, and Corporals Louis Fischer (who achieved fame as an historian and political writer on Russia and Russian leaders) and Joseph Brainin (executive vice president of the American Committee for the Weitzman Institute) were transferred from the training camp at York Redout in Halifax, to Montreal. How much the Canadian authorities valued this recruiting drive is best illustrated in the letter they received from Major General Lessard:

The splendid showing of Jewish manhood of the United States leads me to believe that your endeavors will meet with success. Impress upon the Jewish young men of Canada that this is their opportunity to serve in this hour of need the cause of Great Britain and her allies, and at the same time

David Ben Gurion and Yitzhak Ben Zvi after they volunteered for the Jewish Legion, during their stay in the United States.

quet the parade used to start out from the hotel. A dozen cars and a bus would open the parade down Broadway through Twenty-third Street, down to Second Avenue, and from there to Houston Street, thence to Essex, Rivington, Clinton Streets and East Broadway. The enthusiasm would extend far into the night and long after the volunteers had retired to their homes, the East Side remained alive with parades, flag waving, the resounding choruses of *Hatikvah*. And when the day of the departure of the first group arrived, February 28, 1918,

Colonel Eliezer Margolin, commanding officer of the 39th Royal Fusiliers, later the Second Judean Battalion, composed of American volunteers.

help in the establishment of the Jewish Homeland in Palestine which has the support of His Majesty's Government. As a Canadian, I should be delighted to see the record of the Jewish Legion in the United States equaled in the Dominion of Canada.

The recruiting campaign among Jewish youth of Canada must have appeared of such importance and significance that even Sir Robert Borden, the Prime Minister of Canada,

American legionnaires display an issue of the newly established Hebrew daily Haaretz.

felt obliged to write a letter to one of the recruiting officers, Corporal Joseph Brainin, to assure him of his sympathies with the purpose for which the Legion is to fight.

The Canadian official policy had its most unexpected influence on Jewish fighting men in the frontlines of Europe. Jewish soldiers in various military units were eager to fight on the Palestinian front. These moods were best illustrated in a letter addressed to the publicity bureau of the Zionist Federation by an officer of the American Expeditionary Forces in France, Captain Jablon, who was formerly a physician in San Francisco. Captain Joblon wrote:

I have just said goodbye to two young French Jews who form part of the company of the *Corps d'Elite* or storming troops, both

American legionnaires in Rishon Lézion.

of whom have won distinction in numerous raids and attacks. They asked to be sent to fight with the French and British Jewish troops in Palestine. They told me of many of their friends who had gone there and who had been killed and of many more whom they hoped still to meet. That night I heard of the Australian Jews who had requested, after two and a half years in the trenches of the French, to be transferred to the British forces in Palestine!!! . . . That is the way we will recover Palestine.

And the letter continues,

We, here in America's army, are looking forward to the day when we can go back to the Promised Land, today indeed the Promised Land, with the same eagerness as that of our ancestors. And we will go there as free men who have earned that right by shedding freely of our blood in freedom's cause.

These young men were not plagued by the talk of double loyalty; neither did anybody in the non-Jewish American community consider something else than natural the desire of the Jewish boys to fight for the cause their country was fighting, with a special interest for the cause of their ancient homeland, and the redemption of their people. And those who had any doubts as to the propriety of such twin interests were eagerly drawing on the example of the Irish. The words of Cardinal Farley at the farewell party for the Irish Sixty-Ninth Regiment in New York were quoted over and over again. Paraphrasing the words of Cardinal Farley:

Boys, I needn't ask you to be loyal to the Stars and Stripes, but don't forget Old Ireland.

The Zionist leaders stated:

Boys, we needn't ask you to be loyal to the Stars and Stripes, but don't forget that you are Jews!

And forget they did not. The recruitment turned into an outpouring of Jewish patriotism which spilled over into every province of life. They tried hard to study Jewish history, the geography of Palestine, the Hebrew language. The brief dispute with some Poale-Zion leaders whether Hebrew or Yiddish should be the language of command in the Jewish Battalion was resolved: Hebrew easily prevailed. As consecutive groups of the volunteers departed on March 9, March 21, April 10, they carried with them the basic words of the Hebrew military command which Hebrew scholars worked hard to create. The Yiddish press, and primarily *The Jewish Morning Journal* and *Der Tag*, opened their columns to those linguists who had done their best for the sake of what they called "militant Hebrew." They had source material in the example of the first units of the Jewish Legion already in Palestine. A special commission was established for that purpose. The pronunciation adopted was Sephardic. The papers published examples of this "militant Hebrew": "Company," *haplugah;* "squad," tzror;" move," *hen.* Some of these, such as *haplugah,* were preserved until our very day and are standard words of Israel's Defense Army.

As was fitting, the Legionnaires had their songs. One such marching song for the Judaeans, which achieved considerable popularity, was written by Nina Salamon, the wife of Radcliffe N. Salamon, the senior medical officer of the Legion. For the benefit of the volunteers in America, it was printed and reprinted in *The Maccabean*:

Zion our Mother, calling to thy sons
We are coming, we are coming to thine aid.

Justice Brandeis visits Legion during his visit in Palestine, 1919.

Spread among the nations, we thy loving ones
We are ready, we are coming unafraid.
All along the ages, thou vast lying waste
We were waiting, we were looking to the goal
Thou wast always calling, calling us to haste
We were hoping and we heard thee in our soul.

Not only Jews were overjoyed with these developments, with the success of the Jewish Legion idea. Former President Theodore Roosevelt, a few months before his death, was so impressed by the establishment of the Jewish Battalions, that he could not withstand the temptation of writing a letter of congratulations to Colonel John Henry Patterson, the commander and the Zion Mule Corps, the first Jewish unit of 1915, that fought on the Gallipoli front, and later commander of one of the fighting Jewish Battalions. The great statesman wrote:

My dear Colonel Patterson, I most heartily congratulate you on leading what was not only one of the most important but one of the most dramatic incidents in the whole war: to have the sons of Israel smite Ammon hip and thigh under your leadership is something worthwhile.

It is worth mentioning that by the time the letter reached Col. Patterson, Theodore Roosevelt was already dead. The letter was sent in error to France and was shuffled from one army corps to another, until somebody noticed that it had on the address, "E.E.F."—code name of the Egyptian Expeditionary Forces, as the British army, under General Allenby, on the Middle Eastern front was called.

The high excitement over Jews fighting in Jewish formations for the liberation of the Jewish land was due for an unpleasant disillusionment. The staff at General Headquarters of Allenby's army was not too keen on exposing the Jewish character of the new battalions which had joined the Expeditionary Force. Dispatches relating to the three Jewish battalions — the 38th, 39th and 40th Royal Fusiliers, later known as the First, Second and Third *Judean Battalions,* were never allowed to appear in the Palestinian and Egyptian press. Even General Allenby's dispatches were censored. Only one such dispatch, of October 1918, somehow dodged the censor and thus it revealed to the world what General Allenby had to say about the Jewish warriors:

> I will bring to notice the good fighting qualities shown by the newer units. These include . . . the 38th and the 39th Jewish Battalions of the Royal Fusiliers.

When this commendation reached America, the Zionist Organization of America hastened to send a letter of congratulations to General Allenby who acknowledged the receipt of the letter and wrote on November 1918 to the Zionist Federation:

> You will be glad to hear that the Jewish regiment did consistently good work!

The recruitment for the Jewish battalions was accompanied by a concentrated effort to provide the Jewish units with the supplementary services an army has to have. Detroit, one of the centers of the recruiting campaign, had the distinct honor of initiating the organization of a society which had to carry on among the Jewish recruits work similar to that which was performed among the American servicemen by such agencies as the Jewish Welfare Board and the Red Cross. The society adopted the name *The Red Mogen David,* and promptly started the publication of a Red Mogen David Bulletin, edited by the well known poet, H. Rosenblatt. In this category, though not related exclusively to the military effort, should be mentioned the American Medical Unit. Though part of the practical efforts of Hadassah, organized and equipped by the Zionist Federation, the group of forty doctors and nurses and hygiene engineers, headed by Dr. Rubinov, brought encouragement and joy to the American boys in Palestine.

They needed such encouragement badly. The excitement of the New York recruiting campaign was seriously put to test in face of the realities within the Egyptian Expeditionary Forces. The volunteers from America joined the Jewish battalions for one purpose: to participate in the liberation of Palestine. They wanted to join the front line units; they had behind them months of military training which they hoped to use in combat. But front line

duty was slow in coming. Vladimir Jabotinsky dwells on this problem in his *Story of the Jewish Legion:*

> American young men, he wrote, on leaving the boat at Alexandria, instantly wanted to know, 'Where is the front?' The Englishmen replied, 'First do your training.' The Americans retorted, 'But in your country's camps, they tell you that three or four months' training is quite enough—and we have had six.'

Thus instead of sending the American volunteers directly to the front line, they were commanded to perform various military duties, except fighting.

The fact that these were perhaps objectively, from the point of view of the over-all strategy of the Middle-East front, most important military duties, did not help in alleviating the feelings of frustration and even discrimination sensed by the American volunteers. The fact that at some juncture units of the Jewish battalions were guarding the entire net of communication lines, that they were in charge of the prisoner of war camps, was no consolation either. Every soldier understood the distinction between front line duties and all the other forms of military service.

There was still alive the spectre of the first Jewish military unit of 1915 which was not given the privilege of a fighting unit but had to accept the function of a mule corps, *The Zion Mule Corps,* confined only to servicing the fighting units. The American boys considered such treatment what it was, discrimination in the best tradition of the British general staff not to entrust real fighting to what they called "fancy battalions." Though they were in the words of Colonel Patterson "the mainstay of the British authorities in Palestine," they considered their vows fulfilled only when they were given the opportunity to participate in the final assault against the Turkish army and help to drive the Turks out of Palestine. The American legionnaires considered it the most glorious chapter in the history of their American units when they were included in this final offensive. Entrusted with the task of capturing a ford across the Jordan River known as Amun Esh Shert, for opening the way for advancement to the town Es Salt in the hills of Moab, far beyond the Jordan, they displayed excellent courage, endurance and military skill which was highly praised by the command of the Expeditionary Force. American units under Colonel Margolin were the first infantry troops to march to Es Salt, believed to be the ancient Ramat Gilead, and to establish there their occupation authority. This was a kind of a Jewish liberation army that established Jewish rule in the entire area for the first time in two thousand years.

But the national pride and personal satisfaction those American Jewish units derived from this military fact, and from their part in the final victory, did not obscure the realities of the situation. And these realities did not live up to expectations. Unlike many of the members of the 38th battalion of Royal Fusiliers, the soldiers of the 39th battalion of the American volunteers were professed Zionists, groomed in Zionism, possessed by Zionist zeal and the desire to serve the Zionist cause.

In war they wanted to fight, after the war they wanted to build the country. The could not stand the harsh military discipline of the British army. Although they themselves were of European extraction, the majority of them, after only a few years of life in America, were imbued with the ideas of American democracy and American freedom. The anti-Semitic excesses of the British command made the senseless exercises in endurance in the desert heat even more oppressive. When American legionnaires were ordered to Egypt in order to assist the British troops in quelling a national rebellion, they refused to be pawns of British imperialist interests. They did not flinch over a close brush with what in military terms was sheer mutiny. It was only due to the intercession of the high command and the intervention of London that a major crisis was avoided and the original order rescinded.

Under such conditions, a clash with the British commanders became unavoidable. A insignificant incident which was followed by a cruel and unjust punishment caused a demonstrative break of discipline. The military authorities acted with full rigor of military regulations. This was the famous mutiny in the American Jewish battalion. A court martial ensued. Jabotinsky acted as defense counsel though he did not approve of the mutinous action. Fifty-four and then thirty-five of the American and Canadian legionnaires were sentenced to years of hard labor. The sentence was later commuted. There were examples of extreme courage and nobility when a Canadian corporal named Levinsky shouldered the entire blame and thus saved a group of six of his comrades from a harsh sentence.

The harsh sentence of seven years imprisonment was only another example of the conditions which prevailed in Palestine, in British

headquarters, in the leading circles of OETA (Occupied Enemy Territory Administration). Though the sentence was rescinded after four months, it left a bitter after-taste. The perplexed feelings were well fed by the British command. During the Passover of 1919, the General Headquarters published an order forbidding Jewish soldiers to visit the city of Jerusalem. The outrageous order stunned the legionnaires. While the songs of liberating Jerusalem were still resounding in their ears, they were confronted with a political reality they could hardly grasp. The visit of Louis Brandeis to the battalions was a pleasant interlude. Even Brandeis' intercession with the London government which recalled from Palestine some of the most outspoken anti-Semitic officers, did not change the atmosphere. The arch enemy of the Jewish battalions, of the Balfour Declaration, the Chief of Staff, General Louis Jean Bols, preserved his position and influence.

The official order according the Jewish battalions their Jewish insignia, the Menorah with the Hebrew word *Kadimah*, which was promised at the outset, was promulgated at last, after the Legion had passed its test of fire. Together with this order, the three battalions were granted the official name, *The Judaean Regiment*. But even this belated fulfillment of an early promise contributed little to the alleviation of grievances, of dissatisfaction, of frustration.

With the war over and no proper plans available for incorporating the legionnaires into the mainstream of constructive life in the young Jewish *Yishuv*, the demand for demobilization and return to America grew louder daily. The Americans of the 39th battalion, under Colonel Eliezer Margolin, were still performing a vital duty of garrisoning and protecting the Jewish colonies of Sharon and Tel Aviv, but few foresaw trouble and even fewer believed that the Legion was the most important guarantee of security for the *Yishuv,* and of the proper implementation of the policies envisaged in the Balfour Declaration. When their intervention against Arab rioters in May, 1921, saved Tel Aviv and the Jewish inhabitants of Jaffa from a pogrom, they were already a small group of a few hundred who had stuck it out. The majority joined the general outcry for demobilization. The command's attempt to prepare the legionnaires for civilian life through giving them training in trades was neither convincing nor successful. When the order of disbandment came, in the wake of the Legion's

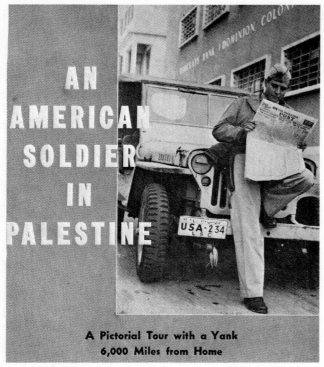

AN AMERICAN SOLDIER IN PALESTINE

A Pictorial Tour with a Yank
6,000 Miles from Home

Cover of pamphlet on American soldiers in Palestine during World War II.

intervention in preventing Arab pogroms, only a skeleton force was left of the 5,000-strong Judaean Regiment.

Before this final act of a heroic chapter came to its close, some of the American legionnaires were given the opportunity to participate in laying the foundations for future political developments in Palestine, consequences of which are reverberating even today. In the summer of 1919, American legionnaires participated in a conference in Petah Tikvah, at which the labor party, *Ahdut Avodah,* was organized. Thus they contributed to the formation of the organization of the labor unions that followed a year later, with the establishment of the *Histadruth* in 1920.

Of the volunteers of the three Jewish battalions, the American legionnaires succeeded in preserving an *esprit de corps* which prevails to this very day. It was they who contributed most to the establishment of a living and permanent memorial for the Legion in Israel, in the Legion veterans' settlement, Avihayil, and the *Beth Hagdudim* (Home of the Legion) there, and these same veterans preserve to this day in the United States the glorious memory of their service. The *Hagdud Haivri* League, American Veterans of the Jewish Legion, an active organization, whose members miss no opportunity to demonstrate their pride in being part of a great heroic chapter in the history of Jewish national redemption. Outworn, outmoded caps, insignia of half a century before, are still to be seen on occasions of great national festivities. Even the military nomenclature was not abandoned. The officers of the League bear the titles of National Commander, National Adjutant, Quartermaster, though they are not appointed but democratically elected at annual conventions. The acknowledgement of their service in the form of a decoration established some years ago by the Government of Israel was a fitting act of recognition they had long awaited and fully deserved.

Perhaps the greatest reward they could have expected came three decades after they have manifested their readiness for the supreme sacrifice, when a new generation of young American Jews picked up where they left off and responded to the second call for the liberation of *Eretz Israel.* This time there were no more legions, no more negotiations with foreign authorities; this time it was the Jewish army and Jewish authorities, all of which came about due to a great extent to the American Jewish youngsters who formed the Jewish Legion and spilled their blood to make their nation alive and free again.

17

DIRECT ACTIONS FOR A JEWISH PALESTINE

THE WORLD WAR I CALL for American Jewish participation in the liberation of Palestine still a living memory, the need for a new American Jewish contribution to a military effort, on behalf of a Jewish Palestine, gained new importance and urgency. Hardly two decades had passed since the last Jewish American Legionnaire doffed his Jewish Legion veterans cap and deposited the insignia of the 39th Battalion of Royal Fusilliers in his family safe, when discussion on a Jewish military unit absorbed anew the American Jewish Community. World War II was on, and with it appeared the promise of Zionist fulfillment together with the threat of physical obliteration of what Zionism had already achieved in Palestine.

Unlike in the days of World War I, the basic differences of opinion concerning the choice of belligerents were out of the question. Jews knew beyond any dispute who were their allies, and whom they had to support. There was also no questioning the importance of the new theatre of war, whose proximity to Palestine made it of prime concern to all. Jews everywhere were concerned not only with the Zionist work in Palestine but also, and first of all, with the physical safety of the close to half million Jews in Palestine.

The Jews of America with few exceptions, were aware of their duty in the new hour of trial. Unfortunately these were the only aspects of the creation of a Jewish military force which differed from those that prevailed during World War I. The attitude of Great Britain to the idea of a Jewish military force, fighting under its own flag, did not change much since the days of the struggle for the formation of the Jewish Legion over twenty years before. Inasmuch as it changed, it changed for the worse. While in 1917 sympathy for the Jewish Legion idea appeared a part of the overall policy of winning the Jews to the Allies' cause, the outbreak of World War II came at a time of a complete reversal of British policies toward Zionism. These were the days of the 1939 White Paper that heralded British resolve to terminate Zionist efforts in Palestine, to liquidate the Zionist dream. Even in its hour of trial, when German troops were threatening the very existence of Great Britain, after the Dunkirk debacle, the British Government found only one answer to

the Yishuvs, to the Jewish offer to raise four divisions for the fight against the Axis: these divisions will be used for defeating the anti-Zionist White Paper.

In this situation, recourse to the political intervention of American Zionists became the only hope for a change in the British policy concerning a Jewish fighting force. The American Zionist Emergency Committee was the natural group to turn to for such intervention.

The political circumstances were not too favorable for American Zionist action. The United States was still a neutral country. And though there was no doubt where American sympathies leaned in the war, the Neutrality Act remained the governing formulation of the American position. These political circumstances were by themselves a serious handicap in inducing the American Government to intervene with Great Britain. But the Zionist Executive that asked for the Emergency Committee's action added another problem when its plan envisaged that not only Palestinian and stateless refugee Jews be considered the manpower reservoir for the recruitment of the Jewish force. American Jewish volunteers were to be considered as well. To the already serious political problem, a legal problem was added. A meeting of a Zionist delegation with Secretary of State Cordell Hull in June 1940, cleared the legal side of the problem when Hull stated unequivocally "there had been no change in the law with regard to the recruitment for military service abroad." The Emergency Committee decided to act accordingly. It resolved that "there could be no recruiting in this country without the knowledge and consent of the Government."

The exclusion of American nationals from the manpower potential of a Jewish military force did not terminate American Jewish efforts to back a force to be composed only of Palestinian Jews and Jewish refugees from Europe. The Zionist delegation that met with Hull won the support of the British Ambassador in Washington, Lord Lothian, who promised to advise his government of the importance of the plan. Simultaneously presidents of eleven Jewish national organizations cabled Winston S. Churchill "to mobilize Jewish units in Palestine under British military supervision to insure effective home defense . . . in the interest of the *Yishuv* and its future, and that of Great Britain." The effort in the field of public relations marked a success in winning the support of Arthur Hays Sulzberger of *The New York Times.* Mr. Sulzberger promised the editorial support of *The Times* for the Jewish Army idea. He even urged the Zionists to circulate as widely as possible the *Yishuv's* desire to send its sons for military service to the front lines. The leaders of the two major labor organizations, William Green, president of the A.F.L. and Philip Murray, president of the C.I.O., urged the leaders of the British Labor Party that they support the Jewish Army plan.

Efforts on behalf of the Jewish Army idea were not limited to the Zionist Emergency Committee. Vladimir Jabotinsky, the founder of the Jewish Legion in World War I, added his own initiative to the struggle for the creation of a Jewish military force. After his arrival in New York, in March, 1940, Jabotinsky lost no time in launching his program of promoting the Jewish Army idea. In full awareness of the changed situation as compared with World War I, Jabotinsky acknowledged that

> the situation has tremendously changed since 1917 when the formation of a *Judaean Regiment* was such a revolutionary symbol: today a step of this kind will be unable to put us on the map.

The imperative of striving for a major military force made therefore the reservoir of Palestinian Jewry insufficient. "The main hope," he contended, "is with the Jews of the United States."

Aware of the legal obstacles, Jabotinsky saw a solution in forming "an association of men in military age under the name *Jewish Army* which will enter into negotiations with the American Government on the one hand, and with the Allied Government s on the other, for obtaining permission and help to join the Allied armies."

The efforts of Jabotinsky, who acted in his capacity as President of the New Zionist Organization, were not to the liking of the Zionist Emergency Committee. A delegation composed of Rabbi Stephen Wise, Louis Lipsky, Eliezer Kaplan and Dr. Solomon Goldman informed British Ambassador Lord Lothian that "responsible Zionist quarters disassociate themselves from Jabotinsky's adventurous scheme."

The political bickering was not limited to the controversy with the Zionist Revisionist initiative. When the Jewish Agency Executive learned of the British Government's decision to consult with Washington "before taking a final decision on the request of the Jewish Agency for a Jewish military unit," Dr. Wise met with Sumner Welles, the Undersecretary of State, to discuss the matter. Welles requested a memorandum which he promised to study carefully. The preparation of the memorandum again demonstrated the deep divisions within the Zionist Emergency Committee. Hadassah representatives objected to the clause "that the Jewish military force should enjoy similar status and privileges as the Czechs, the Poles, or other allies of Great Britain." In Hadassah's view the *Yishuv* couldn't be compared with independent nations, whose territories were occupied by the Nazis, and their "governments-in-exile" representing them. And though the Hadassah request that the military force be recruited exclusively from Palestine Jewry was rather isolated, unity prevailed in American Zionist ranks that any decision on recruitment in the United States must remain their sole competence.

In spite of these internal divisions the pressure on the American Administration to intervene with the British Government continued unabated. The establishment of a Jewish Army became a major issue of the Zionist struggle for Jewish national aspirations. The American Zionist Emergency Committee was not alone in its action. A Committee for a Jewish Army headed by a group of former Revisionists with Peter Bergson (Hillel Kook) as National Director, succeeded in winning the support of many important personalities in American public life, including members of President Roosevelt's Cabinet. On November 28, 1941, Congressman Andrew L. Somers of New York introduced in the House of Representatives a resolution which read:

> Resolved by the House of Representatives (the Senate concurring) that the President of the United States is hereby requested to direct the Secretary of State to petition the Government of Great Britain to take such action as may be necessary to permit the organization of all Jewish military units in Palestine.

Secretary of War Stimson sent word to a meeting for a Jewish Army in which he said:

> Free men everywhere are arming in the defense of democracy. I send my wishes for the success of your movement.

Chief Justice Harlan Stone cabled:

> I am entirely in sympathy with the proposal to raise a Jewish Army to fight side by side with the English Army.

The support of non-Jewish public figures fitted well into the general effort of the Jewish

DAVID BEN GURION

HENRY MONTOR

ELIEZAR KAPLAN

RUDOLF G. SONNEBORN

REUVEN SHILOAH

SAMUEL J. ZACHS

MEYER W. WEISGAL

WILLIAM H. SYLK

ABRAHAM BERKOWITZ

DR. JACOB SHOHAN

SHEPHERD BROAD

SAMUEL CHERR

Participants in the first meeting with David Ben Gurion for organizing American Jewish support for the Yishusv's defense needs. The room painted by an artist is the living room in the Rudolf Sonnenborn residence at which the meeting took place. The committee was later extended.

JULIUS FLIGELMAN

HAROLD GOLDENBERG

JOEL GROSS

CHARLES GUTWIRTH

WILLIAM S. COHEN

MAX LIVINGSTON

BARNEY RAPPAPORT

CHARLES J. ROSENBLUM

ALBERT SCHIFF

EZRA Z. SHAPIRO

Participants in the first meeting with David Ben Gurion
for organizing American Jewish support for the Yishuv's defense needs. The room painted by an artist is the living room
in the Rudolf Sonnenborn residence at which the meeting took
place. The committee was later extended.

community. The Central Conference of American Rabbis adopted a resolution favoring the establishment of a Jewish Army; Rabbi Joseph H. Lookstein, President of the Rabbinical Council of America, Rabbi Leon L. Lang, President of the Rabbinical Assembly of America, published resolutions of support for the Jewish Army idea in the name of their respective organizations; the National Conference of the United Palestine Appeal appealed to President Roosevelt to urge upon Britain "to act favorably upon the request of the Jewish Agency for Palestine . . . so that there may be called into existence a Jewish armed force."

America's entry into the war changed the situation. It was in America's interest that the forces fighting the Axis grow. American Zionists started to use this argument frequently in their appeals for United States intervention with the British Government. Dr. Weitzman's and Ben Gurion's presence in the United States was exploited for bringing the demands for a Jewish Army directly to the President. In Ben Gurion's words, "Unless the President will personally intervene with the British Prime Minister (there is) doubt whether the help promised us (by American officials) will be effective." Indeed the effectiveness of the American support lagged. The British announcement about the recruitment of Jewish (and Arab) battalions in Palestine, on August 6, 1942, "for general service in the Middle East" changed little the situation. The status of these battalions was inferior as compared with parellel units of the British army. The Jewish battalions were to be excluded from direct combat.

In his report to the Emergency Committee, Ben Gurion termed these Jewish units as "the step-children of the British Army" and the duties they were assigned "a slap in the face of the Jewish people." The recurring British argument about the shortage of equipment was not treated seriously, and the proposals of the Emergency Committee suggesting arming of Jewish units through a direct Lend-Lease operation by the United States were dropped as impractical. Failing to give tangible help in achieving British cooperation for the establishment of a Jewish Army, the Emergency Committee decided to support, first of all, financially, the decision of the Jewish Agency in Jerusalem to initiate a program of mobilization and training of Palestine Jews, irrespective of the official British attitude. The Emergency Committee made available, for this purpose, an amount of $200,000. A similar amount was allocated for the same purpose by the Joint Distribution Committee, a

decision that clearly indicated that non-Zionists were fully aware of the security needs of the *Yishuv,* even though they did not subscribe to the political aspects of a separate Jewish military force.

These aspects were, irrespective of the security needs of the Yishuv, of primary importance for the Zionist movement. Zionists were cognizant of the fact that recognition of a Jewish Army would mean the recognition of the Jewish nation as a belligerent, and that there cannot be recognition of a nation without attributing to it sovereign national authorities and national sovereignty over a territory, over Palestine. In the given development of political events the struggle for a Jewish Army enveloped in itself all the attributes and all the aims of the struggle for the realization of political Zionism. Even after the Zionist Emergency Committee slackened its efforts in this area of Zionist activity, and concentrated on pressing for the recognition of a Jewish Commonwealth as the Zionist aim, the Jewish Army seemed to have remained a topical subject of discussions between American and English leaders. Churchill reveals in his memoirs, that on his trip to Quebec in August, 1943, for a meeting with President Roosevelt, he took along Major General Orde Wingate who was "being considered as Commander in Chief of a Jewish Army when formed."

As events developed, the Jewish Army was never created, and the formation of the Jewish Brigade Group in September, 1944, though a considerable step forward if compared with the Jewish Legion of World War I, was a far cry from the Jewish Army concept.

But with this chapter of American Jewish involvement in the struggle for a Jewish military force closed, another form of American involvement in direct action for the implementation of Zionism appeared. World War II drew to an end. The dimensions of the Jewish tragedy surpassed the most pessimistic appraisals. The remnants of European Jewry, wretched bodies which survived miraculously the holocaust, had to be given a heaven. The only country that yearned to receive them, to rehabilitate them, Palestine, was under British rule that intensified its regime of oppression to eradicate any hope for Jews to go there. The direct action of the fighting underground forces appeared as only one aspect of the struggle for the opening of Palestine's doors for the Jews, crowded in the Displaced Persons camps. Storming these closed gates, literally and physically, became imperative. The great saga of *Aliyah Beth,* the so-

The "Exodus" which became the symbol of "Aliyah Beth",
the so-called illegal immigration to Palestine.

The Jewish State with 2,000 "illegals" on board being
boarded by British army personnel after ship was intercepted on
high seas by British vessels.

called "illegal *aliyah*" entered its dramatic stage of a mass movement.

Palestine Jewry could not carry the burden by itself. The hour of American Jewish help, in forms hitherto unprecedented and unexperienced, arrived. There was a need for ships, for skilled seafaring personnel, for financial means to equip the ships and to feed the immigrants. In this general scheme of attack against the British anti-immigration policies care for those waiting for aliyah in the D.P. camps assumed primary importance. In this respect, American Jewish enlisted men and officers, rabbis in uniform, serving with the American occupation forces in Europe, in whose territory most D.P. camps were located, undertook a mission of support and rescue which has written one of the most glorious chapters of Jewish

Reunion of the Exodus crew held in New York on the occasion of the 20th anniversary of the ship's epopee, May 1967. In center Rudolf Sonneborn.

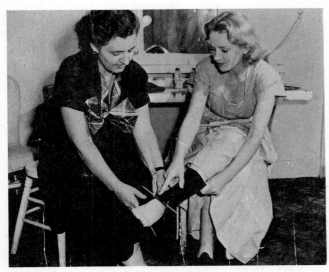

Rebecca Imber (left) chairman of Knitting for Israel with well known actress Jessica Tandy, one of the many non-Jews who supported Israel's struggle for Independence, in promotional photograph.

Colonel David Mickey Marcus, who commanded the Israel forces on the Jerusalem front, the most distinguished Mahal volunteer, who fell in Israel's War of Independence.

brotherly love, of human compassion, and perhaps sometimes unwittingly, of real, practical Zionist zeal. Volumes could be written on the material help given, sometimes of the soldiers' own rations, on communication means made available, on moral support which proved to be lifesavers for people whose nightmare of Hitler persecution receded a new tide of human compassion flowed out to them. And all this was in addition to the unprecedented human salvage operations conducted by American Jewish civilian efforts, by the funds and representatives of the Joint Distribution Committee.

Though much of this help to Jews living in the D. P. camps was given without outside prodding, the conversion of this humanitarian effort into a planned national action, devised to bring closer the attainment of Zionist goals, had to be accomplished by Zionist authorities themselves. The end of the war opened the American doors for emissaries of all factions which fought in their own way for a Jewish Palestine. But among those emissaries who came to appeal for the help of American Jewry, first of all American Zionists, one mission stands out in historic proportions, and its already acknowledged historic achievements.

This was the now famous mission led by David Ben Gurion. Upon his arrival in New York on July 18, 1945, Ben Gurion set out to mobilize American Jewry's support for direct action against the British scheme of strangling

Rudolf G. Sonneborn
300 Fourth Avenue
New York City 10

March 7, 1955

My very dear friend:

"The book is about to be closed" -- a mission which we undertook ten years ago has been accomplished.

It was on July 1, 1945 that a few of us met at my home with several distinguished Palestinians and dedicated ourselves to certain endeavors. Without formal structure, we grew into a radiant, dynamic organization of Americans who undertook, as Americans, the attainment of an ideal, of a vision, and later, of the State of Israel -- compatible, of course, with our American responsibilities.

During these years Israel has proved its right to take its place in the hall of nations. During these years we have served effectively and eminently well. You, as one of this group, have shared equally the dignified, unheralded appreciation of a people who have gained a homeland. You and I have been privileged indeed to participate in this creative experience -- perhaps this was better stated by John Adams in 1780:

"When I consider the great Events which are passed, and that I may have been instrumental of touching Some Springs and turning some Small Wheels, I feel an awe upon my mind, which is not easily described."

And so, on March 31st of this year, Material for Israel will suspend its operations. I know that you will continue to serve your heritage with the sacred devotion and zeal that has characterized you in all of your endeavors on behalf of our people.

Please write as often as occasion suggests, and believe me in all my humbleness to be gratefully and sincerely yours,

Rudolf G. Sonneborn

RGS:gp

The "Mission Accomplished" letter closing a heroic chapter in American-Israel partnership in the direct struggle for the rebirth of Jewish Statehood.

the Yishuv and liquidating Zionist aspirations in Palestine. Within less than two weeks, on August 1, 1945, a meeting was called in the home of Rudolph Sonneborn, whose Zionist services started as early as in the days of the Zionist Commission, at the end of World War I, and who has never since missed an oportunity to serve the Zionist cause. Twenty-three persons were invited to that meeting, according to a list prepared by Henry Montor, assisted by Meyer Weisgal.

Today, over two decades later, there are at least three scores and more of persons who claim that they participated in that meeting. Unfortunately, personal inquiries were not too helpful in verifying the names. Even a photographic recording of this occasion, arranged much later through a photographic montage, seems not to be too helpful. What is beyond doubt are the names of seventeen persons present at that meeting, as recorded by Ben Gurion himself: Harold Goldenberg of Minneapolis; Same Cherr and Jacques Torczyner of New York; Sam Zaks of Toronto; Julius Fliegelman of Los Angeles; Sheppard Broad of Miami; Philip Lown of Louisville; Eli Cohen; Ezra Shapiro of Cleveland; Albert Schiff of Columbus; Alec Leventhal and Charles Rosenblum of Pittsburgh; William Sylk of Philadelphia; Adolph Hamburger of Baltimore; Roger Travis of Atlanta; Max Livingstone of New Haven and Rudouph Sonneborn of New York.

The meeting which was called to order at 9:30 A.M. lasted for hours. Ben Gurion, as chairman of the Jewish Agency Executive in Jerusalem, spoke of the need to prepare the *Yishuv* for a military confrontation with the mandatory power and with the Arabs, as well as of the urgency of organizing a mass exodus of Jews from the D.P. camps to Palestine by the ways of *aliya beth*. Of the assembled he asked to provide the financial means and the necessary connections for implementing this program. As the most urgent demand Ben Gurion mentioned the purchase of equipment for the clandestine military industry of the Haganah, then in its incipient stages of development. Writing about this meeting years later, Ben Gurion pointed out that

the tools were sent to Israel (Palestine) during Mandate days . . . and though the Government in Palestine used to search for arms in the Jewish settlements, all the machines were safely received, without the Government in Palestine knowing about their end uses. The Government did not at all suspect that the heavy and bulky machines which arrived in the country were destined to military uses and not a single machine fell into its hands. Most of the machines and tools which are today at the disposal of the military industry in Israel are the products of this meeting which took place at Rudolph Sonneborn's on August 1, 1945.

Thus was born what Sonneborn's associates later called "The Sonneborn Institute." It engaged in a widespread effort for preparing the hour of trial and military contest in Palestine. In the days preceding the establishment of the State, this group of people were instrumental in the great clandestine effort to provide the *Yishuv* with guns, tanks, medicines, ambulances, planes and even clothing for armed personnel. Assisted by Israelis like Reuven Shiloah, Yaakov Dori, later chief of Staff, Shlomo Shamir, Teddy Kolek, Aryeh Manor, this group was engaged in a gun-running operation of unprecedented proportions. The fact that it was officially unrelated to the Zionist political effort was a well-thought-through device to keep the official representation of Zionism engaged in the decisive political struggle, away from any suspicion that could have handicapped the political efforts.

One of the most urgent responsibilities of the group was the acquisition of ships on which "illegal" immigrants had to undertake their mission of forcing the British blockade of the Palestine shores. But the ships were only part of the operation. The potential immigrants had to be reached, organized, transported to the ships, put on board and taken to Palestine.

The story of these efforts sounds more sensational than any fiction. Movement orders for use of military transport were made out for *B.R.I.H.A.* ("Escape" in Hebrew -- the name of the organization engaged in clandestine transport of immigrants, crossing of borders), and signed by E.H.V.D.

American military authorities did not conceal their sympathy for these American Jewish efforts. Ruth Gruber, "the miracle worker" of a whole series of these *aliyah beth* operations, was given official papers, rank of colonel in the U. S. Army and uniform, and full cooperation of Colonel Ernest White, who was in charge of all D.P. questions at General Eisenhower's headquarters. On one occasion Colonel White cancelled a troop transport and ordered a boat (*Ascenia*) for one journey to Palestine, closing his eyes to the fact that instead of the authorized 900 passengers, 2400 boarded the ship instead.

American Jewish boys were among those who led the ships in their blockade running efforts. On the famous *Exodus* with 4,000 Jewish immigrants aboard were Captain Bernard Marks, second mate Cyril Weinstein, boatswain William Millman, Bill Bernstein, who was killed at the wheel by a blow on the head during the struggle with the British boarding party. Of the spirit that filled the hearts of the American boys one can learn from a letter of Eli Kahn, of the Bronx, who wrote to his parents:

> If life in America will make me more normal and complacent in my approach to the D.P. problem—Well . . . all I can say is God forbid. . . . Sorry for the sermon.

The American League for a Free Palestine also tried its hand in the field of illegal immigration, *Aliyah Beth*. In accordance with its methods of action the League initiated a public campaign to turn the Jewish illegal immigration into Palestine from "a trickle into a mass exodus." A special Repatriation Advisory Board was appointed with Messrs. Ben Hecht, Louis Bromfield and Will Rogers Jr. But the amount of publicity given to this action was disproportionate to actual achievements. Only one ship was bought, manned and sent to Palestine by the Repatriation Board, the S.S. *Abril*, renamed Ben Hecht. It was intercepted by the British on March 8, 1947, near Haifa, and its passengers deported to Cyprus.

Blockade running, rescue of D.P.s, at times joining the "illegals" in the role of immigrants as small as the number of those Americans were, was only a preparatory stage for the coming test.

The test came in the fall of 1947 when the *Haganah* initiated the formation of special units of foreign volunteers, *Mitnadvey Hutz Laaretz, Mahal*, the Hebrew initials of which became the official name of the entire movement. The recruitment had to be carried out unofficially, secretly. Under the guise of recruiting specialists in various technical fields the *Haganah* sought to strengthen its forces by war veterans, tank commanders, pilots, radar technicians, aircraft mechanics. Offices opened under the name Land and Labor in New York, originally meant for registration of specialist-technicians were soon turned practically into recruitment centers for Mahal candidates. Another outfit, under the name Palestine Vocational Service (P.V.S.) registered prospective settlers in Palestine.

The response exceeded availability of military equipment or even swift means of transportation to the far-off battlefields. The intervention of the American Government did not impair the recruiting campaign. The warning of the American Consulate General in Jerusalem on January 30, 1948, that American citizens taking part in the conflict will lose their American citizenship remained unheeded. Of the 5300 *Mahal* volunteers, the largest single contingent was that of Americans, numbering 1700. The American *Mahal* volunteers fought in all three categories of the Israel Forces, in the Infantry, Air Force and Armored units. One of the brigades in Israel's War of Independence, the famous *Seventh Brigade,* had a battalion composed of *Mahal* volunteers and was nicknamed the "Anglo-Saxon Battalion." The Commander of the brigade was a Canadian *Mahal* officer. The highly technical army services, like the air force and the tank corps, were heavily manned by English speaking *Mahal* volunteers. English had, for a time, to be used as the official language of Israel's Air Force.

There were numerous instances of unusual bravery, of heroism in the line of fire. The fact that a relatively large percentage of *Mahal* volunteers were former officers supplied the young Israeli Army with an excellent, experienced officer corps. Due to the accepted standards in the Israel Defense Army, the officers were not only commanding but really leading in combat. This led to an abnormally high percentage of officers killed in battle.

Among the many hundreds of American *Mahal* volunteers some achieved special distinction. Colonel David Marcus, a graduate of West Point, who was given in May, 1948, the command of the Jerusalem front, belongs to the legendary figures of Israel's War of Independence. Ben Dunkelman, an outstanding and often decorated Canadian armored corps commander in World War II, volunteered as a private and served as a number one of a three-inch mortar crew until, after his identity was discovered, he was given a position fitting his military standing and elevated to the rank of major-general.

As in many other fields of activity in support of fighting Palestine, the group of the Hebrew Committee for National Liberation, acting through the American League for a Free Palestine, tried to work separately in the field of recruiting volunteers. Recruitment for a George Washington Legion was proclaimed by the League. It succeeded in winning the co-operation of the boxing champion and Marine Corps hero, Barney Ross. According to the

League's reports it succeeded in registering 5,000 volunteers for service in Palestine in defiance of the State Department opposition.

I don't want to lose my American citizenship, said Ross, but I certainly want the right to fight for a cause that is just. . . . All I've got left is my heart and two good hands to talk for me.

The full saga of this American Jewish role in Israel's War of Independence has still to be written. There is still to be told the story of those American G.I.s who chose the Hebrew University or the Technion as the institution of their studies under the G.I. bill with the clear intent of being close to the scene and putting their military skills at the disposal of the *Yishuv* whose approaching encounter for Independence was a generally predicted certainty. And certainly deserving of explicit presentation is the fact that many American volunteers (as well as *Mahal* volunteers from other countries) refrained from registering when the Government of the State they fought to establish announced its decision to register *Mahal* volunteers so that they may take advantage of special privileges they were to be accorded.

Of course, compared with the number of military personnel that fought in the War of Independence, the number of American volunteers could appear not too impressive. But they were there, and in the words of the official historian of that war, Colonel Lorch

their importance did not lie in numbers, but in the qualifications and experience, their devotion and their sacrifice.

Mahal members piloted the planes, the whole assortment of flying war machines, Messerschmitts, Constellations, Flying Fortresses. They manned the Sherman tanks after three shipments reached Israel's shores in September, 1948, aboard the *Borea, Resurrection* and *Arzin.* They were instrumental in putting at sea Israel's first war vessel, since they were always on the spot when a shipment of arms from the United States had to be assembled from the crates in which it was shipped.

Buying and shipping of arms for Israel's defense is a heroic chapter by itself in the story of American-Jewish partnership in the building of the State of Israel. One of the arms shipments, 450 Brownings, 300 machine guns, 65 Vickers heavy machine guns, were still in San Francisco when the United States Government declared the embargo on shipment of war materials to the Middle East. How these arms were removed from American soil, how a yacht owner who rented his boat to allegedly ship crates to a small island off the California coast, and once on his way, was commandeered to the Mexican port of Tampico from which the arms reached Israel, is a most dramatic story by itself.

Though the dangers involved in these operations are at present recalled with deep sentiment and pride, in the days of their implementation they were quite burdensome and painful. There was wire-tapping, there were arrests, there were court hearings and trials at which judges would announce that if they were Jews they wouldn't hesitate to act similarly for the freedom of their country; there were accidents with explosives, and there were mass demonstrations while materials were being dispatched to Israel with flag-bedecked rostra and mayors and police commissioners participating in the official ceremonies.

Police officers, judges refused to treat harshly those caught in acts of shipping arms to Palestine for the Jewish fighting forces. When a group pleaded guilty of attempting to ship 60,000 pounds of TNT to Palestine after the cases broke open on a Jersey City pier, Federal Judge Sylvester Ryan found that "this offense was not committed for any gain or profit," and another judge ruled that "sending arms and ammunition to Israel is a worthwhile act."

This multiphased operation, though mainly unofficial, and often clandestine, had to care for some formal backing as well. Conforming with American laws an official organization, Americans for *Haganah*, was called into being. The founding of the new organization was announced on July 8, 1947, by its president, Abraham Feinberg. The first issue of the organization's organ, bearing the same name, published on August 15, 1947, presented a three-fold program of Americans for *Haganah*:

(1) To rally the moral support of the people of the United States behind unrestricted Jewish immigration into Palestine;

(2) To disseminate information about the part *Haganah* is playing in bringing displaced European Jews into Palestine in spite of the illegal British immigration quotas;

(3) To clear up confusion existing in many American minds concerning the various wildcat groups which claim to be identified with the Palestine struggle.

These "wildcat groups," the *Irgun Tzvai Leumi* and the *Lehi,* had their supporters in the United States. To combat them was one of the major tasks of Americans for *Haganah.* Additional indication of the seriousness of this problem as seen by *Haganah* supporters could be found not only in pronouncements of Americans for *Haganah* but also in special pamphlets devoted to the same subject. A pamphlet, *Haganah or Terror,* published by the *Hehalutz* Organization of America, supplies a clear indication of the depth of the problem. One of the basic passages in this pamphlet reads:

It is possible that even a clear-headed Jew, who understands the main problems of our struggle for the upbuilding of Palestine, will feel a swelling pride when he reads about the acts and undertakings of the two terrorist groups. This feeling of pride is the result of the inferiority complex of the Jew, who feels insulted and degraded and suddenly is presented with the Heaven-sent opportunity to boast to his gentile friend of the patriotic deeds. But the question is: Shall we pay the price which must be paid in order to satisfy the feelings of pride of a Brooklyn storekeeper?

Such questions were even more pressing in view of the publicity given by the American press to the acts of the two underground groups, and the intense propaganda campaign by which the news were followed in page-long ads by the Hebrew Committee of National Liberation, one of the newly formed groups of former revisionists and Irgun supporters.

It would be misleading to assume that the British Government and the British Embassy in Washington were silent observers of this overt support for the forces that were fighting and were preparing, on a nationwide scale, the armed fight against British policy in Palestine. The British Foreign Minister, Ernest Bevin, and British Prime Minister Clement R. Atlee made representations directly, or through the British Ambassador in Washington, demanding American official intervention in putting an end to the anti-British acts prepared, planned, financed, and partly implemented by Americans, on American territory. There were the old accusations of Communist plotting, of planting Communist agitators among the illegal immigrants, and there were threats and anti-Semitic outbursts. But all this was of no avail. United States Jewry continued to be the depository of Jewish assistance to the struggling front-line of Jewish renaissance in Palestine. It continued on and intensified its role as a virtual hinterland in this direct struggle, a

Presenting the model of Exodus to the Smithsonian on July 16, 1967. The plaque presented to the Museum on that occasion lists the following ships in service of Aliya Beth, which were manned by volunteers from the U. S., Canada and Latin America: Hagana, Josiah Wedgewood, Haim Arlosoroff, Hatikvah, Ben Hecht, Exodus, Jewish State, Geula, Independence, Ingathering of Exiles.

faithful partner in every way, on all fields, in all activities.

The establishment of the State, the recognition of the State of Israel by President Truman, changed the formal means of this help, its legal aspects, but it did not terminate this help as such. Americans for *Haganah* were replaced by Materials for Israel. Everything which was of use was collected and shipped to Israel, military equipment and materials for civilian use alike. From used army hats and field bottles to books, all were collected for shipment to Israel. Materials worth millions were registered at the Materials for Israel offices, at 250 West 57th Street, in New York. *Kibbutz Pentagon* as this head office was nicknamed, hummed with activity. The sight of a man or woman walking into the office to present a meager weekly pay check was nothing unusual in those days. Dollars and cents from people who because of their help to Israel had to deny themselves a decent meal, mingled with the thousands and tens of thousands of the rich.

Thus, when Rudolph Sonnenborn sent his letter announcing the end of these activities, the by now famous *Mission accomplished* note, those who were actively associated with this work in addition to those already mentioned, like Avis Shulman, Moses Speert, Charles Gutwirth, Max Swerin, Nahum Bernstein, Zimil Resnick, Charles Chapler, Isaac Imber, Julius Jarcho, and the hundreds of devoted pioneers of this effort throughout the country, must have felt a pride only active participation in nation building can give.

The dream which the members of the Jewish Legion of World War I had dreamt and fought for, that of a Jewish State, at last became reality.

The Mission was accomplished; its legacy still a binding obligation for all those who followed them and for all those who will follow them in the future.

AMERICAN VETERANS OF ISRAEL FOREST   יער מתנדבי ארה"ב וקנדה למען ישראל

IN MEMORY OF THE VOLUNTEERS   לזכר המתנדבים

FROM THE U.S.A. AND CANADA   מארצות-הברית וקנדה

WHO GAVE THEIR LIVES IN ISRAEL'S WAR   שמסרו את נפשם על עצמאות ישראל

OF INDEPENDENCE   במלחמת השחרור

1948 — 1949   תש"ח – תש"ט

RALPH MUSTER	דאלף מוסטר	SAMUEL HANOVICE	שמואל הנוביק	BENNI BOGUSLAVSKY	בני בוגוסלבסקי
LEONARD PITCHET	לאונרד פיטצ'ט	RAY KUNTZ	ריי קונץ	ZEEV CANTOR	זאב קנטור
SIDNEY RUBINOV	סידני רובינוב	SIDNEY LEIZEROWITZ	סידני לייזרוביץ	WILLIAM FISHER	וויליאם פישר
ROBERT LESTER WEECKMAN	רוברט לסטר ויקמן	SEYMOUR LERNER	סיימור לרנר	AARON HANOVICE	אהרן הנוביק

KALMAN PITTEL	קלמן פיטל	DANIEL GOODMAN	דניאל-יצחק גודמן	HANS ABRAHAM	חיים אברהם
SALLY PALKOWSKI	סלי פלקובסקי	IGO GRIFFEL	יצחק גריפל	JUSTIN ADLER	יוסף אדלר
SHMUEL POMERANZ	שמואל פומרנץ	FRED GROSS	צבי גרוס	WILLIAM ALT	וויליאם אלט
POSNER	פוזנר	ZIPORA GRUNBERG	צפורה גרינברג	STANLEY ANDREWS	סטנלי אנדרוס
CARMI RABINOWITZ	כרמי רבינוביץ	ERICH HELLINGER	אריך הלינגר	PHILIP BALKIN	פיליונ בולקין
HARRY ROH	שבתאי רוח	OLIVER HOLTON	אוליבר הולטון	LOUIS BALL	אריה באל
MOSHE ROSENBAUM	משה אהרן רוזנבוים	OSCAR HYMAN	אוסקר היימון	ISRAEL BERN	ישראל ברן
JACOB ROTHMAN	יעקב רוטמן	JOE KAHN	יוסף בהן	WILLIAM BERNSTEIN	וויליאם ברנשטיין
SELIG RUDOLPH	רודולף זליג	JEROME KAPLAN	יהודה קמלן	YAACOV BIELUR	יעקב ביאלור
MIRIAM SALPETER	מרים סלפטר	HERBERT KERMISH	צבי קרמיש	LESLIE BLOCH	לסלי בלוך
MOSHE SCHMUCKLER	משה שמוקלר	ERNIE KING	ארני קינג	SPENCER R. BOYD	סמנסר ר. בויד
DOV SELIGMAN	דב זליגמן	JACK KLEIN	יעקב דניאל קליין	JOSHUA BROWN	יהושע בראון
IRVING SEVIN	ישראל סיין	HEINRICH KUPPERMAN	חיים צבי קופרמן	BUZZ BURLING	בז ברלינג
JACK SHULMAN	עזריאל שולמן	ARI LASHNER	אריה לשנר	JACOUB CHECK	יעקב בן יצק
YOSEF STADLER	יוסף שטדלר	ALVIN LEVY	אברהם לוי	MOSHE REUBEN COHEN	משה ראובן בהן
AVRAHAM DAVID STAVSKY	אברהם דוד סטבסקי	BARUCH LINSKY	ברוך לינסקי	WILLIAM EDMONSON	וויליאם אדמונסון
SHLOMO SZIGETI	שלמה סיגמזי	JOSEPH MANN	יוסף מן	BERNARD FAJERMAN	ברוך פיירמן
YECHEZKEL TESHER	יחזקאל תשר	DAVID MICKEY MARCUS	מיבאל דוד מרבוס	HENRI FERNEBOK	הנרי פרניבוק
LEONARD TROYEN	ליאונרד טרוין	MANDEL MATH	מנדל מט	ZVI FISHEL	צבי פישיל
ISRAEL YAROST	ישראל ידוסט	DAVID MILLER	דוד מילר	LEN FISHER	לן פישר
MARJERY ZIFF	מרג'רי זיף	HAROLD MONASH	צבי מונש	MOSHE GEBERER	משה גברר
MOSHE ZUCKER	משה צוקר	HOWARD E. MOORE JR.	האואדד מור בן	WILLIAM GERSHON	וויליאם גרשון
		MOSHE PERLSTEIN	משה פרלשטיין	PHILIP GOLD	פיליפ גולד

JEWISH   NATIONAL   FUND

Plaque at the Memorial Forest in honor of Americans and
Canadians who fell in Israel's War of Independence.

SELECTED BIBLIOGRAPHY

AMERICAN JEWISH YEARBOOKS, 1900 THROUGH 1966: The American Jewish Committee.

THE AMERICAN CHRISTIAN PALESTINE COMMITTEE: The Arab War Effort; A Documented Account, New York, 1947.

AMERICAN JEWISH TRADE UNION COMMITTEE FOR PALESTINE: British Labor and Zionism, New York, 1946.

BEN GURION, DAVID: Rebirth and Destiny, New York, 1954.

BEN HECHT: A Child of the Century, New York, 1954.

BYRNES, JAMES F: Speaking Frankly, New York, 1947.

BENTWICH, NORMAN: For Zion's Sake; Biography of Judah L. Magnes, Philadelphia, 1954.

BEN JACOB, JEREMIAH: The Jewish Struggle, London, 1942.

BLAUSTEIN, JACOB: The Voice of Reason, New York, 1950.

CHURGIN, P. and GELLMAN, A. L.: Mizrahi: Jubilee Miscellany on the 25th Anniversary of the Mizrahi Organization in America.

COHEN, ISRAEL: Britain's Nameless Ally, London, 1942; The Zionist Movement, London 1945.

CROSSMAN RICHARD: Palestine Mission: A Personal Record, New York, 1947.

CRUM, BARTLEY C.: Behind the Silken Curtain, New York, 1947.

DE HAAS, JACOB: Louis D. Brandeis, New York, 1929.

FINK, REUBEN: America and Palestine, New York, 1944.

FRANK, E. MANUEL: The Realities of American-Palestine Relations, Washington, 1949.

FRIEDRICH, CARL: American Policy toward Palestine, Washington, 1944.

GARCIA-GRANADOS, JORGE: The Birth Of Israel—The Drama as I Saw It, New York, 1948.

HADASSAH MEDICAL ORGANIZATION: Twenty Years of Medical Service to Palestine 1919-1938, Jerusalem, 1939.

HALPERN, BEN: The Idea of a Jewish State, Cambridge, Mass., 1961.

HALPERIN, SAMUEL: The Political World of American Zionism, Detroit, 1961.

HEBREW COMMITTEE OF NATIONAL LIBERATION: A Call by the Hebrew Nation, Washington, 1944.

HERZL YEARBOOK, VOLS. 1, 2, 3 ,4, 5, New York, 1958-1963.

HIRSCHMAN, IRA A.: Life Line to a Promised Land, New York, 1946.

HUREWITZ, J. C.: The Struggle For Palestine, New York, 1950.

JABOTINSKY, VLADIMIR: The Story of the Jewish Legion, New York, 1945.

LOWDERMILK, WALTER CLAY: Palestine, Land of Promise, New York and London 1944.

LAPIDE, P. E.: A Century of U. S. Aliyah, Tel-Aviv, 1961.

LEARSI, R.: The Jews in America, New York, 1954.

LEARSI, R.: Fulfillment: The Epic Story of Zionism, Cleveland-New York, 1958.

MAGNES, J. L.: Rebellion, Presidential Address on Diploma Day at the Hebrew University, Jerusalem, 1945.

MANDELBAUM, B.: Assignment in Israel, New York, 1960.

MEEKER, ODEN: Israel Reborn, 1964.

MIKESELL, RAYMOND F. and CHENERY, HOLLIS B.: Arabian Oil: America's Stake in the Middle East, Chapel Hill, 1949.

MORRIS, YAACOV: Western Pioneers, Jerusalem, 1952.

MORRIS, YAACOV: On the Soil of Israel—The Story of Americans and Canadians in Agriculture, Tel-Aviv, 1965.

NATHAN, ROBERT R., GASS, OSCAR and CREAMER, DANIEL: Palestine—Problem and Promise, Washington, 1946.

ORGANIZING AMERICAN JEWRY, DEMOGRAPHIC TRENDS IN U. S. JEWRY, American Jewish Congress, 1946.

PALESTINE YEARBOOKS, 1945, 1947, 1950, 1954, Zionist Organization of America, New York.

POALE ZION ZEIRE ZION OF AMERICA: Labor Zionist Handbook: The Aims, Activities, and History of the Labor Zionist Movement in America, New York, 1939.

REPORTS, ANNUAL, DEPARTMENT OF MIGRATION, 1934-1945, Government of Palestine.

ROBINSON, JACOB: Palestine and the United Nations: Prelude to Solution, Washington, 1947.

RUBIN, JACOB, A.: History of the United Nations, Illustrated, New York, 1962.

RUBIN, JACOB, A.: Your Hundred Billion Dollars, The Complete Story of American Foreign Aid, New York and Philadelphia, 1964.

ROYAL INSTITUTE OF INTERNATIONAL AFFAIRS: British Security: A Report by a Chatham House Study Group, London and New York, 1946.

SAMUEL, MAURICE: Level Sunlight, New York, 1953.

SCHECHTMAN, JOSEPH: Rebel and Statesman, New York, 1956.

SCHECHTMAN, JOSEPH: The United States and the Jewish State Movement—The Crucial Decade, 1939-1949, New York, 1966.

SHERWOOD, ROBERT E.: Roosevelt and Hopkins: An Intimate History, New York, 1948.

SILVER, DR. ABBA HILLEL: Vision and Victory, New York, 1949.

SOKOLOW, NAHUM: History of Zionism, 2 Vols., London, 1919.

STATISTICAL HANDBOOK OF JEWISH PALESTINE: Jewish Agency, Jerusalem, 1947.

SYRKIN, DR. NAHMAN: Essays on Socialist Zionism, New York, 1935.

VAN PAASSEN, PIERRE: The Day Alone, New York, 1941.

WATERS, M. P.: Haganah—Jewish Self Defense in Palestine. London, 1946.

WEITZMAN, CHAIM: Trial and Error, The Autobiography of Chaim Weitzman, New York, 1949.

THE WORLD ZIONIST ORGANIZATION AND THE KEREN HAYESSOD CONTROVERSY IN AMERICA, London, 1922.

ZAAR, ISAAC: Rescue and Liberation, New York, 1954.

ZAFRULLA KHAN, SIR MUHAMMAD: Palestine in the U. N. O., Karachi, 1948.

ZEITLIN, R.: Henrietta Szold—Record of a Life, New York, 1952.

ZUCKERMAN, BARUCH: Memoirs, New York, 1963.

This Bibliography indicates only partially the many sources consulted by the author in his search for information on the subject of this book. Among the sources not mentioned, foremost were the many publications and periodicals of Zionist and non-Zionist Organizations in America and abroad in the last seven decades, reports, correspondence, minutes of important meetings, official government documents and diaries.

ACKNOWLEDGMENTS

PHOTO CREDITS

The author and the publishers are grateful to the following personalities, photographers, organizations, institutions and picture services for permission to reproduce their photographs in this book:

American Committee for the Weitzman Institute, Alexander Archer, Association of Americans and Canadians in Israel, American Friends of the Hebrew University, American Jewish Historical Society, American-Israel Cultural Foundation, American Zionist Council, Bar-Ilan University, American Jewish Committee, Joseph Brown, Chicago Zionist Organization, Central Zionist Archives, Cosmo Sileo, Inc., F.P.A.I. Photo Service Foundation Fund (Keren Hayessod), Dr. Israel Goldstein personal archives, Hadassah, Hagdud Haivri, Histadruth, Isaac Imber, Israel Medical Center, Israel Office of Information, Israel Defense Forces, Julius Jarcho, Jewish Agency-American Section, Jewish Agency, Head Office in Jerusalem, Jewish National Fund, Mizrahi, Mizrahi Women, Dr. Emanuel Neumann personal archives, Nate Fine photo, P.A.L. Photo Service, Pioneer Women, New York Public Library, Aliza Rubin, Chovevei Zion Society, Speiser Morris, State of Israel Bonds, The N. Strauss Family Archives, Technion, United Israel Appeal, United Jewish Appeal, Rabbi Jerome Ungar, United Nations Photo Service, U. S. Department of State, Weinstein, Solomon J., Zionist Archives and Library, Zionist Organization of America.

INDEX

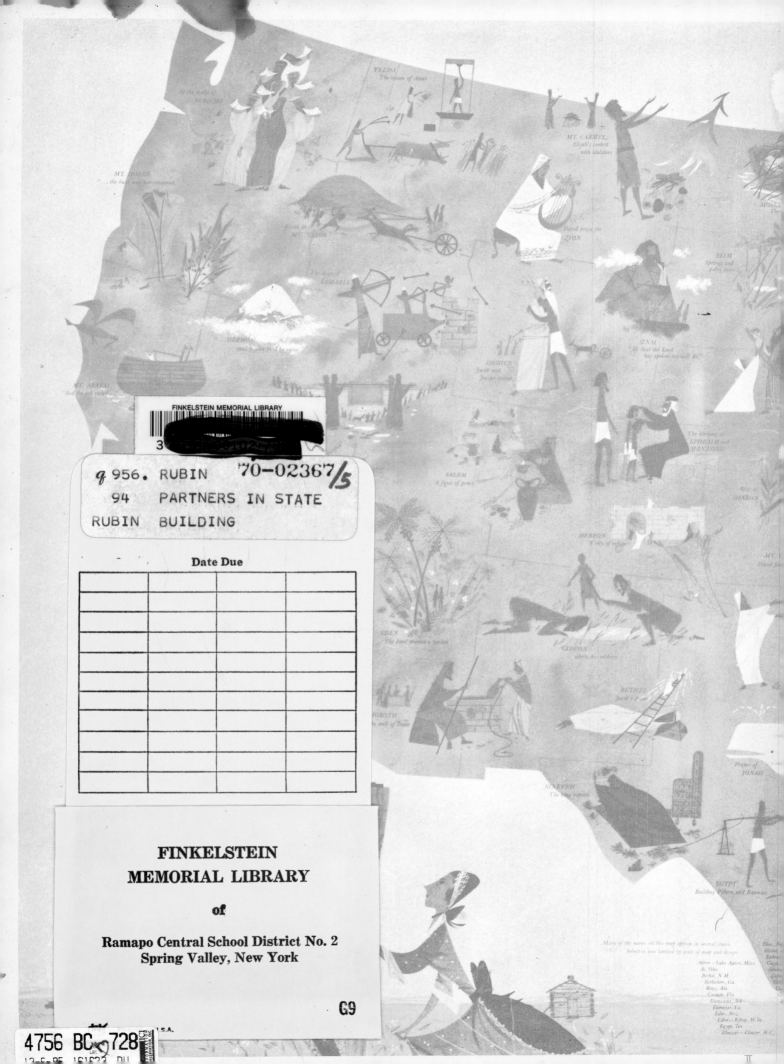